VIRAMMA

life of an untouchable

Vira...   ...cine
an...   ...ne

Tra...   ...on

UNESCO Publishing

Paris

In a series of conversations held between 1980 and 1990 Viramma, a Pariah from a village in southern India, told her life story to Josiane Racine in Tamil, their shared first language. It is because Viramma calls and considers herself a Pariah – a term condemned nowadays by emancipationists and militants, who use the more general word for 'oppressed', Dalit – that we have retained the word, as well as Untouchable, in the narrative.

The names of political figures and well-known celebrities, along with caste names and names of Indian towns and cities, have beeen retained, but the names of the people in Viramma's narrative and the villages mentioned have been changed. Any resemblance that these fictional names bear to existing people or places is purely coincidental.

UNESCO Collection of Representative Works

First published by Verso 1997
This edition © Verso 1997
Translation © Will Hobson 1997
First published as *Une vie paria. Le rire des asservis, Inde du Sud*
© Librairie Plon 1995
All rights reserved

Published with the financial assistance of the French Ministry of Culture

The moral rights of the authors and the translator of this work
have been asserted

Verso
UK: 6 Meard Street, London WIV 3HR
USA: 180 Varick Street, New York, NY 10014–4606

Verso is the imprint of New Left Books

UNESCO Publishing
7 place de Fontenoy, 75352 Paris 07 SP France

ISBN 1–85984–817–6
ISBN 1–85984–148–1 (pbk)

UNESCO ISBN 92–3–103145–7

British Library Cataloguing in Publication Data
A catalogue record for this book is available from the British Library

Library of Congress Cataloging-in-Publication Data
A catalog record for this book is available from the Library of Congress

Designed and typeset by Lucy Morton, London SE12
Cover art and text illustrations by Sophie Herxheimer
Printed and bound in Great Britain by Biddles Ltd, Guildford and King's Lynn

Contents

Translator's note

This book is the result of ten years of conversations between Viramma and Josiane Racine. Viramma's knowledge of popular songs and laments made her a valuable source for Josiane Racine's ethnomusicological research; but, when asked about her life, Viramma's initial tendency was to play down its hardship and, in general, to gloss over any feelings that might appear provocative or critical of the established order. Over five years, a close relationship developed between the two women, which, while acknowledging their differences of class and caste – 'Sinnamma', Viramma's epithet for Josiane Racine, reflects the latter's middle-class, Tamil background – allowed Viramma to speak more openly about her memories and experiences. A sense of trust and affection prompted her to discuss subjects which, under other circumstances, would have seemed either too personal, too controversial or, as her husband Manikkam puts it, 'degrading': that is, likely to play into the hands of those who would stigmatise her caste as 'uncivilised' and deserving of their position in society. What had only been commented on in passing would be described more fully when it was brought up again later, or when a tape of a previous conversation was played back to her and her neighbours and friends. After a decade, working directly from the taped material, Josiane Racine selected and translated into French the narrative which was published in France in 1995 and is the original of this English translation.

There are certain inevitable compromises and omissions when an oral culture is represented in print. It is hard to retain all of the context that informs conversations – gestures, facial expressions, the pitch and tone of a voice, the interjections of other participants – and much of this has had to be left to the reader's imagination, apart from particularly striking moments when Viramma laughed at past misfortunes, as a reflection both of how bad they were and of how she has overcome them. More specifically, Viramma pronounces, contracts and alters words in distinctive ways – ways which, incidentally, the castes of the *ur* consider as falling short of 'correct' Tamil usage. I followed Josiane Racine in deciding not to try and duplicate these by using an English or American demotic or working-class dialect. Instead the intention has been to use a simple, neutral, current English that is neither too literary nor exaggeratedly colloquial. Pointedly, many of my discussions with Josiane Racine were about words or expressions – 'degrading', for example, or 'I lifted up my head, heavy with sadness and flowers' in chapter 4 – which I at first thought should have more informal, or even slang, English equivalents. If nuances in the way Viramma speaks have been lost, the practice of a literal translation has the merit of showing the range of her self-expression and the inappropriateness of those who stigmatise her Tamil as a 'half-language' on the grounds of its lack of self-control.

I have obviously not toned down the other aspect of her language – her use of swearing and sexually explicit language – which has elsewhere been criticised. As Viramma says, its meaning depends on its context, and it is one of the many ways in which, for her, speaking both gives pleasure and is a form of self-assertion. Her fastidious attention to detail, her use of emphasis – conveyed by the many exclamation marks – and the strongly imagistic nature of her language all reflect the same attitude, and I hope that this translation allows Viramma's identity to emerge, not just through her thoughts, emotions and the ways she has reacted to the events of her life, but also through the way she expressed herself to Josiane Racine throughout the 1980s.

Many thanks to Josiane and Jean-Luc Racine, who have been unfailingly helpful and attentive, Anjalai Modi, Marie Derome, Charlotte Hobson, the British Museum Botanical Library, Jane Hindle at Verso and everybody at Granta.

Will Hobson
London 1997

Maps

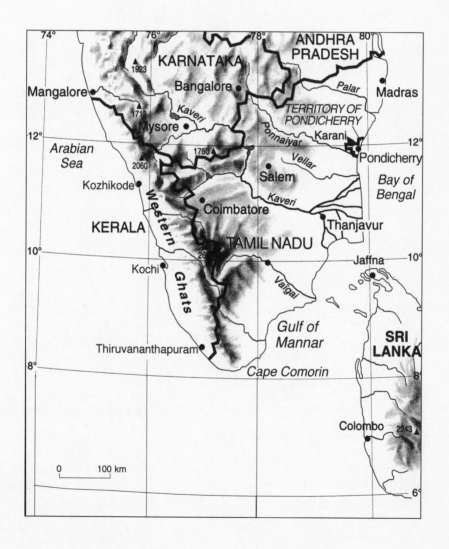

Karani in its South Indian context

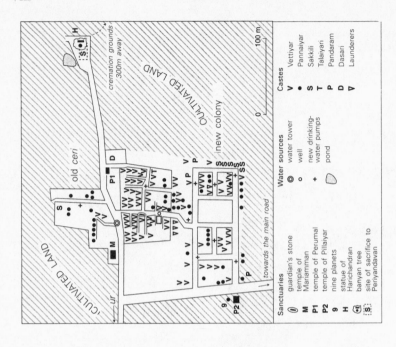

The *ceri*

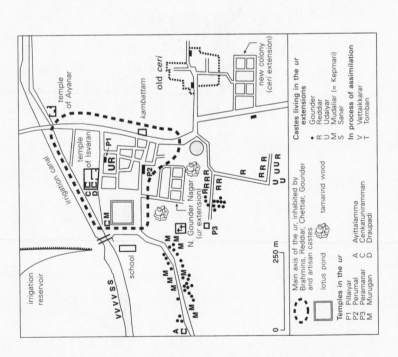

Plan of the *ur* and the *ceri* in Karani

ONE

A childhood in Velpakkam

My paternal grandfather Samikkannu was a serf of Swara Reddi.[1] He was a just man, a staunch worker and loyal to his masters. He was an agricultural labourer but he also practised sorcery. He could cast spells and tame demons. Everyone feared him and respected him too. He had five children by his first wife Kannima, the daughter of a carter from Karai. The demons took three of them: only my father and my aunt Adi survived. One day Grandfather Samikkannu went to see a famous sorcerer to learn more powerful mantras. When he returned, he had with him the daughter of this master sorcerer and she was pregnant. My grandmother said nothing and she was never aggressive towards the newcomer. God alone can tell if she was afraid that Grandfather would cast a spell on her if she argued. She kept on leading her quiet life, raising her children and then her rival's, who had a boy and a girl. The children grew up together and, when their turn came, they were sent to work for the Reddi.

One day a friend of Grandfather Samikkannu came to tell him that there were some jobs going on the coconut plantation in Madras where he worked. Grandfather prepared a little bundle of clothes for each of his sons and they left after sunset with this friend without anyone knowing. Grandfather thought it was a unique opportunity and that the boys would earn more in town. The next day he told the Reddi that they had left to see some relatives in a distant village. He tried to do the

1

boys' work with his two wives and his two daughters but it was difficult
– they didn't always manage to make ends meet because in those days
women touched almost nothing and girls even less. Life became hard at
Velpakkam. But at least we had the sky, the clouds, water, all of nature.
Water gushed out everywhere in those days! We had about three monsoons a year, the land was fertile and everything grew without much
trouble. And that's why, even though his sons had left, Grandfather
managed to hold on to the few plots of land that he owned.

The separation was heartbreaking for Grandmother though. She was
always crying and lamenting and wishing that the boys would come
back, or at least her son Nadesan. Night and day, she tried to think of
ways to bring him home and she decided to talk about it to her sister
who lived in Ranganam. She went to see her with Aunt Kanikkai.[2] Her
sister tried to comfort her and suggested that she marry Nadesan to the
daughter of one of her relatives whose husband was settled in Madras as
well. 'Their daughter is beautiful, as light as a Tamil, in good health,
and she can do a man's work', she said to her.[3] 'Nadesan will be won
over when he sees her and he won't have the heart to leave his wife and
his village any more.' Grandmother listened closely to her elder sister
and returned comforted to Velpakkam.

Women are skilful when it comes to planning marriages. A little
while afterwards, Nadesan visited the village. Grandmother got all the
men together and told them her plan. And in fact my father didn't want
to go back to Madras. He took up his work for the Reddi again and
tried to hold on to the little bit of family land. But all his work was for
nothing, because the children's marriages forced Grandfather and then
Father to pawn the fields and give them up.

From then on, the future depended on the children, on the new
generation. My mother Pattu had seven children who lived, three of
them born at Ranganam. When my brother Muttu was born, they heard
of the death of my maternal grandfather Panderi, who hadn't been in
touch once since leaving for Madras years and years earlier. A friend
who worked with him in a sari warehouse in Madras brought the news
and said that the warehouse owner had taken care of the funeral. So my
grandmother had barely known her husband and my mother never knew
her father. Once she had done her duty as a wife, my grandmother
decided to leave her family-in-law. She gave back her gold *tali* and
returned to Korakkupam, the village where she was born, and where
her brothers lived a more comfortable life. When my grandmother left,
my mother didn't go to Ranganam to give birth any more. Her mother-

in-law Kannima loved her like her own daughter and made her go there: that's why I was born at her house, at my paternal grandparents' in Velpakkam.[4]

It was a night in the month of Markaji, a night when we stay awake fasting and actors entertain us until the early morning. The whole neighbourhood disapproved, but my mother wanted to be there, even with her stomach sticking out like Pillaiyar. She couldn't stay long. The moon had barely risen before she went into labour. My grandmother, who was sitting next to her, hurriedly got up when she saw her breathing like an ox and gathered together all the women. They took my mother back to the house. Grandmother and Aunt Kanikkai prepared what was needed: hot water, rags, castor oil, turmeric, milk weed and the sickle. And then they waited, stroking my mother's forehead and encouraging her.

Day broke. The sound of the hand bell and drum could be heard coming from Perumal's temple in the village, along with the noise of pulleys and buckets: people were taking their ritual bath. The fast had just ended. Here in the *ceri*, the men were getting ready to go to the fields after staying up all night. They stopped in front of the house and seeing my father sitting near the door, his head in his hands, was all they needed to guess what sex the child was. They carried on their way, saying, 'Nadesan has had another daughter!' The women recognised the high-pitched cry of a girl and shouted good-naturedly, 'Hey! Here's another little bitch been born!'

Grandmother, for her part, comforted herself as much as she could by explaining that it wasn't an ordinary day and that, although the month of Markaji was ill-fated, that particular day was auspicious – part of Perumal's festival. A birth on that day could only be a stroke of good luck for the family, even though we say that the fourth daughter brings good fortune only so long as she stays at home and that, after her marriage, she brings no more wealth except to her family-in-law. When she marries, the fourth daughter reduces her family home to poverty; it's as if she'd stripped the house bare!

Be that as it may, I was born on a lucky day, when we worship the gods, and I was given a divine name, Viramma.[5] We Pariahs often use gods' names, because we're not meant to live in a state of cleanliness or take ritual baths all the time. But by using the gods' names, we can purify ourselves many times a day. Don't they say that when you call God by his name, his goodness comes down to you and that just to speak the name of God is an auspicious and worthy act?

Disappointment or misfortune don't last long among us, the poor; we can't live if we brood on them the whole time. So the disappointment of my birth was quickly forgotten and I was welcomed into the household very well.

My childhood passed as if I was living in the kingdom of the gods on earth. Of course, if I compare it to my daughter Sundari's I'm sure it was a little short; we didn't go to school when I was a kid. But I'll always have happy memories of my years in Velpakkam. We spent hours making up games, songs and stories and we picked up everything we could find to make toys. Our days started later than the grown-ups': we'd get up long after sunrise when our mothers came back from the well. The men would be in the fields, the women doing the housework, and the *ceri* would be quiet. Then suddenly it was filled with the squawking and shouting of children. As soon as we woke up, we'd leave the house to talk about what we were going to do that day, about places to explore and paths to discover. But our mothers would put a stop to our discussions to send us off to wash, while they got the littlest ones ready. In my house almost everybody went to work. My grandparents had slaved away in the fields until their dying day to feed the family. Mum went to the Reddi's house in the morning to clean the stable and do whatever else was needed. So she used to hand my little brother over to Sarda, our eldest cousin, who was nursing a child as well, and she'd feed the two babies. Mum would give her a helping of *kuj* and talinga potatoes so she'd have more milk and sometimes Mum would breastfeed the two little ones herself.

Getting ready didn't take much time: a little water on the face, arms and feet and a little ash to brush our teeth. Then we'd swallow some rice in water and millet gruel. My little brothers went around naked. I just put on an underskirt like my sister. Stick in hand, dragging our carts made of coconuts, we went from house to house looking for friends who'd join us, each of them with their treasures: tea sets, marbles, ropes, pebbles, little white shells. And off we went! We'd stop here and there, climb trees, steal fruit, pick grain and plants, collect stones, singing and squawking away the whole time.

The boys always walked in front, faster than us. Little by little we'd lose sight of them. We girls never split up. We used to go across the fields and when it was the millet season we'd stop to pick it. The millet at Velpakkam was fantastic, with big ears that were all round and very yellow. Some of us would hold out our underskirts while the others tore off the ears and threw them in: we only used to steal about ten ears in each field. Once we'd gathered our harvest, we'd climb to the top of a hill not far from there and stop under the shade of a big banyan tree. We'd put down our loads there so we could go back down to the foot of the hill to pick some lentils. The mornings passed without us noticing. There'd be less and less shade and the heat would get more and more scorching. Hunger pangs reminded us that it was meal time. Then some of us would go back to the *ceri* to find something to eat, as well as a bit of salt and a matchbox with two matches – but not so much that our parents would notice that we'd been pinching stuff. The *kuj* was poured into little jars and we had to go through the houses taking a bit from each one. The girls who'd stayed at the foot of the hill shelled the lentils, then climbed back to the top to the treasures that had already been collected. From up there on top, we could see the girls coming back from the *ceri* carrying little jars piled on top of each other. We used to have fun shouting to them, screaming and calling out names, and the echo would make them come back as funny words that made us giggle. Finally, when we were all back together, we put the jars on the ground and sat around them in a circle with our legs crossed. Before starting we'd check that everyone had something to eat, because, particularly in the slack months, some parents couldn't provide any food for the midday meal. Well, in that case we shared. The girls who could gave a little bit of *kuj*. It's not for nothing that people say that Pariahs are like crows, children and grown-ups alike. It's not just the colour. Like crows, we're always in a group. Like crows, we never eat alone. When a crow finds something, he calls his friends to come and share it with him: it's the same with us.

Once we had wolfed down the *kuj* and finished the meal, it was time for the tea party. We adored this game and often we played marriage feasts. I always used to ask to be the husband and Kirti was my wife. The ceremony, that was something! Everyone knew their role. First the flowers. There had to be flowers, of course, to decorate the platform where the bride and groom were going to sit. We found yellow chrysanthemums all year round and, depending on the season, we mixed them with red colville flowers or wild jasmine, which smells so sweet. Kitteri, Rukkumani and Nilamma were the experts. There was nothing they didn't know about garlands and ropes of flowers. They could arrange the shapes, the colours and the smells with perfect taste: we loved their talents and sometimes we called our parents to show them their works of art. Kasturi, Nayaki and Patchamma used to play drums with tins and sing. Nagamma was the priest and the rest took care of the feast.

One group collected twigs, put them between stones and carefully lit a fire using the two matches that had been pinched from the house. Others hulled the millet that had been picked on the way there; a bang on the head with a stick and the grains spilled out on the ground. There was lots of laughing and singing while we prepared everything. We were very happy copying the grown-ups. We quietened down for the meal which ended the ceremonies and we handed out the millet and the lentils on coral-tree leaves.

Then the sun started going down. When we saw it between the coconut palms, we had to set off home, nibbling millet or carrying empty jars on our heads. Usually we stopped at a pond. We put down our clothes and the jars on the bank and threw ourselves into the water, having races like Whites in the sea, diving and coming up further along until our eyes were as red as gourd-ivy berries.

Sometimes when we were bathing, we had trouble with the boys who'd left with us in the morning and who came back by the pond as well when the sun was setting. Those little bastards used to take our underskirts, climb up a nearby tree and enjoy the show. At first we were ashamed and with our hands over our fannies begged them to stop. The big girls, most of all, didn't dare show themselves naked and they'd plead with the boys to give them back their clothes. And then, bit by bit, we'd get angry and throw stones at them, calling those bums every kind of name: 'Hey! Cowherd! You jam rags!'; 'Hey! Juice drinker! Come here and I'll take you to see my mum and dad!'; 'Faggots! What are you messing around here for? What the bloody hell has it got to do with you that we're skinny dipping, you widows' brats?'

That would get to them and they'd get off their perches to hit us, but a group of us would always manage to drag them into the pond and dunk their heads under the water. Then they'd throw our underskirts back, break the jars and scamper off like donkeys.

Often we'd get home before our parents. As soon as they got back, the men would leave again, their *soman* down to their ankles and their *tundu* knotted on their heads. Off to the wine stall! Their day was finished and they didn't hang around at home; often the women had to run after them to get a bit of money. Because there was still a lot for the women to do, starting with the market. We kids loved following our mothers to the market. A market is always interesting, even the one in the *ceri* with just a few little stalls and not much to choose from. The women caught up with the stallholders and they used to chat and sometimes buy us a cake, a *vadai* or a *murukku*. But they didn't waste much time, because they had to prepare the evening meal, the one full meal of the day: some rice, a good strong sauce, some vegetables. Our job, as little girls, was to grind the spices: fenugreek, cumin, chillis which burnt our hands.

The dumb things I've done in the kitchen! One day I sat down totally naked on the grindstone where some chillis had just been crushed. Ayo! My thighs and my ring-doughnut were on fire, Sinnamma![6] (*Viramma laughs.*) My mother was furious and hit me, telling me once more that I shouldn't sit on the grindstone because it's sacred. Mother Lakshmi resides there and it's an insult to the goddess to go and put your behind on top of her! The burning lasted all night, but that time it had really sunk in; words are useless when you're young, you learn by experience.

Burns and things getting burnt: the number of stories I could tell you about that ... The thing is, we didn't always go to the market with our mothers. Often when they got back from work they'd quickly light the wood, put the water for the rice on the fire because it took a long time to cook, and then run off alone to the stalls, telling us to keep an eye on it all. We'd feel important; obviously cooking a real meal with real food was a change from our tea parties. But we'd quickly lose interest because it was tempting to go and find our friends rather than stay and watch the fire. I ruined some rice like that! Alerted by the smell of burning, a neighbour discovered the disaster; she put everything out and ran to tell Mum, who hurried back from the market. Mum took her anger out on me and then, disheartened, she fixed a plainer meal of *kanji* seasoned with tamarind chutney: it wasn't easy when the men would get home half-drunk and find their evening meal wasn't what they expected.

Good intentions weren't always enough: the worst happened one evening when I really wanted to help Mum. She and Grandmother were still in the fields, picking the Reddi's chillis. I got it into my head to start fixing the meal before they came back. There was kindling and wood and I wanted to cook rice. But it was impossible to get the fire to take! Smoke everywhere, yes, stinging eyes, but no flame. Impatient, I decided to try using petrol. I'd already seen Mum use it to get things done faster. I opened the lamp and poured half the petrol in it on to the twigs. Then I put a match to it ... in a flash, flames were licking the palm roof, which had been repaired a few months earlier. Terrified, I ran for help. But big brother Sinnatambi and big brother Kannan had already seen the fire spreading. There was a crowd immediately and the first buckets of water went round. The news spread faster than the fire itself: Mum left the harvest and, devastated, came running. I heard her shouts, 'Ayo! Ayo! Is she burnt? Oh, my little one, my child, my girl!' I pushed through the crowd to get to her. And when she saw me safe and sound her anxiety gave way to anger, she was Kali incarnate, thunder and lightning. She threw herself at me, gave me a thrashing and left me to my tears. I hurt all over. I hid behind Kitteri's house and didn't move, promising myself that I wouldn't try to do good any more if you had to pay such a high price! Thanks to everybody's help, only our roof had burnt but the neighbours had had to get their thatch out of the way fast so that the fire didn't spread to the whole *ceri*. Dad and his friend Irsin had been doing a deal: they'd both repaired the neighbours' roofs and they'd lost at least a day's work. We'd have to borrow money to replace our roof. Grandmother, who never treated anything as a tragedy, came and found me and took me home. 'Viramma's safe,' she repeated to my mum, 'that's the main thing, isn't it?' It was too emotional for everybody and no one was hungry. That night they sent me to bed without eating.

Whenever we kids got back to the *ceri* earlier, we played more games: hopscotch, horses, slaps, hidden hand – but never jacks, because picking something up in the evening brings bad luck and makes the spirits of misfortune pick up everything lying around in the house themselves. The ring was one of our favourite games. We could sing and dance for hours and hours.

The *ceri* was always full of noise and singing and shouting. It's always full of life where we live, but in the village, in the *ur*, everything's quiet, everyone's in their home. The children in the *ur* could only play at set times. They were forbidden to do loads of things and they didn't know the countryside around the village. Only the children of the Kudiyanar went out a bit: their parents were agricultural workers like ours.

In those days we didn't go to school. There was one in the *ur* but it wasn't for us. Our lives were made up of games and stories. Our schoolmaster in his own way was Grandfather Munissami, Kitteri's grandfather. What a storyteller! He could make us laugh and he was happy to tell the same story again and again if we asked him. Each story lasted several days and every evening he'd say to me, 'Hey, Kannima's granddaughter! Tell me where we got to yesterday!' I'd faithfully remind him of the last thing he'd said the night before and he'd carry on. He taught us songs and riddles as well. I still remember some of them. 'Sheep without number which graze in a field without limits – what are they? They are the stars in the sky.' 'The Brahmin who runs with three stripes on his back – who is he? He is the squirrel.'[7] Once I asked Minatchi, the daughter of the Reddi who Mum worked for, one of Grandfather Munissami's riddles: 'My parents are the sun and the sea and they've left me in every house – who am I?' She didn't get it and I didn't want to give her the answer. She complained to her mother who called mine. I was scolded for having wanted to show off my little knowledge in front of our masters who are much better educated than us. Humiliated, I shouted the answer from the door of the stable where I had gone to hide: 'It's salt!'

The stories Grandfather Munissami knew! He knew as much as a schoolmaster but we chose to go to him. He was unstoppable and it was as if us kids were hypnotised by his words, the sound of his voice. Our heads were full of dreams, we never felt tired or hungry. Normally Nayaki's mother's shouting brought us back to earth, 'Aye! These she-devils, these ring-doughnuts! They're almost up with the sun as if they had work to do, and when night falls here they still are with their games and their stories!' She used to shake her daughter and everyone would go home. That's when hunger would suddenly hit, as if we hadn't eaten for days. We'd tear into our dishes of rice as if we were starving and be full before we'd even finished what was there. Another telling off from our mothers and then we'd fall instantly into a deathly sleep. We'd leave for another world, such a lovely one, the world which Grandfather Munissami described to us night after night.

Our days of happiness flowed past like this, our days of games and laughter. And then we became young men or young girls. It wasn't a question of age or build, it was a question of money, because everything depended on what your family owned. The eldest children generally started work earlier. They had to look after the little ones or bring in a few pennies. When we started roaming a bit too far, it wasn't long before our parents ordered us to come to the fields to stay in their sight and start learning the trade. We were told, 'Listen little girls, life is not just songs. You can't play like that for ever. You must learn to use your hands. One day you'll go and make your life elsewhere and people must be able to say, "Here's a good worker! Here's a pair of hands that'll bring in money and not just another mouth to feed!"'

We weren't keen on giving up our games to work and we argued; but once we were dragged to the fields, we set to. It was slow at the start. We watched. We tried. We learned, you know! It was only later that we began to be paid – almost nothing: four *anna*, a quarter of a rupee – for picking aubergines, beans, green lentils, black lentils, cassava, chillis. The owners were a bit worried by us, they were afraid the work would get delayed or, even worse, be ruined. But it was such a good deal for them to pay a kid four *anna* a day that they always ended up taking us on. For our part, we would try to pay ourselves a little bit extra in kind. But it was impossible to steal the smallest grain during working hours. The Grand Reddi had a nickname: we called him Owl Eye. He saw everything and he could sniff out people trying to cheat him. When we left the fields, we had to shake out our underskirts and show that our jars were empty, to prove that we hadn't taken anything.

One day I decided with Nagamma and Nayaki to make some peanut cakes. There was no way we were going to buy the nuts when we spent all day picking the Reddi's, so we decided to hide little piles of them in the ground. When we finished work, we queued up to be inspected, got our four *anna* and took the road home. We didn't go very far. When we saw the Grand Reddi had left the field, we turned off by the tamarind-tree path, cut across the Gounder field and like little ants, not missing the smallest pile, we brought in a second harvest – our own this time. The bunches of nuts grew thick around our little waists. We were so happy at bringing off our plan and tricking Owl Eye that we couldn't stop giggling. Our laughter echoed a long way. The Reddi was talking to Subramanian Gounder and Ramalingam Naicker near the fields and he sent his accountant to see what was going on. We'd stopped worrying by then and were hurrying home when suddenly the white figure of the accountant loomed up in front of us. Terrified, screaming as if it was the Budam himself, we stayed stock still instead of trying to run away. 'What the hell are you doing here?' he shouted. Grabbing us by our plaits and knocking our heads together, he dragged us over to the Reddi. We were in tears, ready to give back what we'd stolen and even our wages so long as we weren't beaten. Our trembling didn't move the Reddi. He ordered the accountant to undo our bunches of peanuts and slap us each a couple of times. We let him, expecting to be hit some more, but the Reddi only snarled, 'Get the hell out of here, little bitches, and don't let me catch you again!' We didn't wait a second longer and ran back to the *ceri* at full speed, where everybody, I don't know how, already knew what had happened. Kuppamma's gang had a good laugh at us and the others did too. To save face, our mothers came out and gave us a couple of slaps, more to punish us for not being shrewd enough than to tell us off for stealing. My head hurt and I felt as if I was burning all over. That evening I didn't ask for any food and I didn't go and listen to Grandfather Munissami. As I went to sleep, I promised that I'd be a bit more cunning at the next peanut harvest and that I'd make those bloody cakes in the end!

As we grew up, our working days got longer and we spent all of them in the paddy fields. We learned planting out and weeding. We watched it being done at first and then, with the owner's permission, we climbed down into the paddy field, sank into the mud up to our thighs and tried to copy our mothers. We were never paid for that. They never hired anyone working so slowly, but gradually we became almost as fast as the adults.

It's so much work, the paddy field! We used to sing to while away the hours and forget the tiredness and the pain in our backs:

> Our legs stuck in the mud make us suffer
> Ellamba ellan!
> Have pity on us, executioner!
> Ellamba ellan!
> It's the hour of our meal,
> Ellamba ellan!
> We've quickly planted out,
> Ellamba ellan!
> A seedling of paddy for each cubit,
> Ellamba ellan!
> Pains in our knees, drawn faces,
> Ellamba ellan!
> We've finished three *kani*
> Ellamba ellan!
> Kannimma is going to the market,
> Ellamba ellan!
> To buy three measures of millet,
> Ellamba ellan!
> And some dry chillis,
> Ellamba ellan!
> To restore us when we're so exhausted,
> Ellamba ellan!
> But she must have grilled nuts as well,
> Ellamba ellan!

We used to tell each other funny stories as well and the gossips' tongues would wag away in the paddy fields! Often we'd add our own selections to the songs everyone knew and it would end up in a terrible racket. In the shadow of the palm tree, from where he'd oversee his world, the owner used to get up from his cord bed and come and chase us, hitting us with his umbrella.

That's how we learned to work, Sinnamma. We would rather have
carried on playing and getting up late. We would have loved to stay
children all our lives, and we tell ourselves that if it wasn't for these
bloody stomachs which we always have to fill, we'd live innocently and
happily. In my day we did our education in the fields. These days it
happens at school. The children are collected, they're given books and
pencils, and even the midday meal as well: the mistresses look after the
little ones while their mothers work. Even so, there are very few boys in
the *ceri* who've stayed right to the end. We sent our Anban to school
until he was nine or ten. But that son of an idiot didn't want to stay
there: he couldn't stand being smacked. So we put him in the fields. We
haven't got another son and we'd just married Miniyamma. He had to
look after the little ones and we always need a young cowherd. You've
got to have time and patience for school. If you've got it, you can
become rich. Children now are shared out between the school and the
land. They don't learn one or the other properly: if we put them on the
land first, they don't have time to go to school regularly; and if we start
them with school, then it's difficult for them to go back to the land.
They grow up, they're not obedient any more, and then, one day, they
decide to go and look for work in town, leaving behind their parents
who've suffered to bring them up. That's the fate of our Pariah caste
and it's very true, that saying 'One span forward, one cubit back.' Education is there, at our disposal, but we still don't know how to take
advantage of it. In my time there wasn't a choice. The line was drawn
and it had to be followed. Learn agricultural work and housework from
a young age: that was work and it paid immediately!

When I'd return to the *ceri* after working in the fields, my day was
still not over. I went with my mother to the Reddi's to clean out the
stable and sweep the courtyard. While she winnowed the paddy and
ground the spices, I did the washing up and drew the water. I loved
going to the Reddi's with Mum because there was always something to
do there. Minatchi and Janaki, the Reddi's daughters, liked me a lot: I
entertained them and indulged their whims. I'd play at being a dog for
them and run around on all fours while they chased me, laughing, with
sticks in their hands. They often asked me to tell them stories: I knew
a lot more than they did.

One day Janaki, the eldest, kept on at me to tell her a story about a
demon. I knew she'd be afraid and I didn't want to. But she hit me and
threatened to tell her mother that I'd cracked a jar that evening when I
was going to get water. I gave in and told her the story of Murugan's

messengers who live in drumstick trees, their favourite tree. I made it very clear that you mustn't go near drumstick trees when the sun is at its height or after it has set. Janaki asked if the drumstick tree near the toilets was inhabited. Of course it was!

Mum had finished her work and she came and found me. We went back to the *ceri*. Next morning, the Reddi's wife called for Mum very early and bit her head off. Janaki had convulsions and a fever. She had been crying all night. Mum fell to her knees and promised to beat me and not bring me with her any more, and she asked what story I'd told. When she knew it was the story of the spirit which climbs the drumstick trees, she was relieved and reassured her mistress, stressing that the demon wasn't harmful, it was an envoy of Murugan. She suggested going and finding big brother Mani, who knew what to do with spirits as well as demons: banging his drum and the right mantra would heal the child. She ran to the other end of the village, near the pond, to big brother Mani's. He was getting ready to leave for work, but he was a simple, peaceful man, always at another's service, even ours. He went home, put down his Sanar's tools, took his little drum shaped like an hourglass and set off with Mum for the Grand Reddi's house. They set him up in the back courtyard and brought him the child. Big brother Mani had no trouble healing Janaki, who felt completely recovered when he'd finished the last songs of praise. The Reddi's wife gave a little measure of rice to big brother Mani who was very happy and everyone went home. I was still asleep. A pair of slaps woke me up. I burst into tears. Mum fixed herself a chew of betel to calm herself down. Crying, I went up to her and told her that it wasn't my fault: I had told the story under threat. Mum replied that it would be better to be slapped a couple of times by Janaki or her mother than let ourselves talk about spirits to our masters. 'Those children don't go out of their houses,' she told me. 'They know nothing about nature and they're afraid of the evil eye. You mustn't talk to them about that!'

She was right. Janaki and Minatchi never put their noses outdoors, not even on to the *tinnai*. Always shut away in their big house, the poor things! Friendship, discovering nature, Grandfather Munissami's stories – they were forbidden all of that. That's the lot of high-born children! Their parents think they're amusing them with toys or expensive things but they're barely interested. I really realised that when I went to a dolls' marriage for the first time.

It was like a real marriage: there was a *pandal* covered in flowers, fireworks, a carriage decorated with garlands and ropes of jasmine, musicians, women and girls in silk with gold embroidery, saffron, rose water, trays of presents, sweets, a feast for the guests. We were stunned to see a parade like that for a dolls' marriage. We tried to get near the carriage with the dolls in, but our clothes and our sweat gave us away and we had to step back. Finally, we settled down discreetly in a margosa tree which was facing the *pandal*. Huddled together like monkeys in our tree, we could watch everything: the ceremonies that went on and on, ladies bustling around, the Brahmin muttering in his corner, busy with the rites, and the men sitting in the middle of the *pandal*, talking and chewing betel. Some children were sitting down, others were following their mothers, but they all looked as if they were bored stiff. It was obviously no fun playing dolls with grown-ups! There wasn't anything wrong, it was all too perfect!

Our dolls weren't as beautiful. They came from the potter in Viramangalam or they were made from healing wood and bought at the festivals of Draupadi to cure wounds and abscesses. Lots of our dolls didn't have any legs or arms left, but how happy we were playing with them!

We became less and less impressed; this dolls' marriage was dead dull. We only stayed for the food. The smell of cooking was making our stomachs hollow but it was given out to the poor quite late. When we got our share, we went back to the *ceri* to divide up what we'd been given.

That's when I found out that the dolls' marriage was not a game for children. A suitor had come to see Janaki, but the meeting hadn't led to anything and it was a bad omen. When there's a dolls' marriage, things should work themselves out and a real marriage should be arranged very quickly; it's a tradition of the castes above us, especially the Reddiar.[8] It's very expensive, but it's effective, because, sure enough, Janaki was married within the year!

TWO

The marriage is arranged

I was still a little girl, innocent, happy and flat-chested, when it was decided that I should get married. Big sister Ellamma, one of my much older cousins, had been given to a family from Karani. When she heard that my future parents-in-law were looking for a daughter-in-law, she let them know that she knew an ideal little girl in Velpakkam, the village where she was born. Big sister Ellamma has always loved my mother very much and she wanted to show her affection by arranging this marriage. It was a happy day at home when she came to say what was going on: I can still see my mother weeping with joy on the *tinnai* and big sister Ellamma comforting her. The idea seemed tempting to Mum. 'It's true that things are going well for Ellamma over there,' she said. 'Viramma could be happy at Karani too and if anything happened, Ellamma would be there to take care of her. My *puja* haven't been in vain, Periyandavan has blessed us.'

She left for the big market at Selvipatti straightaway and brought back some very fresh fish and a large supply of palm wine to prepare a meal fit for the occasion. When Dad came back from work, Mum quickly came out of the house, told him to wash his feet and come back immediately because Ellamma was there with important news. Dad told his friends who were off to the wine stall that a visitor was going to keep him at home. Mum let grandmother explain their idea to him. She did it in a low voice. I knew they were talking about me, but I only heard

15

snatches of sentences: 'She will be happy ... She will work well ... Ellamma will be there to look out for her ... Karani's not far, we'll be able to go and see her a lot ...' I thought they wanted to send me to work for the Reddiars of big sister Ellamma, where I'd earn more and get board and lodging as well.

I called my best friend Nayaki over into a corner and told her the whole story and made her promise to keep it secret, even from her parents. Of course, by the next morning everybody was more or less in the know and was trying to find out exactly what was being planned. My parents remained cautious, saying that nothing had been decided and that there were only inquiries being made about me: if it ended in a refusal, what a bad blow for their daughter's reputation! But Mum was confident, because big sister Ellamma was someone you could rely on. And at Karani, my future mother-in-law was thinking the same thing. She consulted the Iyer who set the auspicious day for a visit to Velpakkam. Things were taking shape.

In the mean time, marriage was explained to me. I was going to leave home, leave my family, my friends and the village where I'd been born, to go and cook and work for strangers. From then on I would only belong to them. I would become their daughter and I would only be able to see my parents with their permission. It was too much for a young thing like me. I sobbed day and night. I begged my mother not to give me away in marriage. I would be good. I'd stop all the games, I'd work hard, I'd bring home lots of money. I also asked Nayaki and my friends to talk to my mother and make her give up her plan. One evening, when she got back from the fields, it was my mother's turn to burst out sobbing. Holding each other in our arms, we cried hot tears. Mum was well aware that I was only a child and that I couldn't understand anything of this but she felt incapable of explaining it to me. She used herself as an example. She had left her mother too to come to Velpakkam: she had had children here and she was happy here, even if we didn't always eat enough. That was the fate of women. Leaving is terrifying, you believe that everything is coming to an end, but everything is only just beginning when you get married. You become a woman and you blossom in the light of your new household.

These words made me think and gave me a bit of strength. My grandmother looked after me as well. She told me that I wouldn't be sent to Karani immediately after the ceremony: I'd stay at home for a while longer. I knew that I could count on her promise and that gave me the heart to face up to the preparations for the first visit.

A half-sari had been cut out from an old sari of my mother's and I let myself be dressed in it, although I far preferred my underskirt with nothing on top. Mum bought me coconut oil almost every day and soaked eclipta and chenille leaves in it to make my hair go dark black and then decorated it with jasmine. Time passed like this: I kept on working in the fields, going for walks with my friends and listening to Grandfather Munissami, until one evening when I was told that the family of my husband-to-be were coming to see me the next day. That oughtn't to have surprised me but the news hit me like lightning striking a young palm tree. The elders tried to comfort me. They spoke to me gently. They gave me advice, 'Make sure you smile ... Bring just a tiny little bit of salt ... Give hardly any lime...' But I spent a terrible night. I imagined awful things. At that age you don't understand what marriage is. I was going to be parted from the people I loved: as far as I could see, it was like a kidnapping. When we were small, we were told to watch out for kidnappers and now, here I was going to be as good as kidnapped with my whole family's blessing! They weren't going to kill me but make me work and 'make a woman out of me'. What was a woman? I was perfectly happy being a little girl. For the first time in my life, I stayed awake the whole night. I heard the first crows announcing that day would soon be breaking. The sky was still black, no moon, no stars, no clouds, no lightning. It was as if it was in tune with my pain. I'd stared at that black sky all night. When a little glimmer of light appeared, I fell asleep.

The visit was set for the afternoon. My grandmother insisted that I be left to sleep very late. No one went to the fields that day. Mum and her cousins bustled about, making *idli*, *uppuma* and *vadai* with drumstick leaves, whey with spices, and pancakes. A great jar of water and a little cup were put at the entrance of the house. Everything was ready when I woke up. Everyone had washed, carefully done their hair and got smartly dressed. I took a long time getting ready and I slipped on the underskirt, still new, which I had been given at Dipavali.[1] Mum took out the pretty coloured glass bracelets which she had bought at the fair. Big sister Ammayi did my hair for a long time. She made me a thick plait with a thousand braids and bound in two good bunches of double jasmine very tightly. My face and arms were powdered. My eyes were made up with a paste which Mum had specially prepared for me and, last of all, a *pottu* was drawn on my forehead with the same paste. I was ready.

My friends were all there, half-naked and smelling of sweat, and they complimented me. Our neighbours trooped past, along with all the inquisitive people. Suddenly we heard the children who were hanging around outside shout, 'Here they are! Here they are!' My father strode out of the house, pushed through the crowd and when he got to the square, the kids burst out laughing, overjoyed that their joke had worked. My father chased them, shaking his shawl with a furious expression and then he let them get away so he could come and talk to the men in front of the house. A good while later uncle Ponnussami came and announced that the visitors had arrived. Dad and the family stepped forward to receive them. I disappeared into the darkness of the house and huddled down in a corner. My heart was beating very hard.

Mum spread mats on the *tinnai* as the guests washed their feet and hands. Both families took their places. The *tinnai* was too small for that many people! Conversation started. The men and women talked about this and that: about the journey to Velpakkam, about the country here and over there. They tried to find out if the families were related and they found one relation, because big sister Ellamma was a niece of my paternal half-uncle who had married a cousin of their line. At last they said that they very much would like to see me.

Without getting up from the *tinnai*, Mum called me and asked me to bring some water. I came out of my hiding place with my head lowered and put a three-quarters-full glass down next to the person who had been pointed out to me. Without lifting my eyes, I went and sat down near grandmother. Silence fell. I felt everyone looking at me, trying to guess, from their first glimpse, what kind of a daughter-in-law I might be: a good one, able to live in the bosom of my new family without rebelling, or a difficult one, ready to run away at the first scolding? The woman who was going to be my mother-in-law asked me in an unconcerned voice to prepare some betel. With my eyes always on the ground and remembering the advice I'd been given, repeatedly, I took a good-looking leaf, broke the stalk, spread very little lime on – a sign of meekness – and sprinkled a little areca nut and ground tobacco. I folded it all up carefully and offered it with both hands to my mother-in-law. A murmur of satisfaction rose from the visitors. Embarrassed and not knowing what to do, I quickly went back to my hiding place. Mum followed me into the house, clasped her hands in front of the trident fixed in the ground and threw me a big smile.[2] Then she brought out the food to eat. Our guests approved of the dishes that had been chosen and the way they tasted. Their reception and the girl seemed to be what they were looking for. When they'd talked about it in a low voice, they let it be known, without spelling it out, that I had pleased them, that the arrangement seemed good and that we must meet again, at Karani this time, to discuss the marriage and the formalities more fully. Mum brought out the trays of betel. The guests helped themselves and then got up. They took their leave with their palms together and headed home, happy with their visit.

Neighbours and friends immediately poured on to the *tinnai*, asking a thousand questions. That's all Grandmother had been waiting for and she described the meeting without sparing her audience the slightest detail. People made flattering comments and then everyone left. The house was full of joy, with everyone repeating that I would find myself in good hands.

Preparations for the marriage started the next day. First the money for the ceremony and the dowry had to be found. Dad borrowed a large sum by pawning the two plots of land which Grandfather owned. After he'd tried to pay the interest for a long time, not to mention the loan itself, he had to give them up. That's how we lost our fields. But I had nothing to complain about. They bought me everything I needed: the jewelry for my nose, two gold bracelets, little silver chains for my ankles, brass dishes, a trunk and clothes and loads of other things as well: my mother-in-law couldn't find fault with my dowry.

On a Wednesday in the month of Kartikkai my family went to Karani: an odd number of my line, a group of nine women in all, neatly dressed with flowers in their hair and a *pottu* on their forehead. They were received very well. The two families talked peacefully and agreed on the dowry, who would pay what expenses for the four ceremonies which would follow one after the other and the date they should take place. I don't know if the people we'd sent had asked to see my intended. In any case, when they came back they were much happier to talk about the terms of the marriage than about the man who was going to be my husband. I would have liked to have known more but I didn't dare ask the question.

The pledge of marriage took place at my home but the cost was my husband's family's responsibility and they came with a huge amount of aubergines, ben-nuts, potatoes, bitter peas and lots of other vegetables.[3] A cook had been hired for the event but friends and relatives gave us a hand too. When the meal was over, there was an exchange of betel and an exchange of commitments between the two families. We said to them, 'Our daughter is yours, your son is ours.' And they replied, 'Our son is yours, your daughter is ours.' From then on, there could be no turning back, unless the head of the *ceri* accepted a withdrawal.

A little later, the Iyer of Karani fixed the dates of the engagement and the marriage, which are always very close together; it would be a Monday in the month of Tai.

There were only a few weeks to go and my parents were busy for the whole month of Markaji. In those days they weren't in deep poverty and they did their best, thanks to a loan from the Grand Reddi and the little savings they'd made. I was covered in jewels and there was a fine reception for everybody: that's what people still say at Karani as well as at Velpakkam! But it wasn't achieved without pain. Grandmother put everything aside that she'd been able to hang on to, from kindling to spices. Dad went to drink at the wine stall less often. After his work in the fields he'd go and find palmyra palms and, with a friend, he'd make winnowing fans, baskets and betel boxes. At the cotton harvest, Mum put a few pounds aside to make me pillows. Dad and Grandfather carded them carefully until they were as soft as silk. They filled two big pillows and covered them in cloth ordered from Sinnatambi, the weaver from Palayam. A marriage trunk was bought from Selvipatti market, a beautifully coloured trunk with geometric designs.

That's how the grown-ups spent their time during that Markaji. I carried on working and playing like before. We had fun acting out my marriage and we'd crack up laughing.

But the weeks passed and the Friday of the month of Tai fixed for the engagement arrived. This time the meal was our responsibility. Mum prepared seven kinds of vegetables, some *sambar*, *idli*, *payasam* and whey flavoured with coriander and ginger. We had a little time ahead of us because the guests had to wait for the unlucky hour to end before setting out.[4] At last the women arrived with the baskets of presents on their heads. Grandmother and the women of our family had gone out to receive them. The eldest sisters of my husband-to-be were the ones who'd come and they had smiles on their faces. After they'd greeted us, they put down their loads in the middle of the house. The baskets were full to the brim. In one, there was a sari, a blouse, a skirt, bracelets, a mirror, a comb and some *kungumam*. In the two others, there were three lots of betel, three bunches of bananas, three clusters of areca nuts, flowers, coconuts, turmeric, an oil lamp and a betel tray.

After they had closely examined all the presents, our women arranged them prettily on banana leaves. They lit the oil lamp and made me take three turns round the offerings: everyone prostrated themselves in front of the god of our line and our ancestors. When everything had been carefully arranged, the meal was served to the guests. Like the first time, the meal was very well received and Mum was complimented. In turn, she thanked our guests for the pretty sari and the presents they'd brought and she offered them on a tray a *soman*, a *tundu* and a shirt, five bunches of bananas, five lots of betel and five clusters of areca nuts. Finally we parted to meet up again the day after next, the eve of the marriage, to ward off the evil eye.

We were going to ward off the evil eye at our house again, with my family paying. This time it would be very expensive. My intended would be there for the first time. We had to plan on feeding fifty people, and feeding them well. The daughter's parents have much more of a meal to lay on than the son's and each meal has to be better than the one before.

We are vegetarians in the days leading up to the marriage. No meat, no fish, no eggs – but plenty of lentils. The saying 'No marriage without lentils!' is right. There have to be red lentils for the *sambar*, green lentils for the *payasam*, chickpeas with coconut and sugar and, most of all, there has to be a green lentil paste for the newly-weds' bath: that softens the skin and makes it shine. My parents had set several measures of green lentils aside for the marriage which they had grown themselves and I had picked with my friends. Our supplies of rice weren't enough. One sack had to be borrowed from the Reddi and a second from the carter in the village who knew us well. Mum, big sister Nettappakkam, my cousins Suriya and Vanaroja, my aunts – all the women in my family had set to work for this meal.

I was going to see the man I was going to marry for the first time next day and I was afraid. My friends made fun of me and that didn't make things better. The same as when his parents first visited, I was still hidden in my corner when my intended arrived. I didn't want to see him, this man who would become my master and perhaps my executioner: I burst out sobbing thinking about it. But, on the other hand, how could I resist my curiosity. Little by little I found the courage to gently push aside the woven palm leaves of the wall. He was sitting on the platform set up for the ceremony, dressed in white, in the middle of a buzzing crowd. I couldn't have been more surprised when I saw that his face was gentle and smiling. He must have been the same age as my youngest uncle, he was an old man for a little girl like me. But it's not the age that matters, it's the person ... My first impression was more or less good ... We'd see! I dried my tears on my skirt when I heard my mother calling, 'Viramma! Viramma! Aren't you ready yet?' I jumped out of my hole like a mouse and my cousins dressed me.

I was given the signal to come out and big sister Sarda led me to the
platform by the hand. With my head lowered, I admired all the *kolam*
that cousins and friends had drawn: the ground was covered with them.
I had never seen the house so neat, so well decorated. Well, perhaps for
my brother's marriage, but I was still very small then and I couldn't
remember it exactly. They made me take three turns round the platform
which was covered in a white cloth lent by the launderer. Then I was
put at my fiancé's side. I was shaking like an old woman, with emotion
and shyness. Mum whispered something in my ear but I didn't understand a word of what she was saying. I guessed she was telling me to
calm down and be brave. Facing us, there was the roller of a grindstone
for grinding rice, a little tray of lit camphor and flowers and a large
brass tray with dishes full of oil, sandalwood, turmeric and green lentil
paste.

My fiancé's mother gave the signal to begin. Behind me Mum
whispered what I had to do. I took the oil and, with it, I anointed my
husband-to-be's forehead, hands and feet. Then I did the same with the
lentil paste and the sandalwood, one after the other. I took the little tray
of camphor and performed the *alam*, turning the flame in a circle round
the man. Then it was his turn to anoint my forehead, hands and feet
with oil, paste, sandalwood, turmeric. The tray of betel was passed
around. Everybody took their share and a banana as well. My fiancé
stood up. I did the same. We prostrated ourselves in front of the tray of
burning camphor, then each of us went off to take their bath. During
the ceremony the young girls – my cousins and friends – had struck up
the marriage songs. Now they kept going while they were waiting for
the meal. My mother, big sister Ellamma and other married women led
me. They washed my hair with *sikakai*, they anointed my body first
with green lentil paste and then turmeric and then they rinsed me. My
fiancé was bathed by the men of his family. When the baths were
finished, we performed a fresh *alam* with the tray of camphor and moved
on to the meal.

The women served the food on banana leaves: *idli*, *vadai*, whey,
vegetables, fantastic ginger, tamarind and coriander chutneys. It wasn't
every day that we ate that well! Our new relatives were happy with such
a feast and proud of the family. This was important because it made
relations between the two families easier. We could go to Karani with
our heads held high since we had performed our duty so well by the
grace of Periyandavan, who had given my parents the wherewithal, even
if it meant hardship and a long time paying it off. A ceremony hasn't

succeeded, Sinnamma, unless it's out of the ordinary and unless everyone agrees that it is. Unfortunately not everyone can afford the same
and so grievances are born and they last until death and even beyond.
In this *kaliyugam*, Sinnamma, money gives the orders, even amongst the
poor! What's the *nalungu*? It's the ceremony protecting a couple about
to be wed from the evil eye. But what sticks in people's minds? That
there were lots of people, that people had spent a great deal, that the
meal was fantastic. Truthfully, that's what people notice and that's what's
talked about afterwards: the original meaning of the ceremony is forgotten. I believed in the rites and I performed them sincerely. I didn't ask
any questions, I was happy to live out the *nalangu* and drive away the
evil eye. But afterwards, I was just the same as everybody else.

The day after was the day of the marriage. We got ready early in the
morning to leave for Karani. My hair and the mats were covered with
flowers. My ears were hung with the five gold jewels. Fourteen bracelets
– twelve glass between two gold-plated – were slipped on each arm,
silver rings were put on my toes and big sister Ellamma did my make-
up. The evening before she had drawn pretty mangoes on my palms and
little flowers on the inside of my fingers and my feet with a henna paste
which she had left soaking for hours. When I took off the paste the next
morning, the shapes stood out clearly a beautiful red against my dark
skin. She had drawn a beauty spot on my cheek and last of all a black
pottu on my forehead.

While I was getting dressed, Mum prepared the marriage chest. She
put in a cup for oil, a little brass pot for water, a betel tray, an oil lamp,
coconuts, bunches of bananas, nine rice flower pancakes wrapped in
banana leaveas, rice and palm sugar. The trunk was put on big brother
Sami's head who carried it to Karani. Big brother Maciyan took a basket
with a pot of whey, a big pumpkin and the marriage mat.

And the procession set off! The musicians of the *ceri* were in front,
then the porters and the women: Mum, Grandmother, big sister Ellamma
and my cousins. I came next, in front of Dad and my uncles. The whole
ceri came with us to the temple of Mariamman, and we broke a coconut
and prostrated ourselves before the goddess. Friends and cousins stopped
there. They wished us a good journey and a happy marriage before going
back home. It was very early in the morning, the sun was about to rise
and we had to hurry to reach Karani before the unlucky hour. In the
half-darkness I guessed all the fields we were crossing and listed, one
after the other, the names of their owners. I knew them all by heart. The

harvest had been brought in. The fields were empty and nature was sad. Sad like me. But what was to be done? I'd been told that it was for my own good that I was being sent away from that land where I was born and led off to people that I did not know. And I started crying softly, while all the talk around me was of marriage.

After several hours' walk, we finally saw the *ceri* of Karani. They had already started working the land there and some fields had even been sown. It was strange, this picture of life beginning. At the start of the road which led to the *ceri*, our musicians began playing. The sound of the *senai* was thrilling and I was distracted from my thoughts by the beating of the drums. We stopped in front of the *ceri* temple and sat down. I sat in the middle, surrounded by my relatives. A few minutes later, my parents-in-law and a few members of their family came to greet us, bringing three pots of an infusion of onion and palm sugar and three trays of betel. They took their places facing us. The head of the *ceri* was with them and stood up. He took a pot and a tray and passed them to my father. Then he turned to my fiancé's side and gave a pot and a jar to the head of his family as well. Then each of our fathers put a five rupee note on the third betel tray and presented it to the head of the *ceri* with the third pot. By accepting them, the man recognised the willing union of the two families.

Then Mum opened the marriage trunk. She took out nine rice pancakes, the palm sugar and eleven bananas which she peeled. She kneaded it all together on a banana leaf, repeating, 'Here it is, as a sign of alliance, alliance, O alliance!' Then she divided the mixture into three equal shares, one for each family and one for the head of the *ceri*. When they'd received their shares, each drank a mouthful of the infusion, while the musicians played very hard to mark the end of the ceremony. The children there grabbed the pots and, with loud shouts, claimed their right to a drink, 'Over here! Over here!'

With the alliance sealed like that, my new family received me into the *ceri*. The procession, with the musicians and porters leading, toured the ward. Everyone was at their door and the women sang songs of welcome:

> Oh young girl without match
> He's received you himself
> Beautiful as you are in your jewels.
> He's given you a garland of purple mountain ebony and jasmine
> He's bathed you
> With rose water, sandal and musk.

Having adorned you,
Having decked your neck and knot of hair
With a garland of fresh yellow champaks
With a garland of wild jasmine,
He has put a *pottu* on your forehead
He has put on your diadem
He has knotted your gold *tali*,
For you, the lotus on his chariot

The children shouted with joy. I used to be a child too and, a few weeks earlier, I used to shout like them. Now I was the strange creature. I would have liked to have been able to join them. I was almost jealous.

I walked forward with my head lowered, my heart heavy and my tears ready to fall. But I was all alone in feeling like this: around me it was a holiday, the streets were swept and strewn with coconut leaves, the sky was blue and cloudless. We came up to the house. A *pandal* had been put up and banana tree trunks had been tied to the entrance posts together with bunches of bananas, palmyra fruit and coconut palms.

My mother-in-law was waiting for me at the entrance to the *pandal*. The musicians and porters stepped back. I was led up to the entrance where the *alam* was performed three times with the tray of lit camphor. Accompanied by three women of my line, I entered the house in the proper way with my right foot first. I was given a tour and put my hand in all the jars and all the stores of rice, salt and bran to get used to my future home and take possession of it. Then the meal was served, a vegetarian feast. It was all good. The men ate first, then the women. Afterwards I was dressed in the silk marriage sari, my hair was done again, my eye make-up touched up, and the garland of flowers pinned to my plait was changed.

I was led round the *ceri* again by the musicians, and then to the marriage platform which was beautifully decorated with flowers. The mat that big brother Maciyan had brought had been unrolled on it. Every object needed was there: mortar and pestle, betel tray, incense holder, a clay tray, the little brass oil lamp with the image of Kamatchi, the big oil lamp on feet, soil from the paddy field, palms, millet ears and two pots of water. A bo-tree branch was planted in the middle of a little square of leaf mould. There were wheatgerms around it and a coconut surrounded by a mass of jasmine, covered with turmeric and *kungumam*. The gold *tali* was threaded on a yellow string next to two little bracelets, a plate of cooked rice and a cup of oil.

The Iyer was sitting on the right of the bo-tree branch. He muttered, then he stopped and signalled that we could begin. He gave a handful

of rice to my husband who brought it to my forehead and my thighs
and then passed it to me. I did the same to him and put the rice back
on the plate: the priest keeps that rice. The priest then sprinkled us
with sesame oil and mango buds to ward off the evil eye for a second
time. He lit the tray of camphor, prostrated himself in front of it and
told us to grasp it and present it to the bo-tree branch and all the other
objects. Then we went back to our places on the platform. The priest
put the two bracelets over the wrists of my husband. He gave me the
pestle, which I was supposed to take in my sari. I didn't understand
what this rite meant and all the teasing made me hesitate. I heard people
laughing and saying, 'Oh, she's just a child! She's still an innocent!' We
got up again to walk round the bo-tree branch three times. Then we sat
back down. The initial rites had been performed: the *tali* could be put
round my neck. Now the musicians were playing with all their strength
and people were talking, laughing. The priest recited the *Jaya mangalam*.
My heart beat to the rhythm of the drum, pada, pada, pada … As if I
was in a trance, I felt a foot pressing on my thigh, hands putting the *tali*
around my neck and tying three knots in the string. The sound of the
horn rose highest above the din. Without thinking I prostrated myself
before the burning camphor.

We were married.

I almost had to be brought back to life again to walk round the bo-
tree branch for the last time. My head was empty as I went round. I
don't know now what I was thinking about, but I was too moved to
show whatever it might have been. My eldest sister-in-law went ahead
of us with the tray of camphor. The evil eye had to be warded off again.
The *alam* was performed at each of the cardinal points, we prostrated
ourselves and then went back to our places on the platform. The guests
and relatives filed past to give us money. The last test was to see who
could find the coin at the bottom of the marriage jar: whoever did took
all the money home. I pretended to go along with the game but I didn't
even want to try and win: I let my husband. Afterwards the branch was
dug up, the women took down the platform and swept the *pandal*.
Dinner was served, as generous as the first meal. When everyone had
had their fill, the only thing left was to perform the rite of the growth
of the cereals before going back to Velpakkam.

I was given a new basket, filled with a mixture of about ten grains, a
coconut, areca nut, betel, flowers and bananas, as well as a jar of rice in
water with a pinch of salt, three grilled peppers and a banana leaf. I put
the jar on my head, the basket on my hip and went and joined my

husband. He was behind the house. Near the stable, a little patch of land had been cleared and cut up into four very small plots. I put down the basket and the jar and I sowed some grain in two of the plots. My husband sowed the other two. He broke the coconut, offered the bananas and the flowers to the earth and lit the camphor. The two of us prostrated ourselves. He stood up and washed his hands. I poured the rice in water into his open palms as a reminder of a wife's duties towards her husband and each of their daily tasks. He drank the rice while the kids all around were doubled up with laughter and making fun of us, waiting to pinch the leftovers. I rinsed the jar and filled it with water. I folded a piece of my marriage sari on my head and put the jar on it. My husband took the basket and we returned to the house, with the musicians leading the way. My mother-in-law was on the threshold and performed another *alam* to receive us. Once again a well-filled tray of betel was prepared with three shares, one for each family and one for the head of the *ceri*. We were given a basket with a measure of paddy, a bunch of bananas, three coconuts, some betel and some areca nut. The marriage mat and one of the pillows we'd brought were given back to us. Then my family and I said our goodbyes to my family-in-law and we set off for Velpakkam with my husband. The orchestra led the way. When we arrived in the evening, all the *ceri* was waiting for us. A lot of people had heard the music and come on to the main road to receive us. My husband stayed with us for seven days, then, after a last celebratory meal, this time non-vegetarian, he returned to Karani.

I stayed at Velpakkam for another two monsoons. From time to time I'd go with Mum to pay a visit to my family-in-law, setting off in the morning and coming back in the evening. Nothing had really changed. I was still a child. My friends had almost forgotten, or they acted as if they had forgotten, that I was married. We carried on playing like before. One afternoon, while I was bathing with my friends in the pond at Pakkanur, I lost my gold *tali*. I didn't realise. When I got home, Mum saw my neck bare and panicked. Half a sovereign, which she had gone into debt for, lost so fast and so stupidly! I was beaten but that didn't bring the lost *tali* back and there was no question of buying another in gold. But the situation had to be explained to my family-in-law and the loss made good: my mother decided to buy some new brass utensils to make up the dowry.

Apart from that incident, I was pampered because everyone knew that I was going to leave soon. When I went out in an underskirt with my chest bare, the women of the *ceri* would say to Mum, 'Eh, Pattu!

The areca nuts are pointing, eh! It's going to be the *puttu* soon!' I didn't understand any of all that and I didn't worry. I was happy with my relatives in the *ceri* where I was born and the idea of leaving them had left my head. But now and again, there are certain duties you have to perform. At the first Dipavali after the marriage, presents and clothes have to be sent to the husband. My parents were worried: this time they had to go to the moneylender, because the Grand Reddi wasn't going to grant another request after he'd lent a heavy sum for the marriage a few months earlier. But what I wanted for Dipavali, like any kid, was firecrackers! Mum gave a great sigh and said to Grandmother, 'How's she going to live down there? She's still a child!' Grandmother told her off and said it would happen by itself.

The weeks passed. Some conversations occasionally reminded me that later I would have to leave. Everybody was waiting for a sign, but I didn't know which one.

And one day it appeared.

THREE

'Becoming a woman'

It was the afternoon. I'd set out, with a full dish of sorghum broth in my stomach and a rope and machete in my hand, to go and collect firewood with Rukkumani and her grandmother Subbu.

We had only just left the *ceri* when I felt something running down my thigh. Something cold. I lifted my underskirt and found, to my horror, blood, fresh blood. Fear seized me. I hadn't cut myself, I hadn't scratched myself. I must have been ill to be bleeding like that, but I didn't hurt anywhere. Seeing what was happening, Grandmother Subbu didn't panic at all. Quite the opposite: she told me that it was a happy event and that she was proud to witness it. We turned back. I ran up to Mum to show her the blood on my thigh. She was a bit surprised but she was happy more than anything. She called Aunt Kanikkai and said to her, 'Have a quick look at my daughter. I'm her mother, I shouldn't see this! And tell my mother-in-law.' Aunt Kanikkai lifted up my underskirt and trumpeted, 'Viramma's got her period! We're going to have *puttu*.' I still couldn't understand any of it but I could tell that everybody around me was happy. A celebration was on its way and once again they were going to be invited. My parents felt a mixture of joy and anxiety because they'd have to find the money and do everything to make sure the ceremonies were a success.

Without wasting a second I was taken into the house and ordered not to leave it until the ritual bath had been prepared. Still as sharp as ever

despite her age, Grandmother took everything in hand and briskly set
to work. She was the oldest of the family, rich in experience and capable
of taking decisions on her own and, sometimes, of giving orders to the
men of the house. She showed how important she was once again by
taking care of the invitations and the bath.

First of all she trotted off to the paddy field which Uncle Krishnan
was ploughing, my father's half-brother who was in Velpakkam at the
time. She told him the news and asked him to bring four or five fresh
palms to the house as soon as possible and weave them for my confinement. It's normally the maternal uncle's job, but Mum was an only
daughter and so Uncle Krishnan was the most suitable person for that
role.[1] Grandmother continued through the fields and the *ceri*, talking to
everyone who had to take part in the rites. She gave betel to Kannan,
the drummer, and to seven married women of the family. Out of breath
and parched in the afternoon heat, Grandmother only stopped at home
for an instant, swallowed a little cup of water and then set off again,
with a jar on her head and one on her hip, to collect the bath water
along with Muttamma and Aunt Konakkali.

Mum, meanwhile, was preparing the tonic you're meant to give young
girls for eleven days from the start of their first period: a gruel of green
lentils, rice, unrefined sugar, sesame oil and eggs – a tonic which
strengthens the uterus and the brain, allows women to fight illness and
tiredness all their lives and makes sure they have safe pregnancies and
births. When she'd prepared it she offered it to the god of our line. We
were alone, each of us in a corner of the room. I took the opportunity
to ask what all this meant. Mum told me that I had become a true
woman and that now I was going to live with my husband. I felt cold
suddenly; the news gave me goose bumps. I argued but it was no use.
Mum told me how important what had happened to me was and she
started saying the same things she'd said before my marriage. I burst
into sobs. This time, it was over! No one could promise any more to
keep me after the ceremony as they'd promised at the time of my
marriage. I was so happy with my people! I had even forgotten I was
married. I'd hardly seen my husband for two years and now everything
was starting again so brutally. Mum said she'd come and see me regularly at Karani and at the same time she told me, in an irritated voice,
to stop crying on such a happy day.

Then Grandmother came in. She hugged me to her skinny breast
and covered me with kisses. Wiping away my tears, she found some
words of comfort, 'Come here my little kid, my sugar candy, my queen

of heaven, my coconut bud. Come and cleanse yourself in this lovely cool water, my piece of gold, my pearl, my ruby...' She took me by the arm and led me behind the house, near the stable, where the seven married women who she had sent for were waiting. I was sat down on the ground, and the women took turns to sprinkle water on me through a sieve above my head. I was rubbed with turmeric paste and then rinsed with plenty of water. As soon as I joined the women, Kannan beat his drum to a regular rhythm to drive away the evil spirits. He beat it faster and faster while I was being given the last bath. When I had been rinsed, I was taken back to the house and I prostrated myself in front of the lit oil lamp. Each of the women stuffed me with this famous gruel, which I had difficulty getting down!

Meanwhile Kalimuttu the launderer was blocking off the *tinnai* with the palms woven by Uncle Krishnan – that was where I was going to live over the following days. He only left a narrow passageway to get in and two lemon-shaped holes as windows. The sun mustn't come into my little room. He's a male god who is unlucky at this time: he can make women sterile! In the same way I wasn't meant to see a man for eleven days. Kalimuttu was given what he was owed: a measure of rice, a banana, some betel, some areca nut and, most importantly of all, my stained underskirt. Losing the brand new underskirt I had been given for Dipavali made me furious. Manjamma, the launderer's daughter, was going to be happy to get her hands on that!

An old sari folded into four was put between my thighs and fixed to my waist by a string and I was taken into my shelter. Each of the women who'd bathed me was given a piece of turmeric, some betel, some flowers and a banana. Kannan was entitled to one rupee, some betel, a banana and some flowers.

Everyone went away happy. I was in my cage. Mum and Grandmother were waiting for Dad to come back. As soon as he'd heard the news, Dad had gone to the Reddi to borrow some money which the master couldn't refuse: whether you are Pariah or high caste, you have to cleanse yourself when you reach puberty, because evil spirits are attracted by the strong smell of periods. They come and prowl around girls and if the rites are not performed in the proper way, the spirit enters into you. We see young girls who've been possessed! Everyone knows that and the Reddi didn't wait to loan the money. Just because we're poor doesn't excuse us from doing what we have to and we know that we can count on the Reddi at important times in our lives.

With fifty rupees in his hand, Dad went to Karani to give the good news to my parents-in-law and to invite our kith and kin to the turmeric water ceremony, set for the eleventh day. He was served a drink and something to eat, then they quickly took him to the Iyer to get a clearer picture of my horoscope. A tray was brought for Mani Iyer with some betel, some areca nut, some camphor, a banana and a one rupee note. He was at home and he brought his visitors into the house to shelter them from the inquisitive who were already crowding round. He asked the day and time of my birth and the day and time of my puberty. Dad told him and waited anxiously for what was coming next. You never know what the future has in store. If the horoscope foretold problems, if misfortune was lying in wait for me or the family, there would have to be more money to pay for rites to ward off the threat. Mani Iyer quickly found the two stars which matched the dates and times given. He consulted the horoscope and reassured everybody: no incompatibility, everything was for the best, this time of poverty would end with my arrival in the new household. The time of my puberty was fortunate, both for me and my family-in-law. I would be a strong healthy woman and the mother of many children. Dad was happy and proud to hear the Iyer's predictions. He'd always kept himself in the background amongst his relatives, and now suddenly he felt himself swollen with satisfaction and pride at the thought of giving such a precious gift to my family-in-law. He insisted that the ceremony of the eleventh day take place at Velpakkam and not Karani and then he returned to the village. On the way, he stopped at Tirulagam market to buy what was needed: mirrors, lime boxes, brooches, flowers, bananas, sugar, betel, turmeric, *kungumam*, a cloth bag. He also stopped at the wine stall on the main road: I can still see him, a gourd of palm wine to his nose, proudly telling the story of his consultation with the Iyer, without missing out a single detail, and Grandmother and Mum listening, deeply moved.

So I was confined for eleven days and forbidden to receive anybody in my shelter, forbidden to leave it except for my daily bath, forbidden to go into the house, forbidden to touch the household crockery. I spent my time sleeping and thinking about what was going to happen to me. In the evenings, a group of old and young women, including Arayi's and Nagamma's grandmothers, would come and sit near the *tinnai* and sing funny, rude songs. By their singing, they were teaching me what was in store and how my husband would 'use' my body. I was glad to be out of sight in my cubbyhole because hearing them made me ashamed.

Each evening someone came up with a new song, but some would crop up again and again, especially the song of Kuppu which everyone sang in unison:

> Oh sweet little one, you've had your first period,
> When did you have it, little girl?
> Tell me what you're feeling,
> Don't be ashamed as you find out.
> Girl, now you've reached puberty
> Your doughnut should cover itself
> With curly hair, with soft hair.
> The first day, you'll eat broth
> The fifth day, you'll eat *puttu*
> The eleventh day, you'll take a turmeric bath.
> O little girl, afterwards you'll leave
> With your husband, for his home.
> Lots of good things will come to you,
> Your husband will do everything he should.
> He'll caress your pretty, firm breasts,
> That will make you feel good, little girl.
> He'll push his thing in your pretty fanny,
> He'll put it in the hole above,
> That will be good, it will be delicious,
> That's how he'll make you pregnant,
> And the child will come out by the same hole,
> And will hurt your pretty fanny, O sweet little one.

Everyone was laughing and I was crying in my corner, unhappy that I was a girl. The idea that a child could come out of this little hole made my stomach heave. Even in that hubbub, sometimes my sobs could be heard: then Grandmother made the women quieten down.

I knew a lot of those songs and I'd sung them myself during Nilamma's, Nagamma's and Kasturi's confinements. I particularly liked one in those days. (*Laughs.*)

> He goes up the hill of Annamalai and notices ...
> He climbs up Clitoris mount and sees ...
> Squeezing your breasts with both hands, my beloved,
> He enters your hairy, curly fanny,
> He's hurt you by entering the hole above,
> But how good it is, my beloved, how good!
> You are mature, it's marvellous, my beloved,
> It's marvellous!

Before, I used to laugh singing those songs, just like the others were doing now. I used to find those songs rude but they never made me frightened until now. Why had things changed? Was it because of my friends who wanted to know everything? 'What colour are they, your periods? And what hole do they come out of?'

Was it simply because the days were passing and that soon I was going to be given to my husband? I don't know, but for me, apart from the physical changes, puberty was a signal that I was going away. It was the last stage of marriage.

Our old women were talking to me about sex in their songs. Mum and Grandmother were working to make a woman out of me in eleven days. They were careful with my diet, which was vegetarian because meat and fish give periods a strong smell which can attract evil spirits! They cut out certain fruits and vegetables too, like banana tree heart or fried green bananas which colour periods and leave stains that can't be washed out. Because we're poor, we Pariah women make do with dirty clothes to save money, and that's why we attract demons more than other women. My mother understood this and strictly followed the rules of what's forbidden. So I was made a fuss of, well fed, well looked after and bathed every day. My brother and sisters didn't understand why I was being pampered like this and were jealous of my meals and teas. Every day I had my helping of *puttu* of yard grass or rice, with sugar and some grated coconut. *Puttu* is the most important part of a girl's diet when she reaches puberty. It strengthens the hips, the womb and all the organs and if you want to ask if a little girl has reached puberty, all you need to say is, 'Has your daughter made *puttu*?' On the day of purification, a cone of *puttu* is given to each of the guests. The green lentil broth is also a good tonic with lots of properties and Mum made sure I had it.

So a lot of time was spent preparing my meals. Dad insisted on the best and he always found the money to feed me well. I have never been as spoilt as I was in those eleven days! It was a strange moment in my life: on the one hand, I was rejected and confined because I was un-clean; on the other I was constantly surrounded. I felt that the reason I was being cared for so well was to tear me away from childhood and throw me into the real life of an adult. A woman had to be made out of me in those eleven days.

They were also the last days that Mum could mother her child and she saw our separation hurrying closer and closer. She kept on saying to me, 'Eat well, my daughter! You have to gather your strength to face up to the difficulties of life and to work. I won't be able to be by your side from now on; make the most of the last time I'll ever be able to take care of you!' I began to understand her feelings and the reasons for all her hard work. I didn't break down and cry as I used to. I listened to her advice, 'Obey your parents-in-law, from now on they are your gods. Obey your husband, he's your master. Be faithful to him. Don't be arrogant, don't provoke anybody, don't speak wildly but earn yourself a good reputation: it's difficult, you know, it doesn't just happen by itself!' I had time to mull it all over in my cubbyhole and little by little I was getting myself ready for the big day.

On the tenth day of my confinement, Mum and Grandmother, betel in hand, went to repeat their invitation to the seven women who were going to give me the ritual bath on the day of purification. The musicians had been told and all the relatives invited to the turmeric water ceremony set for the next day, Wednesday morning, at ten o'clock after the unlucky hour.

On the morning of the eleventh day, Kalimuttu the launderer took down the shelter where I had been confined, prepared the platform needed for the rites and gathered up everything that I'd touched during my confinement: the mats, my pillow, my crockery, the palms. My family-in-law had turned out in full, carrying trays laden with bananas, betel, coconut, flowers, with a gold embroidered sari as well, a blouse, an underskirt, some *kungumam*, some turmeric, a comb and a mirror. The musicians had received the visitors at the village entrance and serenaded them up to the house. The trays were offered to the women of the family, who put them in a circle in the middle of the house and lit some camphor on a little tray. Everyone prostrated themselves.

Some cooks had come to prepare the meal, while the women steamed a huge amount of *puttu* for all the guests. Then Mum and the seven women gave me the ritual bath. First I was rubbed with a green lentil paste. I was rinsed, then rubbed with turmeric. I was rinsed for a second time. The other women who'd made me up for my marriage, dressed me: I was put into new clothes which my parents had bought and my hair was dried with incense smoke. Afterwards each of these women got a rupee, a banana, some betel, a lime box, a comb and a mirror, which Dad had bought at Tirulagam market. At the same time, my parents offered my husband a *soman*, a shawl and some betel. Then Mum gave the guests some *vadai* with whey made with spices.

I was ready. Aunt Kanikkai performed the *alam* for me and I went into the house. My Uncle Krishnan brought forward his tray while the musicians started playing. My husband and I sat down on the platform. Uncle Krishnan performed the *alam* and put his tray with ten rupees down in front of us. Then my parents gave him a tray with twenty rupees in exchange: the uncle must always be given twice as much as he gives. It's his due, because he's the one who'll take over from the parents if they die or can't take care of their children. Each of the guests threw rice at us as a sign of their blessing and gave us a present – money, mostly. Each of them was given a cone of *puttu* and a banana, with some flowers and a *kungumam* box for the women as well. The celebration ended with just the family having a good non-vegetarian meal, with palm wine for the men.

The time to leave was getting closer. My trunk was ready with the crockery, mats and clothes. Mum couldn't take any more. Her eyes were red and she didn't leave my mother-in-law's side, begging her to take good care of me. The people of the *ceri* had gathered in front of the house to see my mother entrust me to my mother-in-law. Mum came back over to me and went over her advice to me one more time. I was sad to see her like that. I couldn't cry any more. I had no more tears. I had become serious, my old cheerfulness had disappeared.

The musicians took their places at the head of the procession. The signal was given. I was going to leave. My grandparents, my parents, my brothers, my sisters and my friends had tears in their eyes. The whole *ceri* was moved.

The procession set off for Karani. This time it was for good. It was my turn to start crying.

FOUR

The wedding night

I knew the way to Karani by now. I had my landmarks. I knew you had to turn left by the clump of areca palms and pick up the main road bordered with tulip trees. Over there, within eyesight, was a palm-wine stall marking the road to the village.

The musicians started playing as soon as we entered the village. As they always do, the children were the first to run up and they shouted, 'Here's the wife! She's a little girl! We can play with her!' Their shouts reassured me a bit and I lifted up my head, heavy with sadness and flowers. I wasn't used to wearing a plait of flowers down to my back, earrings, little chains hung from my hair and a pendant on my forehead. It was all heavy and irritating and made it hard to look around. The kids were more or less my size. I felt quite comforted that the children in my new village were giving me a warm welcome. I said to myself that at least I was going to have some playmates because, although I came across as shy, I was a joyful girl, always laughing and I made friends easily. And there I was, off thinking about new games and new stories to tell and forgetting all my mother's and grandmother's advice. How can I explain how innocent I was in those days?

As we got nearer and nearer to the *ceri*, inquisitive women flocked to see us and added their comments, 'Oh she's just a child!' said one. And another, 'What a big wife for Manikkam! She's as round as a top! A real *ujakku*!' And a third, 'It's all right, she's got beautiful features even though she's dark.'

A woman came out of the house, carrying a brass tray made up for the *alam*, and handed it to my mother-in-law, who passed it three times round my head. Then they had me enter the house, checking that I did so with my right foot first.

Everybody settled down on the *tinnai* or wherever they could. The women gathered round my mother-in-law who was telling the story of how they were received at Velpakkam. When I saw that everyone was caught up in the conversation, I quickly undid my flowers, took off my jewels and my half-sari. I folded my skirt around my waist and edged my way into the middle of the crowd to go and find the children who were playing on the outskirts of the village. No one noticed I was gone.

I fell on a group of girls, who greeted me with 'Here's the Old Man's wife!' I was sad to hear that. Once again I'd forgotten I was married. If I had been at Velpakkam, I would have given them some crude answer straightaway. But here at Karani I'd become shy and I lowered my head without saying a word, looking pitiful. Then one of the girls came up, took me by the hand and said, 'It's OK, don't be angry, you'll be our friend, OK?' I nodded. I joined in with the group and was immediately asked loads of questions: 'Why were you married off? Were you naughty?'

'Oh no! It was because I was too big to go on staying at home in Velpakkam. Do you know him, the Old Man?'

'Which old man? Big brother Manikkam?'

'Yes.'

'Oh yes! We make fun of him a lot, because some of his teeth are missing. We call him Toothless. When he's really furious, he runs after us or throws stones at us.'

'Oh right, he's missing teeth is he? I didn't even notice. Why do you call him "the Old Man"?'

'Because he's got white hair.'

'And you, you're not married are you? Aren't any of you?'

'Yes! Kannima, Sakkamma and Danamma ... Their men are over there, at Kannan's, singing ...'

'Right, what about playing hopscotch?' shouted one of them. And we all said 'yes' in unison.

And so we started having fun, jumping, running, shouting, laughing. It was good, I was happy with my first evening in my new *ceri*, when suddenly I heard a voice calling me. It was my mother-in-law's. But I was so out of breath that I couldn't answer her. I headed off to the

house without even saying goodbye to my new friends. I got there in a
sweat, my hair all tangled, my knees showing because I'd forgotten to
let my skirt down.

The women all burst out laughing when they saw me, 'What a sight!
Big sister really has found an obedient, well-brought-up girl for her
son! She's only just got here, and here she is scampering around like a
runaway donkey! How's Manikkam going to live his life with a girl who
can't keep still?' Hearing all these unpleasant remarks I started trembling. I walked along the wall like a little mouse and went into the
house with my head bowed. I put myself in a dark corner and cried hot
tears. My mother-in-law came to find me, calling, 'Hey! Little girl!
Where are you? Are you there? In the dark?' And in a voice that was
half-strict and half-cajoling, she said, 'But why are you crying, little
fool? Stop shedding tears now that the lamp has been lit, it brings bad
luck! Hey! Kacimma! Give her something to eat, it's late: we've been
chatting for ages.'

Big sister Kacimma, my eldest sister-in-law, took me by the hand,
wiped away my tears and brought me something to eat. I wasn't hungry.
I was very tired and sleepy. At Velpakkam I often went to sleep without
eating. Here that was taken badly. 'We'll save some money on food if you
carry on like this,' my mother-in-law kept on telling me, 'but our line
will stop here and there will be no one to pour out our *kuj* tomorrow.'

In those days I couldn't understand anything she was telling me: I let
her talk and kept up my little hunger-strike.

The women of my new house were very kind to me. In our caste, the
mother-in-law and her daughters start bullying the daughter-in-law
much later, when she's become a woman. But at any rate, it's nothing
like what goes on with the Reddi. Recently one of the families made life
hell again for one of the daughters-in-law who'd just given birth to a
second daughter. What could she do about it, the poor thing? You don't
choose the little one who's in your womb. Isvaran decides and then
there you are, you have to accept it. Anjamma, the barber's wife who
takes messages, told me. The poor girl had cried and told her about it.
Apparently they don't even call her to come and eat any more and they
leave her to look after the baby on her own. I see her as well when I go
and sweep the stable. She always looks sad, the poor thing. It has to be
said that we work outside: if we spread our stories around the fields, all
the women get involved, say who's in the wrong, the mother-in-law or
the daughter-in-law, and then it's over. Or else there's a big argument in
the *ceri* itself and everything is sorted out. It's different with the Reddi.

It all happens on the sly, through signals, words, moods and snide remarks. They sulk, it lasts a whole lifetime. Or it ends badly. Even here in Karani, two daughters-in-law have committed suicide since I arrived, though they haven't been Reddi. One threw herself into a well. Her misfortune was not to have children. Her mother-in-law and her family-in-law had pointed at her so much that the poor thing ended up in the well.

The other soaked herself in petrol in the kitchen and burnt herself alive. They couldn't do anything at the hospital. The affair was covered up by saying that her nylon sari had caught fire while she was walking past the rice. But our men who went to play the drums at her burial heard the people from the hospital say that it was suicide. She was from a humble family and her father hadn't paid the dowry he'd promised. So she was scolded and bullied. The poor child couldn't stand it and decided to burn herself. Just because they're higher caste doesn't mean that they know how to live a better life. They can behave like animals as well. I don't say that we Pariahs are perfect, but we always find someone to defend us and we support each other more. There are some people who commit suicide, but it's very rare and mainly because of adultery. Sometimes a man can do it, but I've never heard of it happening in the neighbouring *ceri*. We hear people talking about things like that at the hospital.

To get back to my first night at Karani, my mother-in-law was very kind to me. She did my hair as if I was her little daughter. She was gentle. After dinner, I started crying again and I was afraid of sleeping in the dark. My mother-in-law reassured me that everybody was soon going to sleep and I wouldn't be alone. She stretched a mat on the ground and put a white cloth on it. She put the oil lamp beside me and said, 'You can go to sleep. I'm going to sit down by the front door and chew a little betel. You've got nothing to be afraid of. Sleep well!'

Outside, one or two women had come to chat with my mother-in-law. I heard them laughing and singing. 'Manikkam will be celebrating today,' they were saying. I couldn't listen to their conversation any longer. It was reassuring not to be on my own. Overwhelmed by tiredness and emotion, I dropped off immediately.

I was in a deep sleep when I felt someone take my arm. Terrified, I screamed, 'Ayoyo! Ayoyo! He's touching me! He's crushing me!' My mother-in-law got up immediately and whispered, 'Don't shout, little girl, you'll wake everybody up!' And I shouted, 'I saw a ghost! Someone's just gone out!' She calmed me down, telling me that there wasn't any-body there and that I'd had a nightmare. I went back to sleep immedi-ately. But soon somebody was smothering me again. I screamed so much that the weight got off me immediately. Even though I tried, I couldn't make out anything in that night as black as charcoal. Behind my tears I saw only points of light, flickering like when you rub your eyes until they hurt. Nothing was moving around me. I was afraid and I stayed awake. Little by little I began to make out a white shape beside me.

I lifted my head to get a better look. Just then, a rough hand stroked my hair. 'Hey! Viramma! Why are you afraid?' Then I recognised my husband's voice and his white *soman* which my parents had given him. My crying fit started again and I mumbled, 'I want to go back to Velpakkam, I want to go back to my mum, I'll tell her everything that's happened to me here.'

'Be quiet! Be quiet, little fool! We'll see about all that tomorrow morning!'

I didn't shut my eyes for another second that night. I waited for the sun to rise to get out of that hole and I quickly went and sat down next to the drumstick tree. There's a story to that drumstick tree. From that day on it became my confidant and even now, when I've got a problem, I go and talk to it, tell it my sadness and it comforts me. On Fridays I light camphor for it, the same as for the trident. It's a god for me.

I was there at the foot of this tree. The men going by with their hoes on their shoulders stopped in front of me and said, 'Hey! What's this then? A young bride!' But they didn't dare ask any questions. The women started arriving with their jars. Aunt Konakkali, the nosiest and chattiest, asked me, 'What's happened to you, little girl? Have you finished your wedding night?' I didn't understand what she meant, but I answered her immediately, 'Last night the boy of the house pulled me by the arm, aunt!' My mother-in-law came out then and turned to the women, 'Did you hear that?' Everyone burst out laughing. Oh! I was disappointed by that! Hearing women who were my mother's age laugh-ing about what had happened to me!

'No! I know the way to Velpakkam. This morning I'll go and tell my mother what's happened and you'll see if she'll leave this man in peace! She'll cut off his head. My father will chop him in two!'

'Yes, yes! Your father and mother are heroes. We're all afraid of them! While we're waiting, go off and have a wash!'

Of course the news spread to the whole *ceri*. My playmates were the most curious of all, they didn't stop asking me questions and I answered them all. Which meant that instead of going to Velpakkam as I had promised myself, I went and played with the girls.

That's how the first days passed. I went out and played. I only returned at mealtimes. I started crying at the slightest remark and every night I rejected my husband. My mother-in-law was very patient and didn't rush me. She tried to reason with me loads of times, but I had the spirit to keep up the fight. I didn't manage to overcome this fear of being given to a man. It was too cruel! My mother-in-law asked big sister Ellamma to talk to me as well, but I didn't want to hear anything. The women were sympathetic when they saw me and they'd say, 'Everyone knows her in the *ceri* except for her husband Manikkam. She's so childlike, the innocent! Ah! We've all gone through that! That's the fate of women.'

All the same my mother-in-law ended up having enough of my ways. She started by forbidding me to play games outside. Then I had to help her with work around the house. Meanwhile, my playmates were off roaming the countryside. My mother-in-law said, 'This can't go on. Your parents haven't spent so much money to marry you for you to go and play with your friends!' And from that day on, she started being severe with me and scolding me whenever she saw me playing. To keep me busy and at home, she used to mix a measure of rice and a measure of lentils and tell me to sort them. And while I was doing it, she sat next to me and lectured me. She reminded me of everything Grandmother and Mum had told me.

And then, one day, she announced very calmly, 'Your father-in-law and I are going to live separately. We'll divide this big room in three. Your husband and you will be on the left: we'll be in the middle: Marimuttu and his family on the right. There'll be three rice jars now. Each of us will make our own meals.'

What a thunderbolt! I looked at my mother-in-law with tears in my eyes. She'd been so kind up till now, she'd been a mother to me, and now here she was, being tough and laying down the law. I had nobody left I could confide in. Big sister Ellamma advised me to obey my mother-in-law and my husband. 'Go along with them', she used to say. 'Your mother's name will suffer if her daughter doesn't fit in with her new life with her family-in-law.' I felt really lonely and unhappy. Big sister Ellamma kept on telling me that a husband is a protector, that after marriage you belong to him and so you have to satisfy him. I kept on being given this advice. But at that age, listening is not enough to make you understand. Why should I belong to that brute who'd touched me at night, rather than to my father and mother who'd brought me up? I wondered whether my parents had sold me to these people from Karani. In my family, a cousin of my mother was sold to agents who were buying coolies for tea plantations in Ceylon. My old aunt always held it against her husband that he'd sold their son and, what's more, for almost nothing! The agents had promised loads of benefits and money, but nobody saw them and the son never came back. That story had stayed in my head and I often felt myself in the same situation: I said to myself that perhaps my parents had got rid of me. But then why so many ceremonies, why the celebrations, the orchestras, the presents? Tears, sadness: I couldn't be consoled.

That very afternoon my father-in-law and his sons, all in loincloths and turbans, set to work and put up the mud walls which would divide the house in three. I helped the women move. Of course when the neighbours went past, they stopped to make comments, 'It had to come to this, you realise! Eh, little mouse, it's not good enough playing with a doll, you know: you've got to move on to the real thing! Your parents didn't spend so much money marrying you for nothing. Go on, give in, you'll see, you'll be asking for it again! People know about these things!' And everyone laughed.

'You're young and your husband is already old. Make the most of it, time flies when it comes to these things!'

From up on the roof, a man's voice shouted, 'Females today are stubborner than in my time!' It was my father-in-law, and that was the first time I'd heard him speak!

I wasn't hungry that evening. My mother-in-law forced me to eat a few handfuls of rice. Then she stretched out the mat and put the white sheet back on it. She told me that I could go to sleep and that she was going to sleep in her part, next door. I shouldn't be afraid, my husband was going to be with me soon. Then she shut the door and went off. This time I didn't protest. I'd entered a new phase. Now I was waiting and my heart was beating hard.

The man came in at last. I shut my eyes straightaway. I was curled up like a shrimp, my head in my hands. He brought the lamp nearer. I was as still as a corpse. He muttered something and lay down next to me. He took off his *soman* very quickly and with the same speed he undressed me. I was humiliated to be naked. He stuck to me like a leech and took a firm grip of my breast. I was suffocating under his weight. I was trembling. I was terribly wet as if I'd pissed. At last he let go of one of my breasts, took his tail which was as hard as a sugar cane and pushed it in at the top of my thighs, which he kept apart with his own. It felt like he was tearing me. He roared like a lion, giving great thrusts and for once, I suffered in silence.

Even today, at my age, I still tremble when I think of my first time: it's stayed as a horrible memory. The Reddi are more civilised, and they don't do it like these savages, these Pariahs. I know how it's done with the Reddi. Trays of fruits, *jilebi*, *laddu*, *Mysore pak*, *bonda*, *uppuma* and two glasses of milk with almonds and saffron are brought into a bedroom decorated with jasmine garlands. A white sheet is put on the bed. The elders lead the married couple into the bedroom and shut the door. Then the young ones have a whole day to talk, win each other over and make love gently. It's too crude with us, too brutal. It's true we don't have the time or the space to do it like that. But my experience was too awful!

When my husband calmed down, I said to him, crying, 'No. It's not possible that my parents have allowed something like that. I want to go home. I want to tell my mother!' And he said, 'Calm down, little girl. This is your home. You're going to live with me. I'll make you happy, you'll see. It's because it's the first time that you feel bad. It'll be better next time.' My husband whispered these words in the blackness which troubled me. But I kept on crying because I felt like I was burning. I had other strange feelings as well: my whole body felt sticky and dirty. My husband was disturbed by my distress. 'There's some water in the bucket outside. Come and wash,' he said. So as not to leave me alone, he came out of the house as well and waited on the *tinnai*. I took the big bucket and poured it all on my doughnut. That did me good and soothed the pain a bit. Without even drying myself, I slipped on my underskirt and my shirt. I really resented my husband for what he'd just done to me so brutally and although he called me to come and lie next to him, I went off into a corner of the room for the rest of the night.

When I woke up I was alone in the house. My husband had left to plough the Grand Reddi's field. I heard big sister Ellamma asking, 'What's happened to the little one?' And my mother-in-law replying, 'Come and see if she's behaved herself well!'

Big sister Ellamma, my sister-in-law Kacimma and Aunt Nettakkali came in, 'But where is she, that little wasp?'

'Ah, there she is, in her corner as usual!'

'Hey, look! The cloth is next to the jars!'

They rushed at this rag and I wondered what could be so precious about it. 'Such a carry on for these drops!' they said, then they went out and Aunt Nettakkali called my mother-in-law, 'Big sister, your son must be very happy. It's done! This little one isn't at fault at all. But you've got to admit that she's a stubborn one, eh! She stood her ground for such a long time!'

That's how it was done in the other *yugam*, the *yugam* of the innocents. Today all that has ended with us. It still goes on with the Reddiar. It's disappearing with the Kudiyanar. Poverty makes them work in the fields like us. They meet in secret and go together before marriage. You can't stop them any more! In the countryside, there are thousands of places to go together! And also, in this *kaliyugam* when girls wait several years after their first periods, it's given much less importance. When I arranged the marriage of my daughter, I can tell you that the family-in-law made a bigger point of the dowry than of her virginity. Times change. I've often regretted not having always paid attention to my mother's advice when I was little. But what can be done? When you're young, you're awkward and resentful.

As I was now living in a separate room, I was forced to do everything for my husband: serve him his meals, heat the water for his bath, take his meal to him in the fields, give him betel. There was no go-between any more. All my mother-in-law had done now came back to me. Once again, it wasn't the work that made me recoil, it was doing it for this stranger who hurt me at night and disappeared in the day. But the only answer was to obey. If I refused, then I had smacks in store: I was definitely not going to be sweet talked! So I sulked, I scowled, I never laughed, I took my revenge in my own way. I'll give you an example. There were seven of us girls who took lunch to their husbands in the fields. All of them rolled up the fold of their sari on their heads and put their pot of *kuj* on top. But I used to say to myself that that executioner didn't deserve it and I'd arrive with the pot flat on my head: I didn't show him proper respect and I annoyed him every time. So, in the evening, he'd find some reason or other – there was not enough salt in the rice or the water for washing was too hot – and he'd start insulting me, 'You poxed, badly fucked whore! Will you take a look at that cunthead!' I'd be ashamed and start crying. People would come and calm him down and they'd say, 'Don't get angry, Manikkam! She's a tiny little girl!' And he'd answer, 'No she's not. You don't know what a nerve she's got!' And he'd say what I'd done that morning. I was humiliated but, at the same time, satisfied with my game.

I had another way of annoying him. When I'd go and take him his *kanji*, I'd put the pot near him on the ground and I'd sit farther away, turning my back on him and scratching the soil with my big toe. That made him beside himself and he'd shout, 'All these women have come and brought *kanji* to their husbands, they've served them their food and they stay by their side while they eat! And look where Velpakkatta is![1] Ten feet away from me!' Everyone started laughing and they'd shout back, 'Hey! Manikkam! The scales aren't tipping your way. You don't know how to get it right. If you gave her a good hiding, she'd get back on the right track!' I was furious and I'd throw them a look of contempt and mutter, 'What the fuck has it got to do with the rest of you, you herd of buffalos!'

I never dared answer back to my husband's insults, I was afraid he'd hit me: you see me, me an earthworm against a Mahadisvaran![2] But I always laid into the people who'd set my husband against me, 'It's not hard to see that it doesn't hurt you anywhere to say things like that! I hope your tongues rot!' No one held it against me. But mind you, I only allowed myself all that in the fields in front of groups of young people. I would never have done it in the *ceri* in front of the old people: there I always kept my persecuted look.

After coming back from the fields, I'd put down my jar, take a basket and go looking for firewood. I didn't hang around like I used to because I was afraid of being scolded by my mother-in-law. I didn't go and play with my playmates any more and I hardly saw them. They'd started by sulking and they ended up simply ignoring me. It was hard. Then I got closer to a group of married girls like me and later, to Kannima and Anjalai most of all. One came from Manigappakkam, the other from Murungappakkam. But I only saw them when I was going to take the meal to the fields. So I used to feel alone and abandoned. The older women were always teaching me a lesson. I'd had enough of that.

The person I saw most of all, in the end, was my husband, who tried to win me over. He'd often come back to the *ceri* before the others. He always justified it by this or that job he had to do when people said to him, 'So, Manikkam, you seem to appreciate your house and your wife, eh?' He'd answer, 'No, no, it's not that at all!' and he'd go in. He'd call me, 'Aye! Little girl! Come out of your hiding place!' I'd say to him, 'No! I'm not coming!' and refusing to move, I'd start groaning. He'd get worked up and insult me. 'If you want me to flay the skin off your back, then stay in your corner! If not, get out of your hole quickly, you bitch!

Perhaps I don't suit you as a husband? What's wrong with me? What's somebody else got that's better than me? Do you need a maharajah, a son of Manmadan?'

I never answered back when he lost his temper like that. I knew that repeatedly refusing his advances and provoking him made him furious. Hearing him insult me like that I boiled with rage. I wanted to beat him! Between ourselves, Sinnamma, it's not so difficult to beat a man ... In our *ceri*, there was a woman who did nothing but that and what's more, she drank. The couple was a laughing stock. Everybody called him a milksop and her Patrakali. When we Pariahs call a woman Patrakali, it's really no compliment! All the gods are afraid of Kali. She's on her own. She waits around by pyres, condemned to eat corpses. The Koratti don't put up with it. If the husband raises an arm, the wife raises a foot! But they're different castes, they're nomads. We don't move around. We live in a colony and we follow rules.³

In fact, my husband was kind. He tried to get to know me, to make friends with me. I was the one who didn't understand anything. I was too young, and the slightest thing he said or move he made seemed to me aggressive. At the same time I watched him while I was moaning in my corner: he was handsome, his face was gentle. His big muscular body, covered in pearls of sweat which shone in the sun didn't leave me cold. Seeing him did something to me ... feelings. He was good-natured: he was always laughing with his friends, swapping jokes. He knew loads of funny songs and love duets. I was the little crow who couldn't fly and didn't dare throw itself into life alone. Being older than me, he put in a lot of himself and threw me grain, as we say, to tame me.

In the evening I'd cook rice for two meals: the evening meal first and the rest for the morning – in those days we could allow ourselves that. I served them on a brass dish which my father had given me in my dowry. My father, who was then working in Madras, hadn't sent me away empty-handed: water jar, brass dish, oil lamp, large *puja* tray, little oil jar, pillow, mat: they were all part of my dowry. My father was civilised and he'd managed things well.

Yes, I used to prepare a good strong tamarind sauce with aubergines or salted fish. I could cook and nobody could criticise me about that. Then I'd sweep the room, I'd put water on to boil for the bath and wait for him by the door, inside. He didn't dawdle around on the way and he never came back empty-handed. He always had something: some grilled chickpeas, some *murukku* or *vadai*. He'd also buy some betel from the Mustachioed for the evening. As soon as I heard him, I'd rush to my fire. He'd wait for me by the door, I'm sure wanting me to come and welcome him. But I didn't move. 'Aye! Here! Aye! Come and take this,' he'd say to me nicely. Without turning round, I'd let him know that I hadn't looked after the cows with him just so he could call me 'Aye'. Irritated, he'd raise his voice, 'Do you want to take what I'm giving you or do you want me to ripen the skin on your back?' I'd answer that I didn't want what he'd brought me and that, anyway, I hadn't asked for anything. Then, moaning, I'd stand up and go and get the treats. But, flirting, I wouldn't eat them and I'd put them on the ground. And it would start again, 'Why don't you want to eat what I've brought you, you ass?'

'No! I don't want to. I'm not hungry. I'll eat them later. What? Have I got to eat them straightaway? Maybe I haven't got the right to eat them later, is that it?'

My crying fits had ended and I almost looked forward to these arguments, because, little by little, they were bringing us closer together. My mother-in-law and the others who said that I was withdrawn took a dim view of the way my husband spoiled me and the insolent way I answered back. Of course everything we said was heard through the partition and I quickly learned that we should keep our quarrels for night-time when we were alone.

When my husband had had his bath, I served him his dinner. Then while I was eating, he'd go for a walk and chat with his parents or the young people in the *ceri*. I'd hurry to do the washing up and put away the pots and pans. Then I'd lay out the beautiful mat which I'd been given for my marriage and I'd lie down while I was waiting for him.

My husband didn't use to hang about too much at that point either. He came home pretty fast and stretched out next to me. I'd get up immediately to massage his legs and then he'd ask me to tell him stories. I was very happy with that, especially because I knew a good number of them and because it relaxed me: at last I was the speaker and I liked being listened to. While I told him stories, he'd pull me to him and I'd be stretched out next to him, legs against legs. I didn't feel embarrassed at all. I felt fine. My husband caressed my body with his rough hands. His movements were quite nervous, but not at all brutal. We caressed each other for a long time, a very long time. I don't know how to tell you all this, Sinnamma. At those moments, he was ready to do anything. Once, to punish him for having been so brutal at the start of our marriage, I made him lick the soles of my feet and my toes! It made me feel very good at the same time. I found out with him that the ears and the hollows behind the knees are places that give pleasure. Not only that. I looked admiringly at his little hairy balls and his sting which was thick and hard as sugar cane with its violet head. I was always very moved at those times, and I felt feelings that I had never known before. He'd say to me, caressing my thatch, 'You are my mount of Tiru-vannamalai and its wick.'[4] Ayo! ayo! We got up to some things when we were young! His favourite position was 'peeling the coconut'![5] Ayo! I'm ashamed to tell you all that but too bad, everybody does it. In the end, we were happy, we satisfied each other. I felt good with him. I'd been told that I'd be very happy with my husband but my first experience had been so hard that afterwards I'd become very worried. And then, it's no good other people advising you, you don't understand much. Nothing matters as much as your own experience! It was from that time on that love was born between us. In any case, it was then that I began to love my husband as the dearest being in my life.

FIVE

'He still desires me!'

Everything was starting to go well between us. I liked being married now. I waited impatiently for my husband to come home. I enjoyed his company. He was gentle and good to me. It was too beautiful and in the country you must never forget the evil eye. When they saw that everything was going better for me, the women in my family-in-law used me more and more to do their work. How could I refuse? Grinding spices, fetching eight jars of water a day, looking after my nephews: it all made me behind in my own work and when my husband would get home, I'd still be busy with some job here or there while my sister-in-law was hanging around by the well. If the work wasn't done, I got the blame and was called lazy. I didn't say anything because I could see perfectly well that it was jealousy. My sister-in-law didn't have the same relationship with her husband as I did with mine: he was old and he wasn't interested in her. He spent all his time drinking and talking with the men of the *ceri*. The good years were over for them. As for my mother-in-law, she felt abandoned by her son. My husband knew that I was the victim of these women's jealousy, but the poor man was in a difficult position. I understood: whose side would he take? His family's or a newcomer's? I put up with it all and didn't bear a grudge against anybody, because I found happiness and courage at night next to my husband. I'd thought my mother-in-law was unfair to put us in separate rooms, and now I was telling myself that it was a real stroke of luck we

50

had a room to ourselves. You know, Sinnamma, that I didn't plot to get it and that we ended up there because I was innocent and childish: manipulative is one thing I'm not.

I never talked about my problems to my husband at night. We 'did it' well. My doughnut was sore because it took a long time to satisfy me. I'd pour on lots of water to soothe the burning. It all gave me the patience I needed for the days. Sometimes we'd meet on the track leading to the well behind Aiyanar's temple – the Pariah's well used to be round there surrounded by cactuses. We'd have some betel, he'd take my hand or feel my breast: he'd send me a kiss and then quickly get going before anyone saw us. I loved those nights when we were lying there, naked as the day we were born, with our threads round our waists.[1] I used to listen to him panting. I felt good.

That's how time passed in my new village. I began to get to know everybody and feel comfortable in the *ceri*. I went to the *ur* a few times. I didn't know anybody there, apart from the schoolmaster's mother who is from Velpakkam as well. A new Pariah in the *ceri* – nobody's interested in that, as you can imagine. But at the Grand Reddi's they knew I was Mannikam's wife. I used to go there with my mother-in-law to sweep out the stable and collect cow dung. My family-in-law have been serfs at the Reddi's for generations. One day my mother-in-law was sick and she sent me to his house to work instead of her.

In those days, I was beautiful, young and healthy. My hips and thighs were as smooth as the trunk of a banana tree. I was small and black as a crow, but my curves were attractive. For a Pariah, I wasn't so bad and, even in the *ur*, everyone said so: I used to hear it as I walked past. Coming back from the Reddi's, I'd stop at Pajani Gounder's, the schoolmaster's father, and ask his wife for news of Velpakkam and the boys from the *ceri* who were working for her father there. She'd ask me to do little jobs every time: 'Here, Velpakkatta, come and give the courtyard a sweep', she'd say, and give me a handful of salted chickpeas, or toss me a coin.

The registry office was next door to her house: there was a wall dividing the two. One day I'd done my hair well, with flowers, I'd drawn a beautiful *pottu* and I was very neat. The civil servant was sitting at a table near the window. When he saw me walking past, he signalled to me to come in. I said to myself that he was a top man, a Sir, a civil servant, and that I should stop out of respect. Maybe he wanted me to sweep the pavement or the courtyard. I went into the room, covering my back with my sari and putting my palms together

respectfully. And what did I see when I raised my eyes? His dick! A fat
dick! He was holding it in one hand and he had money in the other. I
screamed. I was trembling all over and I didn't know how to get out of
the situation. The schoolmaster's mother and her husband were watching
the scene from their courtyard and wondering if I was going to accept
his offer or raise the alarm.

We Paratchi have the reputation of being easy women who'll jump
into bed with anyone if they whistle. It's true that our young are happy
to have sex before marriage. I even know some who sleep around afterwards. But that's between us. We work in remote fields, young guys
come past … But we're not whores. Those gentlemen of the *ur* talk a lot
about the uncleanness of Untouchables, but our holes always turn them
on. We're the ones they get up to all their dirty tricks with; it makes
you think our juices taste better than their wives'! It's the same in the
hospital. All of them make passes at us, from the doctor to the sweeper.
'Aye! What do you say? Are you coming?' The doctors pretend to listen
to our hearts so they can feel our breasts. Others just go ahead and get
their packet out and tell us to touch it. That's happened to more than
one of us. We're harassed non-stop down there. But we don't dare shout
or make a scandal: we'd be called liars, our names would be crossed off
the hospital registers and we wouldn't be given any more treatment.

What would it be like if we were as civilised as you, always clean and
beautiful? But don't worry, we can't stay beautiful as long as you. Young,
yes, we're as strong as tamarind seeds, but after children start coming,
it's all over. We lose blood with each child and, on top of that, there's
all the work we get through: planting out, weeding, harvesting, looking
after the cattle, collecting cow dung, carrying eight jars of water, and
then pounding, winnowing the millet, hulling the paddy, taking it to the
rice mill in Tirulagam, and all the work at home and in the *ur*. A Pariah
woman loses her strength and beauty very early. The Reddi women only
have to sleep, eat and do a few little jobs in the kitchen: they can keep
very clean, very civilised. We come home in the evening exhausted,
covered in sweat. We don't take the time to wash, we go to bed as we
are. The women in the *ur* wash several times a day. We don't have the
same life! And yet we're the ones they try and sleep with!

To get back to my civil servant, that donkey fucker made me die of
fear more than anything else. They all thought I was going to accept his
offer. I hadn't seen the Gounder watching me from their courtyard, but
straightaway I walked out screaming, without daring to tell the whole
story. The schoolmaster's mother called me and asked me what was

happening, of course without telling me that she'd seen everything. I said to her, 'Ayo! Mother! Mother! The registrar called me: I went in there thinking you must obey a village official and here's what he showed me: his dick and some money!' I burst into sobs. She comforted me and said, 'Go on, Velpakkatta, you've behaved well. That's what they're like, city people who come to the country. Never stop when a man calls you!'

I was on my way back to the *ceri* feeling very ashamed, when I saw my husband on the road, drunk and with a knife in his hand. He was shouting, 'He won't get out of here alive, that son of a whore! I'll finish him off this evening, that cuntlicker! He dared call my wife to be his woman! I'm going to talk to him, that's right, with a good smack across the face with my old shoes, bastard, mother fucker, sister fucker!' The news had got round quickly and my husband, upset at finding out what had happened to me, and angry that it should have happened to his wife, had gone drinking to get the courage up to take everything he was feeling in his heart out on this guy. A Pariah had no rights in those days; he'd always lie flat on his stomach in front of his masters. He couldn't make any claims like now. So he'd go and get drunk and shout abuse at the entrance to the *ur*. That's what my husband was doing. No one would take it seriously: they'd say it was drunkard's talk and that's all there was to it. The people shouting abuse never went further than the *ceri* and the matter would be buried. Nowadays, if we wanted, it would be different, because the party men are always ready to help us. Mind you, they don't do it for free, they've got all our votes. Anyway, Sinnamma, the elections, that's another story.

A group of old men had calmed down my husband. One of them was the father of Malliga, who was the head of the *ceri* in those days: 'Forget that man, he didn't even touch your wife! And even if he did do something, you know perfectly well that we couldn't do anything against him, he's high caste!' 'Ah no!' shouted my husband, 'those aren't arguments! This dick here' – he lifted up his *soman* – 'this dick here won't be scared of him! We'll see if he can tear out a single hair!'

But people kept on soothing him, laughing all the time at seeing his things showing. In those days he was young and rebellious like people his age. It's when we get older that we realise it's no use fighting people like that ... It has to be said that everybody had a good laugh in the *ceri* that night, not about the civil servant who'd showed his dick, but about my husband who'd answered by showing his own!

The next day that son of a whore civil servant did the same thing again to big sister Tacimma, a Kudiyanar who I knew well because she

worked in the fields too. She wasn't afraid, she immediately shouted
and made a great fuss. So that made two scandals: one with me, a
woman from the *ceri*, and the other with a woman from the *ur*. And a
scandal in the *ur* isn't the same! In those days, the father of the Grand
Reddi was *kambattam* and he had power. They went and complained to
him and he had that guy transferred immediately. We never saw him
again in the area. They say that he was a Muslim: those people are
never satisfied.[2]

When I heard the news on my way to get water, I ran back to the
ceri, telling anybody who wanted to listen, 'You know that the civil
servant has been sacked because of me!' I was very proud! I thought I
was going to be congratulated. But oh no! The jealous women turned
the whole thing against me. 'It all happened because you're too much of
a flirt!' That's what they said to me!

I still had everything my father had given me as a dowry and trousseau and my sisters-in-law used to help themselves as they pleased. For
poor people like us, the daughter-in-law's dowry is mainly used to marry
the daughters of the house: what else can you do when you haven't got
a penny? But luckily for me, my husband's two sisters were already
married and so I could make the most of my trousseau and I had outfits
that were still brand new ... The other women were jealous as well
because things were going well between my husband and me and because he spoiled me. Girls now used to whisper and giggle when they
saw me. And the old women would say, 'Eh! You know how frightened
Velpakkatta used to be of her husband, well that's how much she loves
his tail now!' It hurt me to hear that and to be left out of things.

Even so, I was happy in my new *ceri*. I thought less and less about
Velpakkam and my family. It all seemed very far away, although it was
only one harvest ago that I'd left them. I realised that I was happy
thanks to my husband and that he was important in my life.

He was happy as well. Sinnamma, I'm ashamed to tell you this, he's
lost his teeth, our children are married, but he still desires me! It's true
we've slept together a lot. He wouldn't let go of me and he was asking
me for it the whole time. I'd say to him, 'Stop behaving like a donkey
on heat: you'll lose your strength and I will too!' Sinnamma, there are
men in our *ceri* who hang about without the strength to work. Panderi
is a guy like that. He loves women, everyone knows that, and he's had
so many relationships that now he's weakened by 'bad water': his limbs
are swollen and all his blood has turned. One of his sons is the same:

they say that he caught syphilis and the only way that'll go, Sinnamma, is when it takes your head with it.[3] The poor man, he can't touch meat or fish. His mother really has tried every medicine. In the end, the Nadar healer in the *ur* advised him to take niruri juice. That sickness also does a lot of damage to the Kepmari in the *ur*: those people travel a lot. They cross foreign countries, they visit Bombay and Delhi. No one knows who they sleep with and they catch syphilis. Mani, the son of Ramamurti Kepmari, looks normal, he hasn't got thin or anything, but people have noticed that he's been walking bow-legged for a while. Anjalai, Pakkiam and I said to each other, 'Oh! Hot piss, that's what that boy's got!' Two days later, the barber's little one came looking for me, and when I asked why, his mother, big sister Anjamma, came out of her house and took me aside to say, 'Aye, Viramma, I need white laurel leaves and niruri.' I said to her, 'Is it for someone at home, big sister?' She answered, 'No, it's for Mani, the son of Ramamurti Kepmari. He's got syphilis. They say his gland is all red, all eaten away, and that his tail has shrunk terribly: he showed it to my husband. The Nadar is looking after him. He gave him some castor oil that had been heated up with cumin to rub on to his tail, and he's looking for some niruri, white laurel leaves and euphorbia buds to make him a paste that he can take for three days.' When I heard that, I said to myself that I really do have a sharp eye.

We say here that those pox turn into the great sickness when they get worse.[4] That's another reason why, when we started getting older and my husband was on at me to sleep together even when it was my period, I'd say to him, 'Why are you acting like a dog on heat who hangs about in the street? Am I a whore? What's worrying you? I am always here at your side. When you want me, we can do it. At your age, aren't you afraid of going mad? You'd look pretty smart with a stiff neck and swollen feet! You think your stomach will fill up all by itself when you're in that state? Calm down a bit, my old friend! Why are you worrying? Is it to do with the millet or the *ragi* – are you worried someone will help themselves? You know perfectly well that a red ant couldn't make a move here without my permission. Is there anyone more handsome than you? You think your thing is twisted and that I like the neighbour's better?'

I had become more confident, and I still really like talking like that, crudely, even to young people or relatives like an uncle or a cousin, 'Hold on a bit, you bastard! Wait till I pour my juices over your face! Get your packet out and come outside with me! I'll give you an eyeful!

I've had a full bushel of children!' When they hear me, the young ones hide their heads in shame and say, 'Ayoyo! That woman is just too rude! She's got a son and a grandson, but even at her age, she's still talking dirty!' And that makes us laugh very much, all the women and me!

Sinnamma, it's been a long time since I cut down relations with my husband. It was very good at the start, but who paid for it later? I did. For him, it was nothing: he climbed on top of me and that was the end of it. But I found myself with a child in my womb afterwards every time, having trouble standing up, sitting down, sleeping! So much trouble! The old people had good reason to tell me, 'Don't let yourself be taken all the time, Velpakkatta! You'll lose your beauty and your strength.' And it's true, all the blood you lose with each child. Men don't care. They eat well and are as strong as the clubs the gods' guards hold.[5] Screwing doesn't scare them, but we have to think of the consequences and we prefer to go without. Even rich women are the same: rich or poor, you give birth through the same hole, and you lose as much blood. Of course those women will live longer, with the food they eat. But I just don't think that I'll hold out for long after so many children; I really don't have the strength for anything any more.

In the *ur*, even if men are aroused, they can control themselves. Look, the headmaster of the school only has one son, the little Gounder has two children, the Grand Reddi has three. But they can afford family planning: they've got money, their *kanji* is guaranteed. It's not the same for us: our stomach's full the day we work, otherwise it's empty. If there's a lot of us, then we can eat and live in a *ceri* without too many difficulties. But if you don't have anybody to feed you when you're old, you're not going to go looking for work in town at that age, are you? Virassami's father, the cobbler who used to play the horn, gave everything up and went off as a *sanyasi* after the death of his wife and two sons.[6] Otherwise there's nothing left to do but to take up an earthenware cup and go out begging.

They're always talking to us about family planning 'to be happy' and 'to bring down the population rate'. I spit on that lorry which comes from Pondy hospital. They gave out transistors and money and our people went there at first. But we get more nowadays at each election. Besides they've stopped giving anything for sterilisation and it doesn't attract many people any more. Sinnamma, they wanted to take my husband to do that operation on his balls. He was already in line to get on the lorry when a kid came and told me. I left the cattle straightaway and ran to the *ceri* with Anjalai and Pakkiam: we always stick together at times like that. We went to find the doctors in the lorry and told one of them, 'Leave our husbands in peace! We've been brave enough to have ten children and feed all ten of them. We're all happy! Go and find some goats, cows, donkeys or horses and do anything you want with them, but don't touch our men!'

'Come on you women, get up here!' they said.

We answered back. 'We can still have another ten children! Go back where you came from and take your lorry with you!'

They insulted us, but they went away.

It's a very dangerous operation. At Sivapatti it drove a man mad after he'd had migraines every night. They say that after the operation they can't get their thing up, even if they spend hours: men have no passion. Is that being happy? My daughter told me that. She's only got five children and she thought that that was enough. My son-in-law had the operation. She's a beautiful woman. Well, he lost his teeth and he's like an old man. Some die of it immediately, the ones who are mal-nourished. Others can cope with all the strengthening food they eat: oranges, mandarins, other fruits, this and that, everything which gives you strength. But we can't eat like that, our health suffers and it's easy for us to fall ill. And then they stop having any desires. Nothing comes. All they're good for is to sit on top of. Look, even a little child, if you catch his willie and give it an affectionate kiss, well then, it stands up straightaway! If you cut that important nerve, then it's all over! You can ask anybody that, anyone high caste. But it's because there are births on all sides, real flocks of children, that they've decided at the hospital to cut everybody, whether they want it or not, men or women!

They say the operation for women causes even more trouble, because women swell up and get tired quickly and so they can't do the work they used to. It's normal because the bad blood hasn't been cleared out. It's all fine for women who work in creches or offices, but not for Pariahs who roast in the fields. It was different in the *yugam* when I had children: in those days we were blessed for having little ones. Today, in this *kaliyugam*, it's all back to front! Even the government says we must stop at two children. And our young, carried away by the party men and the cinema, accept that and shrink from work: they're a useless bunch!

Why would anyone expect me to get sterilised, Sinnamma? I've had so many children that now I'm like a tree which has borne fruit. Desire only abandons human beings when they die. And even then ... My mother-in-law used to say that a corpse would have tried to beat its tail when it was being put on the pyre!

So, the fact that my husband still desires me is not a crime, I just don't think it's reasonable at this age, even if it's true that I still get my period. I say to him, 'Listen: we've had so many children; we've had a son, we've given him a name and we've brought him up: now he goes and sleeps with his wife, and instead of being happy and proud of that, you want us to be husband and wife! Aren't you ashamed? Are you a man or not? What are you eating, straw or rice? Don't you have the brains to understand that? Do you want me to end up with another child in my womb at my age?' And arguing like that I turn him down. And if he really goes on about it too much, I say everything I've just told you at the top of my voice out on my *tinnai*. People immediately burst out laughing in the neighbouring houses and there are always some young ones who make fun of him, 'De! Uncle Manikkam! You're old and you still want Aunt Viramma to be your wife?'

SIX

A mother to twelve children

I loved sleeping with my husband. We were good together and everything was working out for the best between us. But one day my mother-
in-law asked me, 'Hey! Viramma! Have you bathed this month?'[1] I
answered straightaway, 'Yes, why?' and she said, 'No, no, I just wanted
to know.' Soon big sister Ellamma and the others were asking the same
question and I told them 'yes, yes' as well. They didn't drop it, 'But
we haven't seen you hang your sheets on the cactus.' To stop the conversation, I took my jar and went to the well. I'd lied to everybody: I
still hadn't had my period that month and, since I was ignorant then,
I didn't understand why. Perhaps I'd been making love too much with
my husband recently? And why were these women so interested in my
periods? Perhaps they'd guessed that I'd had too much sex by looking
at my face? I'd been happy not to have my period and now I was
starting to get worried. What could be behind it? I didn't dare talk to
my husband about periods. Once again I was alone. Big sister Ellamma
was old and had plenty of experience, but I still hesitated and I didn't
know how to bring up the question. I felt as if I'd done something
stupid. Palm fruits with sugar were in season. Had I eaten too many
or had I been with my husband too much? Why didn't I have my
period any more?

Before I'd even decided to talk about it to big sister Ellamma, one
evening after supper I was violently sick: I just had time to get out and

do it on the *tinnai*. My mother-in-law, who was chewing betel nearby, ran over with water, 'Come, Ma', she said to me, lifting me up.

She wetted my face, laid out a mat and made me sit down, 'Lie down, Ma. It will be like this for a while and then it'll go.'

'But what have I got, aunt? My heart hurts.'

'No, no, it's nothing. Ma, it's good news: you are pregnant!'

I didn't understand a thing: my stomach was normal and flat and here she was telling me I was pregnant! She went outside straightaway, where my husband was chatting, to tell him the news, 'Hey! Manikkam, your wife is pregnant!'

'Hey! Manikkam, you've done your work well', his friends said and everyone started laughing. The women came out of their houses. They tried to work out the first day of the pregnancy with my mother-in-law to find out the date of birth. I'd gone inside and, lying down, I listened to all their conversations. I didn't feel ill or pregnant. My husband came in a bit later and said, 'Come on then, show me, apparently you're pregnant?' I started laughing when I realised that he was as inexperienced as me. But he insisted, 'Show me!'

'But what do you want to see? It's like an earthworm in my womb and it'll only grow bigger bit by bit!'

That's how I learned what pregnancy was. My mother-in-law was proud of me and she said to everybody, 'Our Viramma is pregnant!' The news was carried to Velpakkam and my parents, happy and proud as well, came to see me with lots of sweets. My mother wanted me to go to her house in the seventh month – that's the custom in our caste – but, so that I'd stay longer with him, my husband refused, claiming that there wouldn't be anybody to make his meals. For the first birth we go back to our mother's family quite early because we're never very sure the date the pregnancy starts. It lasts ten months in all and we celebrate the feast of *simantam* in the seventh month. But I only left for Velpakkam in the ninth month.[2]

In the fifth month my parents brought me the first trays of food specially made for women halfway through their pregnancy. There were five measures of rice and all sorts of vegetables and sweets. All of it was put in the middle of the house and camphor was burned. All the relatives were invited to see that my mother had done a good job. Then my husband and I were sat down and they started to share out the meal on to two banana leaves. A little of everything was put on: rice with yoghurt, rice with whey, rice with sorrel, doughnuts well fried in oil ... Then all the rest was given out to the family, friends and neighbours, just like you do: don't you send trays of sweets to each other's houses? We have to honour our friends as well!

In my case, we only celebrated the *simantam* in the ninth month but we did it right. My parents brought the food in a copper vessel as big as that! There has to be lots of it. If you're poor or destitute, you should still send at least half the normal amount. You have to save face. You borrow a vessel from one house, some rice from another. And when it's a question of honour, people are happy to lend: just because we're poor doesn't mean we have to humiliate ourselves in front of our family-in-law! What's been borrowed is given back when a daughter goes back to her mother's to give birth. We cooked three sorts of rice in big copper pots and put *laddu*, *jilebi*, *Mysore pak*, *vadai* and *murukku* in another one. In the past we'd bring it all in big osier baskets but the world has completely changed in this *kaliyugam*. Now any old destitute owns stainless steel pots and pans. We transported it all from my mother's house to my family-in-laws' in big copper basins covered with yellow cloths.

We celebrated a very important ceremony before the birth. This time my husband and I were sat down facing two jars that were filled with water and covered with banana leaves. On one jar there was a tray with a sari on it, and on the other, a tray with a *soman*. Everything was ready. I was asked to bend down so a banana leaf could be put on my back. Then the women in my family-in-law came and poured a measure of cow's milk on the leaf and each time someone announced who had just poured, 'The milk of Viramma's mother-in-law! The milk of the eldest sister-in-law!' When that rite finished, I put on the new sari from the tray and my husband put on his new *soman*. We went back and sat down for the donations of money: the men put the money on my forehead and the women put the money on my husband's forehead and again someone called out each time who had just given and how much, 'The mother-in-law's money: five rupees! The brother-in-law's money: three rupees!' Meanwhile the meal was being prepared. When we'd finished, we were taken back into the house. Banana leaves were put on the ground, and my family was invited to sit down and eat. After the meal, my father went to consult the Iyer to see if we could go back to Velpakkam straightaway or if he saw any unlucky stars which could trouble our return. Most importantly, was Venus facing us? The Iyer replied I don't know what, that Venus was in her descendant or in her ascendant, and asked what side the opening of our house was, telling us that we had to go round by the north if the entrance was to the south, or by the south if the entrance was to the north. And that's how we all left on foot for Velpakkam.

I waited there until the tenth month. I didn't have a clue what was happening to me. My stomach grew bigger from day to day. I was small with a fat stomach like a baby elephant and I moved around just like one, taking little steps. People pitied me. They'd stop to ask, 'Hey! Little girl, where does it hurt?' And I'd show them here, the pubic bone, telling them, 'That's where it hurts. I don't hurt in the stomach, or anywhere else, I only hurt there.' (*Laughs.*) I was ignorant in those days! I couldn't cope with the pain and I'd grumble, 'Ayo! Some widower or other has gone and given me away in marriage and look what's happening to me!' The women said to me, 'Poor little thing, the first child is like that; afterwards it'll be much easier!'

And then one day, while I was sitting on the veranda, my mother said to me, 'Viramma, go and pick me some of the purslane leaves on the roof, we're going to make a *kuttu*.' I got up and, leaning against the wall, I went to the edge of the roof. I could only pick two or three leaves: my lower stomach was pulling, a type of pain I'd never had before, something like being stung by red ants. Even so I picked the leaves and went and sat down, saying to my mother, 'Ayo, mother, my stomach hurts! Ayayo, my stomach hurts! Put some dry ginger paste on it for me.' My mother answered, 'Don't move. It's begun. You have to wait a little while for the first child.' I asked my sister-in-law Saroja to make me an infusion of ginger. She brought it to me after she'd let it cool a bit. I like the smell a lot and I thought it would relieve the pain, but no, nothing happened. Leaning on the wall again I headed for the drinking trough and there I said, 'Ayayo, mother! I feel like I want to go to the garden.'[3] Han, yes, I remember women who came to the hospital and gave birth for the first time felt like this: they'd go and sit down in the toilets and they'd give birth in that position into the bowl! I'd just managed to get near the drinking trough. I couldn't bear it any more. I squatted down, saying, 'Ayo, Sami!' I heard, 'Podukku', like the sound of a running tap. That was all. The child had fallen into the folds of my sari. I was all dressed, the end of my sari over my chest. He was stuck in the folds and crying. I was very scared and screamed, 'O mother! O mother! Ayo, the dirty widows! Come quickly! Come quickly!' Panic stricken, my mother ran up, 'Ayo, my daughter! Ayo, my daughter! You idiot, you could have told me that you were feeling bad! You could have told me!'

My mother was a midwife. She went to find a sickle to cut the cord. She dug a hole quickly in the drain with a hoe and buried the placenta and the cord straightaway. At the same time my sister-in-law was heating up water and preparing saffron paste. The baby was washed with soap, rubbed with the paste and then rinsed in hot water. It was all clean and wrapped in a nice, soft old sari so as not to hurt its delicate skin. A big black *pottu* was put on its forehead and another on its cheek to ward off the evil eye, and it was laid out on the mat.

I was massaged with oil, first my head, then my stomach, to bring out the bad blood. I was washed everywhere with hot water and my stomach was bound up very tightly with a piece of cloth so the air didn't get into my vagina. That's how it is for everybody, eh, even women of your caste! Then a good thick layer of rags was put between my thighs to collect the discharge. My baby and I were laid down in a corner. I couldn't stand up, my head was spinning. In the morning I was given some ash and a little water to brush my teeth. I spat into an earthenware pot which was held out for me and I washed my face like that, sitting down. I wasn't allowed to go out. After washing, I had some freshly made *selavu* powder on an empty stomach, I drank some warm water straightaway and then I lay down again. No meals for two days. I fed myself on bread and ginger coffee, that's all. I lay flat, without turning over too much. When I wanted to sit up, I asked my sister-in-law or my mother to help me. The baby was put in my arms for feeding. I was very weak. Two days and two nights without eating: my ears blocked up with tiredness and my pulse was too weak to pick up the child. I'd say, 'Amma, lift up the child a little and give him to me, Amma!' That's how I breastfed. Then, when we start eating again, we get some of our strength back and it's easier. Soon I could sit up on my own and talk to my visitors. I told them every detail of how it had gone.

That's how I gave birth to my first child, Sinnamma. I was well fed at my father's and I was in good health; that's why my labour went so quickly and so easily. The child slipped out like a banana and I didn't even tear. In the hospital you see some midwives, some brutes who break an arm or twist the baby's leg.

After the birth, I didn't go outside until the ninth bath. All that time we fed our launderer: he's the one who washes the soiled linen after the birth, whether it's new or silk, and it goes to him too: it's his by right. At the ninth bath, he's given some *sikakai*, some oil, some betel and a two rupee note on a tray and then we've done our duty to him. The last bath, the ninth, is with ammi. A measure of oil mixed with a handful of seeds which have been heated up is put on our hair. That feels very good. Our body is massaged with the same oil and then we wash ourselves with *sikakai*. The most important thing is not to doze off after the bath, otherwise the water collects in the head and you can be very ill: we don't see any sun for all that time and it's hard for us to get rid of the water we drink, and that's why it can stay in our body, in our head, and give us *sitalam*. The water mixes with the blood; you cough, you breathe badly, you get a strong fever, you're delirious, you become very weak. Sometimes the blood can even evaporate!

My mother took very good care of me when I was at Velpakkam. On the third day she made me lots of rice with a good *selavu* sauce which is cooked with a grilled powder in a brand new earthenware vessel and made with dry ginger and cumin, mustard and ammi seeds. My mother had prepared plenty of this powder. She had kept half in an iron box to use in the sauce and mixed the other half with palm sugar so I could have some on an empty stomach when I woke up. It's a very effective remedy, Sinnamma: it gets rid of all the impurities in the womb and at the same time heals the part which is on fire. When I was at Velpakkam, my mother was very attentive to my diet. She never gave me cooling foods so as to avoid *sitalam*, which can make you delirious and kill you.[4] She didn't even let me drink cold water for the first three days, and gave me boiled, warm water. Up to the ninth day, I only had rice with *selavu* sauce and then some *kali*. We poor people cannot eat rice every day. For a month, I wasn't given any *kuj*, pumpkins, okra, marrows, tomatoes, green leaves, rice from the day before, or whey: all of that is very cooling and you have to steer clear of it otherwise the baby suffers and gets diarrhoea. Warming foods are what you have to eat and I was given more and more *selavu* sauce, aubergines, lentil puree, salted fish, meat and goat's milk. There was lots of garlic, cumin and fenugreek as well, prepared every day, but I wasn't given much palm sugar or sugar cane, because that gives babies diarrhoea as well. My mother didn't want anyone to blame her about this or for them to say at my mother-in-law's, 'What! Viramma went to give birth at her mother's. She wasn't looked after, she was left to eat any old thing, and look: now the baby's ill.' Sinnamma, even if the daughter-in-law is hardly looked after at her parents-in-law, they never hesitate to criticise her family.

I stayed at Velpakkam for another three months. My family-in-law came to see me once after the birth and they came to find me when three months was up. My husband came twice in between. He wanted to see the baby and he asked me gently, 'De, when will you be sent to

Karani?' He was in a hurry for me to come back and I was as well, because I'd had enough of all the things I was forbidden. I didn't even go and work in the fields, so as not to risk catching *sitalam* by putting my feet and hands in water. I wasn't allowed to go to the well either, so as not to lift heavy things or make sudden movements. There was a woman my mother's age in Velpakkam itself whose sack hung down between her knees: apparently she had moved a big vessel of paddy too soon. And we were told, 'Be careful, girls. If you are careless, you'll find yourself with an egg hanging down like a pendant between your thighs like Kuppu.' That made us laugh a lot, but even so we tried to be careful because we were afraid. We're always a little afraid for the first child and we do what we're told.

You know, Sinnamma, babies get diarrhoea easily and often they die of it. Two or three of my children died like that. My mother had planted some bitter apples on the edge of a field to cure babies who'd caught a *dosham*. We make the little ones sit down and we put some diluted lime, some turmeric water and some bitter apples on a tray. We carry the tray three times round the baby's head, then we pour it all on the ground and break the bitter apples on some land outside the *ceri*. We give the baby an infusion of cumin and mulberry leaves in the morning and the evening. That's for the most common *dosham*, the one you catch on dark roads. But there are more serious *dosham*, which we can't treat. The launderer takes care of them: he plays the drum, sings mantras and gives the baby a knotted string or talisman. There are so many dangers in our countryside! We go out collecting wood, we go everywhere, even to the cremation grounds. If a mother who's breastfeeding is possessed there, there's nothing you can do, the baby gets the *dosham*. You can see it clearly in his face: he only half-opens his eyes, he is very tired, he doesn't smile any more and cries the whole time. That's the *kujidosham* every time. I said that the other day to Sisata. She was coming back from the dispensary at Naliveli with her baby and said to me, 'Big sister, I've taken him to the dispensary for injections for three days running, but he isn't any better.' I answered, 'Your child won't get better at the dispensary. Look at him, it looks to me like a *kujidosham*. Go to big brother Peramban's, he'll cure you and your child with his mantras. Injections and tablets haven't been invented yet for that trouble!' Today, in this *kaliyugam*, everyone runs to hospital for a yes or a no. No one bothers with the old diets, when there were no injections, no compresses, no hospitals. Everything that's given out now at the dispensary is so warming that you have to take cooling foods to make up for it!

Nowadays, doctors make the rounds of the villages and give medicines and tonics to pregnant women from the start of their pregnancy. In the sixth or seventh month they're meant to go to the dispensary themselves for a check up. Yes, everything has changed now. They come and see us, they bring us medicines, Sinnamma. A nurse comes to the village. First she does the round of the *ur* with Anjamma, the barber's wife who is a midwife. She records the names of all the pregnant women and all those who've given birth recently, then she comes to the *ceri*. I'm the midwife here and in the same way I take her to all the women who haven't had a bath or who are in labour. I also say if the newborns are boys or girls. Then the nurse goes and enters all that in the registers at Pondy hospital. Tablets and injections are sent to Naliveli. The people from the dispensary hand them out in the villages and do their rounds of the *ceri* with their tray of medicines. For births, we're meant to go with the mothers to the dispensary, but often there's no room, or the doctor isn't there and we have to go by bus to Pondy. In the past women were only taken to hospital in real emergencies. We went there in an ox-cart or rickshaw and often the woman died on the way.

We midwives help the nurse during labour and we're paid twenty rupees a month by the State. They even suggested that I come and work at the dispensary permanently, but I didn't want to. I've got enough to do at home and I couldn't do that work full-time: who'd look after my cows and calves? If I was alone, well then, yes. The head doctor, the nurse, everybody came to the *ceri* to tell me to do a course, but I told them no. I work at the Reddiar's, I irrigate three quarters of a hectare of his land. I couldn't leave him. Anjamma, the barber's wife, went on a course and apparently she learned lots of things there. When it's a serious case, she comes and gives me a hand here in the *ceri*. Eh, what can you do? Pariahs or not, you have to help each other when there's danger: we are women first and foremost! She's never made any trouble about coming. The child shows itself badly, the placenta goes back up, the cord is round the neck: it's better to be two, don't you think? But we make it up to her, we pay her properly.

In the *ceri* I'm given five rupees for each birth nowadays, plus half a rupee which is the cord money. When a woman goes into labour, they come and find me: 'Eldest sister-in-law! The woman's in pain at home!' So I drop everything, I go and see her, I examine her, I turn her round one way then the other, I pester her a bit and then I tell her more or less when the child is going to be born: in two hours or before daybreak or after the first screening at the cinema or after the second. And it turns out as I said it would. I quickly cut the cord with a knife and tell the women attending to go and find a hoe and a crowbar and dig a hole in the drain near the house. I wait for the placenta to come out and go and bury it myself straightaway. Then I take care of the mother. I stretch her out on the mat, wedge her in with pillows, wash the baby with soap and hot water and lie it down next to its mother. Then I put a sickle and some margosa leaves at the head of the mat, next to the pillow, so spirits don't come near them. Yes, those rogue spirits love to prowl around the lanes in the evening or at night, eating any food on the ground and trying to possess people.

It's well known that they follow us everywhere we go, when we're hoeing or planting out, when we're changing our sanitary towels, when we're washing our hair. They sense that we're going to visit a woman in labour and then they possess us, because they need an intermediary to pass into the body of a woman who's just given birth. That's why we put down the sickle and the margosa leaves which keep them away. After that I quite often go and visit to keep in touch, to see if everything's going okay. Sometimes, if impurities have stayed in the womb, I cook the leaves of the 'cow's itch' plant, extract the juice and make the mother drink it three times.

There, that's how a birth happens with us. Here in the *ceri* we prefer to give birth at home. It's only in really difficult cases that I advise women to go to hospital. But I've told you, they come to the *ceri* more and more now telling us to make sure we take the tonics during pregnancy and to give birth at the dispensary. But our women don't go there: the experiences some of us have had don't encourage us at all. First of all we get a bad reception. We have to wait a long time before someone comes and takes care of us. When we're admitted, we country women always talk a bit loud, and when we're in pain, we say it, we shout, 'Ayayo! Mother! I'm in pain!' And the nurses make fun of us, 'Eh! It felt good back then, eh? Aah well, now's the time to suffer!' It's all young nurses who tell us that, Sinnamma! And what's more they're harsh, 'Get up! Walk! Get out of bed! Go to the toilet!' The mother has to do everything or sometimes the family can look after her. But it's not that we're afraid of work; basically, we're lost over there. We don't know what's what or where things are. Men are not allowed into the women's block and, because we don't understand, we're yelled at the whole time. As well as the pain in our womb, we have to put up with everything we

hear: we're humiliated. Or else the nurses send us away or tell lies about
us to the head doctor. He doesn't see what goes on. He listens to what
the nurses tell him and he says to us, 'Ma! Why don't you do what the
sisters say?'[5] How do you expect us to open our mouths in front of the
head doctor? It's our men who reply, 'No, Sami, my wife comes from
the country, she doesn't understand anything, forgive her, she'll do
everything you say!' The head doctor isn't harsh but he's got so many
people to see that he's never there. Looking at it another way, it's true
as well that the nurses have to deal with villagers a lot; there are so
many illnesses that people come from everywhere.

All the same, we prefer to give birth at the *ceri* after what happened to
Irsamma and Kaliyamma. You'll understand why we're mistrustful. You
see Nadan's wife, the one who's as thin as a twig on a broom? She's
called Irsamma. She was pregnant with her second child. Her first had
died. She was weak and she was still losing blood. At the dispensary at
Naliveli she was told that she must go to Pondy hospital to give birth.
We thought so as well: at least at the hospital she could be given some
tonics or a bottle of blood could be put in her veins. Irsamma, Nadan
her mother and I left for the hospital a few days before the birth.
Irsamma had a room but there was no free bed. She had been set up in
a corner on the floor. She was fine, food was brought to her and she was
taken care of. We three lived in the park facing the hospital. We'd
brought utensils to cook and we took turns to go and see Irsamma. One
morning I was told she was in labour and that she was in the birthing
room. I quickly went down to tell the others. Then a nurse came to tell
us that Irsamma had given birth. But because they'd had to use the
forceps to bring the child out, Irsamma had lost lots of blood and she
was very weak. So she was in a separate room with her baby, who was
a boy. We were very frightened and we started crying. At that moment
the head doctor came out and reassured us that the reason she'd been
kept separate was so that they could really restore her strength with
glucose and get her back to good health. It's comforting when a head
doctor says that! For more than a week, she stayed on her own and then
she was put back in the general ward. When we went to see her we
found her crying. But she looked well, she didn't have any tubes in her
or anything. We went up to her and asked her, 'What is it, Ma? Are you
in pain?' She started screaming, 'It's not that, it's my baby!'

   'What's the matter with your baby? Hasn't he had a drink? Is he
sick?'

'No! No! My baby is a boy, he's all black!'

I hadn't seen the baby yet and I said to her, 'What is all this? Crying because your baby is black? Who ever heard of that?'

Meanwhile Nadan and his mother had leant over the child, 'What? He's pretty light, this little one! And first things first, black, light, is that what matters? You think we're light, us? No, are you mad?'

So I said to them, 'No, no, it's not her fault, there are too many spirits in these places! Maybe it's those dogs who are doing it!'

Irsamma started crying again even harder. The people nearby came up to her bed and she shouted, 'Give me back my baby, it's an all black boy! I saw him! Give him back! Give him back to me!'

We couldn't understand. I took the baby in my arms and said, 'But what is this? This is a girl!'

Irsamma was crying on one side, on the other the nurses were furious with us and we had to give answers to all the people who were gawping and surrounding us. You couldn't hear yourself in that racket. I didn't know what to do any more. The nurses were insulting us, 'You don't just come here and give birth in comfort, you shout like fishwives! You are real Pariahs!'

The head nurse, the one with the butterfly hat, came up just then. I was afraid she'd send us away and the poor little girl needed tonics and rest. So I stepped in, 'Mother! Mother! It's nothing at all, it's about the baby: our little one thinks she had a boy, that's all.'

'What? What is all this? We're working here! We can't waste our time with your stupidities! Let's see what the mum's number is and the baby's!'

It was only then that I noticed that both of them were wearing a numbered tag on their wrist. And the head nurse said, 'Eh well! It's the same number for both of them, come and see! What more do you want?'

But we didn't know how to read. The people around us looked and said, 'Yes, it's definitely the right number. What could that woman have seen in her condition?'

I added, 'No, no, mother, she didn't say that, the one who's possessing her did.'

The nurse left shrugging her shoulders. We didn't make a great thing out of it – quite the opposite, we even told Irsamma off and said to ourselves that she should have a black thread round her neck to protect her, or to weaken the effects of the *dosham* she might have, because you find all sorts of illnesses at the hospital. Perhaps Irsamma saw a woman miscarrying and that will have made her delirious and given her the *dosham*. We wanted her to be well cared for there and then take her to our exorcist to have her affliction removed.

Irsamma was given injections every day. She was given medicine every day. But that halfwit, instead of making the most of the food which they brought her, wouldn't eat! The head doctor told her that if she didn't eat, she'd have to come back to the hospital again and he gave us a pass so we could come in ourselves and give her food in the mornings and evenings. She ended up feeling better and when she had made a good recovery, we thought she could return home. Nadesan went to the market to buy everything needed for a *puja* and before leaving the hospital, we burnt some camphor and broke a coconut on the stone by the entrance. And then there was Irsamma having another crying fit in front of us, 'Ayo, Andava! What you do is not just! You take back what you've given me!'

We were really furious with her. Thanks to God, she had been well cared for, she'd recovered her strength and here she was starting the same old story again! Her husband gave her a good telling off and her mother-in-law did as well. I stopped myself from shouting any abuse in that place, in front of a god. But a caretaker who was standing near the grille came up and said, 'Leave her be. Don't scold her. It's her maternal instinct coming out. Maybe she isn't wrong but crying won't make her child come back! Go on, go on, go home, you live a long way away.'

Nadesan slipped him a coin, as he'd done to all the labourers, and I said, 'Let's go. We have to hurry now to get home before night falls. The little one mustn't get the evil eye or be touched by one of those evil breaths of wind that prowl around everywhere!'

We stopped a rickshaw which asked an enormous sum just to go to the buses. We had a heavy load with all our jars, and since we women didn't want to find ourselves alone down there with all our things in the middle of so many people, I said to Nadesan, 'Little brother, get in the rickshaw with the two women, the baby and all the things. I'll follow you on foot.' And they all left like that.

Walking along, I thought over what the caretaker had said – that story was on my mind. So I turned round and I went to see him. I knew him a little bit by sight, because I'd come to the hospital several times and he was always at the gate in the afternoon. So I trusted him a bit and I went and asked him, 'Big brother! Big brother! What did you say about that little one only a minute ago? That she's not wrong?'

'Do you really want to know everything?' he said. 'And what will you do afterwards?'

'What am I going to do? Listen with this ear and send it on its way through this one! Eh! What can we do, people like us?'

And so he told me that a high-born woman had given birth a few hours after Irsamma. This woman already had three daughters and she absolutely had to have a boy, because she'd been told that she wouldn't be able to have any more children afterwards. So the family had paid all the doctors and nurses for the girl to be swapped for any newborn boy. Irsamma was in a separate room with tubes everywhere at the time and so they took advantage of it to make the swap. Otherwise what mother would have the heart to swap her son? It's true that people sometimes abandon their child because they're too poor or because they've done wrong, but who would swap her little one? Even in the state she was in, Irsamma had had a good look at her boy, and it must have been some nurses who weren't in the know who told us the baby was a boy. But no, because the trick was only decided on afterwards! Who knows? We could be made to believe anything in those days, you just had to raise your voice. Anyway, there's the son of Irsamma in a rich family and this little girl in the Pariahs' *ceri*! It was written on their heads that their lives would change like this as soon as they were born. Who knows what they were before being born into this human life? In any case Irsamma raised the little one like her daughter and she even gave her away in marriage in a village next to Karani.

Several years later, a similar thing happened to Kaliyamma. But this time it wasn't the nurses who made the swap but a mother herself who took the child. The mothers are in such a big room in the hospital! After she's given birth, we can stay with a mother during the day but in the evening we have to leave her to go and sleep in the corridor. The night nurses sleep in a room next door. They don't hear what's going on with the mothers and anyone can do anything in their room, it's easy. Kaliyamma was asleep when it happened, but, of course, she was the first to realise when she put her child to her breast in the morning. She said to me instantly, 'What is this? De! He's got a different head!'

I had slept badly all night and I wasn't fully awake when I heard that. I said, 'Aye! Give your eyes a good rub and have another look!'

But she was already undressing the baby: it was a girl instead of a boy. Kaliyamma started lamenting and beating her chest. I couldn't understand and I started trembling. I had clearly seen that her baby, her real baby, was a boy. What had happened? The nurses ran up with Mariamma, Kaliyamma's mother, and Ganesan, her husband. I explained to them what was going on. They were amazed, but they didn't want to

take a decision because their shift was almost over: they told us to wait
for the head doctor. Kaliyamma let them talk, but she went round the
room on her own and, suddenly, she cried out, 'It's him! It's him!
That's my child!' pointing at a well-dressed baby, all covered up with
socks and a bonnet. The woman who was with the child started insulting Kaliyamma, calling her mad, and protesting, 'What? Swap with a
Harijan? Us!' She was a Muslim. Meanwhile the team of nurses had
changed. The head doctor had been informed and he came into the
room. I prostrated myself in greeting. I was getting to be known at the
hospital because I often go there with the sick or mothers. The doctors
were on our side that time: the scheme didn't come from high up. The
doctor gave the order to undress the children. He looked at the register.
It was clearly marked 'boy' for Kaliyamma, and 'girl' for the other
woman. Ganesan could read and write; he also went up to the register
and saw the same thing. The boy was given back to Kaliyamma. The
woman tried to explain herself, saying it was the night nurses who'd
mixed up the cradles. You know, all newborns look alike, dressed like
that. But for a mother it's different, her instinct and her love open her
eyes! The woman and the doctor kept on arguing. We were very happy
to have got our baby back. Oh now he's a handsome boy who's called
Ramakrishnan: he's big and he goes to school with a pile of books!

You can understand why we don't like the hospital very much,
Sinnamma. For my twelve children I did it all alone, I didn't let anyone
near me in case they tore the hole or dislocated one of my baby's bones.
I've always said to the nurses at Naliveli, 'Leave me in peace, it'll come
out on its own! Why do you want to rummage around in there?' I
always give birth very gently, like stroking a rose. It never lasts very
long: I'm not like those women whose labour drags on so much – for a
whole night or even for days – that you have to give them some water
or *kuj* or coffee to drink. No, it's not like that for me at all!

  First of all I make a point never to forget to prepare the tray for
Ettiyan and his huge men with their thick moustaches who carry a club
on their muscular shoulders: a tray with green mangoes, coconuts, other
fruits as well and some tools – a hoe, a crowbar, a basket – so that they
can set to work as soon as the child comes out of the sack in our
stomach. Yes! I've seen enough to know what I'm talking about! I've
had a full bushel of children! Everything we eat goes into that sack and
that's how the child grows. Just think what a mystery that is! With the
blood he collects over ten months, Isan moulds a baby in our womb.

Only he can do that. Otherwise, how could a sperm become a child? And it's Isan who sends Ettiyan and his men to soothe our pain after the birth. They take some mud and throw it on our womb so the pains ease and that's how all that part that's as red as hot coals, and the skin that's as soft as cotton heal up so quickly!

So the first thing I prepare is a tray for Ettiyan. Then I quickly heat up the water. I take off my sari. With a cup I pour water on my waist and my hips. I dry myself and I wipe myself with a little cloth. I walk a little, leaning against the wall. I feel it coming down and to be dead sure, I wait for the pouch of the waters to open and, oh!, I hear it burst, 'podu!' and then start flowing, 'sala, sala, sala ... ' and afterwards everything comes quickly: first the child, by the head, then the placenta and there we are, it's finished. Apparently Devi says to Sami, 'Lord! Give it a kick with your foot! Don't let this child hang around a minute longer in this womb, this is a clever woman!' Yes, experienced women like me have the Lord's special favour.

I don't make any mistakes, I treat all the labours I'm in charge of the same way. I know that the way to the resting place of Vishnu is open for us midwives and marked out in full. If I die today or if I die an old woman, Yama or his guards won't be there to stop me and tell me my sentence. Isvaran won't sentence us midwives to hell. We see too much suffering with our own eyes! The blood that we see flowing! The blood that we collect in our hands! The pain! That's why there won't be any obstacles for us. The sixteen gates will be flung wide open and we'll go straight through and shut ourselves away in the residence of Yama. He won't send us to be reborn! No, not this damnation of rebirth.[6]

SEVEN

The destinies of children

I've always had plenty of milk during my pregnancies and even more afterwards. It used to flow so much that the front of my sari was all stiff. I'm sure that even now, if I was pregnant, I'd still have plenty of milk. My daughter is like me, she has even more. You had to see the weight of my breasts when a baby was dying: the milk hardened in my breasts, I suffered so much! In the *ceri* people don't dare apply poultices for fear of not having any milk for the next child. Ah yes, Sinnamma! No more milk ever after poultices! So we go to the dispensary and they put a transparent cup on us with a pipe and a pump at the bottom. The milk is sucked out and the breasts become all slack.When we want to wean the child, he's already big and we don't have as much milk as at the start. So we go and collect a large amount of jasmine, put it on our breasts and tie them up very tight with a bandage. We do that three days in a row and then that's it: the milk's dried up and, at the next pregnancy, it starts again.

You know that we breastfeed our children for a long time, for at least three years. That allows us not to have another child straightaway. We are women condemned to bake in the sun. If we went and got a baby in the womb each time, how could we manage to work and eat? You Sinnamma, you're a rich woman: you can allow yourself to stretch your legs and take a rest. But to have my *kanji*, I have to take it everywhere, my womb: planting out, hoeing, grazing the cows, collecting wood. And

when we've got a little one in our arms, it's the same: we take it everywhere and we worry, because while we're working we don't really know
what he's doing or where he is. That's why we try to wait three years
until the child grows up, walks, talks and can say, 'Dad', 'Mum', 'That's
our cow', 'Aunt's coming'. That's a sign for us. We let a period go by
and afterwards we can start 'being on speaking terms' and 'doing it'. If
we stick to this gap, the child will be strong and chubby. We Pariahs
breastfeed for a long time and our milk is in great demand, Sinnamma!

People come and ask us for a little when a baby or its mother are sick
in the *ur*. One day in Madras, in the Pariahs' market, a Marwari – a
pawnbroker – who'd set up his stall down there got someone to stop me
to ask for a cup of milk. Han! I was walking in this market with my
baby on my hip. He found me and sent someone to ask me for a little
milk for his wife and baby who were very ill. He needed to dissolve
some powdered medicine in my milk. I was ashamed when I was told
that in front of everybody, like that, in a big town, but my husband said
to me, 'Give it, de! Someone is ill!' So I went into a corner and collected the milk. Sinnamma, the Marwari gave me ten rupees for such a
little cup! Ten rupees! Yes, our milk is in great demand and when it's
given to your children, they get better quickly, because it's very rich
milk. We can eat everything, nothing's forbidden for us. When we can
afford it, we eat chicken, beef, mutton, all sorts of fish and green leaves.
That's what makes our milk so special and nourishing. You only eat
vegetables. Of course you have lots of bread, lots of milk and fruit, but
in spite of all that, you have a little less strength than us. Because we're
poor, we cook simple meals: a handful of lentils with lots of leaves
picked on the lanes in the fields, a quickly made, very strong sauce of
salted fish with a green mango. Sometimes some beef. That's what makes
our milk rich. When you lift up one of your children, they're always a
bit limp, flabby and light. But when it's one of ours, you'd think you
were lifting up a stone Pillaiyar!

You don't have to look far, just have a look at the son of our Reddiar.
He's a handsome young man now, good and strong. He was born the
same time as one of my children, my first one I think. I gave him the
breast. In those days, when he was a baby, his mother had lots to do in
the house. She had to prepare *idli* and *uppuma* for breakfast, heat up the
bath water for her five brothers-in-law and get the *kuj* made for the
seventy workers who were working in their fields. The women of that
house had so much to do that they handed the baby over to me. I was
told, 'Look after him in the garden. Give him a bit of your milk!' I used

to take him to the *ceri* and I fed him like my own child. If I'd cooked beef, I gave him some. He liked the taste and he'd ask for it! And now he's a man, he doesn't respect me and if I'm at his house, in the courtyard, he says to me, 'Aye! Stop there, you! It smells of Pariah here!' One day I'd taken the cattle to graze in the sun and I'd come back parched, without having been able to stop and have a drink on the way. I tied up the cattle and said to him, 'Little brother! Pour me out some water, I'm dying of thirst!' He turned to his mother who was in the kitchen and said to her, 'Mother, Velpakkatta is asking for some water.' And his mother told him to go and get some in a tumbler. He'd drunk at my breasts, and now here he is, thinking twice about giving me a little water!

All that is to tell you how much our milk, the milk of the Pariahs, is in demand. And we raise our children on that milk until they grow and talk.

After the birth of a child, the husband must not go near his wife. No, even his shadow mustn't go near her. If his five fingers touch his wife, the milk will turn immediately and just be water, like cold water, you know! Then the child will die. It will fall ill and won't recover: it will stay thin, through lack of mother's milk. That's true for all women, Sinnamma! Whether it's your mother or someone else's, if a woman falls pregnant while she's still breastfeeding, the child she has in her arms will become stunted!

Once I almost lost a little one like that, through lack of milk. That surprises you, doesn't it? Because I said that I've always had lots of milk. But you'll see. One day while I was sweeping our Reddiar's court-yard, I heard a priest's handbell ringing near the place where people are buried sitting down. So I went up to the wall to see. Our Reddiar's family had come from Pakkanur and were having a *puja* performed to the god of their line. I finished sweeping and then I took my baby on my hip and went back to the *ceri*. It must have been my third child: I don't know any more if it was a boy or a girl, it was such a long time ago! Anyway, it started crying. It was hungry. I took it, sat down and nursed it, but nothing came. It was no good nursing it: nothing, not a drop! And it was sobbing fit to burst! It was the evening. Hearing the baby crying like that, the neighbours came out to see what was happen-ing. They thought the baby was all alone. I couldn't understand any of it and I told them that suddenly I didn't have any more milk. They said to me, 'Some spirit, some Katteri prowling round our *ceri* has possessed you or terrified you! Tomorrow you'll go and see the Gounder: he'll put a little thread round your neck and some ash on your forehead and it will be all right!' But what was to be done while waiting? I gave my baby some rice gruel. I couldn't sleep that night: I wondered what was happening to me. And suddenly, thinking about the Katteri, I remembered that the *puja* I'd seen performed that day had to be in honour of Katteri, because she is the goddess of the Reddiar's line. But their Katteri is good, she raises children.[1] I didn't know what it all could mean. As soon as the day broke, I quickly got ready, took my baby on my hip and ran to the Reddi's. When the lady saw me, she said, 'Well, Velpakkatta! You get here with your baby on your hip as soon as the cock cries, do you?'

'Yes, mother! I didn't close my eyes all night: I haven't a drop of milk left to feed my baby!'

And I told her everything, crying. She answered, 'Han! Your uncleanness has displeased our Katteri! Bring me some camphor, some betel, a coconut and some little black bracelets!'

It was the morning. I didn't have any money, nor did my husband. I quickly ran to my friend Ambigai and asked her to lend me a rupee and then I was able to bring what the Reddi's wife had asked me to. She went back into her room with it all and performed a *puja*. While she was doing that I cleaned out the stable, trembling with fear. A long time afterwards she came out again with a packet of ashes and the black bracelets and she said, 'Hey! Velpakkatta! Here you are, put that on your baby's wrists and spread the ashes all over your breasts. But most importantly, don't play around watching us when we're performing a *puja*! Our Katteri is good: she has been restrained with you. But if she's crossed, she can make pregnant women miscarry or strangle her children instead of raising them. Have you forgotten who you are? All your sort are unclean!'

I respectfully took the ashes in my hands and as she had told me, I rubbed my breasts and even my forehead for three days and I spread them on my baby's forehead too. The cow's milk, the sugared water and the rice gruel which he'd been given in a tumbler hadn't satisfied the little one, and he still wanted to feed. I had tears in my eyes seeing him. I lay him on my thighs and sang him songs. Once I'd started a lullaby and, without realising, gone into a mourning song and I cried. And then, when I wanted to blow my nose in my sari, I felt it all crisp. Just by touching it I guessed what was happening. It was milk, Sinnamma, milk which had dried on my sari! Ayo! I was happy, very happy to be able to breastfeed my child and see it smile at last with a full stomach!

Since then, for each pregnancy and after each birth, I have asked our launderer – Katteri is the god of his line – to perform two *puja*: one to protect me during pregnancy, the other to keep my children from illnesses and evil spirits. It's been expensive, but too bad! What can you do without milk? How can you bring up a child without milk? My milk has run out only once, as I've just said. But Isvaran has given me a baby a year and, even so, my blood has stayed the same, it hasn't turned and my children have never been really emaciated. But it also depends on the way you look after them.

For me, that used to be my great worry! I managed to feed them well. As soon as I had a little money, I'd buy them sweets, candies. I made them rice whenever I could, some *dosai*, some *idli*, I'd put a little sugar in cow's milk. That's how I took care of my children, who came one after the other, so close together! There are some women who just let their children be without giving them regular meals. A human being can only live if you at least put a little milk in their mouths when they're hungry! Some of our women skip their children's meal times when they're in the middle of the housework or earning a little more money. But then how do you expect them to grow? How do you expect them to shoot up?

For me, that's been my fate! Isvaran has done his work well: he's put plenty of children in my womb. But it's been different afterwards. A lot of my little ones have died.

I've given birth to beautiful children, born in perfect health, Sinnamma. It's only afterwards that some have died: one of diarrhoea, another of apoplexy. They all walked! Two of my children even came to the peanut harvest: they weeded, they went and picked green leaves for me in a little white wicker basket. I pierced their noses for a jewel. I gave them a plait on each side and put flowers in their hair and a pretty *pottu* on their forehead, made with paste. I took good care of my little ones, even if I let myself go because I work in the fields: I never neglected them. I dressed them neatly. They were well dressed and if people like you saw them running in the street, they'd talk to them kindly, thinking that they were children of their caste.

You ask me how many children I've had in all? Wait, I've had twelve children! The first born was a girl, she was called Muttamma. Then, a boy, Ganesan. After that a girl, Arayi. Ayo! After that I don't remember any more, Sinnamma! Wait, wait a bit. But I've definitely had twelve, we even registered them at the registry office. Yes, when there's a birth, you have to go there and declare it. 'Here sir, I've had a boy or a girl and I name it Manivelu, Nataraja or Perambata.' Down there they enter all that into a big ledger. Ayo! If we went to that office, perhaps they could tell us how many children I've had and what their names were as well. Ayo! Look at that, I don't remember any more. They're born, they die. I haven't got all my children's names in my head! Sometimes they die before I even give them a name.[2] I don't know them all by heart. At the registry office we tell them a name, but when the skull's shaved for the first time and the nose pierced, we give them another name, and that's the one that stays.

Wait, let's start again. The first is Muttamma. The third is a girl. Hey! Hey! After one it's two, so the second is Irsamma. But to remember the names properly, we name them after the order of their birth: Muttamma comes from *mudal*, that means the first; Irsamma comes from *iru*, that's the second ... No, even so, I can't do it. The fifth is a girl, Anjalai. So the first is Muttamma, the second is a boy and ... I swear, Sinnamma, I can't manage it. You think that I've got them all in my head, the names of my children who've died! Wait, wait. It's coming! The third is a boy, Muttukrishnan. The fourth is my daughter who lives in Koraiyur: that's Miniyamma. The fifth is Anjalai, the sixth Arayi, the seventh Murugesan, that's a boy. That makes seven, no? After the ninth, it's a girl. Ah! No! No! After seven it's eight: that's my son Anban. So the ninth, that's a girl, Omkkanni. Then the eleventh is a girl. That's it, isn't it?

'No, it's ten next!'

Ten? Well then. I don't remember any more. Yes I do, yes! it's Palayi. That makes ten in all. The eleventh is Sundari, a daughter. The twelfth is a boy, Govindan. There, that's the end.

The order of children is very important, Sinnamma. For us, and for everybody, when it comes to marriage you always ask the girl or boy's order of birth. If the order's bad, it can bring misfortune: if it's good, it can put an end to years of misfortune. I've had difficulty telling you the order of my children because many have died: all I have left are Miniyamma, my fourth child, Anban, my eighth and Sundari, my eleventh. But I know their order well! Take my daughter Miniyamma: for a fourth birth it should have been a boy who would have brought luck to everybody. Whereas all a girl born fourth does is clean out, clean out, completely clean the house out. It's not her, Miniyamma, who does it, it's simply that her star and her sex don't match. If a well-off family has a girl as its fourth child and continues to prosper, then the family she goes into will be cleaned out after her marriage. But if the family she's born in suffers bad fortune, then her family-in-law will prosper after she arrives. Look what happened with Miniyamma: we married her well to people richer than us in the village of Kanjapakkam who owned cattle and even a little paddy field. But as soon as my daughter set foot there, it was all over and today, they're in poverty. It didn't do any good my helping Miniyamma, nothing would make any difference.

To have good fortune, Sinnamma, a boy has to be born eighth. And in this case my wishes were granted with Anban. I raised my son with as much care as something as precious as gold! And since his birth, Sinnamma, we really are less poverty-stricken. You can see for yourself: I've got cows, goats, and I work every day. We're getting back on our feet, you know. My only regret is that his wife hasn't got any children yet. But I'll spend what I have to for her to have them. I'll do all I can to take her to the temples. Afterwards, we'll see. Isvaran will make it known. Anyway, the Iyer of Perumal's temple confirmed for me again the day before yesterday that things will go well for my son Anban: his cattle will be in good health, and the goddess Lakshmi will live with us in this house. What more is needed? It's written in his horoscope that during his life – perhaps for only half an hour of his human life – we will see him triumph by the sword and somewhere lay a foundation stone. That's true for all the eighths: whether they're sons of a maharajah or sons of the poor who don't even have water to drink, they all have the same chance. We should have called that boy Ettyan, the Eighth, but when his skull was shaved for the first time, I said, 'No! I longed for him, this eighth child. I've saved him from every illness. I want him to be called Anban, the Beloved.'

As for my daughter Sundari, my eleventh child, I was again the one who chose the name. Sundari is the character I love best in the Bharatam.[3] She is such a powerful mother! You've seen how her face hardens cruelly and tenses as she comes down in the fire when the narrator sings, 'Pattini Sundari Devi ... ' 'O virtuous goddess Sundari'. The darkness of her face then! Black with fury. This mother is anger itself: she was born a woman to show the true nature of anger!

Every year I manage to go and listen to this story which I love so much. Coming home from the fields I sit by the lotus basin for a little while and listen. Or maybe I stop after collecting wood. When the sun sets, I put my bundle of sticks back on my head and go back to the ceri to do the evening's work at home. Wherever I am, whatever sort of work I'm doing, I never fail to go and listen for a bit: I drop everything. I really like going into the Madhava Reddi's field, the one next to the wall of Draupadi's temple. I can hear the Iyer reading the *Bharatam* clearly from there and at the same time I can't be seen. Apparently it's very good for you to listen, it absolves your sins. But that only happens in the *ur*. No one will ever agree to read for us, we're too unclean for that, and there'll always be some son of a whore who starts cursing during the reading. But again, who knows? In this *kaliyugam*, money's what matters. Perhaps if you paid a good price, a better price than the people from the *ur*, you'd find a priest who'd agree. But that hasn't happened up till now. So, I'll tell you how it's done in the *ceri*. We all clubbed together to buy a big book of the *Bharatam*, where everything is marked. Our men who know how to read take this book, go and sit down near the *kulam* and, while the temple narrator reads and explains the *Bharatam*, our lads, who are intelligent and smart, write down all the details on the book: here's the palace of wax, here the descent into the fire and so on. In the *ceri*, on days when there's no work, four or five of them sit on a *tinnai* and start reading in front of about ten men. Hearing their stories we women go and listen as well. That's how I got to know Draupadi. Since then I've always wanted one of my daughters to have one of her names, especially if it was an eleventh child!

We say that with the daughter born seventh, 'even the lean-to will have a gold roof'. Her family will be blessed and lack nothing. The town she'll live in will be like Ayodhya.[4] When she reaches the age to be married, everybody will fight over her. But a boy born seventh is the opposite and he will bring bad luck to his family. It will be really difficult for his family: even if it was on the way up it will go back down again and he will suffer many failures himself. No, what's needed as a seventh child is a girl! For the fifth child it's the same. If it's a girl she'll fill the loft. But then she'll have quite a character! She'll make the five elements tremble. She'll be scornful and bossy. But if it's a boy, he won't weigh heavy in the scales. He'll wander like one of Siva's beggars. He'll be able to work like a dog, he won't have either satisfaction or blossoming. Wander, wander, that's all he'll be able to do.

'*Arayi purayi ambattila nallayi*', 'Where the sixth goes in, the husband will not be happy!' That girl born sixth, even if you shut her up in a box, she'd still get herself speared by someone apart from her husband, and even though it's easy for her to cuckold her husband, she won't be happy. That's true for all the castes: the Reddi, the potters, the Gounder, mine, yours.

The daughter born ninth will be happy. She'll always be called Omakkanni. The third-born girl will bring stability to the family. But she mustn't have spirals in her hair, either in the front or the back. Otherwise her first husband will fade away and her second as well. Only the third will be able to enjoy the knot which he's tied at the back of her neck, because she'll have three marriages in all. Oh, it's not her choice, the poor thing! It's Him who has drawn these spirals on her skull: when you've got them, you have to live with it! For a boy born third, it'll be the same: if he's got the spirals, his first wife will die, his second as well. His marriage will only work the third time.

> She's a girl born eighth
> Don't marry her!
> You are a girl born tenth
> Don't look at me!

That's what the men sing in their irrigation songs. When you get close to a girl born eighth, you are ruined. And if she's a tenth child, she can even destroy a palace: no trace of it will remain! The names of those two are always changed. Normally you should call them Ettiyamma and Palayi, but we call them Saroja or Kamatchi or anything. That's the only way a man will marry them. It's true for all women, even the ones born from your mother's womb: she would change her daughters' names as well, I'm sure of it, to be able to marry them. In the end, it all depends on lots of things. The time you're conceived and the time you're born can change everything.

The first child, whether it's a boy or a girl, always brings good luck, that goes without saying! The main thing is to have a child. If you don't have even one child, you're called a sterile woman and all your life people will keep away from you because you bring bad luck. You lose your honour, your reason for living. You're not yourself any more. A sterile woman suffers very much, Sinnamma, more than any of us. It's on her mind the whole time. What can she have done in a former life to deserve this? Her parents can't have performed their *dharma* well and it's ended up with their daughter! When we plant out the rice, we always like singing the song of 'the woman who didn't have a child'. It's a sad song and all of us cry, even the women who are mothers. Here, it goes like this:

In the forest, *yelalam*, being brave, isn't that so?
   Yelama yelam
   Being brave, isn't that so?
Kaliyamma, *yelalam*, I've modelled
   I've modelled.
Ayo! Even so, *yelalam* ...
They had no children,
   Yelama yelam,
The five sons, *yelala*, the Pandava
   The five sons, the Pandava.

In the sanctuary of Puttupputtan
   In the sanctuary,
I even brought, *yelala*, a basket of offerings,
   Ayo! Even so ...
They had no children,
They had no children,
The five sons, the Pandava,
The five sons, the Pandava!

In the temple of Selliyamma
   In the temple
I left, *yelala*, a cock.
   Ayo! Even so ...
They had no children
The five sons, the Pandava!

In the temple of Patchaiyamma,
I even brought some milk.
The milk had not curdled, *amma*!
My past wrongs have not been atoned for!
   Even so ...
They had no children,
The five sons, the Pandava!

Ayo! Telling myself that I have no child,
I even walked to Chidambaram.
   Tillai *nana* hasn't,
   Yemma, Him of the forest,
He hasn't given me the grace of a child!
   Even so ...
They had no children,
The five sons, the Pandava!

Saying to myself, *yemma*, that I had no turmeric
I even walked, *yemma*, to Mayavaram.
   Maya *nana* hasn't
   Yemma, Him of the river bank,
He hasn't given me the power of the turmeric!
   Even so ...
They had no children
The five sons, the Pandava![5]

Then, because the woman doesn't have a child, she adopts a nephew:
the child of her husband's sister. But when she wants to marry him to
her brother's daughter, her sister-in-law refuses. This is what her brother
says to her and what she answers:

> I would have gladly given you my daughter, *yelama yelam*,
>   Gladly given, my sister,
> My daughter, *nana*, o Mother! I would have gladly given to you,
>   *yelama yelam*
>   Gladly given, my sister,
> All decked with flowers, for that prince, *nana*,
> If you had come to me eight days earlier, *yelama yelam*,
>   If you had come, my sister
> The virtuous daughter, *nana*, I would have given her,
> I would have given, *nana*, my daughter, *arigari*,
> For your handsome boy, my sister,
> O my sister, if eight days earlier you'd come,
>   *Arigari*, eight days earlier,
> The virtuous daughter I would have given her!
>
> O my brother, if your daughter, *nana*, you don't give,
> I'll take, my brother, the full jar,
> I'll break it, my brother, against your door!

Don't you find it sad that song, Sinnamma? She's gone into all the
temples, this poor woman, and no one has granted her wish, no one has
honoured her with a child. She hopes to have her brother's daughter for
her adopted son to keep her ties with her mother's house, and since she
can't, she ends by saying that she'll break the water jar against the door
to really show that she is not worthy to be the daughter of that family.
That's what life is like for a woman without children: you're nothing
any more. You're not respected any more, even by the kids who say
when you walk by, 'Look at her, No Children!'

People in the country really do everything they can to have a child. You
know very well that we haven't got the power to make a child. A doctor
can't make a child come into your womb. It's Isvaran alone who decides.
So people run to the mantra sayer or the *samiar*, who give them amulets,
ash, lemon, threads or other stuff and tell them to make offerings to such
a god and to such a goddess. Wait, just yesterday, I saw some relatives
of mine leaving to perform a *puja* to Periyandavan, the god of our line.
It was for their daughter-in-law who comes from Pakkanur. She's been
married for three Julys and she still hasn't had a child. Everyone was
leaving for the pond, with some *pongal*, coconut, bananas and a cock. The

Iyer was with them and the musicians as well. I pray that Periyandavan hears her and moulds a child for her, for that poor woman!

As I'm the midwife in the *ceri*, people also come to me for vows. Yes, when someone wants to be honoured with a child, they make a vow to a god. To make this vow, you get everything that's needed for all the usual offerings, but you need a baby modelled in rice flour as well. And I'm the one in the *ceri* who makes that baby for women who haven't got children. The son of the head of the *ceri* asked me for the last one I modelled. I know his wife, Ponni, well. She comes from Kattrappakkam, a village not far from Velpakkam. When she was very small, she came with her mother to Pakkirippakkam. She married Mani and now she lives here. It's been five Pongal that she's been at Karani, but not a single pregnancy. The poor girl made a vow to Patchaissami, the god of her village of birth, to have a child. That's why they came and looked for me. This is how we did it.

We took four measures of unhulled rice. We were four women pounding it with four pestles. We were so skilful that the pestles never caught each other and we never stopped while we were doing it: dang, dang, dang, dang ... That drowned out all the noises of the *ceri* with a nice and regular rhythm. Then we sieved the rice several times, before making a paste out of it with a little water. The baby was modelled out of this paste. Each one of us made part of the body. I moulded the head: I'm good at making heads, with a pretty smile which shows the teeth. I modelled the eyes, the ears and the nose as well. Then I stuck all the bits together. It was like a real baby! Water was being boiled in a great pot at the same time. We wedged four bamboos in a cross-shape into the opening of the pot, laid a cloth on top, and put the baby made out of paste very gently on the bamboos before putting back the cover. I quickly made twenty-one little oil lamps and put them around wherever I could. And then we left everything steaming for a long time. While we were waiting, the family prepared the rest: the coconuts, the incense in grains and in sticks, the bananas, the camphor. After half an hour, I took the baby off the fire: it was good and firm and I let it cool down. I put some wicks and oil in the lamps of rice flour. Then Ponni went off to put on a yellow sari. When she was ready, I put a big rice sieve on her hip and I put the paste baby inside. Then she left with her family and the musicians in procession to make the offerings in the usual way. Straight afterwards, the baby was thrown very high up into the air and everyone there – men, women, relatives or people who were just inquisitive – rushed forward, one stretching out his *soman*, another holding open the fold of her sari, to get a piece of the flour baby. The man or woman with the good luck to catch even just a crumb of the baby will have a child within the year. Ah well, Ponni got practically all of the baby: the head and the stomach fell into the fold of her sari. Her wish has been granted, Sinnamma, and now she's on her third child. It happened like that with my last daughter: at the festival of Draupadi, someone had thrown a flour baby. I was lucky enough to get a piece and I gave birth within the year.

We have a saying that if you call on the ancestors and, when a house is in mourning, if a married woman gets the pot of funeral milk from the person leading the mourning, then the woman will become pregnant immediately the sixteenth day ceremonies begin. We did that for my sister-in-law Saroja when my mother died. Saroja had dressed like a Brahmin. We women went with her to the pump, because the river at Velpakkam is very far away, and we poured three buckets of water on her. When the men arrived with the pot, Saroja, completely soaked, walked towards the man leading the mourning and she exchanged the pot for a one rupee note and some betel which she put in his hand. She carried the pot very reverently and put it on a measure of paddy scattered in the centre of the house surrounded by all sorts of lighted oil lamps. As the deceased was a woman, a sari, bracelets, and earrings were put there as well. Saroja put them on. Then Saroja prostrated herself, revering the pot because it's said the spirit of the dead is inside it. At the end she came outside to change clothes. That rite is very good for sterile women. The following year, Saroja gave birth to a girl and then she had a boy.

That's how we do it in the country. Who do you expect us to clash with but the people up there? I've already told you that a woman without children is lost. You can't take medicine to have a child. So, these doctors tell us to stick to family planning, eh? If women without children asked them for medicines to do the opposite, could they come up with them? Answer me! That's why sterile women take milk to the Naga, offer *pongal* to the god of their line, dedicate painted statues, visit temples and do everything that this man or that man advises them.

On the one hand, sterile women do everything they can to have a child, and on the other, there are more and more women in the *ceri* who want to have an abortion after two or three children! They swallow *selavu* powder by the handful and you see them writhing in agony because of the pains in their womb. They lose clots of blood and, for three or four days, they're as tired as if they've just given birth: besides, they have the same diet – bread, ginger, and then a good sauce with lots of garlic, aubergine and salted fish – before going back to normal meals. Sometimes girls who are on speaking terms with men and don't have their bath any more eat green mangoes and papayas because these are very warming foods. They hope that it will make them miscarry, but it doesn't always work! So they come to me to make them miscarry by putting a milk weed stem inside them. But I tell them, 'No, my little sister! It's impossible! Go to hospital, I'm not going to do that.'

I'll tell you something. The last time I was pregnant, I wanted to have an abortion as well. I wanted to do it a different way, because it's too painful with the milk weed. I already had a son-in-law, grandchildren, a son ready to marry and I was three months' pregnant: I was dying of shame at having one in my womb. Han! I still remember, I used to hide. I refused to let myself be taken, I humiliated my husband in front of everybody. But he ran after me so much that I took pity on him. I said to myself, 'He can come on then if he's up to it. He desires me so much, let's do it!' The thing is, some men get weak if they go without the smell of women. I was afraid that he'd fall ill. They say that there are even some men who pass away from grief. So I let him do it. And Isvaran modelled that into a child and put it in my womb. *Selavu* powder, black cumin, green mangoes, green papayas, hibiscus flowers, all the warming things that should have made me miscarry! But Isvaran had decided that nothing would have any effect on me. And since I was afraid of putting that milk weed inside me, afraid of being in pain, I went to see Anjamma, the barber's wife, to get a tablet from her which would make me miscarry. She has done a training course at the hospital. She got me that time, good and proper, and ever since I've held it against her. She asked me for two rupees! And afterwards she brought me some little balls, like goat droppings, to swallow with palm sugar. I went to buy the palm sugar at Tirulagam market, I ground it into a powder like sugar, coated the droppings with it and swallowed that. I did it for three days. And look! Not even a hair down here miscarried! I went to the sisters' dispensary as well, because I'd been told that there was a nurse down there who did abortions, a fat one who had no children. Yes, I didn't think about the expense, I went down there and not to the government hospital where they make fun of us and insult us. Anyway, that fat woman from the dispensary dragged five rupees out of me, but she didn't make a thing move. A good sturdy child was born, my twelfth, my last one, who came after I'd got a son-in-law! Oh! Since then he's died as well, that one.

I know that a foetus mustn't be destroyed. If I touch a foetus, ten billion generations of my descendants will suffer from it and, first of all, my own children, my daughters, my sons. That's why I say to myself, 'No! I won't do it with my own hands! I pick fruits not buds.'

EIGHT

Irsi Katteri,
the foetus-eater

You see, Sinnamma, a pregnant woman who wants to have an abortion doesn't always succeed. A pregnant woman is the prey of everything that roams around her, I mean the ghosts, the ghouls, the demons, the *pey picacu*; she has to be very careful. Especially if she is a Pariah. We Pariah women are forced to go everywhere, to graze the cattle or collect wood. We're outside the whole time, even when the sun's at its height. Those beings take advantage of it, they grab us and possess us. Either that, or we're terrified and we fall ill, or we have a miscarriage. Something like that happened to me when I was pregnant with my second child. My nephew, the son of my eldest brother-in-law, died young, suddenly, the day after his engagement. He was a handsome boy, the spitting image of my husband. One night when my husband and I were asleep – I was a few months' pregnant – I saw this boy sitting on me, I felt him! My husband told me that I squeezed him very tight in my arms, that I was delirious and mumbling something. I couldn't understand any of it. The next day we said the boy needed something and that's why he'd come. My husband quickly went to get a bottle of arrack and a bottle of palm wine. I arranged the offerings in the middle of the house: betel, areca nuts and lime (my nephew chewed betel like a woman) a big banana leaf with a mountain of rice, some salted fish, some toast, a cigar, bottles of alcohol, a jar of water full to the brim and a beautiful lamp with lots of oil and a big wick. In the meantime my

89

husband went to find the priest from the temple of Perumal; he's the one responsible for funeral ceremonies. The priest asked us to spread river sand next to the offerings. He called on Yama, drew a letter in the sand like the sign of Yama, then he left. We ate that evening as usual and went to sleep in a corner. You must never put yourself opposite the door, because 'he' might slap you when he comes in if he finds you in his way. You really have to be brave when the ghost arrives! In fact you don't see it. You only hear its footsteps. It's like the sound of little bells, djang, djang, like when an ox-cart goes by. It goes han! han! han! as if it wanted something badly. It always comes with its messengers, each of them tied to the other with big ropes. You hear them walking with a rhythmic and heavy step: ahum! ahum! ahum! We were very afraid. Some get diarrhoea when that happens. As soon as the ghost came in, the lamp went out in a flash, even though it was full of oil. We heard it walking and eating its fill for a good while and then suddenly it fled. We heard it running very fast and, a few minutes later, it was light. We rushed to see what had happened. The rice had been scattered every-where. On the sand we found the print of a cat's paw and part of the letter had been rubbed out. 'He' had come in the shape of a cat! While we were waiting for the priest to come and give his opinion, we collected the offerings in a big wicker basket so as not to attract the dogs that hang around in the street. The priest himself was very satisfied and said that 'he' couldn't come back. But afterwards I fell ill several times. I was weak and I had a miscarriage.

There's worse than that: there's the Katteri, who spy on us con-stantly when we are pregnant. You have to be very careful with them. There are several sorts of Katteri. Rana Katteri, with the bleeding wounds, who drinks blood; Irsi Katteri, the foetus eater; other ones as well. Irsi Katteri is terrible. She's the one who causes miscarriages. As soon as she catches the smell of a foetus in a woman's womb, she's there, spying, waiting for the first chance to suck up the foetus. We can tell immediately that it's that bitch at work if there are black clots like charcoal when the baby miscarries: she sucks up the good blood and only leaves the bad. As soon as someone miscarries like that, we prepare a sauce straightaway with aubergines, salted fish and all sorts of vegeta-bles. We mix the sauce with large quantities of rice and throw it out, handful by handful, at each crossroads in every corner of the *ceri*, to satisfy her so she'll leave without touching our children. Breast milk attracts her. Once she emptied my breasts, and she's done that to lots of other women in the *ceri*; we hadn't even a drop of milk to give as medicine! Children died day after day; how do you expect them to be strong without their mother's milk? We can't do anything to protect ourselves. We have to see a *samiar* or a mantra sayer – they've got all the power over her. We have to bring everything that's needed for the *puja*. Then the exorcist writes formulas on copper leaves. He puts the child's name and draws a conch shell or a trident on one of the leaves.[1] He does the same on the other, but puts the mother's name instead. Then he rolls up the leaves to make talismans and he gives them out with some ash. Anjalai did that for her youngest daughter. For one of my children, Sundari, I bought two talismans in Tirulagam market: there's a seller there who knows that mantra and prepares amulets in advance. He sells them for a quarter of a rupee. He gave a peacock feather to my daughter rolled in a metal cylinder and he gave me a piece of tree root, which only he knows about. He sang us mantras and put a bunch of peacock feathers on our head. Later I lost that talisman.

To go back to Irsi Katteri the foetus sucker, the terrifying, I had a strange experience with her. When I was pregnant with Miniyamma, my husband went to work in Madras for a while. He took me along to cook for him. There were a few of us from the *ceri*. In those days there weren't as many buildings as now and there were cactus bushes and sleeper trees everywhere where rogue spirits of all sorts sheltered. Oh! Madras is a big city. My husband was moving alcohol from one place to another. It was temporary work and so we hadn't rented a room. We were camping near a cactus bush. There were lots of other people doing the same around us. In those days there was the land to camp on. It was better than now when people are forced to stay on pavements in the middle of town with all the traffic! The showers and public toilets are built just anywhere down there: nobody pays attention to the orientation. Those spirits are happy about it and they spy on us in all those places. That's how Irsi possessed me one day when I'd gone to wash in a public shower and for nine whole months I lost blood and I thought I was going to miscarry.

There are so many people in Madras! Beggars, people with no work, the sick. They come and take shelter and sometimes die there all alone. No one's around to perform their last ceremonies: they are just buried by the city corporation. Then all of them prowl around as spirits, waiting their true death. Ayo! There are a thousand times more than in our countryside! Those poor people often have family in a village, but who will take the trouble to tell their parents and how? If the dead man had regular work, his boss may take charge of telling the family who can then come and find him. But the day workers can't rely on anybody, they don't know anyone. So it's the corporation which sees to their burial. It can also happen that the dead man's fellow poor, who share his piece of pavement, decide to look after his burial themselves. You see them in the markets with an oil lamp on a tray and they say to you, 'Alms for a poor corpse! Alms to bury him!' The money rains down. Once I even saw people putting in a ten-rupee note. With that money the collectors hire an orchestra, buy flowers and hold respectable funerals. But the abandoned, whose bodies end up with the corporation, they change into spirits, into *pey picacu*.

Anyway I found myself in that state, losing blood continually. The people around me had guessed that Katteri was possessing me and they pressed me to go and see an exorcist. My brother-in-law was with us. He asked around and found out that a launderer at Vannarapet healed everything to do with Katteri. My husband and my brother-in-law took me to him in a rickshaw. The exorcist drew a great circle on the ground and sang some mantras. He surrounded me with incense and covered my forehead and arms with ash. Then he stood up. He wrote something on a metal leaf, drew the figure of Anjaneyar and a club on it and rolled it up to make a talisman. They say he invoked Minisuprayan, the male form of Katteri: he's good and protects children. The exorcist said to me that the child to be born had to be called Miniyamma if it was a girl and Miniyan if it was a boy. Since then I have been possessed by Minisuprayan. I don't really notice but apparently when people play drums and the horn I dance and sob heavily. Oh! Otherwise, it's no trouble and I'm not trying to make him go away. That's Minisuprayan: I pray he'll stay, since he protects children! Anyway I was protected with this talisman round my neck and gradually I stopped losing blood and could keep the child. But I didn't want to give birth down there in Madras at all. I was too afraid of all those spirits. The women with children round me always kept them in their arms. If they'd lain them on the ground, the spirits would have rushed to devour them – that's what it seemed like. When they told me that, I wanted to go straight back to the *ceri*, where we've got our own house and we're safe. At any rate my husband decided to take me back to the village. So I made a vow that if my child was to live in good health, I would return to Vannarapet to offer *pongal* to the goddess Katteri. Careful, not the demon Katteri, the foetus eater! No! The goddess. Coming back to the *ceri*, I gave birth to a girl who we called Miniyamma as the exorcist had told us. Later when she began to talk and to walk well, we went as we'd

promised to Vannarapet with the musicians of the *ceri* in procession. I
was dressed in black, like my daughter. I took a *soman* and a shawl for
the exorcist, an all-black cock and everything needed to make the offerings. Down there we prepared some rice with a vegetable sauce. The
exorcist put three bricks under a banyan tree, slit the cock's throat and
performed the proper rites. Then he shaved Miniyamma's skull. Everything was done by the rules, without any mistakes. That mantra sayer is
dead now, the poor man! He had fine *bhakti*! If he was still here, I'd take
my daughter-in-law Amsa to see him, who has still not had any children
since marrying my son Anban. At the moment she goes to Murugaiya
Gounder who's become *samiar* in the *ur*. He gave her two lemons
charged with mantras: she ate one and kept the other. He also told her
to walk round the temple every day: Aiyanar's temple, Pillaiyar's temple
or Mariamman's. We'd thought Amsa would be possessed. He gave her
a string with white knots to put round her neck: that's charged with
mantras as well. Yes it's true what he says, the *samiar*! It was plain to
see the other day, when the travelling musicians came to the *ceri*. When
they played the drums and the horn, Amsa started dancing and spinning like a top and my son had lots of trouble calming her down. We
still don't know what's possessing her, but I haven't lost hope.

My three first children were born at Velpakkam, at my mother's. Their
births went well and they were in good shape when they died.[2] The imp
who lived in our house at Velpakkam devoured them. My grandfather
on my father's side knew sorcery. A friend who was a sorcerer taught
him. But we are not of that calling at all. What my grandfather really
knew was how to 'bind' a person, how to draw somebody to him by
magic. People came to see him at Velpakkam. He didn't ask for money,
but they'd bring him a gourd of palm wine, some camphor, some betel
and some bananas for offerings. They used to say that he called up the
imp, talked to it and asked it to go along with him when he went out.
He lived with him, basically! When my grandfather died, we tried to
drive that spirit away because he really was a pest. But it was no use.
He'd come back and sit down, assuming the form of my grandfather;
he'd join in conversations, calling my grandmother by her name like her
dead husband used to. My grandmother used to answer back, 'Ah! The
only answer I'll give you is with my broom, you dog! I recognise you!
I know who you are! Get out of here!' As for him, he'd just throw
tamarind seeds in her face. When a sorcerer came from Ossur to try and
get rid of him, he became plain vicious. The sorcerer told us he couldn't

do anything against him. The spirit had taken root in the ground. He was old and cunning: we were the ones who had to go. He destroyed everything! Everything! Not even a garlic clove would grow! My father had to sell his paddy field. I gave birth three times there: none of those children survived. He ate them as and when they were born. Nothing prospered. That's how it is with the spirits. Once you start working with them you have to carry on otherwise they'll turn against you. That's also why I haven't gone and given birth at Velpakkam any more.

All my children have been buried where they died: the first ones at Velpakkam, the others at Karani. My mother insisted we burn the first-born and throw her ashes in the river so a sorcerer couldn't come and get them. The ashes or bones of first-borns are coveted by magicians. A tiny little bit of ash or hair is enough for them. You see them with a hoe on their shoulder prowling around where a first-born has been burnt or buried. Even a little bit of ash mixed with sand attracts them. People whose custom is to bury their dead also put the first-born in a jute sack, before going and burying them secretly. For my eldest, we made sure that everything disappeared. We have a saying that if you dissolve those ashes completely in water, you'll have another child straightaway.

When you're pregnant with your first child, Sinnamma, you have to be very careful with the palmists, fortune tellers and all those sort of people who travel through villages. We never go out alone because they can cast a spell to make us follow them. Then they make us swallow something which makes us forget all attachments, all relations: father, mother, brother, sister, village! You must have seen those sorcerers who come from malayali country.[3] The men and women are terrifying: the women are palmists, the men cast spells. They don't understand our language much. It's no good calling them juice drinkers, mother fuckers or anything we want, it doesn't do anything. We have a good laugh insulting them but we're very afraid of them at the same time and we hide after abusing them. They always walk along holding a first-born's hand covered with turmeric, with talismans hanging from it, which they sell us in the *ceri* for a rupee or a rupee and a half to keep away evil spirits, *pey picacu* in the paddy fields and to ward off nightmares. Those are all things that happen to us Pariahs, so we're always tempted to buy their talismans to protect ourselves.

When they've sold their talismans, they go and sit by the banyan tree and do magic. They catch one of our children and, putting a talisman on his head, they make him read things in a make-up box, 'Little brother! What do you see in that box?'

And the child answers, 'I see Arayi, Kannima or Panderi ... I see seven people.'

But when they take off the talisman, it stops, the child doesn't see anything any more. The talisman's power makes him see the whole world in the bottom of a make-up box!

They've got another trick as well: they catch a child and say in their malayalam accent, 'Look! Look! Look! Look! Open your eyes wide to see this prodigy!' Then they play their little drum very hard and say, '*Janakkattu, janakkattu, janakkattu, janakkattu!* Come out quickly! Come out quickly! Come out quickly! There you are!' and they take an egg out of the child's little bum! Our stomachs hurt from laughing at that trick, but we're afraid as well. Then they say to us, 'Don't run away! Don't be afraid! Stay here, otherwise I'll let loose a spell and blood will flow in your houses!' What can we do then? We are poor terrified destitute people and we give them a quarter of a rupee, a half a rupee or a measure of paddy, or millet or *ragi* as alms so they'll clear off. They do something else as well! They call a woman, ask her to lie down, and with a large, sharp knife, they open her belly. Blood spurts out, but she doesn't feel anything, doesn't say anything. We're shouting, we're afraid for her. They take out her organs like that, one by one and put them to the side. At the end they sing a mantra and say, '*Janakkattu, janakkattu, janakkattu, janakkattu!* Come quickly, come quickly, come quickly!' And everything puts itself back together and the woman gets up as if it was nothing. Those are their magic tricks. While we're all gathered there watching them they find women pregnant with their first child to kidnap. That's why a pregnant woman is never allowed out when magicians are passing. We're also afraid that seeing their tricks will make her miscarry.

The people from malayali land are not the only ones to pass by. We see others who walk through our countryside with a little imp and some skull bones from first-borns; they do black magic. And then there are those crooks who come with their cobras. They sit down just near here in Guardian street. They make their cobra come out of the basket to the sound of the *magudi*. The cobra comes out, 'takes the photo', turns round three times, then hits his head on the ground.[4] That's all: the performance is over. But afterwards those bastards pick up their cobra and release it outside the door of every house as they're asking for alms. People don't wait to be asked! They're on their doorstep pouring out some grain for them before the snake's even there! Out of our wits! We're scared out of our wits by their cobra! If it got into our houses

which are all dark, the only thing for us would be to get out. Can you
see what it would be like if they went and hid in our paddy jars? You
can understand why we rush to give alms. So they make their cobra get
back into the basket and to get it over with quicker, we pour the grain
directly into the basket on top of the snake. That's how we get rid of
those juice drinkers.

I started off telling you about women who are pregnant with their
first child and now look at all this talk of magicians. But the point is
how careful you have to be when you're pregnant. In our village, a child
has never been kidnapped or sacrificed, but we know it happens in other
places: the travelling singers have sung us more than one story about it.
Even to you I'll give the same advice, Sinnamma: stay well hidden with
your first child! There are too many cunning spirits prowling around at
times like that.

Oh, until they grow, until they become as big as that, we mothers always have a fire in our belly for our children: we must feed them, keep
them from all sickness, raise them to become men or women who are
going to work. My niece died sixteen days after my mother, on the day
of the rites. Normally there should have been different ceremonies for
each of them but we held them for my mother and that child on the
same day. How do you expect us to pull through when there are two
deaths at the same time? We are not rich people! My brother is the only
boy of the family. He hasn't an elder or younger brother: what can he
do, the poor thing, all alone without anybody to help.

In the month of Panguni in the same year, one of my three sisters
died. She was coughing a lot: she had a kind of tuberculosis. Her illness
had started a long time before. When she was a baby, she'd been bitten
by a rat. You know you don't feel it when a rat bites you because of its
breath. The rat had completely chewed her ear and its poison had stayed
in her body. People said to themselves: it's only a baby and a rat after
all, it's not very serious! They let it go without giving her the medicines
she needed. The poison ended up by getting into her blood and that's
what gave her tuberculosis. She used to cough a lot and have sort of fits.
An iron was heated in the fire to relieve her and she was marked everywhere on her back. The poor thing, she had burns all over! But that
didn't cure anything. She swallowed all sorts of herbs in a paste which
a hunter exorcist gave her. When she swelled up, she was taken to all
the healers. One of them, a hunter as well, had specialised in poisons.
He sang his mantras, holding a bunch of peacock feathers to bring the

poison down. But nothing worked, she died. She had been married and she left a child, a son, who it had been very hard for her to have. I kept him after the death of his mother. As this boy was often very ill, just like her, my sister had made a vow to help him get his health back but she had died in the meantime. So I took up her vow. I went into three houses. In each one I asked for a cubit of fabric. I put the three bits of fabric on the ground and laid the child on them. Then I went into three other houses and exchanged the child for three measures of bran, saying, 'The child is yours, the barley is mine.' Of course this was only for long enough to get the bran, and afterwards I took the child back. Then I went to three other houses to collect a handful of dirt. I mixed the three handfuls, spread them out and rolled the baby in them, saying, 'Your name will be Kuppa! You are Kuppa! You have been born of dirt!' Then I pierced his nostril with a silver thread which I twisted into a ring. That worked very well for him! He's still alive, and he still wears that ring in his nose today. These are ceremonies which make sure the child doesn't die. The elders say so and I do as well. Didn't I do that for Anban? I've given birth to four boys and they've died each time. It was when I did that ceremony that the boy stayed alive. I called him Anban. None of the castes are any different in this. Even the rich do it: a caste like the Reddi for example. Once the Reddi asked me to do that for one of their children: he's called Kuppa as well now, Kuppa and some other name of the god of their line. Families don't think of doing it straight-away. It's only when several children have died: and every child I've done that ceremony for is alive today!

But swapping the child for bran or rolling it in dirt are not always enough. The child can fall sick again. Take jaundice: we take the little ones to hospital, but at the same time give them our medicine, a niruri infusion which is very effective. But children stay very weak after they've had jaundice, like after poisonous fever. Since they don't have rich food like other people, they stay like that all their lives, or they die.

When an illness is very serious, there is one thing that we can arrange: 'the burial of the bricks'. We've just done that for Sengueni's little daughter. In the middle of her house, in front of the oil lamp, Sengueni placed three bricks covered in cloth soaked in yellow turmeric water. The little girl was lying on the ground in a corner, under a big wicker basket. Everybody in the ceri went to visit that house as if someone had died there. And we women, sitting around the bricks, sang laments, beating our chest, 'Ayayo! Sengueni's daughter is dead!' Meanwhile, the totti responsible for announcing the death had gathered together the

musicians of the Pariah orchestra and they went through all the streets
of the *ceri* shouting, 'Today, Monday the eighth day of the month of
Purattaci, in Sengueni's house, the little girl died. The burial will take
place at four o'clock in the afternoon, at the cremation grounds of the
ceri at Karani, dum, dum, dum, dum, para, para, para, para.' At the
appointed time, we formed a procession and carried the three bricks in
a hammock made out of the cloth soaked in turmeric water. Reaching
the cremation grounds, we performed the same rites for the bricks as
we do for humans and buried them. Three days later the family went
back there for the milk ceremony, and the Iyer came on the sixteenth
day to perform the last rites. The man leading the mourning had brought
a copper pot in the procession with a coconut on top of it decorated
with flowers. The Iyer sang mantras at the cremation grounds. After
that he was given a loincloth, some betel, some areca nut and five rupees. We paid the musicians as well, then a meal was served to all the
relatives and friends. All this needs a lot of money. But what wouldn't
we do to save our children?

I've had so many children, more than the fingers on my hand, I've
got at least three left, thanks to the *puja* and the vows I've performed.
I did the burial of the bricks for my son Anban, but I didn't have
enough money to pay the musicians. They knew that and they didn't
ask me for anything. All the same how can you let people who work for
you go away with nothing? I bought them a big gourd of palm wine and
they were very happy. My daughter Miniyamma, I've already told you,
she escaped that Katteri of Madras. So I made a vow, right here in the
ceri in the temple of Mariamman. I said, 'Mother! If you give me the
son I want, I'll give you a bell to be rung!' Mother heard me: she gave
me a son. That's Anban. But I couldn't keep my promise straightaway.
So the year he was born, at the festival of Mariamman in the *ur*, I put
a 'child in a cradle' all dressed in yellow like Anban in my arms. We
didn't really manage to save the money needed to buy that brass handbell for the temple. In those days, besides, it was almost abandoned, the
temple. When our K.S. was elected, he gave the money for the temple's
renovation.[5] Then the Reddi of Naliveli offered a bronze statue of the
goddess. It's only since then that there've been regular *puja*. But even so
that I couldn't save anything. So, to show I hadn't forgotten my vow
and to make the goddess wait, I had a potter from the *ur* make a pretty
child in a crib in baked clay. We may be poor but we know how to go
without to keep our word ...

NINE

The god of Tirupati

We are Pariahs, we're unclean but we believe deeply in the power of the
god Perumal of Tirupati.[1] The year of the great cyclone, my whole
family was sick. My husband was coughing a lot. My grandson had a
fever which didn't go down and he was delirious: it was tetanus and he
died. I felt so sad. I didn't consult anybody, any *samiar*. I went to the
Guardian's stone. I lit some camphor and I said, 'Heal us all and give
my daughter a child. I will offer a cow to Perumal at Tirupati.' I went
into the stable. I took the grey heifer, sprinkled it with turmeric water
and put a fat *pottu* on its forehead. Then I went to see my husband to
tell him my vow. 'You've done well!' he said. Making an offering of a
cow is the best offering we poor can make to that great Tirumal. We
have to be in good health, grown-ups and little ones, to put something
in our stomach every day and my daughter has already lost two children.
I know what it is to carry a child for ten months and not be able to keep
it to the end! I offered a cow to Venkatapati for all these reasons – we
call it 'leaving a cow for the mountain'.

The day I made the vow, I coated the house with cow dung. My
daughter and I fasted. The next morning the priest came to fix a yellow
thread round our wrists – the sign of people who've made a vow. He lit
the camphor, broke a coconut and sang mantras. I put a rupee on his
tray and he promised to come to Tirupati. I'd prepared a *sambar* of
drumstick beans and fried aubergines for the meal, which we offered to

the god before eating. During the week my husband asked around to
find a trainer of performing cows. He was told there was one in Aiveli.
He took the bus and went to find him. The trainer agreed to teach the
cow all the tricks he knew: she'd be trained and be able to answer all the
questions he'd ask her when they stopped in front of a house. For
example he'd ask her, 'Will there be a marriage in this house?' And
while he'd play the drum, the cow would answer 'yes' by moving its
head. Or he'd ask, 'Will a virtuous prince be born in this house?' Lots
of questions like that. I needed money to go to Tirupati. So we sold the
cow to the guy from Aiveli for a very low price, one hundred rupees,
and whatever money we didn't spend on the journey we gave as an
offering at Tirupati. Before handing the cow over to the trainer, I washed
it with fresh water, covered it with turmeric paste and made a great
pottu on its forehead. I also treated it to a good *pongal* of rice flour
mixed with palm sugar, bananas and coconuts on a banana leaf. And I
gave the trainer a new *soman* and shawl. People who don't go to Tirupati
give the cow away for free. Rich people who make the pilgrimage also
give the cow away and pay for their journey as well. But we couldn't do
that. Everyone does what they can. Anyway my grey cow left looking
beautiful, a garland of flowers round her neck. She and the trainer
seemed happy.

After I'd made that vow for all of us and especially for Miniyamma,
I asked the goddess Mangavarttamma to give my daughter a child. We
went with my son-in-law's family to perform the *puja* of the cradle at
the temple of Mangavarttamma. We had brought three metres of white
cloth, a brand new brick, a fat, beautiful turmeric root, some flowers
and some *kungumam*. The temple is in a large wood of huge banyan
trees on the road to Tirupati. We travelled all night and arrived very
early in the morning. The air was cold enough to catch your throat as
we got out of the bus. Then we walked for a long time, asking everyone
we met the way to the temple. Once we were there, Miniyamma and I
prepared the brick, drawing red dots on it. Then my son-in-law jumped
up to bring down a branch of one of the banyans. While he was holding
it, I knotted the white cloth on the branch, just like we make a cradle
in the village by tying a sari to a beam. Then Miniyamma laid the brick
in the cradle. She put the turmeric root on top and then the flowers.
And when my son-in-law let go of the branch, we all prostrated ourselves, touching our faces and saying, 'Mangavarttamma! The favour of
granting us a child is now in your hands!' That made one extra cradle
amongst the thousands that sway in the wind in this wood. The next

year, Miniyamma was pregnant. She gave birth to a boy. And we got our health back.

We waited until the little one grew and knew how to say, 'Grandfather, that's our cow!' We hadn't cut his hair for all that time: we'd promised it to Tirupati.

We managed to save five sacks of paddy. We sold them and with the money we set off to fulfil our vow.

It's a long journey to Tirupati. It's far away and you have to have a lot of money to perform that *puja* and you can't come back empty-handed either. When someone makes a vow to go to Tirupati, sometimes his family joins him. It's an opportunity to go on a trip because people of my age don't get about much, especially not us, the women. So lots of people go. And then, before going, you must offer our Ejeumalaiyan here in the *ceri* half of what you'll give Perumal down there. All of it needs a lot of money and so you always take a collection. This is how. You buy several metres of white cloth which you dye with yellow turmeric water. Our temple's priest puts a garland of basil round the neck of everyone who's made a vow. For ten *paice* more, he marks the sign of Vishnu on the men's foreheads: the *namam* and the stripes.[2] For the women he just does a line on the forehead. A little jar is prepared too, covered with a yellow cloth which is split down the middle. When everything was ready and we were dressed in this yellow cloth, we set off in procession. Our Iyer led the way and played the gong and his little drum. Behind him came the people who'd made a vow, with their garlands of basil round their necks and the sign of Vishnu. The others, just with the sign, were at the back. We shouted, 'Govinda! O Govinda! Govinda! O Govinda!' and started by going round the *ceri*. Everyone gives something, money or grain. Then we went into the *ur* and five neighbouring villages where we get work. Of course the *ur* was where we got the most money, paddy and grain. Everything we collected was divided into three: a third for the god of Tirupati, a third for our priest and a third for us, to make the meal for the end of the fast and receive the god of Tirupati into our household on our return.

The day of departure, we did another collection at the bus stop and in Tirulagam market, shouting 'Govinda! O Govinda!' My husband was the one holding the tray and the jar and lots of notes fell in! When the bus arrived, we loaded up everything we needed for cooking: the sack of rice, spices, lentils, mustard seed, tamarind and oil. I got on first, dressed in yellow. And then all the feelings stirred up my womb: I felt something running down my thighs! I was very afraid and I asked the older women there their advice straightaway, 'Mother! What is this sign? I've got it just when I'm leaving for the temple! Can I go there or should I stop here?'

'There's no harm in that', they said to me. 'You'll be able to climb the steps of Tirupati after the third day's bath.'

So I got down to clean myself and stock up with towels. When I got back on again, the bus set off and we all left for Tirupati ...

It was the first time in my life that I'd travelled so far! When we arrived at the foot of the mountain, we started climbing the steps that lead to the temple. Just before we got there, our priest started singing about Perumal. When he stopped, we shouted, 'Govinda! Govinda!' and we did so very reverently because it was the first time that we people of the *ceri* had gone into a temple. We followed all the priest's advice, we watched our language, we didn't chew betel. We mustn't do anything that might count against us because we are unclean. Our priest didn't leave us for a minute and that reassured us: he was used to it.

Ayo, Sinnamma! What struck me most on the way was the statue of Kali in the temple of Mangavarttamma! Ayoyo! She had sixty arms on each side, Sinnamma! When I saw her, I came out in a sweat with fear. It had such an effect on me that straightaway I had my period again! That's the last time I was unclean. The last time that I bathed myself was on the way back from Tirupati at the temple of Mangavarttamma. I prayed hard to Mangavarttamma. I went and plunged myself in the basin with my period. I put my hands together and said to her, 'Manga-varttamma, I've had twelve children. Now I don't want any more. Wash my womb and rinse it well with this water. I am a woman like you: I don't want any more children at my age!' Sinnamma, it's finished: I've never had a period again!

What surprised me a lot there is the amount of melted butter which is poured on Kali's statue to clean it. They give it a bath of melted butter! And there's another statue of Kali, covered in gold, right in the middle of a basin. It shines like the sun. The water is white and icy like a snail's slime. We also saw some waterfalls on the way which made a terrible noise. Yes! What astonishing things we saw on that journey!

We reached Tirupati at last and I could keep the promise I'd made. My grandson threw a handful of coins into the basket surrounded with stakes. Ayoyo! That basket can hold two sacks of money, it's so tall and big. The Koravan wove it. And my grandson's skull was shaved as we promised. It was only then that I realised what 'work like the barbers of

Tirupati' means. Han! So as not to lose their clients, they take a few locks off each and then make them sit down in line to wait their turn to be shaved completely! The barbers aren't short of work down there, but they always want more.

When we got back to Karani, there was the last *puja* to perform, the one that marks the return from Tirupati. The members of the family who'd stayed in the village had got the house ready. They had covered the ground with cow dung, then sprinkled it with cow urine to receive us. We got back with our heads shaved on a Saturday. To prepare the meal for the end of the pilgrimage, we'd bought some new jars and some vegetables: aubergines, drumstick beans, broad beans, tomatoes and so on. There has to be seven kinds of vegetables. In a big pot marked with the sign of Vishnu, we cooked a *pongal* of unhulled rice first. During cooking, everyone around the pot shouted, 'Pongalo! Pongalo! Govinda! O Govinda!' Then the *pongal* is taken off the fire and a good measure of sugar is poured in. It's only afterwards that the vegetables and the sauces can be cooked. The oil lamps, the offering trays, in fact everything copper is well polished and put out. Red spots are made with *kungumam* on the back wall, which is covered with cow dung as well. When everything is ready, we go and find the priest. He comes with his little drum and before starting to sing, he surrounds the offerings with pieces of camphor! Then the priest sings songs in honour of Venkatapati. A mountain of white rice is put on a big banana leaf, with sweet *pongal*, a jar of milk, a jar of curds, a jar of melted butter, cooked vegetables, nine coconuts broken in two, *laddu* bought at Tirupati and a big flour lamp made with rice mixed with molasses. Melted butter is poured into the lamp, and it's lit with a thick wick while the camphor burns. The priest gets up and draws the form of the god of Tirupati on the wall and, beside it, a huge *namam*. No one comes to the pilgrims' house when they get back from Tirupati and watches the ceremonies on the day of the sweet *pongal*. It's the one and only time in the *ceri* when the inquisitive don't come flocking round a house where something's happening, because no one must block the way of the god of Tirupati who is going to go into the house: he mustn't meet anything unclean! The *bhakti* is so great at that moment that the bird at Tirupati, Garuda, comes and wheels just above the house. I swear to you it's true! The priest sings until Garuda passes over our heads. When the eagle arrives, we shout, 'Govinda! O Govinda!' And it's only then that everybody comes out of their houses, to join in shouting, 'Govinda! O Govinda!' Everybody, men, women, children and the old, all have to shout. The

priest then shouts louder and louder beating his drum. Oh Sinnamma!
It's good fortune just to see that! And there you are! It's the end of the
fast. The men go in first and are served. Then the old, the impotent
and the widows are sent for and served food on banana leaves in a
straight line. Twelve litres of rice are cooked that day to feed so many
people! Then the Tirupati water and the sweets brought back from
there are handed out to the neighbours, with a piece of coconut, some
sweet *pongal* and a piece of the flour lamp on a banana leaf.

That's how we did our duty to Venkatapati. You know, Sinnamma,
I've just made a new vow for my son this time. I've already told you, he's
been married for four Pongal but nothing's come out of my daughter-in-
law's womb. Nothing, not even an earthworm! Every Tuesday, Murugaiya
the *samiar* gives him ashes and makes him an amulet of different metals.
I also took my daughter-in-law to a Muslim of Tirulagam. He gave her
a knotted string. But nothing up till now. I hope very much that
Venkatapati will hear me and continue my line. I have behaved myself
perfectly towards him, he has nothing to blame me for. Govinda! O
Govinda!

What's more important for us women than children? If we don't
draw anything out of our womb, what's the use of us being a woman? A
woman who has no son to put a handful of rice in her mouth, no
daughter to close her eyes, is an unhappy woman. She or her parents
must have failed in their *dharma*. I have been blessed that way: Isvaran
has filled my womb. Ah, if all my children were alive, they'd take up all
the trades there are in the world! One would be a labourer, another a
carpenter. I would have made one of them study. We could have given
two daughters away in marriage and enjoyed our grandchildren. I could
go and rest for a month with each of my sons. Yes, we would have been
proud of the children.

TEN

Mariamman and Kali

When Mariatta moved into the *ceri*, I had a child in my arms. Don't ask me which one, I don't remember any more. I remember it was a girl, not very old: I was still breastfeeding her and she had *mariatta*. You know what *mariatta* is, it's chickenpox or smallpox. In the country we call it *mariatta*, because it's Mariamman, the Mother, who comes in this form to make people give her a jar of gruel. She goes from person to person, from house to house, from *ceri* to *ceri* and everywhere she goes, she takes one or two people. And when everybody has made her an offering, when everybody has given her what she wants, she leaves this world.

Mariamman came to earth one day when her husband Isvaran was furious and drove her out, covering her with twenty-one types of spot. He cursed her and said, 'Peuh! You're not worthy of my household! Get out of here! Sow the spots all around you and live on what people will give you to be cured!'[1] Poor people like us saw this woman arriving all naked and covered in spots, and wondered who she was. Some launderers at the wash house quickly soaked a white cloth in turmeric water and gave it to her to cover herself and treat her spots. Then she saw some cobblers. They prostrated themselves at her feet and gave her a pair of sandals so she could go round the world without hurting her feet. A bit further on, people from our caste were harvesting rice. They quickly picked a few ears, made flour out of them, offered that to the Mother in

105

an unpolluted coconut shell and gave her *kuj* to drink. And the Mother carried on her way, granting good favour to everyone who offered her underskirts, saris, *kuj* and balls of flour. So then temples were built everywhere to honour her and that's why, when you have *mariatta*, you go and get gruel from the launderer and cooked rice from the cobbler. Normally we wouldn't touch food cooked by them: they're lower than us. As for the launderers, they wash our dirty clothes. They work for us, basically! Mariamman is a very important goddess for them. She has given them the power of the drum. They come and play in front of houses and sing invocations to Mariatta, so that she'll leave quickly.

The possessed warn us when the Mother storms into the *ceri*. One of the gods comes down, not just on anybody, but on someone in their favour. The possessed starts dancing and announces to us, 'Dei! Dei! Mother has arrived! Dei! Mother's just entered your *ceri*! Dei! Pay attention everybody! Above all no uncleanliness! Behave yourselves well! Nothing unclean!' He goes through the streets, stops at the crossroads, shouting like that. All of us leave our houses and crowd round him to listen and find out if Mariatta is in the *ceri* or the village. Yes, those people always cover it up when Mariatta's reached them. They're too afraid, too ashamed to say it. But the possessed tells us and then we take our precautions. The old woman of Kuppam or other old people from the *ceri* question the possessed, 'Mother, Mother Mariatta! How long will she stay in this village? When will she leave the *ceri*? In ten or twelve days? In five or seven days? Will she cause losses on the land? Should we hold sacrifices? Will Mother leave if we carry out *puja* to the gods of the territory?'

The toothless man from Guardian Street used to ask the most questions. But quite a few of us burst out laughing whenever he talked – now he's dead – because he'd lost his front teeth and so every word was followed by a *pfeu*! 'Mother *pfeu*! Mother *pfeu* Mariatta *pfeu*!' When we made fun of him, the men insulted us, 'Aye! Bastards! Whores! Monkey bitches! Shut it!' Then the possessed did a jump and screamed, 'Pariah dogs! Your language! Your language! You've got lost, Dei! Be careful!' The elders apologised and we'd put the fold of our sari in front of our mouths and snigger. You laughed when you heard him, Sinnamma. It's true, he was really funny with his empty mouth. Sometimes when we women were on our own, we'd strike up conversation with him and make him sing: hearing him always made us burst into mad laughter. So he'd stand up, adjust his turban and walk away, telling us, 'She-asses *pfeu*, she-asses *pfeu* on *pfeu* heat *pfeu*!' That made us laugh even more.

We'd catch up with him to calm him down and give him betel and areca nut to chew. He'd take it, happy as anything, still saying, 'Bunch *pfeu* of *pfeu* whores *pfeu*!' I couldn't control myself when I was young, even at very serious times like the announcement of Mother Mariatta's arrival. Anyway, later on, Toothless wasn't allowed to talk in public any more, because he made the young laugh too much and even the old found it difficult to be serious. But he was still asked for advice, he knew a great deal and people listened to him a lot. It was his way of speaking that made people laugh, even girls as little as bees.

To get back to the possessed, he answers all the questions and says what has to be done. 'The frontiers have to be marked out.' Then he collapses: the god has left him to return to the mountain. We bring him round with water and prepare the *karagam*. The possessed stands up. Margosa branches are tied all over his body and, inspired again, he sets off with the two drums of Mariamman and about ten men to support him because Mariatta won't give in: she'll fight to stay there. The possessed fears her a little because she is very powerful. She can slap him and break his limbs like you break a stick. But he is under the gods' protection: he carries the *karagam* on his head, walks to the limits of the village territory and at the eight cardinal points he plants a flag, shouting, 'Govinda! O Govinda! Remove Mariamman from this village, Govinda!'

The next day we all club together – ten or twenty *paice* per house – to carry out the thread *puja*. We buy a ball of thread, which we have soaked in turmeric water, and offer it to Mariamman in her temple. Then the possessed goes through every house and ties a piece of the thread on everyone's wrist to protect them. He even ties the thread on babies born that night and on the cows, oxen and goats. That won't stop Mariatta staying or doing what she has to do, but it means she'll do less damage.

You can be a maharajah's son or the son of a Koravan but if Mariatta has decided to come down on you, she'll come. No one can escape her. I'll tell you a story that everyone knows here.

A woman only had one son and she didn't want Mariatta to take him. So she says, 'My son, Mother is playing in our *ceri*. Go and hide at your grandmother's. Mother won't touch you there in the other *ceri*!' And the child set off. But someone's waiting for him under a banyan before he gets to his grandmother's. Yes! Mariatta, under a banyan tree! Seeing this boy coming, she took the form of an old woman trembling all over. When the child passed in front of her, she called him, 'Who goes here? Stop a while! Come here! I'm a poor old woman. Which town are you going to, Sami? My head is itching very badly; will you pick out my lice? Be kind, little brother, pick out all these beasts for me and scratch me hard, I'll grant you a favour, a good favour!' The child agreed to pick out her lice. He put down his bundle, started unknotting the old woman's hair and then all he saw was eyes, eyes, countless eyes like holes in a flour sieve. The child took fright and said, 'Grandmother, I can only see eyes on your head, eyes everywhere! I'm afraid!'

'Don't be afraid,' the old woman said to him, 'I'm Mariatta herself. You wanted to run away from me, but I can be in front of you wherever you go! I am everywhere and I see everything!' Taking a tuft of his hair in her hands and shaking his head, she said to him, 'I promised you one favour and this is it: you will only have five pearls on your forehead, no more, and you will not suffer!' Then she disappeared. The boy reached his grandmother's *ceri* with a high fever and only five spots on his forehead. That's why we call those five spots 'the pearls of duty'.

Even now when she enters a house and wants to stay there, Mother Mariatta still chooses her victims by pulling their hair and shaking their heads. If the hair tears off and comes away in her hand, she goes away. But if it doesn't, she gives the usual spots, well spread out over the body and shining brightly. If she isn't crossed she'll just give what she has to and they look pretty. The spots will bud a few days later and even the smallest will grow enormous. Towards the fifth day, the pearls on the forehead will burst and the others will quickly follow. On the ninth day Mariatta will get down from the body and leave only scars.

You never go out when you've got *mariatta*. Even children stay shut up until the last bath. You have to wait for the Mother to leave before you can put your head outdoors, otherwise the evil eye or meeting an unclean person could drive Mariatta into a rage, and then she'd mark us for life! You mustn't go near anyone who's had relations, not even the place where a man and a woman have been together. Unclean food or other uncleanlinesses don't bother her. But she doesn't put up with the pleasures of the mat! You know why, Sinnamma! This mother was never happy with her husband. She was innocent, but Isvaran cursed her and that's why she wanders from country to country.

When Mariatta came down on my baby, she also settled in on me. The poor little thing was covered with spots and sticky as glue because of the milk coming out of all the spots. 'Mariatta's milk' is like cashew milk. I couldn't take the little one in my arms, we were both so sticky!

My mother-in-law handed me the baby wrapped up in a banana leaf for breastfeeding. I had a pot of cow's urine mixed with turmeric beside me: I sprinkled the little one with that to soothe its irritated skin. I had begged Mariamman: I'd promised to pour a jar of gruel one Friday in her temple if she'd leave peacefully. I hummed the invocations of the *kumbam* myself. Kalimuttu, our launderer, normally ought to come three times a day to sing praises to the goddess, but he didn't have enough time. He was accompanying supplicants to Mariamman's temple to make offerings of gruel and he was running from one house to another with his drum. He came by the house once, in the morning. He started his rounds here and he said to my mother-in-law, 'Sister, you can sing, you've got a voice: your daughter-in-law has as well. Sing lullabies to Mariatta yourself: she is bound to hear you. I'll come every morning with my drum. I don't know where to go any more, that Mother has moved in everywhere!'

My mother-in-law said to him, 'Go on! Off you go! Now you can make the most of it!'

The fifth day arrived, but Mariatta still didn't seem to want to go. I said to my mother-in-law, 'Ayo! That pighead is still here, eating the launderer's broth and the cobbler's cooked rice!'

My mother-in-law, having paid homage and done penitence ten times in front of the *kumbam*, begged the goddess, 'Ayo, Mother! You make us suffer, you keep on staying with us, you put us to the test, Mother! We trust you, we love you. You've come to my house: that's enough, now. Leave here, go somewhere else!'

And I kept on protesting, 'Ayo! I've got such a young baby, and that widow has come and moved in on us! How am I going to fill my belly! I am poor! How can I stand her being so stubborn?'

I cursed her. While she was there we didn't light any camphor in the evening. We didn't draw *kolam* in front of the door. We didn't make sweet things, like rice with molasses. The lamp stayed out and the house was dark.

Round about the ninth day, Mariatta said to herself, 'Ayo! I've come to this cursed woman's house who won't even burn ten *paice* of camphor for me! There's no point staying here. Let's leave!' Yes, Sinnamma, if you treat her like that in every house, she ends up by leaving the *ceri*.

By the ninth day, at last, the pearls on the forehead had burst. Gradually the others did as well. Towards the eleventh day, the *mariatta* had completely disappeared, but of course there were some scars left. The bath had been prepared. My mother-in-law had gone and bought a new jar from the potter. She decorated it with turmeric and red dots, then filled it with water which she'd left to heat up in the sun. She'd gone to pick margosa leaves and couch grass roots. Margosa trees are stripped bare at these times, Sinnamma! Everyone picks their leaves: they eat them to clean out their intestines; they use them in the bath, to heal the skin and help with the itching; and they purify their houses with them after Mariatta has passed. So my mother-in-law made a big lump of turmeric, margosa and couch-grass paste. She took a little bit of it, mixed it in water heated in the sun and purified the whole house with it. The baby was given a bath first. Then it was my turn. I was covered with plenty of oil and washed with the paste, carefully rinsed with warm water from the jar and finally wrapped in a white cloth. All damp, with a margosa branch in my hand, I set off to raise a collection. I stopped and asked at each house, 'Alms for Mariatta! Alms for Mariatta!' I went round the whole *ceri* like that collecting gruel from each house. People gave very thick gruel – no one refuses. Coming back here, I poured it all into a big rice jar and added water to bring it to the consistency of a normal gruel. Meanwhile my mother-in-law had prepared 'Mariatta's flour'.

When a child has *mariatta*, you offer flour. When an adult does, you offer gruel. We offered both since my baby and I had had *mariatta*. Kalimuttu came with his drum to go to Mariamman's temple with us. We sang some prayers and dedicated our offerings to Mariamman. The baby was given a little flour and a mouthful of gruel to eat, as we said, 'Mariatta, eat this flour and drink this gruel, Ma!' Then we shared out the gruel with everyone else, starting with children, the old, widows and sterile women. I was entitled to a good meal: white rice, fish sauce with aubergines and drumstick beans.

One year Mariatta played a long time in our *ceri*. We'd stripped I don't know how many margosa branches to cover the whole courtyard of Mariamman's temple, a real mattress, as thick as that! The adults with spots were taken there packed tight in rows. They were all naked. The men didn't have their talisman any more, the women had taken off their jewels. Each had a coconut shell to eat their gruel out of. A *kumbam* was put at the temple entrance. Kalimuttu, Uncle Murti and Grand-father Vellai started describing Mariamman, singing her story. Night and day, all three sang praises of Mariamman. But Mariamman had some children and two adults on her list, one at Naliveliya's and one in the street of Perumal's temple. She didn't want the rest; she kicked them and then left ...

Nothing was done for the ones who went to *vaikundam*. You mustn't do anything for those dead: no tears, no songs, no music, no flowers. They are simply rolled in a yellow cloth and handed over to the grave-diggers. Even the mother of a child who dies of *mariatta* is not meant to shed tears. You can ask anybody, Sinnamma. No, no! You must never cry for those dead because that would only make Mariatta more furious and she would do even more damage.

There are several kinds of *mariatta*: little spots, which we call corian-der seeds; black ones like palmyra fruit; *mariatta* with plaits where you can see three feet which weave in and out of each other: others which are all flat like my earrings. The *mariatta* of the throat is very painful: the goddess and her husband come and sit each side of the ears. Your throat swells up as big as that and you can't move your head or swallow anything – not even your own spit. There's no cure for that, you have to wait. You just use poultices made out of margosa, turmeric and couch-grass paste to relieve it a bit, that's all.

To tell the truth, Mariatta only comes because she desires the *tali*. The gold's what makes her come. You know that she hasn't enjoyed her *tali*. Paramasiva drove her out. He even cut off her head and cursed her. 'All your desires will be granted by the people on earth until your time comes' is what he said to her. And that's why she comes like this, in all her different forms, to ask us for what she wants. To satisfy her, we take a white cord and dye it yellow with turmeric water. We thread a new *tali* on it decorated with a red spot and after dedicating it to Mariamman we tie it round the neck of Mariatta. Satisfied, she goes on her way immediately. But you have to be very careful, and especially not go where a couple have been together, or else this Mother will assume her terrifying form and maybe suffocate us in one go. What you must do is wait piously without making her furious, so she'll leave as she came, peacefully.

Everything's changed now. Doctors go through the villages with the *mariatta* injection. They catch the little ones most of all to inject them, even those who aren't a foot tall yet. They say that this injection is a protection against Mariatta like the thread you put on your wrist. But the doctors don't make any offerings: they catch us like calves, do the injections and go away! No one can stop Mariatta coming but you could say that she wasn't playing as much as before in the *ceri*. At first we hid when the doctors came to the *ceri*. We were afraid their talk would provoke Mariatta and she'd turn against us. The world has changed with time. But even now there are still people who flee the doctors. In

the past I hid Anban during the time of *mariatta*: when the doctor did
his rounds, I said to him, 'No one's got *mariatta* in my house, sir!' I
didn't want my boy to be taken to hospital! Do you think we poor have
got the time to go with someone to hospital and stay sitting there next
to him, just like that? And who'll do the work here? There are plenty of
other sicknesses worse than that. We can understand that people are
taken to hospital for them. A few years ago there was an outbreak in the
ceri of what we call 'local fever'. That one's horrifying. People who
catch it die every time. Last time at least five people died and that was
only here. Next to all those sicknesses, *mariatta* is nothing. She turns
up, does her duty, gives what she has to give and goes away. She's not
like cholera which kills without counting.

Govinda! O Govinda! Sinnamma, you're much too young to have experienced cholera. I was still at Velpakkam when it struck. I saw five or six
people die every day with my own eyes! Everything started at Velpakkam
with Nayagam's son. It got him very early in the morning. He kept on
being sick and having diarrhoea. He couldn't take any more, the poor
boy: he was almost old enough to marry. His mother had called the
family and showed them her son, when they heard, 'Govinda! O
Govinda! Govinda! O Govinda!' I remember that it was in the month of
Markaji and our priest had been playing the gong in the village. Everyone had rushed outside to see what was happening. The old man of
Pombur was in a trance. He shouted, 'De! Wake up! Build the fire to
drive away the spirits! Cholera has come to us! Build the fire to drive
away the spirits! Burn everything! Govinda! O Govinda!' Ejeumalaiyan
had come down on this old man to warn us.

   Cholera is Mother Kali. They say that she comes down to earth with
a jar filled with dark blue oil in a woven basket. She goes into every
house looking for the ones she wants to take: men, women, children or
animals. She pours a spoonful of oil in their mouths and goes away. The
old man of Pombur showed us that cholera was there, because he was in
a trance: how would we guess otherwise?

   Hearing what the old man was saying, we immediately went off shouting, 'Govinda! O Govinda!' We rushed to the margosa trees. Everyone
had a branch in their hands and shouted, 'Govinda!' We met up in
every street, at every crossroads, to build fires out of everything we
could find: palms, twigs, whatever. We ran in every direction, knocking
into each other and shouting, 'She's over there! – No! She's here, that
widow!' It was as if the *ceri* had burst into flames. It was burning in

every corner. They say that when you start fires like that, Mother becomes afraid and runs away to another village. If fires were started
everywhere she'd leave this earth!

But it turned out differently at Velpakkam. The *ceri* over there is to
the north: that's to say it's higher than the *ur*. I don't know what asshole
built it like that but anyway, he put the *ur* to the south. So, when there's
an epidemic of *mariatta* or cholera, what direction do you expect Mother
to run away in, eh? Well, when the fires are lit in the *ceri*, Kali can only
run away....into the *ur*! That's exactly what happened! They started to
get cholera in the *ur*. They made fires too to drive Mother away, but she
hid by a drumstick tree. They sent for the old man of Pombur. He went
into a trance and, accompanied by the musicians and scores of people,
he went to dig up the jar of oil and the basket and the spoon. Of course
the goddess of the village, Draupadi, helped him drive Kali away. She
drives out Mariatta and other evil spirits: she protects our village.

Only the possessed can approach the jar of oil. No one else, because
Kali would slap them and that would be the end of it – we could all
take the road to *vaikundam*. When he'd dug it up, the old man of Pombur
took the jar a long way away to a tamarind tree by the pond. There he
broke it and burnt it: the fire lasted until sunset. Since then I've had
children, two sons-in-law, grandchildren, but thanks to God, cholera
hasn't come back here again.

All this was after the seventh month ceremony during my first
pregnancy. We were hulling cotton at the house in Velpakkam when we
learnt the news. My father rushed towards the cotton husks and threw
them into the street to burn them with anything else he could find. We
all went back into our houses and shut the door. Only the people with
cholera were in the temple courtyard, totally naked, without their
talismans. Their bodies had been rubbed with white ash. The poor
things were emptying out through their mouths and their bottoms. They
were wasting away from day to day. We could see it was this Mother's
work: oily diarrhoea was coming out – basically just oil, the oil Mother
had poured into them. That's why you always have to sleep on your
stomach to catch Kali out. If she comes in, she takes us for a tree
branch and rejects us with a kick, saying, 'Pah! That's nothing but a
piece of wood!' But if you sleep on your back, she has no trouble realising that she's dealing with humans: she pours her oil into your mouth
and runs away. That's how you catch cholera …

But it's all written, Sinnamma! Look how crowded our *ceri* is! I've
had twelve children: how would I have fed them and brought them all

up? And it's the same in every family! How many people would there be in this *ceri* if everyone had stayed alive? That's why Mother goes into the *ceri* each year. She gives cholera to some and *mariatta* to others. She takes five or ten people in each *ceri*, and about ten more in each *ur*. She does that in every *ceri* and every *ur* in the world and that means there's that many fewer people to feed!

ELEVEN

The festival of Mariamman

We have a festival for Mariatta every year, Sinnamma. We're not the only ones, the whole world does it, the fifty-eight countries. Have you seen how many temples of Mariamman there are in the villages?

The one here was already up in my husband's grandparents' day. They say the government built it. I don't know anything about that. But two Adi after my marriage, the elders of the *ceri* met up. In those days the Chetti's father was the head. The elders decided to make the temple bigger. At the time there were about a hundred houses: each household gave ten rupees. Lots of money was collected in neighbouring villages as well and the *ceri* committee decided to hire a contractor who was experienced in the art of building temples. Not just anyone can do that: there are rules and rituals which we don't know. The contractor said, 'Give me two thousand rupees and I'll get my masons to build the temple walls by the book, but you'll have to pay for manual labour, bricks and mortar.' He came up with such a high price by counting twenty rupees for a whole man, fifteen for a half and ten for a quarter.[1] We accepted without any fuss.

We *ceri* people took turns working on the building-site right till the end: one person from each household every day. Six women pounded the lime, three facing three, and the poles fell to the rhythm of the songs. The men carried mortar to the masons. Building it took a long time!

Our temple only had one little room at the start. Our generation made it bigger by building a tower and outer walls. Lots of people who'd made vows came and offered earthenware babies, saris, silver jewels and gold *tali*. With all that we were able to get a copper statue of Mariamman made by the Thanjavur craftsmen the next year. A Brahmin came for the consecration ceremony.[2] Again lots of money had been collected and a troupe of musicians had been hired for seven days: you know that a festival of the goddess must have theatre. The troupe from Pombur is very well known: they are invited far and wide in the month of Adi, the month of Mariamman's festival. But our people had booked them several months before by taking them some betel and giving them an advance. They organised everything with White-Soman's help, the leader of the *ur*'s troupe. The Pombur actors are Vanniyar, they can't eat or sleep in the *ceri* so we gave them all the money they needed to eat and sleep at White-Soman's. And we got a priest of Mariamman to come as well to sing a lullaby for the goddess every evening before the performance. We gave our temple of Mariamman a good inauguration!

After that everyone did what they could to give the temple what it was missing. One year Kaliyan, all on his own, gave the wooden statue that's used for the procession. Darasuram and Manivelu offered the statue of Kattavarayan. Another year we all clubbed together to have the statue of Munnadiyan sculpted. At Anban's birth I offered a handbell. And one evening, coming back from Karikkimedu fair, I saw a bulb shining at the top of the temple. I was amazed and asked the kids playing there, 'Hey! Little ones! How come electric light is shining on top of the temple?' My husband who was coming to meet me answered, 'Murugaiya Gounder has had it put there. He said to us, "Dei! You *ceri* people! Don't you worry! I'll install electricity at my own expense." There's light now thanks to him. Our temple to Mariamman is finished!'

We've paid to have other temples built. Mani Iyer took charge of the temple of Pillaiyar by bringing stone dressers from Tiruvannamalai. For Perumal's, we didn't have a priest with *namam*: we sent for one from Kokkur. He moved in here and he's the one who lights up the temple in the evening. As for the Guardian, he came out of the earth all by himself and nobody built anything. You know the stones at Pondy hospital which have come up all on their own? Well, it's the same here in our *ceri*! Anyway, none of these temples has big festivals every year. Only Mariamman is entitled to that!

So, once a year, we perform the sharing out of Mariamman's gruel. Four young boys are disguised as girls to collect everyone's share. We dress them in an underskirt and a bra and put jewels in their noses, and a *tali* and pearl necklaces round their neck like tribal women. They have a beautiful margosa branch in their hand and they throw themselves into the dance of Mother Ganges, backed by a drum and cymbals. Then the pair of Koravan come: it's always two men from the *ceri*. Virappan is disguised as a Koravan, Ranga as a Koratti. They've got little bells on their feet and they dance without stopping: they're tireless, those two! And they sing:

> That necklace of glass pearls, aren't you going to buy it?
> If you buy it and wear it, it will be very beautiful!
> Ayoyo, ayoyo, o, o, o!
> When we've thrown the net into the pond,
> We stay hidden ...
> Don't you want us to be together then,
> Narikara, a a a ...[3]
> Aunt, listen to what she said: my wife is six months' pregnant.
> O Mother! What shall I do if she gives birth on the way?
> O Mother, give us money so we can buy some medicine!

Yes, the Narikara go by every house begging and singing the whole time. And then suddenly Virappan and Ranga change rhythm. They start jumping as they're dancing and singing:

> In the Narikuri market, Narikara,
> I went, well dressed, to sell some fox teeth.
> Down there a Narikara dwarf signalled to me ...

When they dance like that, it's madness, everybody leaves what food they've got on the fire to come and watch them. Then Elephant-Foot, the palmist, arrives. With his little drum in his hand, he sings:

> In this house good fortune will be born!
> Give what you should to Mariatta!
> We are going to make the gruel for Mariatta
> The measures of grain hidden away,
> You should give them to us!
> Kudukkudukkudukudukka ...

Then Sankaran comes. He plays the sorcerer. He disguised himself very well this year: a blood-red face with a cardboard crown decorated with crow's feathers and cock feathers and holding a big switch of fake hair in his hand. And even though his dancing took your breath away, his crown stayed on his head!

There's the pair of hunters as well, with their faces all black. Krishnan and Kuppan play them every year: I don't know how many measures of

charcoal they put on their faces! The crowd follows them and everybody laughs – you laughed as well, Sinnamma! They sing and beat their
drum very hard, the beat is fast, the dance catches fire. What a show!
The two shepherds are much quieter: they hardly say anything. They
have to be there, that's all, just a presence, like the launderer, as a
reminder of all those people Mariamman has met on this earth.

The masquerade tours Karani and the neighbouring villages. You
have to plan for two whole days just to take the collection in our *ur*.
The Kudiyanar are the same: the collection takes two days when they're
holding their festival for Mariamman. We hear the sound of drums
everywhere in the month of Adi and the shouting, 'Mother Ganges!
Mother Ganges!' Everyone takes collections to celebrate the festival of
the goddesses, because in every village there's a temple of Draupadi and
one, two or three temples of Mariamman.

Each year, the Pariah orchestra goes with the dancers for the collections. First they must accompany the *ur*'s dancers, who are the first to
go collecting, and of course they don't come here to the *ceri* but to all
the Kudiyanar in the neighbouring villages. A fortnight later the Pariahs
take their collections. Two men carry a large wicker basket to collect
cereals. Another man – it's always a Chetti – carries a big copper tray
to collect the money. First they go to the houses in the *ceri*. Everyone
should give what they can afford. The head of the *ceri* is there as well
with the dancers. He notes down in his big book the people who've
given, how much they've given and the people who haven't given yet,
because not everybody is ready to give something. So those ones say:
'Wait a little bit, come back in a while, I've asked the Reddiar for
grain.' The head notes in his book that he has to go back to this one
and that one. But there are some people like me who look ahead and
put a measure or two aside for Mariamman during the groundnut
harvest. You can put yard grass or other grains in the basket and of
course you can put money on the tray. People are generous in the *ur*,
especially the well-off: they give cereals and money. The big basket
quickly gets heavy and fills up. The musicians aren't paid for the days
of the collection, or only very little, but they make sure they're given as
much to drink and eat as they want. They go from house to house,
asking a Kudiyanar woman, 'O lady of the little master's house, pour
out a little gruel!' Or, further on, 'O lady of the Reddiar's house, pour
out a little gruel!' And everyone pours out gruel for them without
having to be coaxed. Yes, the festival of Mariamman is the festival of
the musicians, our own festival.

We also take the collection in all the neighbouring villages where we go and work. The dignitaries of Naliveli and Mangappakkam hear us coming a long way off and recognise us, because our men are good singers and our dancers are famous. When the whole troupe gets there, the *kambattam* give the order to hand out the gruel to everyone, then the musicians and the dancers each get two measures of *ragi* and two rupees. The *kambattam* of Mangappakkam gives as much as three rupees to each of them and *ragi* as well. And the *kambattam* give twelve large measures of *ragi* for our Mariatta and as much money as their heart tells them: fifty rupees or a hundred rupees. Those dignitaries own half the fields of Karani and almost all the *ceri* works for them. So they treat us well at our festival every year. It's true, Sinnamma, that our Mariatta is good to them and protects them all well. 'Go and celebrate Mariatta in style! Hire a good troupe, and if the money's not there, come and ask us for it!', the *kambattam* of Mangappakkam says to us, and on the day the gruel is shared out, he comes on to his terrace and follows the festival from up there. Last year he even came to the entrance of the *ceri* on the day of the festival and nowadays, you see Kudiyanar and Reddiar asking permission to go and worship Mariamman in her temple in the *ceri*. People who've left Karani, whether they're from the *ur* or the *ceri*, send cereals or money, or both, to celebrate the sharing out of Mariamman's gruel ...

When the collection's finished, the money's counted and the cereals are put in sacks: it's all enough to prepare the sharing out of the gruel. The head, the accountant and Six Fingers go and sell the rest at Tirulagam market. Last year they came back with seven hundred and fifty rupees. Mariamman's gruel needs lots of money! There's no shortage of expenses: put in lamps and neons; hire a troupe of dancers for three nights, records, loudspeakers.

This year, the little fools wanted to show a video instead of having the troupe play on the last day – right here, in the *ceri*, where the dance should take place. It's because they're ashamed, they don't know how to do anything any more, those young fools! Before his marriage, my Anban still knew how to play the role of Lakshmanan. Now he says he doesn't want to do that any more, that he's forgotten it all. None of it interests them any more. What they want is to slick back their hair with lots of oil, dress up in nice outfits and go to the cinema (they're not even outdoors like they used to be: even in our part of the country you can find cinemas, there are three in Tirulagam). They don't like the theatre any more like the rest of us do. Uncle Coconut-Grater, the old man

from Kanur and Grandfather Duck all learned to read from theatre
books, there, on the ground in the square. Six Fingers' father-in-law
drew the letters for them on the sand. They understood: by adding the
letters together, little by little they started to read and one fine day they
knew how to read fluently. They formed the *ceri* troupe. Yes, in the past
we had a theatre troupe here in the *ceri*. My husband acted for a long
time, but now he's too old for it. He played Karna, the husband of
Anjalai played Bhima, Chetti's uncle played Arjuna and Manivelu played
Draupadi. My husband had a voice which carried and he had stamina!
He could act all night and go and work the next day. In those days I'd
get into a corner and I'd admire him, my man! He didn't just act the
story of the five Pandava brothers. He could play Kattavarayan, Vira
Pandya and lots of others as well. He knew all the stories, my husband!
He'd drink a good gourd of palm wine and he was ready! He'd jump
and dance. The words flowed like water. He never stammered, he never
got it wrong, he never stopped to ask what was next.[4] Sometimes he'd
go with Six Fingers' father and act in other *ceri*. And, when it was their
turn, they trained the youngsters, but now it's over, the troupe has
broken up bit by bit. Four boys work at Pondy; two have gone to
Madras, and there you are! The ones who've stayed aren't interested.
They prefer videos. They even say that they're cheaper than the troupe
of Kudiyanar from Kodukkur who have to be well looked after.

This year the troupe from Pombur were already booked when we got
in touch. So we went to take betel to the Kodukkur troupe. They came
but they brought their cooks. They set up in the temple courtyard. The
kambattam lent them some utensils and they made their meals with
lamb. We supplied the alcohol. They sleep in the day, drink in the
evening and are ready to dance all night. We know who the best actors
in the Pombur troupe are, so we give them a drink separately and they
dance just for us in a corner. Don't you think all that's fun, Sinnamma?
You were pushed around by the crowd, but you liked it, didn't you?
And now they tell me that with the videos we would only have to pay
five hundred rupees! Let them do what they want, those stupid bastards,
but there really has to be some theatre, at least the first day the gruel is
shared out.

To prepare this gruel, six women have to pound the *ragi*. I am hired
every year because I lead the others with my songs. The pestles fall
quickly and the work progresses! We clean, we pound, we grind, we
sieve: we set up on the cement floor of the temple and we sing the whole
time we're working. A little measure of *ragi* is given to each of us as pay

and no one would pinch a grain in their sari: it's Mariatta's grain and
she could make us seriously ill or blind. At the Reddi's it's different:
we've even got a gift for it. When I'm asked to winnow something at his
household, I drop a few grains with the bran and the black grains and
I get them afterwards when I'm sweeping up. Or when we're harvesting
peppers, bitter oranges or palmyra fruit, I take out what's been nibbled
by insects or rats and put it to one side and when my son comes by, I
give it to him to take back to the house. There you are, that's all! It's not
a big deal. I don't go into houses to steal! Ayoyo, Sinnamma! Anyway, we
don't steal a single one of Mariatta's grains: we tally them up exactly.

The elders come and measure the flour and have eleven different-
sized jars brought, which they fill to the brim. They leave them in the
first room of the temple until Thursday, the day before the sharing out.
The rest of the flour is divided up between all the families of the *ceri*.
On the Friday, the ten clean women who have been chosen at the start
of the ceremonies go and cook the gruel which they've left to ferment
the day before, while each family prepares their own gruel at home.
Towards midday, we put it in the middle of the house with oil lamps
and camphor. Then my husband, my son, my daughter-in-law and I
prostrate ourselves in front of our jar and we dedicate it to the goddess.
Anban goes and finds the launderess and I pour out a share of the gruel
for her. Afterwards we drink the rest. The launderers are the ones
entitled to the first mouthfuls of gruel, whether it's the temple's or a
family's, because they're the favourites of Mariamman, they saw her the
first. They serve us all year, they wash our dirty linen, they take the
news of girls' first periods to the mother's family. We owe them meals
at every festival and every great *puja* to the gods.

But this year something happened when you weren't here, Sinnamma.
Oh! nothing very serious, there weren't any big fights, but just ...

This year our musicians, who should play for eighteen days during
the festival of Draupadi, asked for a wage.

'Sami,' they said to the Gounder, 'we're awake for eighteen days and
we get up early to play. You only give us ten rupees in all, for everything. This year we're asking you for ten rupees for each of us, Sami,
for the eighteen days, no more!'

'Ten rupees for each of you! Are you forgetting your duty as a Pariah
or what? How dare you demand as much as that?'

'Sami, Draupadi is our Mother, we have to play for her, that's true,
it's our duty. But life today is expensive. We play day and night for the

whole festival, so for eighteen days we can't go and work in the fields, Sami, and we earn ten rupees a day there!'

'You Pariahs have no gratitude! Aren't you fed for eighteen days? Perhaps cereals don't count?'

'Don't be angry, Sami, but if I'm fed, who will feed my people for those eighteen days?'

'Ah! Bastards! It's that guy from Pondy who's given you the nerve to come and talk like this![5] We don't want your music! And if one of you comes and sets foot here during the festival, I'll break him, I'll cut him into pieces! You watch out, you bunch of bastards! As for your festivals, go and ask for help from your supporter. Don't set foot here any more. Fuck off, you dirty fools!'

That's what happened this year. Afterwards we had a meeting in the *ceri*. The young said, 'It's a good thing!' But I stood up and asked them thousands of questions, those young idiots, 'Now what? You mugs! Sons of whores! So here we are without the right to be at the festival of Draupadi any more, our goddess, the goddess of the village! You think that's good, do you? Juice drinkers!'

Lots of people backed me up, 'Velpakkatta's right!'

But the young ones calmly replied, 'Sit down, aunt! We'll build another temple to Draupadi and we'll have a festival as well!'

'Ah! Donkey fuckers,' I said to them, 'you listen to those politicians too much! They go to your head and now what we say doesn't matter any more!'

My son stood up, 'Why are you shouting like that? Do you think that it's still the old days, that we have to give in like in the past? Calm down! It's our turn to be musicians this year, but we don't know how to play. What do you want us to bloody do down there?'

'Rip your hairs out, you sons of whores!'

So this year the festivals of Draupadi and Mariamman took place without Pariahs. We couldn't collect anything in the *ceri* or in the neighbouring villages. No one went to work in the *ur* for three months. We all looked for work in other villages. The Kudiyanar cultivated their fields themselves and took our places working for the Reddi. Our own festival of Mariamman wasn't as beautiful because we couldn't collect cereals as we normally do. K.S. gave money to bring a troupe of dancers on the first day and on the next day there was a video.

It's true that they could have easily slipped those eighty rupees to the eight *totti* and everything would have been fine! But both sides are stubborn! That's what's going on between the *ceri* and the *ur* while I've still got my eyes open, and what'll happen after my death? I always tell Anban and all the youth of the *ceri* not to go against the will of the goddesses. They look after us, they protect us. Thanks to them we work and have enough to eat. Why would you want to break that tradition?

TWELVE

The seven virgins

That argument about the festival of Draupadi sunk all us old people into a deep sadness. The young ones joke about it, they're not that bothered!

If you knew the changes we see these days in our countryside, you'd really be amazed! The government is all for us poor and especially the Pariahs! We've got lots of facilities now! All the political parties fight for us, and the K.S. party even says that there are no castes any more, no Pariahs, and that we must mix together to live like they do in Pondy. They don't just say it, they do it too. When a poor Kudiyanar asks the government for land to build a house, he gets it free, in the *ceri*. But what Kudiyanar is going to come and live here, eh? Tell me that, will you! And have you noticed the changes at school? There are three or four new teachers now. They say that two of them are Harijans. Of course they're not Pariahs from Karani, but they live next to the school in the *ur*. And do you know where the two families of pig rearers have been given a place to live? Behind the lotus pond, near the potter's! You remember that empty land behind the Reddi quarter? Well, it's there, right in the heart of the *ur*! The government ordered it and no one in the *ur* argued. One of the pig-keepers doesn't raise animals any more, he's an agricultural worker like us. The other has kept his pigsties in the middle of the paddy fields opposite the temple of Aiyanar. Those guys are the lowest in the *ur*. They were accepted because the government, the K.S. party, ordered it.[1] It was the same with the teachers.

124

The authorities kept on saying: 'If you want to send your children to school, you must accept the teacher we choose, otherwise keep your kids at home!' And the teachers tell whoever wants to listen that education isn't polluting. Everything's changing like that in this *kaliyugam*!

Anyway the people in the *ur* take it all to heart and that's why they took their revenge for our men asking for a higher wage. They drove all of us, not just the musicians, out of the festival of Draupadi. It's not right to keep us away for a few rupees and Mother Draupadi has already come to several people from the *ur* in their dreams and told them so. Anyway, the leaders of the *ur* decided not to use Pariahs any more for the work we traditionally do. There have been two deaths in the *ur* since then: a cow and the father of Ramassami Gounder. Well, none of our seven *totti* was summoned, either to be the quarterer or the grave-digger or to play as musicians! The hunters replaced our *totti*. Not the hunters you know, but their relatives who live out in the fields on the track to the south of the temple of Poraiyatta.

The hunters have changed a lot nowadays. They're more civilised. They listen to the radio while checking the harvests. They ride bicycles. They dress better. In the past they were in the fields and the woods all day, the men in loincloths, the women in short underskirts down to their knee. They caught rats, all sorts of snakes and very fat lizards. They lived on that and they sold their catches for very high prices: skins were worth a lot in Pondy or Madras. We'd hardly see them in the village. At the festival of Draupadi in the *ur*, they'd light camphor and break coconuts. You went to them if you'd been bitten by a rat, a scorpion or a snake. They were good at curing bites with leaves and exorcisms. They have that power because the Seven Virgins are always with them, protecting them in the forest. You'd go to them too when a snake had made its hole near a house or was playing around one. They'd spread some stuff round the hole to put the snake to sleep and then they'd take it out of there and catch it easily. The old hunter played *magudi* for the snake charmers. The others didn't.[2]

Those were the only times you'd have anything to do with the hunters. When we were working in the fields we'd see them in the distance, walking in a group: because the hunter never goes anywhere without his wife; everyone knows that. He always takes her with him, no matter where he's going, no matter what the kingdom. Because as soon as they're on their own, the hunters' wives sleep with all the men on earth! They're known to have thirty-eight men a day: they've got real powers of seduction over everybody, no matter what caste, from

Koravan to Reddi, and including Pariah, Komutti and Gounder. And
they do it quickly: just time for their husband to shut his eyes and open
them again: they're so gifted and they know all the little nooks of the
country so well! You can ask anyone, Sinnamma, and no one will tell
you different! If the Seven Virgins have given their husbands the power
to charm serpents, they've given their women the power to charm all
the men on earth! (*Laughs.*)

The hunters have given up their old trade as well. They're agricultural workers now like us. Houses have been built for them and that's
where they live. They don't run in the woods any more and they get a
wage like us at the end of the day. But they're happy with what they're
given, while we fight to be better paid. They're ready to do anything
now, even our traditional jobs. Look, this year the people from the *ur*
called on them to bury the dead! I hope they make the most of it,
because they haven't got much money either! The other day the wife of
one of the hunters said to me, 'Listen, Velpakkatta! There were many of
us in the past and collecting from our relatives brought in enough money
to perform the *puja* to the Seven Virgins. Now we're fewer and for some
time the *puja*'s only been carried out at our relatives' in Kanniyur near
Tiruvannamalai. We'd like to perform the *puja* to the Virgins right here
like we used to. Look, the children are properly grown up but their ears
still haven't been pierced: their first hair still hasn't been offered to the
Virgins. If we do some work here and there we can earn a little more
money at the Reddi or at the Gounder: that's why our men have accepted that work in the *ur*. You know, Velpakkatta, the wooden statue of
the Seven Virgins which was used in the processions has been put away
in the shelter of an irrigation pump in the fields. It's rotting away ... '

When the old man was still there, the hunters took the Seven Virgins
out in procession only in the *ur* and not in the *ceri*. One man was in front,
with a *karagam* on his head, and the women carried the statue of the
Virgins on their shoulders. They'd sing and two men backed them on a
drum which they'd play with a muffled beat. Oh! That's a very special
way of playing: no one else ever plays like that for any other god. When
we heard that we'd run to see them. There was always a hunter whipping
the women with a plaited whip when they were in a trance. Blood flowed
but they didn't feel anything, it was the Virgins who took the lashes. The
women's hair was untied, they'd stagger, breathing like oxen. It was
terrifying! Just then one of the women in a trance would always start
singing, 'Dei! Half an acre from here it smells of the wind which smells
of the Pariah! Oh! Flee from here, all of you!' As soon as we heard that,

the first of us to get there turned back and the people behind turned around quickly as well. We were afraid our presence and our uncleanness would disturb the Virgins and we were afraid most of all of being whipped. Because it wouldn't be the Virgins taking the lashes of the whip for us! We'd have our flesh ripped to pieces!

All that's over nowadays. There's still a few families of hunters at Tirulagam who regularly celebrate the festival of the Virgins, but these days the countryside has become so civilised the people let themselves go less. The hunters' wives wear pretty nylon saris down to their ankles like you, Sinnamma, and they have a big *pottu* on their foreheads. They still carry the Virgins on their shoulders in the procession but now they stay near their home, going from village to village where their families are employed as agricultural workers: because they're settled now! The procession still doesn't come into the *ceri*, but we go closer and the women have stopped saying anything. They worship the Seven Virgins, singing and begging them for their favours. Some cut their children's hair for the first time, pierce their ears or give them a name. The women ask for alms during the procession and collect lots of money and grain before offering the Virgins the gruel which will be handed out to everybody. All the sick run up to get a share of the offerings which will cure them immediately.

So, the hunters carry out their *puja* to the Virgins very reverently! It's because they are in contact with them every day. Every day they wash and every evening, at nightfall, they call on the Virgins with their drums. That's why they're not afraid to go into the woods, the forests, the fields or the mountains at the hottest time of day as well as at night: that's the domain of the Seven Virgins, who are the goddesses of their line and love and protect them. All of them, men, women and children, wear a talisman with a drawing of the Seven Virgins on a copper leaf. They wear that round their waist, even when they're making love! (*Laughs.*) They're lower than us by caste and anyway, like I've told you, when we take the collection for the gruel of Mariamman, there are always two of our men dressed up as hunters and they make everybody laugh by imitating their drawling accents like the Koravan's: 'Wooman! Wherrre diiiid youuuuu puut thee croowbaar?' But as gods, the Seven Virgins are more terrifying and more demanding about cleanliness than our Periyandavan who is more tolerant, more generous.

The Seven Virgins belong to the Kingdom of the Gods, but they were born on earth. They are a sort of water spirit. They adore the water, they adore bathing. They say that a hill very near Velpakkam used to be very high in the past but the Seven Virgins wore it away by rubbing turmeric roots against it to cover their bodies. And now, Sinnamma, the rocks of that hill are as smooth as your cheek! The Seven Virgins are all the same size, all the same age: you won't be able to find a single old woman between them. It's the same when they want to possess someone: they'll never choose an old woman, they'll take someone like my daughter or you. If they're not pacified, they attack women the most and they make us suffer from painful, heavy periods or melt us like palm sugar. We go all hard like dried fish. It's worse for pregnant women: they run the risk of being cut into seven pieces! We hear the Virgins dancing and singing as they go off to hunt, because we're often in the fields collecting wood or grazing the cows when the sun is at its height. If their shadow touches us on the road, then we've got a chance of living. But if we pass them face to face, then it's all over: they send us to the resting place of Vishnu straightaway! It all depends on the god of our line. If he protects us, he can fight them. But if he's on their side, there's nothing to be done! Once they slapped about ten women in the *ceri*. None of them could be saved. The women were as yellow as a sunflower when they were dying, and that's how we knew the Seven Virgins had slapped them!

They don't only attack women. They can also turn against men, who they prefer to possess: they get into them, they inhabit them but they don't show themselves for three months. Once Anjalai's son was possessed like that. He was with another boy checking the irrigation pump while a field of the Grand Reddi's was being irrigated. At midday, both of them heard singing and dancing and they smelled jasmine, silky rose and strongest of all, turmeric that made their heads spin. Kichtan even saw the glimmer of their torches and said to himself, 'There, that's the goddessses going hunting'. The son of Anjalai fainted: he's as fearful as Kichtan. Later, both of them went home as usual. They didn't have a fever the next day, as normally happens when an ordinary demon possesses you. But then this boy who had been so strong, so active, just wasted away. After three months we saw he'd gone yellow: his hands, his nails, his toes – he was like a statue painted yellow! Anjalai, her husband and some of their relatives ran to the hunters. When they exorcised the boy, the hunters understood that it was the Virgins' doing but that the boy had a chance to get through. That's the main thing we ask the hunters: to tell us what it is and guarantee that the *puja* to the Virgins can be carried out. When we know that, we can do the *puja* ourselves. But there has to be a celibate adolescent to conduct it. In the *ceri*, we always send Bommaikkannu. He's not an adolescent any more but he's stayed celibate and we've kept him because he's very brave and isn't afraid to go to the places where the Virgins are.

Anjalai carefully prepared the tray for the *puja*, with seven brand-new bricks, seven betel leaves, seven areca nuts, seven cubits of flowers, seven coconuts, seven bananas, seven beautiful thick turmeric roots – they love that, the Virgins – seven coins, seven pieces of palm sugar, seven bitter apples, seven thorn apples, seven measures of crushed chick-peas, seven measures of rice petals and a big jar of a sweet onion infusion with palm sugar. Bommaikkannu took the basket on his head to a wood very far away, behind the river, where no one goes. And over there he did the same as always: he put the basket under a tree and stripped naked, completely naked without even a talisman round his waist. Then he set out the seven bricks and washed them with plenty of water. He made a paste out of the turmeric roots and coated the bricks with it. Then he gave them a big red mark and surrounded them with flowers. He put all the offerings out in front and prostrated himself. When the *puja* was finished, he stood up and got dressed again. He took some ash which he'd knotted in his *soman* and set off with the jar of infusion on his head, leaving all the other offerings behind. While he was doing this, Anjalai's son had gone to sit at the village entrance beside a field near the river, so that Bommaikkannu would see him before anyone else. When he got to him, Bommaikkannu put the ash on his forehead and gave him a few mouthfuls of the infusion which had been offered to the Virgins. He poured the rest of the infusion into the little jar Anjalai's son had brought. The boy and all his family drank that infusion for seven days when the sun was at its highest. And that's why the Virgins left Anjalai's son and he was cured. If all that had been neglected, he would have died young, taken off by the Seven Virgins.

We can trust all the gods that exist in this world, but the Seven Virgins, Katteri, Mannarsami and Viran are unfathomable, terrible and dangerous. You must have seen the statue of Viran on the road coming here? Don't look at him too closely otherwise you run the risk of having trouble and miscarrying. He is enormous, with his bottle of alcohol in his hand and his great red eyes!

There's always a woman at his side: they are husband and wife. Haven't you noticed? They're thigh to thigh. When I think about his eyes again, his eyes as red as blood, it makes me shiver! Each time I go by that statue I bow my head and put my hands together!

At Karani there are people who worship Viran: he's the god of their line. The day of the *puja* to Viran they offer him dozens of bottles of alcohol: he's a god who loves drinking a lot! They also kill a goat and a cock and they make *ragi* bread. Like the Seven Virgins, Viran keeps a very sharp eye on uncleanliness. If a woman who's got her period visits someone with Viran as the god of their line, then it's all over, Viran makes her melt like palm sugar and her periods will run like a tap! And if it's a pregnant woman he'll make her miscarry straightaway!

The other terrifying god I know is Mannarsami. He's in the middle of a wood of illupie trees on a hill at Velpakkam. It's a remote place, where there's no noise of pestles or the mill: the village is a long way away. He's the youngest of seven *muni*. He has been fed by his six brothers and he's become bigger than them. He has a temple, but the Seven Virgins, Viran and Periyandavan don't. But because he's a *muni*, his temple is in the woods. He's alone down there, cut off from the world of men. At Velpakkam his festival happens in Cittirai. He's the god of the village, the same way Draupadi is the goddess of Karani. But he is terrifying! Just by looking at him a pregnant woman will give birth straightaway! Yes, her baby will fall to the ground, just like that, in a second! The *totti* goes through the whole village, *ur* and *ceri*, announcing his festival with his drum. He says that Mannarsami will be worshipped on such a day and asks all women pregnant with their first child to go back to the villages they were born in because Mannarsami fills us with dread! We Pariahs observe the festival from a long way away, because we're not allowed to be there. We keep our distance from his temple and make our *pongal* separately. We don't prepare any flowers for Mannarsami but, since he's very greedy, we offer him garlands of fritters, huge garlands of fritters made with chickpeas and black lentils. That's what he wears round his neck! And people walk on fire for him, like they do for our goddess Draupadi. By people I mean the Vanniyar, not us of course. You can go anywhere in the whole world, but you'll never hear of Pariahs walking on fire! No, no, you'll never see that! Look, the government does lots of things for the Harijans. Now there are Pariahs, as I've already told you, in the *ur*, and even pig-keepers, but that doesn't mean they'll be allowed to walk on fire!

We wouldn't even think of walking on fire in our dreams, Sinnamma! We know perfectly well it's impossible. We're not clean enough for that! Pariahs walking on fire, no, I don't believe we'll ever see anything like that in this *kaliyugam*!

THIRTEEN

A family funeral

The last time I went to the festival of Mannarsami at Velpakkam was when my mother died. To tell the truth, she died just before it and I stayed on after the mourning ceremonies for the festival because I knew it would be a long time before I went back to Velpakkam. It's never the same after your mother dies, you're never received in the same way. The village I grew up in has almost become foreign to me now, even though my brother still lives there. It's well known that, for us women, a mother can't be replaced, even if we leave our mother's house to join a new family. They always say that a woman should only visit her mother as a guest after her marriage, but what sort of mother would make her daughter feel that? Rules and duties are one thing, but feelings are another! I would have given my life if I had to, to save my mother, but she was in good shape when death took her.

I had been ill for a long time. My mother had come to see me, bringing preserved bitter oranges, brown rice and sweets for the children. I'd planted some cassava that year and my mother had wanted to go and check the field, which was beside the main road, while I went to the market at Tirulagam. Coming back from the market, I met Anjalai who said to me, 'Viramma, hurry up! Your mother fell into a ditch on her way back from the fields. She couldn't get up or walk! Kannan carried her back to your house on his shoulders!' Then my brother came to find her. They made her some poultices. They took her to the bonesetter at

131

Otterippalaiyam but even he couldn't do anything for her and she died
soon afterwards. That's the only thing that was wrong with her! She
could see well, she could walk well, she had all her teeth. Not a single
illness. Until that damned fall she didn't need anybody's help. There
you are! Her end had come: it was time to go and she was in good shape
when she went!

She was all there before she died. She asked my brother to send a
messenger to tell me that she wouldn't last. A man from Velpakkam
brought me the news. 'Come, big sister! Your mother only has these
words on her lips, "My eldest daughter! My eldest daughter!" She's
asking for you: her last wish is to see you, her eldest daughter. Hurry
up! Come and grant your mother's wish!' I prepared some *idli* and *dosai*
straightaway so as not to go empty-handed and I left for Velpakkam
with the messenger. When she saw me, my mother took my hand and
said, 'Viramma! Are you here at last? You've been able to come and see
me, have you? Is Anban well? And Sundari? My son-in-law, is he all
right?' She asked me all these questions and then I made her eat a very
light gruel. It's a gruel made from rice flour, sieved several times, thin
and white as a cloud. It helps the digestion and stops diarrhoea. This
gruel is one of the things you give the dying to eat. It gives them a bit
of strength, makes them hold out longer. Afterwards I washed her and
made the evening meal with my sister-in-law. Then the two of us sat by
my mother and stayed there without leaving her.

She died two days and two nights after I got there. I suddenly saw that
it was difficult for her to breathe. She beckoned me nearer, 'Viramma!
You've been able to come to my side, have you?'

'Yes, Ma!'

'Viramma, lead your life intelligently! Take good care of your family.
While I've been alive, my son-in-law hasn't wanted anything from me.
So it's up to you to get by all on your own, don't expect anything from
your brother. I haven't got much longer. I won't see Sundari's marriage
or Anban's. And my son-in-law hasn't even come to see me one last
time. Viramma! Viramma!'

There you are: those were her last words. I gave her a drop of milk
and she died peacefully. Messengers left straightaway for Karani, first of
all, to tell my husband and my family-in-law, and then for all the places
we have relatives at second and third remove. We respected my mother's two wishes: not to tell her family-in-law and that her last clothes
should come from her son-in-law instead of her son. That's what she'd
said and she repeated it to all the *ceri* elders of Velpakkam and Karani,

'I'm telling all of you that, even if I have to die tonight, I don't want my son's sari but my son-in-law's!' The trays of offerings have to come from the mother's side with us, like they do elsewhere: that's to say from the daughters of the house who have been given away in marriage. For example, if my husband died, the trays would have to come from my mother's and daughters' households. If my son-in-law died, I'd have to send the tray and the *soman*. If there are ten girls in the family, each of them has to bring a tray in the dead person's honour. So you can see why people are afraid to have daughters! It leads to a lot of expense, that's for sure!

So, when my mother died, my sister and I each brought her a sari, and a *soman* and scarf for my brother as well. But we dressed her in the sari my husband had brought her because it was what she wanted. It was a beautiful, twenty-five-rupee sari and, to accompany the tray of offerings, he hired a *naiyandi* orchestra as well as the funeral orchestra of the *totti*. Lots of people came from Karani. The head of Velpakkam *ceri* and the dignitaries laid garlands of flowers. A crowd gathered in front of the house. Yes, Sinnamma, my mother was gentle, generous, discreet, obliging and very kind. Everyone knew the story of her life as a wife mistreated by her husband, everyone knew her courage and how hard she worked without grumbling. She was very respectful. She never got involved in a conversation in front of her son-in-law. She didn't even stand up in front of him and if my husband insulted me in front of her, she didn't open her mouth. At meal times I used to say to Sundari, 'Go and find grandmother, dinner is ready'. And she used to come and sit down timidly on the *tinnai*, very uncomfortably, all huddled up in a corner next to the goat.

When the messengers had left to take the news, my brother and the *totti* did everything needed to raise a *pandal*; cut the bamboo, make a funeral stretcher, plait the ropes and dig the hole as quickly as possible. I took care of the washing. My sister-in-law, her daughters and my sisters were all young, the poor things: it made them a little frightened. I didn't want other people to touch the body. After all, I was the eldest daughter and it was up to me to do it. Normally you don't wash the body straight after death, you wash it just before putting it on the stretcher when the offerings arrive from the mother's family. If a husband dies, that's when you perform the ceremony of exchanging betel: the widow puts some betel in her dead husband's hand and an eldest son takes the betel and gives it back to her: it's to show that married life has ended and the light-heartedness, the joys and the games of love are all over. The brother-in-law then puts a new sari on the widow's shoulders, everyone shouts 'Govinda! Govinda!' and the body is lifted up, while all the musicians play to a very fast beat.

Since my mother was a widow, there was no exchange of betel and we could wash her straightaway. After the bath I closed her vagina with cow dung – if she'd still had a husband I would have used long turmeric roots. While we were waiting for the sari my husband was meant to bring, I put a white sari on her and drew a *namam* on her forehead. I thickly coated her hair with coconut oil to dress it well. Then she was carried out to lie under the *pandal* on a couch covered with a sari. I broke a coconut straightaway and prepared a tray with some lit camphor. We put the tray on her chest and the pieces of coconut at her feet. All the women prostrated themselves and then sat around the body, embracing each other. And we cried talking about my mother, about her life.

Suddenly I heard, 'djing, djing, djing, djing … ' and I saw tiny children dancing to the rhythm of the drums. My heart started beating very fast and my tears started flowing. In a while there were other shouts, other drum rolls in the distance. Karani's offerings were arriving, along with our musicians from Velpakkam which my brother had sent to meet my family and receive them at the entrance to the village.

I was worried. I wondered if the offerings were going to be all right, because I was the eldest daughter and people inspect the eldest daughter's offerings the most. I was afraid they would find fault with my husband's offerings and with his family. The procession took some time to reach us, because when the musicians are getting near to the deceased's house, they stop, sing two verses and set off again. After a while I clearly heard Ranga's voice singing. My husband's tray was arriving. I came out first, followed by the other women, beating my breast to greet them. There were lots of people. My eldest sister-in-law was carrying the sari. The youngest was carrying huge garlands of flowers which I'm sure were plaited by the flower seller in Tirulagam: I recognised his way of weaving roses and wormwood flowers. About ten women carried the rest of the offerings: vegetables, rice, seven new jars. Everything for the evening meal after the funeral, except for salt and water. I saw my husband behind the women and about twenty elders from the *ceri*. In the end they'd got there quickly because there isn't a coach that runs directly between Karani and Velpakkam: they'd had to walk several kilometres and cross the river. Behind me I heard people making comments, 'Come and see! The eldest daughter's offerings are arriving with the music!' I was pleased that people were appreciative.

The women soon left the procession and came to put the trays down at my mother's feet. Again I took a coconut from one of the trays and I broke it. With a little camphor I put the two pieces on the tray resting on my mother's chest and I sobbed, 'Ayo, Mum! You're going away to a good place leaving me all alone on this earth! Protect me! Look after me well!' My sisters-in-law and the other women immediately took me in their arms and the songs of lament started. They began as usual with the story of the crow:

> Ayo, the crow has not flown for me!
> Those who saw it told me nothing about it!
> Ayo, the eagle has not flown for me!
> Those who saw it told me nothing about it!

Crows always bring bad news. When a crow runs in front of your house more than once, a visitor will come. But if a crow comes and caws on your roof, or if you see two crows kissing, it's a bad sign. That means the women of the house will cry and embrace and so someone will die soon. That's why crows, the bearers of bad news, are always mentioned at the start of the laments.

When we had finished, the funeral orchestra from Velpakkam played and then they made way for the *naiyandi* musicians of Karani. I heard our boys clear their throats and get their drums ready. I went out straightaway to listen and the other women followed me. Rangam had dressed as a woman as usual. He wore a tiny bodice. For breasts he'd used two halves of a coconut shell, leaving a tiny tuft at the end to stick out like nipples. Around his waist, just above his pubic hair, he wore a little skirt like a young girl's, all gathered up so it would swirl easily, swell and lift up while he was dancing. Under his little skirt, of course, he had his pouch. His make-up was immaculate, his face well-powdered, his eyes well done, red lipstick and a beautiful *pottu* on his forehead. He wore bracelets on his forearms and had a beautiful thick plait ending in velvet pompoms embroidered with pearls. He was a great success, very attractive, more than an ordinary woman, more like a woman in films. Vinayagan, who is stockier, played his young lover. He had a big moustache painted on his face with the tips twisted right up and a red turban. Don't go thinking that they're queers, now! They're all young lads from Anban's bunch: six well-matched boys, the same height, the same build, four musicians and two dancers. They are married now, anyway. They're a beautiful sight and they've travelled a lot.

Oh what a rhythm, Sinnamma, what a rhythm when they started to play! At first they weren't really singing: it was some rhythms, some steps:

> Hey! salak, salakek salak, salakan,
> Hey! salak, salakan
> Hey! salak, salak
> Hey! atchag, atchagatan, tillagatan.

They jumped, they were as light as tamarind seeds. They were warming up the atmosphere. Their eyes were as red as gourd ivy berries. The crowd grew bigger. No one had gone to work in the *ceri*. The boy went up to the woman, playing it up, and touched her nipples. Both of them made rude gestures, still marking out the rhythm with their voices:

> Hey! alak, eh tilak
> Hey! salak, eh salak ...

And the boy started the first verse:

> Walk across these roads lined with trees, *nanna*, come,
>   o girl!
> Cross and come from Sandipet
>   o girl!
> Walk along these roads lined with trees, *nanna*, come,
>   o girl!
> We will flee, the two of us, to Kollaru.

After that first verse the drums beat very fast. The dancers were miming the lovers, dancing cheek to cheek, mouth to mouth. Ranga was exactly like a woman, you see. With his smooth skin he must have turned Vinayagan on! They were rubbing up against each other, groin to groin, dancing as if they were delirious. The little bells on their ankles followed the rhythm of their steps, faster and faster. They breathed in gasps:

> Hey! ahum, hey! ahum, hey! ahum, hey! ahum ...

just like a couple 'doing it'. We women put our saris in front of our mouths, laughing and giggling. And, seeing us laughing, they added more rude gestures, saying, 'Atchagat, tillagat!' and making their breasts go up and down. They're beautiful, those two boys, and a little bit wild: that's why they're comfortable doing all that. They sing another verse which I love:

> Beside the wine stall, hey! your mother,
> I went to weed the field of oats,

Inside the wine stall, hey! your mother!
He tied a little *tali* on me:
Hey! alagata, hey! atchagata, hey! alagata, hey! atchagat ...

And the rhythm set off again even more beautifully. All the kids gathered round and started dancing like them. Everyone was there. To tell you the truth, it's only the dead who aren't watching on these occasions! That's how it happens with us in the country, whether it's a *kambattam* or a Pariah, people sing and dance while they're waiting for the relatives to arrive and up to the burial: the point is to finish life cheerfully. It's not the way you do it or the Brahmins. There was nothing for your father's death, Sinnamma. I wanted at least to sing a lament and take you in my arms, but at the entrance they said, 'Viramma, Viramma, no laments here!' When I told them that evening at the *ceri* that father had died, they all wanted to bring trays and come with the orchestra, of course. But I stopped them, saying, 'No, no! Everything happens in silence with them, like the Brahmins!' I was very sorry, Sinnamma, not to be able to sing laments for your father because you made me sing them on an ordinary day and then, on that day, you did nothing! In my sorrow I would have sung beautiful laments. Well, I do understand: you were in pain and that's not how you do it. As for the Brahmins! Not only is there nothing – no drums, no music. But what's more, they carry the dead on their shoulders and run with them like thieves! (*Laughs.*) They pick up speed leaving their houses and don't stop until they reach the cremation grounds, without making any noise. We are cheerful people and never hold any funerals without songs, without music, without laments.

Burials are even more cheerful than marriages. It's a sort of tribute, a feast which we offer to the dead before they leave us. We don't know if we'll be together again in our next life. And then, as far as other people are concerned, beautiful funerals are a sign of pride on the part of the dead person's family. Friends, relatives and neighbours will appreciate the display. If you don't do it, they'll say, 'Poor soul, with no country or cardinal points, there's no one to give him an honourable burial, no one to hire an orchestra.'

We Pariahs are a caste who express ourselves by noise. You'll find the best weepers among us. Everyone knows each other in this village and each time someone dies, we go and sing and cry and tell beautiful stories about the dead. We also sing these laments amongst ourselves as part of our everyday life or in the fields. The women who know beautiful laments teach them to others. We make them up. They just come to us and we really start crying, just from singing.

The other day our Great Reddiar's mother died. We women of the *ceri* brought trays. I took the Reddi's wife in my arms and we wept. Of course we began the laments in Tamil, with great sobs after each regret. But the women in the Reddi's family sing in Telugu and at the end they just give a little sigh, 'ahum!', no sobbing like us at all.[1]

Anyway, everything went off well for my mother. The *naiyandi* orchestra and the orchestra of *totti* took turns to play. While the young ones went off to drink, the funeral orchestra played again and their laments sunk everybody back into sadness. The *totti* may be old but they dance as well and to a rhythm that is a match for the young. Drunkenness carries them along. Everyone drinks at funerals, from the the leader of mourning to the musicians. It's the rhythm and alcohol that inspires the musicians. They sang,

> Mother had a dwarf birch tree
> A tree where the cuckoo came to nest!
> If someone should cut off its branches
> Where would our cuckoo nest?

> While taking some butter in a saucepan, o my uncle,
> O Manmadan worthy of Rati, o Rati beautiful as the parrot,[2]
> While churning in a ringing churn for our mother
> We hear the drums of death in ceremony.

These are not really laments: they're the song of the dead. Drunk men can't sing laments like us. They improvise on the life of the deceased or sing what comes into their head and the alcohol inside them is their guide. They each get five rupees as well as the meal and they've got at least three rupees of palm wine in their belly on top of the five rupees. They were tireless at Mum's funeral.

When the whole family arrived next morning, we drew a second bath with the seven jars and all the women of the family took part. After the bath we dressed the body in the beautiful sari my husband had brought. Then the launderer spread a white *soman* on Mum and every member of the family put a handful of rice on her body: the rice brought by kith and kin. Finally the body was put on the stretcher and well tied down so it wouldn't move on the way. That's when I cried with all my heart, Sinnamma! That's when grief seized me by the stomach, when I felt abandoned, that my blood was leaving me. People who saw me crying were also very upset themselves, because when a daughter is without a mother, that's always sad. Everybody started groaning, 'O aunt, you're going away! O big sister, you're leaving! Ayo, grandmother, you're abandoning us!' When the body left, we stayed at the door of the house, beating our breasts until the procession turned the corner, led by the musicians, who were in a frenzy.

The procession went to the statue of Harichandran.[3] The body was carried round it seven times. Then the men put their palms together in greeting. I think something's read then as well. The *totti* asked Harichandran permission to go to the cremation grounds.[4]

Before burying my mother, the men went round the trench three times, then lowered the body in with the head facing north and the feet south. Finally, to clearly mark the end of the ties that everyone had with the deceased, each of them threw a handful of sand on her and said what their tie was, 'The son-in-law's handful of sand! The eldest nephew's handful of sand!' Afterwards they covered over the hole and shaped it into a mound. They scattered margosa and treebine leaves over it and planted a branch at the head of the tomb. Then my brother walked seven times round the tomb with a little jar filled with water and, on the seventh time, he threw it on the ground. People who cremate throw the jar on the front of the pyre but we bury our dead – apart from the first-borns – because it works out as less expensive. We couldn't afford to cremate everyone! When the rites were finished, our men took a bath at the well in the cremation grounds, because there isn't a river at Velpakkam like the one at Karani.

Meanwhile we had prepared the mourning meal with the rice and vegetables brought on the trays. For the first time since my mother's death, we picked a broom up, just to sweep in front of the house. It's wrong to do any more housework than that. The water jars hadn't been filled and the house hadn't been coated in cow dung. There was only one full jar in front of the door for the men to wash their feet when they came back from the cremation grounds. The women prepared everything while my sister-in-law, my sister and I were sitting there crying. The meal was ready and laid out on a big banana leaf. All my mother's belongings were next to it: her clothes, her betel pouch, everything she liked having on her. We lit an oil lamp to burn for sixteen days and nights. If you don't do that, the soul will become a demon instead of being reincarnated.

At last the men came back from the cremation grounds. They washed their feet and put ash on their forehead before entering the house, my brother-in-law first. He put my mother's jewels next to her clothes and he prostrated himself before the oil lamp. The others prostrated themselves as well and then the people who weren't spending the night left

without saying anything. We served the meal to the other relatives and
the launderer.

On the seventh day my sister and I hosted a meal. While we prepared
it, all my brother's family took an oil bath. Before serving it, we offered
the meal to my mother, putting it on a big banana leaf in the place
where she had passed away. We all prostrated ourselves and prayed. We
embraced each other, my sister-in-law, sister and I, and cried. When
they saw us, the other women joined us. Then we served the meal to
everyone and went our separate ways, fixing the date for the milk
ceremony.

The day before the end of the mourning rites, a messenger left to tell
the whole family. My brother went to tell the Iyer so they could perform
the ceremony. The Iyer of the *ceri* perform the end of mourning rites
for us and also play the funeral drum for certain families in the *ur*: they
go to our Reddiar's and to some very pious Gounder who read the
devotional works. Here in the *ceri*, no one prays, no one reads books like
that.

For the end of the mourning rites, we came back to Velpakkam with
some trays, some rice, vegetables, oil, camphor, cereals, lentils, cumin,
sesame, clothes for my brother, ten little jars, mango branches and blades
of blue grass. We'd also prepared a big tray of sesame balls and sun-
and moon-shaped cakes. There was a crowd under the awning in front
of the house that afternoon. Everyone was talking about Mum.

The next morning my sister-in-law, my sister and I got up very early
to cry. The two Iyer arrived and left for the cremation grounds with my
brother and some men. One Iyer carried a jar of milk with margosa
leaves and milk weed leaf in it. He also carried a tray of sweets and little
statues of Pillaiyar made out of rice and ammi. The other carried what
was needed for the sacrificial fire and a jar of water. The first Iyer put
the jar of milk, the tray of sweets and the statues of Pillaiyar on the
tomb, at the head. Each man then stepped forward to sprinkle the sweets
with milk before prostrating themselves and then taking a bath. My
brother came back with a turban on his head and a *soman* on his shoulders, followed by the other men.

We waited for them next to the statue of Harichandran. A square of
earth under the banyan tree had been covered with cow dung and surrounded with oil lamps, camphor and sticks of incense. A measure of
paddy had been poured into the middle of the square. The jar of water
was put on top and the second Iyer started the fire ceremony. Everyone
had a blue grass stalk wound between their little finger and ring finger,

and another knotted round their wrist. One after the other we walked towards the fire. Each of us said our name, then threw the two stalks and some cereals into the fire, spilt a little cow urine round the water jar and gave the Iyer a coin. The Iyer recited a mantra to each of us. When everyone had finished, my brother broke a coconut in front of the statue of Harichandran. He took the water jar and we all went back to the house. I've already told you that if a sterile woman is given this jar, she'll become pregnant that year. But because none of us was in that state, my brother piously put the jar in the centre of the house next to the oil lamp. Then we quickly spread the banana leaves on the ground and we put all sorts of vegetables on top, uncooked rice, lentils, tamarind, peppers and a one-rupee coin, before prostrating ourselves at the feet of the Iyer who then left, taking what they were owed. These priests are just Pariahs like us, Sinnamma, but we call them Iyer because they officiate for us and we respect them because there are gods in their houses which they serve. They eat fish and chicken, but not beef. We don't have any gods in our houses, apart from this lance.[5]

FOURTEEN

Demons and *dharma*

The dead man's soul waits for the decision of the Kingdom of Yama until the sixteenth day. That's why his relatives keep all his belongings in the place where he gave his last sigh. We prepare the dishes he used to like and the lamp burns day and night. The sixteenth day is the day of separation. The soul leaves the body and the grave and flies off to the new life Yama has given it.[1] I could tell this with my sister-in-law: she came to see the house, her clothes, her crockery and all of us before flying away, and she left without making a noise. Everything had been moved about but nothing was broken. But we heard the lash of the whip Yama gave my eldest brother-in-law. It must have been midday when we heard someone breathing as if he was in a hurry: 'Ahum! Ahum! Ahum!' He was in the street and then he went behind the house. The cow that was tied up there got free and started running all over the place. My eldest brother-in-law went round the house and then in front of the drumstick tree, which broke in two as if it had been sawn apart! We get to know more or less what Yama decides for the deceased because the dead are always coming and telling us in our dreams.

People who commit suicide are different. They become demons, that's for sure! Here at Karani several people have brought about their own death. All of them have been changed into Mohini, Budam, Mini-suprayan or Katteri and then they've come back to disturb us. That's how we knew.[2]

I'll tell you a story about this. It happened at Perukkarur, a village near Velpakkam. One day, the people of the *ceri* over there clubbed together to buy a pig – not for a festival, but just to eat pork. One man called Viramani, when he'd eaten his pork curry, foolishly set off for the market when the sun was at its highest instead of staying at home. You must never set foot outside after eating pork. In those days our men didn't go and look after the harvests or check the irrigation: no one wanted to risk being slapped by a demon lurking in the fields and fall seriously ill. But Viramani had gone to the market. Night had fallen, he'd eaten and gone to bed. But before dawn, he heard someone saying to him, 'Eh, Viramani, are you getting up? Go on, come and irrigate! Then we'll go to the well.' Viramani had to irrigate a field of chillis. When he heard himself being called, he woke up straightaway thinking that it was very late. He quickly got his things and set off for the well. The man who'd woken him up was walking in front, a stick in his hand, the rope and water skin on his shoulder. In those days there wasn't a pump like now: there was a shaft-well. The man got there first and without saying a word, took his place on top of the pole. Viramani caught up with him and took hold of the bottom. And both of them started working the shaft-well. When the field of peppers had been irrigated, the man kept going without saying a word. The water flowed into the field of aubergines next to it and then into a third plot. The man went up and down so fast on the pole that the shaft-well seemed to be working all on its own. Viramani watched the well run completely dry while he was overcome by tiredness. He started wondering how the man could work the pole for so many hours without getting out of breath, without sweating and without stopping. All he could do was guide the water skin into the channel. He shouted 'Pa! Stop for a little bit, Pa! I want to go and pee. Wait for me for a minute!' The field of chillis wasn't very far from the *ceri*. When the man stopped working the pole, Viramani ran home as fast he could and shut himself in. A little later it was the man's turn to arrive running and he banged on the door saying, 'Hey, Viramani! Give me a little pork curry, da! You stuffed yourself all on your own without thinking of me. Give me a little curry, da!' Then Viramani understood what he was dealing with and he answered bravely, 'Here, come and get your curry! Come nearer!' And when the other stretched out his hand for the pork, Viramani cut it off with a very sharp knife. He picked up the hand, covered it with a wicker basket and put a heavy grindstone on the basket. When Viramani lifted up the basket the next day to see if the hand was still there, there

was only a cat's paw in its place. The next night he heard a voice calling
him, 'Dei! Viramani! Give me back my hand! Give me back the hand
you cut off!' For three days and three nights, Viramani kept him running around like that without giving back the hand. Finally, brave as
ever, he answered with the question, 'Will you start asking me for pork
curry again?'

'No, no!' the other said, 'I won't ask you for it any more, I'll go away
immediately! It's because you smelled so good of pork curry when you
were going to the market that I followed you. I want pork so much.
Give me back my hand now, I'm on my way, I won't come back any
more.'

Viramani threw him the cat's paw and he didn't hear from him again.
He was a healthy man who'd committed suicide after arguing with his
wife. He had become a Mini while waiting for his true death and he had
been tempted by the smell of pork curry on Viramani, who had been
very reckless.

The souls of those who commit suicide always wait where they killed
themselves, whether they threw themselves in a well or hung themselves
from a tree. In our countryside we don't go near those places when the
sun's at its height or when it's late. If it's a tree, we cut it down immediately, making sure we uproot it completely so there's nothing left:
then we cut it up and make logs. We burn the rope in petrol. In the *ur*
the daughter of a Gounder hung herself on the rod of a fan after an
unsuccessful love affair. The blacksmith took down the rod and had it
melted down before putting in another. Yes, that's what's got to be
done, otherwise the dead person's soul will stay where they killed themselves and trouble the whole family. If it happened outdoors, the dead
will hang around until the end of their time looking for their food and
if they don't find any, they'll eat any old thing like a pig.

Another woman in the *ur* committed suicide a few years ago by
swallowing baeltree fruit. She was a married woman who was having
relations with a guy from Tirulagam and she found herself pregnant.
She never used to go out, but she went to the edge of a *ragi* field where
there was a baeltree. She quietly collected the fruit and went behind a
copse. There she reduced the fruit to a powder and swallowed the
powder in a little castor oil which she'd brought. She went back to her
house and went to bed as if nothing had happened. An hour later she
was writhing in pain, burning with fever and salivating heavily. Panic-
stricken, her mother-in-law called all the neighbours. In the country
there's always someone who sees everything, who knows everything.

The old woman Kuppu came up and told what she'd seen, 'Ah, grand-mother! Don't you know where I saw her when I was going to graze the cows? She was in the copse behind the *ragi* field, grinding up baeltree fruit. That must be what she's swallowed!'

As soon as they knew that, no one wanted to keep this woman in the house. The poor thing died in hospital at Pondy and they didn't even take her back home afterwards! In the *ceri* we would have given her a glass of droppings dissolved in water to make her be sick straightaway, or a glass of tamarind juice in which a piece of copper had been soaked. That makes you vomit up everything you've swallowed and it acts as an antidote. Poor woman! She did wrong, but she could have been saved. The family didn't want to face up to the shame of it and they let her die. That's how it is in the *ur* when a love affair is discovered, there's no other way of escaping the humiliation. Anyway the poor thing hasn't come and bothered anyone since.

That happens: demons who don't do anything and don't attack any-body, like the Paunch. The Paunch is his nickname. His parents, with all respect, had called him Sukumaran but we nicknamed him the Paunch because of his enormous belly. This story happened to me one day when my son had dysentery. As the little one couldn't walk very far to go, I had taken him to the field behind the house and I was sitting in the stable beside it waiting. Suddenly I saw a white shape! I opened my eyes wide to see better: it was a man dressed in a brilliant white *soman* which hung down to the ground. My heart started beating hard, as if it was going to fall out. I had recognised the Paunch, the husband of Ammapponu. He had died at Pondy hospital after a stomach operation: apparently the air got in when he was opened up and he died after suffering a lot! He was a good carpenter who used to work in the *ur*. He was good at making meat-safes and cupboards for jars of sesame oil. He had never had children with Ammapponu. She had a lover who she lives with today. And there he was, the Paunch, standing facing me! He didn't move. I didn't shout and I didn't say anything to my son for fear of terrifying him; he was very young and was just starting to look after the cows. I was afraid he'd spill his stomach in one go if I told him what I was seeing. But he'd seen the Paunch as well and hadn't said anything either so as not to terrify me, thinking, 'If I tell Mum, she'll be afraid and start screaming!' I quickly took my little one by the hand and we went back to the house. I lit some camphor straightaway and an oil lamp which we didn't put out at night. That very night my husband had to go and check the fields being irrigated and sleep the night out there. After the evening meal he set off with his lantern and all three of us stayed behind, my two children and me. The evenings my husband's away, the neighbours bring their mats over and keep us company. We chew betel and tell stories and sing songs. Everything was going well, but before going to sleep I went behind the house to have a look. The Paunch was still there, standing stock still! That time I screamed insults at him, 'Come on then so I can hit you with my shoe! Why do you come and see me, eh? What have I got to do with you?' And I turned round to the others to tell them everything, 'It's true, you know! He hasn't got any reason to come and find me! I've got nothing to do with him: he lived over by the launderers' and I live here, by the common land!' When I shouted, he disappeared, I don't know how.

The next day he came back again and that time he terrified everybody in the *ceri*. Then people knew that I hadn't been making it up the day before and that I'd really seen the Paunch. The poor man, he'd come to see what had happened to his belongings which he hadn't been able to make the most of. He'd earned a lot of money when he was alive, but he hadn't been able to enjoy life and he didn't have children: now somebody else was reaping the rewards.

Another time I was at Koraiyur, at my daughter's. Just opposite her house is a big well. I was drowsing in the house when suddenly I saw a man on the edge of the well, a short-set, swarthy guy, and a tree was coming out of the well, a tulip tree with beautiful branches which was casting its shade over this man. And there he was showing me his ten fingers and saying, 'Oh! I'm not going to leave you here! I'm going to take you with me, yes, I won't leave you behind!' I started screaming, 'Ah! Come here so I can beat you with my broom, with my shoe, you donkey! Who are you? And do you know who I am? I am a guest here of my daughter's! I'll twist off your ten fingers if you touch me, you bloodstain!' Sinnamma, nothing was moving around me. The lamp next to my mat had stayed alight, the pot of rice was still on the hearth and the store with its two sacks of paddy was untouched. The others were asleep. My daughter woke up and understood what was going on. When day broke, she took me to an exorcist, a brick seller who cured me with margosa branches. Well, at least cured me for a while.

Because I saw him again, that swarthy one! Another time I had taken twenty kilos of well-hulled, well-cleaned tamarind to my daughter's. Miniyamma doesn't let me do much work there and she's always making me take it easy. So, that afternoon I was having a rest in the house. And then Sinnamma, I'm not making anything up, I'm being very straight with you: that juice drinker came back, black as a bitter apple. It's the truth, Sinnamma, I'm telling you with my hands clasped: he took off my clothes and put his tail in my sex! I started trembling with my whole body – I swear on my *tali*: I couldn't find the words any more, I didn't have the strength to speak. I ended up calling out in a quavering voice, 'Miniyamma! Miniyamma! He's sat on me. He's lifted up my sari and put his tail in my sex!' Miniyamma answered, 'It's got to be my eldest brother-in-law, Mum! He was a bum who wasn't afraid of anybody impor-tant in the village, any Reddi or any Chetti! A rogue who spent his time drinking and playing cards. He died after terrible suffering, Mother! He's the one who's attacked you. Come on! We're going back to the brick seller, he'll give you a talisman!' Do you understand, Sinnamma? That guy was the actual brother-in-law of my daughter! He had a wife and two children, who now live in the next door house. But one time he lived in Mini-yamma's house. That piece of dirt who loved cards so much and died in terrible suffering at the wine stall. Apparently he wasn't even taken back home, he was buried over there. That's the queer with his fat moustache who came back to where he'd lived and violated me! So I had myself exorcised again. I was given a talisman which I always keep on me. And since then, whether I go to my sister's with my husband or without him, whether it's for a joyful time or a time for mourning, I never spend a night there. After this business, when I got back to Karani – I tell you this, Sinnamma, but even my son doesn't know it and he doesn't have to – I dug a hole under the doorstep and I buried some ammi in it to stop that guy getting in. I'm afraid that juice drinker will come and possess me again. That dirty widower died young without enjoying his wife and without having his full share of the pleasures of life. After his death he became a Mohini like people who die at a crossroads. And the Mohini are terrifying – they're furious like that son of a buffalo!

Not all our dead turn out like that. Only certain people who've carried out their *dharma* badly end up in that state and so they attack us while they're waiting to be reincarnated. They disturb us, they make objects move – winnowing fans, slippers – to show that they're there. And the main thing is that they visit friends and acquaintances rather than their relatives. That's why we insult them at the top of our voices in the country, 'Hey, whore! Wait till I catch you with my broom! Go on off to your mother then! Go home! What are you doing here, coming and pestering us?' Yes, that's how you've got to talk to them. We people in hell are afraid of these breaths of wind, these shades.

But we're not afraid of people who've had an ordinary death. Quite the opposite: we think of them a lot: they've always lived with us on this earth and we never forget them. Even now, when I buy something – some new clothes, some cloth, some sweets – as soon as I get back home I put it down straightaway where my little ones breathed their last sigh. I light a little bit of camphor, I offer them what I've bought and I prostrate myself. It's only after that that I hand out what I've bought to the others and help myself. The children I've lost! How couldn't I think about them? When they were with us, they enjoyed eating this fruit or that sweet and wearing those clothes. Now they're dead, who knows how they are or where they are? Good fortune or bad fortune, our dead are like gods to us. We call on them at difficult times, we pray to them to help us. For the marriage of my daughter Sundari for example, I'd got almost all the money I needed but I was still a hundred rupees short. I prayed to my mother, my sister-in-law and all my children. I said to them, 'Ayo, all of you who are dead, you my children, enter into the heart of the Reddiar so he'll let us have another hundred-rupee note! Let me celebrate our Sundari's marriage the right way!' And I got what I wanted.

Those dead have carried out their *dharma* well, Sinnamma, and the fruit of their *dharma* protects us.

It's my parents' *dharma* which protects me, and my *dharma* will do good for my children. What is *dharma*? It's behaving well in life, being upright, virtuous, generous, patient and not being like Kali. It's being humble, obedient, discreet and affectionate. It's speaking politely and decently, with discretion; it's using fine language. If I behave like that, people will say, 'There's a good woman! She came here as a little girl, she grew up here, she brought twelve children into the world, she has even cared for five grandchildren, she's led a respectful and dignified life and here she is leaving for the cremation grounds with just as much dignity!' What people will say about me is the *dharma* I'll have carried out and that's what will protect my son. People will say to him, 'Dei, Anban! It's because of your mother's *dharma* that things are going well for you now!'

Performing a good act is also carrying out your *dharma*. You're the one who should do that for me, Sinnamma, because you can afford it. And anyway, you've already done it! Here! The sari you offered me, the money you've given me, those are good acts which you performed to-wards me. I was given your presents, but I can't give you ones like them. So I give you my good wishes, that's to say I give you a share of my *dharma* so it follows you and protects you in that country far away where you're going with Sir and your children, and so you'll be fortunate and in good health.

Everyone has their duty in life. For example, you say to me, 'Relax! Make yourself at ease, sit down and have a good stretch of your legs!' Well, I have never done that, have you noticed? And I'll never do it! It doesn't matter that I'm like a mother to you or that in the bottom of my heart I think of you as my daughter, you've been born into a higher caste than me. I owe you respect: I'd never stretch out my legs talking to you. That's my *dharma* as well! One day, when I came to your house and we were talking on the terrace, your father came up to bring you a letter. I shook when I saw him. I got up, covered my back with my sari and lowering my head, I went into a corner. He said to me straightaway, 'Stay sitting down, Viramma!' and then he went downstairs. I only sat down when he'd disappeared. That, you see, Sinnamma, is respect. When he said to me, 'Stay sitting down, Viramma!' he must have thought, 'Here's a respectful, humble woman. She's not insolent.' And that good thought about me is *dharma*, whose merits will be useful to my descendants.

Those who carry out *dharma* badly lack respect. They're wounding and slanderous, even in arguments. Now you have to keep a sense of moderation. I say that, even though in our caste people argue so much that they'll say anything in moments of anger. So, when a woman is living her *dharma* badly and losing all sense of moderation in an argument, people will say of her, 'Ah! Listen to what she's saying! I hope death takes her, that dirty widow who won't stop hurling abuse! I hope a snake burrows a hole in her breast! I hope abscesses fill up her mouth! I hope someone takes off her *tali*! Will she still be able to make offerings on a banana leaf? May her first-born swallow it!' And everything that can be said about someone like that will weigh on her *karma* and her descendants will feel it. When someone's suffering from an incurable sickness or is stuck in black poverty even when he's given all the help that's possible, people in the country say, 'What on earth can his father and mother have done? It's the weight of their *karma* that he is atoning for now!' And people say to young people out of work, 'If your mother had carried out her *dharma* you would be benefiting from it now. If you haven't got work it must be because she didn't do what she should!' But they tell me, 'Dei! That old woman is still stuck in the old days!'

They don't believe in anything any more, those youngsters. But the truth is that you must behave correctly in life! They'll see: they'll have accounts to settle with Yama! You can be rich and still die on the pavement because of the weight of *karma*. But when you're on the pavement

and you carry out *dharma*, you can go to the Kingdom of Siva! Look at
people who've got money and gnaw away at the poor's share: who insult
us when we go and work for them; who don't pay us enough. We poor,
what can we do? We curse them, 'Ayo! May the thunder of Heaven and
the Heights fall on your skull! May you be reborn as a dog or a lizard!'
That's all we can say. But that will make the weight of *karma* that their
offspring will have to endure heavier. And in the Resting Place of Yama,
they will have to answer the god's questions. And depending on what
they have done, they will be reborn as a dog, a donkey, a horse or, if it's
very serious, as a lizard, a serpent, a chameleon or a scorpion, while those
people who've carried out their *dharma* well will go and take their place
in the Kingdom of Siva and they won't have to be reborn again.

Since we're talking of rebirth, I'm sure that Isvaran will make those
juice drinkers who killed our mother Indira Gandhi come back as snakes!
The good she did for us poor! When I heard the news, I couldn't hold
back my tears or my rage! We were at the well filling our jars when we
were told: she wasn't dead yet. People were crying on the radio as well.
Loudspeakers were put up so that we could follow the news.[3] A *pandal*
was put up here and in the *ur* with a big photograph of our Mother
surrounded by a large garland of flowers. Incense sticks burned day and
night. We women sang funeral songs for three days in a row. In the *ur*,
cars drove round the streets without stopping. The important people
met up at the Reddiar's and another group assembled at the Gounder's,
the brother of the schoolmaster. I kept my son at home, I was afraid
he'd get mixed up in the troubles at Tirulagam. But in fact everything
stayed calm here, despite the coming and going between Pondy and
Karani. There were more fights at Delhi, the radio said.[4]

The day the ashes were scattered, fried chickpeas were handed out to
everybody in the *ur*. Poor Mother! Poor Indira Gandhi! She had suffered
so much for us! They say the people who killed her were part of her own
guard. The papers said that they were from a caste of brawlers, wait, they
said the caste of Sikhs, guys who look like Viran with a thick moustache
and a beard. Did you see their photographs in the paper? They say that
it was for some caste business that the guys took their revenge. That
caste rose up against our Mother who was in power in Delhi. They
couldn't accept being governed by a female and they killed her. I saw the
film of the funeral in Tirulagam: it was the first time I'd gone to the
cinema and all I did was cry. How beautiful she was in her red sari and
all the flowers!

FIFTEEN

The caste of thieves

The Kepmari are the caste of thieves. It's their families' trade. The women go stealing from town to town, especially in very big cities like Delhi, Mayuram, Kumbakonam, Bombay and Madras. They never steal here in the village. The men steal cheques and rob banks. The women steal from temples and at festivals and fairs. They speak several languages and when they're at work, they dress as if they're rolling in it: chains, necklaces, arms covered in bracelets. Besides, they really are rich. The real rich couldn't match them!

There's a street of Kepmari in Karani, a little out of the centre. They've got lots of paddy fields and we work for them as agricultural workers. The women don't eat beef. They perform a *puja* to Kakkappattan, the god of their line a few days before going out stealing. The sanctuary's near the river, in a silent place where you can't hear a grindstone or a mortar. Kakkappattan is terrifying, terrifying enough to make you miscarry! They retreat there into his sanctuary with their husbands and children for three days and three nights. They take all they need to cook while they wait for the god to give them permission to go and steal, and they bathe three times a day in the river and keep their clothes wet. They only go back home and get ready to go out stealing when Kakkappattan on his horse goes tac tac tac with his tongue. They can stay there a whole month waiting for his permission.

They mostly go to the big temples during important festivals. People don't mistrust them because of the way they're dressed with all their jewels. Apparently they use a medicine, a spray which they put on people's neck or arms and then they take off the chains and bracelets with a gold-cutting stone. They do it very quickly, just long enough for you to shut your eye and open it again, and people don't feel a thing. They know all the techniques, eh, it's their trade! When the jewels have been cut off, they don't go away. Several of them always surround their victim and their children are with them, some even as young as your son. It's the little ones who take the jewels to a man who stands a little way off. When they've got enough, the man takes them back to the village with fifteen- or twenty-thousand rupees' worth of jewels or money!

Those women aren't afraid of a thing. They're ready for anything! The police van came to Karani several times to arrest them. We women of the *ceri* would go to the roadside to see them leave for prison. Sometimes we were sad for them and we'd cry: poor women, taken away by the police like that, the shame of it! We'd say to them, 'You're as beautiful as sugar candy, why do you steal? Why do you have such a trade?' But it didn't embarrass them at all! They'd get all comfortable in the van without feeling any shame and let themselves be taken to the station. It has to be said that they'd never stay there very long. Two days later they'd be back in the village. Someone had stood bail to get them released.

Even so, one year Indira Gandhi had all the country's thieves hand-cuffed and arrested![1] The Kepmari were really afraid when they were told the police were coming. They quickly threw everything in the aubergine and groundnut fields: money, gold coins, jewels, everything, everything! And when the police left, they picked it all up. Well, almost all, because two of our people had got their hands on the gold. Valli didn't know what had happened. When she was going to graze her cows near there, she happened to find two half-sovereign coins shining in the sun. People came and threatened her but she held her own. She said, 'I didn't steal those coins: I didn't take them out of anyone's bag. I found them on the ground when I was walking along: I'm keeping them!' And she was able to marry her daughter with them! Tangavelu also found a gold chain on his way back from ploughing Bangaru Reddi's field. He held out against the threats as well and he didn't give the chain back. He sold it and had a brick house built for him. You must have noticed it. There's only one brick house in the *ceri*!

Viramma singing

Manikkam,
Viramma's husband

Anban, Amsa
and their daughters

Sundari and Miniyamma,
Viramma's daughters

The main stre

ceri in Karani

The main stree

r in Karani

Planting out rice

The seven *totti* of the *paraimelam*

Viramma crushing
the paddy

Preparing the oxen for the Pongal

The penitents' procession

DMK electioneering in Karani

That's the only time the Kepmari have been afraid. Since then, I'll tell you, the police don't come and arrest them any more. They say the Gounder put in a word in high places and made sure that the vans didn't keep coming here the whole time. It was giving the village a bad reputation. But still, if a police van did come, there'd be one particular Kepmari woman who'd take care of it: the one with seven children who's stayed as fresh as a water-lily. She can handle the police, from the Collector to the Deputy Inspector, from the pen-pusher to the subaltern. Everyone knows her, I'll show you her one day, Sinnamma. No one informs against them in the *ur*. First because they never steal in Karani. But also because, when times are hard, they go, one by one, and sell their jewels to the Gounder for a little less than the goldsmiths charge, and so all the money's kept in the *ur*.

I only go to the Kepmari for some agricultural jobs, but Arayi and Larpayi are *padiyal* for them. When we're wondering how these women manage to steal money or jewels when we work for the Reddiar and are scared to steal even a little paddy or some peanuts, Arayi tells us that it all depends on how you dress. If you're just like this, in rags, people are suspicious. You're already called thieves before you've stolen anything. But they go in the front door in cities! They knock on the doors of beautiful houses and ask for something to drink. Then they come out with their routine, saying they come from a long way away and that they'd like to rest for a while on the *tinnai* before setting off. Seeing these well-dressed women, covered in jewels and travelling without men, people don't dare leave them to have a rest outside and they bring them in. So then they go on with their conversation and get into a good position to check the place and find what there is to take. Once they've pulled it off, they come back to the village. At home, they're completely at ease, they talk about their successes and laugh! That's how we know about their methods in the *ceri*!

You should see them when they come back to the village, weighed down with bundles and baggage! They get off at the bus stop and when our men go past with their cart, they make them carry their loads to their houses and they give them two rupees! Once an old woman even gave me three rupees to carry her bundle! As soon as they get back to the village, you can see them in the bar at Tirulagam, even the very old women. They put away litres of brandy: the tables are full of empty bottles and egg and chicken curries. I'm not making anything up, Sinnamma, you can ask anyone in the *ceri*! Coming back from the market, we hang around a bit in front of the bar. They're drunk, talking

loud and bursting out laughing: it's not hard to guess their expedition
was a success! Seeing us there by the bar, they call us. Once Arayi's
boss, who knows me as well, said to me, trying to find the words, 'Hey,
Velpakkatta! Hey, Velpakkatta! What are you saying? You're looking at
me drinking, are you? You want to drink as well? Are you used to
drinking? Do you drink brandy?'

'No, mother', I told her, 'no, I don't like all that. I'm a wife, a woman
who stays at home. I don't have the same habits as you. But if you give
me two rupees, I could chew some betel thinking of you!' And she
threw me a two-rupee note.

A few days later, the Kepmari prepare the *puja* of thanks to Kakkappattan. They have some cocks and three goats killed and they cook a
great *pongal*. Pariahs who work for them get loads of meat that day.
They shave their skull in front of the sanctuary, coat it with sandal
paste and come back with their crockery, all of them, in a tractor trailer.
Then they go and hand out the meat or the offerings to the Kudiyanar:
they accept food from the Kepmari. Besides this *puja* the Kepmari take
charge of one day's expenses during the festival of Draupadi. They do
that in their own way. It's pretty funny.

Nowadays only half of them carry on the trade of thieves. The rest
stay in the village and they've become farmers. Many have bought paddy
fields with the money they've got from their robberies. The fields behind the temple of Ayittalamma belong to them now, they've got several
irrigation pumps and their fields are cultivated.[2] They've become ideal
masters. They've got cattle and they produce milk. To make the work
go faster, they pay a little more than the Reddiar or the Gounder. If our
Reddiar gives six rupees for planting out, they'll give up to eight to
women who know their work and who plant out fast. When we're offered
wages like that, we don't hesitate. We find an excuse for not going to
the Reddiar and we run to work for whoever's offering the most. It's
only normal, but it all leads to arguments between the Reddiar and the
Kepmari. The Grand Reddi calls them together and says, 'Innappa, why
are you giving the coolies such a high wage? I earned my money in my
fields by the sweat of my brow, while you, you go and steal it! You don't
know what it is to earn money! If you suffered to get it, you'd know, but
without tiring yourselves out, you go and steal a stranger's fortune.
We're giving six rupees for weeding out now, ten or even twelve for
working the fields. Why come and put up the prices that everyone pays,
eh?'

The other scratches his head and says, 'Don't get angry! It's true, I was wrong to give more but I had an important job to be done before the rain. That's why!'

That's their defence. This year I asked Arayi's boss to rent me half an acre. I said to him, 'You won't have anything to fear, sir. I've got ten animals in all, that can make ten carts of manure. And I'll grow millet or *ragi* – it's up to you. I'll take good care of the harvest and you'll definitely get your share!'

And he answered, 'We'll see! I'll decide after this year's rains, Velpakkatta.'

SIXTEEN

High and low castes in Karani

All my family is employed at the Grand Reddiar's. My husband takes care of the pumps. The Reddiar owns two which irrigate every day. I collect the cow dung and clean the stable. My daughter Miniyamma helped me until she got married. Sundari has done the same and now it's my daughter-in-law Amsa who works at the Reddiar's. Anban started by looking after the cows. Now he does the important cultivation work with my husband. The reason is that we don't own any land. God only left us these eyes and these hands to earn our living. By working hard at the Reddiar's we've been able to lead our lives in the proper way. We've been able to give Miniyamma and Sundari away in marriage with silver ankle chains and some clothes. We've paid our share of funeral expenses when we've had to. I've been able to buy these jewels for my ears. And when we married Anban, the Reddiar gave Amsa her gold *tali* and her sari. Thanks to the Reddiar, thanks to his fortune – and it's a great one, especially in land – we have enough to eat without worrying. The Reddiar is an important man. Every day or nearly every day he goes to Pondy. The serfs who work at the Reddiar's have their rice guaranteed!

Of all the castes in the *ur*, the Reddiar caste is the highest. They have no equals. The others come after them: the Mudaliar, the Naicker, the Gounder. The Reddiar are the people who don't go to work, they put others to work: fifty, sixty, ninety, two hundred people. Their women don't work and they never go out.

156

I take twenty Paratchi to plant out the Grand Reddi's paddy fields, and they are paid by the day: it takes four Paratchi to plant out four hundred square yards. When we work for the Reddiar, there's no question of us singing. We keep our mouths shut out of respect for the Reddiar, because they're always there in the field watching over us, sitting on their cord bed under a coconut grove or even closer, on the dyke under the shade of an umbrella. Their serf – for the Grand Reddi, that's me – directs the work and checks to see that everything is going right, 'Hey, plant out here! Hey, Saroja! That corner over there's not done!' But towards midday, as soon as the Reddiar goes home to eat, I start up with the first song. After our husbands, the Reddiar are the people we respect and fear the most. We are their serfs. It's different with other land-owners, we sing as much as we want and anyway, they like it. Sometimes when we work for the Naicker, we joke with him. We can even make fun of him. We shout, 'Yennayya! You never stop giving your wife children! She's pregnant every year like a bitch and you'll lose your strength, you won't have anything left, even if you eat melted butter and curds. Come over here a bit, ayya, come and see if your strength is a match for us beef eaters when it comes to real work like this!' It makes him laugh to hear us going on like that! That's how we joke with him, Sinnamma, and with the other landowners for whom we're not serfs. The Naicker own lots of land. They've got some rented out, and pumps and stables full of ani-mals: cows and goats, and they make plenty of milk.

We make fun of Brahmins as well, Sinnamma. When the *pappan* is about to walk past on the dyke, we quickly make up a little song about him like this:

> It's the *pappan*, *adi-pappan*
> Who irrigates by digging a hole,
> Who fishes in there for a dish of crabs,
> Who fishes in there for a dish of crabs,
> While drinking the juices of a young girl
> That very night, there was no moon
> And his sleep was troubled,
> That man with the *pottu* in the shape of the moon,
> Wants to welcome Virayi so much!!
> Nanna, nanna, nanana,
> Nanna, nannana, nananana ...

The bile wells up in his mouth when he hears that. It disgusts him, he spits on the ground, wipes his lips and hurries on. Have you seen Brahmins eat crab? Even just hearing about it makes them want to throw up! Brahmins own nothing or almost nothing apart from the temple land. We never go and work for them, they only employ Kudiyanar. That's why we can make fun of them. The *pappan* are the Reddiar's priests for marriages, the *puja* of the ancestors, for this or that rite and for the funeral ceremonies on the sixteenth day as well. They are lower than the Reddiar and like the other servants, they get un-cooked food from them. They take it raw because they're in contact with God and they must be pure: they have the food cooked at their homes. We prefer to get it cooked: it saves us the time and cost of cooking. One day at the Reddiar's, I heard the Brahmin mumbling his prayers as he raised the sacrificial fire. (*Laughs.*) I was looking through the window when the Grand Reddiar's mother saw me and chased me away: 'Eh, Velpakkatta! Get out of here! Get out of here! Don't look at that!' And it's true that we mustn't see any of it. The Reddiar and the Brahmins speak both languages, Tamil and Telugu. They are vegetarians, they eat lots of melted butter, yoghurt and fruit, and they drink milk. In the country there are no other castes that can match them.

But Karani has definitely got castes! Reddiar, Mudaliar, Gounder, Udaiyar, Tulukkan, Vaniyan, Ambattan, Komutti, Vannan. In the *ceri* there are Koravan, Sakkili, Vannan as well, *talaiyari*. There are Tomban towards Selvipatti and Pakkanur. No one accepts them into the castes.[1] They're pig rearers. They live with their animals. The Tomban is very low, but I've already told you, Sinnamma, he's become very rich. His pigs breed fast, he feeds them on abandoned ground, it costs him nothing and he earns plenty of money selling them. One year we had a big argument when I had rented a plot of land near the temple of Aiyanar from the Reddiar and I'd sowed it with *ragi*. One afternoon I was at my door oiling my hair when Sinnappayya ran up to tell me, 'Aunt! Aunt! Tomban's pigs are wrecking your *ragi* field! Come and see, quickly! Quickly!' I put up my hair, tying it up on one side, and followed Sinnappayya who ran ahead. The kids who used to graze the cows over there had discovered the pigs and sent Sinnappayya to tell me. 'You know, aunt, when the Tomban kids saw there was nobody in the field, they brought their pigs right up to it and went swimming in the river. When we were going past with the cows and saw the pigs in the field, we let you know straightaway, aunt!' I was boiling with rage. I told the kids to catch the pigs, but those dirty beasts, they're smart! They made us run all over the place and they kept on getting away. The Tomban kids saw what was going on from a distance and quickly got out of the water to round up their pigs but even so Sinnappayya managed to capture a piglet which we tied to a stake. Then the Grand Tomban arrived and beat his little pig-keepers. I said to him, 'Innappa! Your pigs got into my field. They've ruined part of my crop. What are you going to do?'

'Please don't get angry,' he answered, 'I didn't know what was happening. We didn't let them loose in your field on purpose. I'll be very careful next time!'

'Ah! That's what you think! You think we're going to let it drop. A crop ruined, a crop filled with such beautiful ears! I want compensation. I'm going to appeal to the Reddiar: he'll decide for himself!'

That's how I answered the Tomban and Sinnappayya ran to tell the Reddiar but he was having a rest. Sinnappayya waited for the Reddiar to get up and told him the story and he told him he'd come after he'd drunk his milk. Meanwhile we'd left the piglet tied up and gone into the shade. I had enough time to make myself a chew of betel. When I heard the Reddiar arriving on his motorbike, I got up and spat out my betel. I went towards him and said, 'Innanga! I've had my grain ruined! How do you expect us to pay you rent now? What do you think of that?'

The Reddiar turned to the Tomban and said, 'Innappa! What do you have to say to that? I see only two answers: either you let her have the piglet or you compensate her in money for her losses.'

The Tomban, squeezing together his legs and hugging his chest with both arms, begged the Reddiar, 'It's my fault but what's to be done? I didn't do it on purpose. I can only give ten rupees. Next time I'll make sure the kids don't bring my pigs this way, Sami!'

But I didn't want to hear any of it and I argued, 'How do you expect me to pay you the rent, Sami? How could I give you five sacks of *ragi* after this damage? I want thirty rupees in compensation!'

The Reddiar calmed both of us down by suggesting twenty-five rupees. Then the Tomban said, 'Have that pig untied and give it to the woman who cultivates your field. I cannot pay that amount!'

And that's how I came home with a piglet. I gave half a rupee to Sinnappaya and ten *paice* to each kid. They went and bought doughnuts at Kannimma's. As for me, I raised the piglet, and he grew big and fat very fast. My husband and Selvam the cobbler killed it, quartered it and sold it at Tirulagam market. We got twenty-five rupees – the same as Tomban's fine – and on top of that we treated ourselves to a pork curry – and Selvam too: of course we gave him a helping. Because we like pork very much, Sinnamma! Sometimes we club together to buy

one on the days of festivals, for Dipavali, Pongal or for the festival of
Kartikkai, and we share it.[2] There's a little song about it:

> The one who's bred the pig is the Raja Pandya
> The one who's made the most of it is the Chetti-who-burps ...

It's pork eaters who know how tasty it is and not the people who breed
them on their land. Anyway the Tomban have got rich. They're farmers
now: they grow rice, sugar cane, aubergines, chillis and they all get me
to hire the manual labour. But in the end, even if they're rich, they're
still very low. The Kudiyanar agree to work for them but they don't get
any cooked food. Although all that's changing in this *kaliyugam*. Now
you see Tomban living in the *ur*. They used to be only just a little bit
above us and now they're much higher thanks to their money! Or rather,
we've stayed poor and we find ourselves even lower than before, still
accepting cooked food from the Tomban.[3]

In this *kaliyugam*, money's the master and when you know how to earn
it, you make yourself higher than you were the day before. It's the same
in the city – everywhere it's a question of money. Look at the Kudiyanar.
In the past they only worked at the Reddiar's. They did housework,
they cooked the gruel for the serfs and the agricultural workers, they
did the washing up, they helped in the kitchen. Always at the Reddiar's.
Nowadays they'll do hard work in the fields like us, at our side, and
they'll even do it for the Tomban. Because you have to fill your stomach
and so you'll work for anybody as long as he pays! But one of these
Kudiyanar families moved to Madras and a girl from our caste has been
doing their housework for a while. It's a different world far away from
the village where you were born, especially in the city.

Just as there are the rich high castes, so there are the poor low castes.
God gave the land to the rich high castes and he gave the poor low
castes the duty of cultivating the land. The duty of the rich high castes
is to employ us, us the Palli, the Pariahs, the Kudiyanar. But there are
some Kudiyanar who own land, sometimes as much as twelve acres:
they don't go and work. Other low castes have their particular trade.
They are a little higher than us because they don't eat beef. They eat
eggs, vegetables, fish, poultry, they drink milk like you. But meat is
unclean, it's waste. Milk is pure. And as we eat waste, we're unclean.
That's the difference between low castes and high castes.

There are all sorts of low castes in Karani that are higher than us.
There are three families of barbers, brothers, who moved in next to the

temple of Perumal. They're barbers for the Reddiar and the Gounder. They cut their hair, shave their armpits, cut their nails, massage them with oil. Generally they work on the steps of the lotus pond and for our Reddiar they move to his house and do their work on the *tinnai*. These families work as barbers for the people of the *ur*, but the Sanar and the hunters sometimes go and borrow their scissors or razors secretly. We do that as well when our barber is away. We quietly borrow a razor from a barber in the *ur* and we quietly give it back to him, because if people ever knew that the same razor had shaved a Pariah and a Reddiar – ayoyo! there would be one of those arguments! That's impossible! But all the same, a barber agrees to it for some money or a little bit of grain. Those barbers are the temple musicians as well and they get some grain for that during the year. They play at puberty ceremonies, engagements and marriages; only auspicious celebrations. It all gives them extra income. Each of them plays a different instrument: the eldest plays the *ottu*, the youngest the *nadesvaram*, and the youngest child the drum, dum, dum, dum, dum …

Two families of potters live opposite the barbers. They're not high or low, because everybody needs them, from the Reddiar to us. In the past the potter used to make enormous jars which contained thirty or forty measures of *kanji*. If you knew how long it took to move those! If anyone carried them on their heads out to the fields, that made the shit come out of their hole! Nowadays the *kanji*'s put in a big aluminium pot which is fixed to a pole. Two men on each side carry it and it's much easier. The potter makes much less crockery than in the past; he mainly makes jars, tea sets for celebrations and dolls. I had all the crockery for my children's marriages made by him. The jars for Anban's marriage were very prettily decorated! I paid the potter in cereals: he's higher than us, but he accepts our grain.

The joiners have built their houses behind him. They are lower than the Gounder and they only marry amongst themselves. Next door there are the carpenters as well. Who else is there? If you come out of their houses and go straight ahead, two blacksmiths have moved in near the Reddiar's quarter. They're never short of orders and they work for us as well. Before the harvest they're asked for thirty to forty sickles. They sharpen old blades and repair carts. One also forged the trident under the banyan tree and the one in our house: you saw how well I decorated it! I never forget to perform the *puja* to that trident, to light some camphor for it. When a house is built in the *ur*, the blacksmiths are asked to make bars for the windows, hinges and bolts for the doors, pulleys for the well, all that sort of thing. The blacksmiths aren't low caste, they're free to go into the Gounder's and Reddiar's houses. They even get to eat with the Grand Reddiar, I've seen them there for a wedding. One of their sons is in teaching now. He married a girl from Pondy where he works and he lives there.

Opposite the blacksmiths are the goldsmiths. There were two families in the past, the big and the small goldsmith. The first made *tali* for the Reddiar and the Gounder. The small one made them for other castes, including us. But he wasn't very honest, that one. I could see that for myself when I gave him an earring to mend. He gave it back much shinier but it was very light. Danam took him her *tali* and she got it back much lighter as well! But we didn't dare complain. They say he cheated a lot of people in Karani and stole a little bit of gold dust from each of them. He got rich that way and chose to leave the village to flaunt his wealth somewhere else. Apparently he set up in his wife's village but sister Virayi who comes from there never saw him again. No one knows what country he's in, that thief! The big goldsmith stayed. Since he had more work than before, he went and got a little shop on the main street of Tirulagam: now he employs three people. Goldsmiths are lower than the Reddiar but, like blacksmiths, they can go into their houses and eat there.

Near the pond, at the entrance to the *ur*, there are two families of traders, they're Komutti. That caste has no other trade apart from business, you can see them in any town. The Komutti speak Telugu, like the cobblers and the Reddiar. But they don't mix either with the Reddiar or with us. We never go to their houses and we don't get food from them. When they celebrate a marriage, they only give betel to the cobblers and even then it's behind their house. They get married discreetly, without making a big noise. Unlike all the other castes, they marry in the month of Adi. I like them a lot, because their wives are always very friendly when they talk to us.

I'd forgotten that the launderers are one of the low castes in the *ur*! They live in four or five houses next to each other and they own a donkey. We have launderers in the *ceri* as well. They're lower than us and we take turns giving them the evening meal. They are pretty poor, but they still manage to hold their yearly festival. They worship Mayilaru and their god resides in their laundering oven. On the day of the festival of Mayilaru, the one in the family who carries out the *puja* takes a bath, puts on new clothes, changes the oven and lights camphor in front of the stone for beating linen. The families cook four jars of

pongal with rice flour and coconut. Some slit the throat of a chicken or
– less often – bleed a pig. There's never any shortage of betel, bananas
and flowers. Everything is handed out between them. We don't get anything, even though we contribute to their festival, just as the Reddiar
contributes to our own festival of Periyandavan. It's the same, anyway:
the launderers work for us and we have to give them something for
their festival. No one can refuse. When Arayi, the launderer's wife,
arrives with her basket to collect what she's owed – a measure of grain
or a cup of oil – we give it to her but we don't miss the chance to have
a moan, 'Those people, they're always ready to worship Mayilaru but
they haven't even brought our clothes back yet! They're nothing like the
launderers in the *ur*: now *they* work!' Then Arayi goes into a corner,
scratches her head and always comes up with a reason: it's rained and
the linen hasn't dried: or it hasn't rained and there's not enough water
in the river: or any old thing. We don't get a share of their offerings but
sometimes our kids do. They always want to know what's going on and
if they're there when the *puja*'s performed, the launderers give them a
little *pongal*. As it's sweet and tastes good, the little ones eat it without
thinking or realising that the launderers are lower than us. Don't forget
that the launderers of the *ur* are higher than us as well as lower than the
Gounder. I always speak with respect to the launderers of the *ur*.

The Sanar are also people of low rank. They're only just above us. A
Sanar ought to act pretty much the same as us when the Reddiar goes
by: he should stand up and speak to him humbly. Sanar and Pariahs talk
to each other almost like equals in the fields. We call out to each other
and say, 'Hey, big sister Kuppu! Ho, big brother Kannan! Uncle Viran!'
You know my friend Vanaroja well, the palm juice seller. We love each
other. Every day in the summer she goes through the *ceri* shouting,
'Palm juice! Palm juice!' She gives me a glass of it and in return I leave
her a measure of paddy each year. Sometimes if the harvest looks like
being scarce and I think our share is going to be small, I pinch one or
two measures of paddy which I go and drop off at her house. Vanaroja
keeps them well hidden for me and gives them back to me the next day
without anybody seeing. To thank her I leave her a little share. We get
on well, the two of us, even if our castes are different!

There's also the Sakkili, the cobblers. They're much lower than us.
You know Selvam, the horn player: he gets cooked food from us. When
there's a marriage, we give him a measure of rice and a rupee. His duty
is to play the horn for us every time it's needed. We never go and drink
or eat at his house, but we talk together normally, and we're warm to

each other when we meet. He also often comes and sits on our *tinnai* to talk and joke (but never in a crude way) or simply to chew. Then he asks us, 'Give me some betel, aunt' or 'uncle' or 'big sister' – that's how he talks to us. That reminds me, Sinnamma, I'm going to stop for a bit. I want to chew some betel as well. Hey! Look: your little Rajini has two spirals on her head. That means she'll have two husbands! (*Laughs.*)

SEVENTEEN

The Paraiyar

Yesterday evening I said to my husband and the group of men taking the air outside the house, 'This morning I was talking to Sinnamma about all the castes who live in this village, in the *ur* as well as the *ceri*, from the Reddiar to the Sakkili, but I forgot to talk about the Pariahs!'

'The Harijans!' my son corrected me, coming out of the house.

'You can keep quiet, boy, that name will never cross my lips!'

He answered, 'Ah! You are stubborn, de! It's people like you that mean we'll never get out of the state we're in!'

'Go away, boy, I wasn't asking you!'

And turning to the men there I went on, 'It was easy talking about the other castes: each has a trade: each has its own customs which it lives by, without mixing with the others, without arguments and in harmony. But what about us? We don't know how to weave winnowing fans or baskets, or repair shoes. We're not from those castes. We are Pariahs. We work the land. But who doesn't know how to do that? Now even the launderers and cobblers are doing it. And why are we called Pariahs?'

'What,' the men said to me, 'haven't we got a trade? And so what do our musicians, our gravediggers, our tax collectors do then?'

'Oh! Don't go into all those details! In the past, in the time of the ancestors, someone called us Pariahs and that word has stuck for generation after generation. Eh, boy! What do you want to hide from

Sinnamma? She's like my daughter, she's a sister to you. I'm telling the
story of my own life, why do you want me to say – what? – Harijan
instead of Pariah and not be open with her about my own caste?'

'Ayo, ayo, Amma! You forget she's married a White and he doesn't
need to know all that!'

'Dei, boy, get away from here and let me talk to your father!'

And then there was my husband agreeing with him! 'Yes, he's right,
it would be degrading for us if Sir learned all that.'

'Han! Are you drumming this into me as well? I'm wondering why
we're called Pariahs and you're telling me all sorts of nonsense like your
son?'

So my husband answered: 'You know very well it's God who makes
the day be born and the night fall. It's God himself who decided this:
men didn't make it up. When Mahakrishna, Adisivan and Vinayagar,
who ruled over this universe, left, they sent Nakulan, Sakulan and
Arjunan here. They shared the world out into three. But a group of
men came and stole one share and they called these men Pariahs. That's
what our elders say.'

That morning, Sinnamma, I went to see Grandfather Muniyan, the
oldest of all of us in the *ceri*. 'Grandfather, we're called Pariahs. Do you
know why we're called that?'

'Listen, Velpakkatta! In the beginning, the divine beings ruled over
the universe. Several *yugam* ago, men took over from them. In those
days there were no castes. Well, if you like, there were two: men and
women. As soon as humans took possession of the universe, there was
the problem of how to share it out. It hadn't been a problem before –
the gods never needed to share it out to rule over it, because they are
everywhere at the same time. There were quarrels when men wanted to
divide it up. One of them, seeing it was turning ugly, began to hide
things, belongings. And just when he was about to hide a drum, the
others saw him and shouted, '*Paraiya maraiyade*', 'Hey you with the
drum, don't hide'.[1] Since then we've been called Paraiyar and we've
been rejected for being descendants of the thief who stole that drum. If
that son of a whore hadn't stolen anything, we would all have lived
together in the *ur*, eh! Why did those dog fuckers do that? They could
have waited to be given their share, couldn't they? All of this for a drum!
But Velpakkatta, it's our fate and nothing will make it change, not even
those politicians who say there mustn't be Pariahs any more! You see,
I'm going to leave soon. I was born a Pariah. I have done my duty
during the time I've had, and I'm going to die a Pariah. Perhaps I'll be

reborn in the womb of the Reddiar, in the household where I was a serf, or perhaps I'll be a wandering dog. Who knows? I'm not the one who decides! And it's not the people from the political parties who are going to change the lot of the Pariahs and mix them up with other castes. Tell Sinnamma that those men want to destroy everything, the harmony and peace we have here. Everyone does their trade: the one who cuts hair will be in the barbers' caste: the one who washes linen will stay a launderer; the one who quarters dead cows will be a shoemaker; the one who crushes sesame will be in the oil pressers' caste and he who sells that oil will be a Chettiar. And there will have to be a Reddiar to be *kambattam* and to put twenty people to work. That's how castes are made.'

'Grandfather', I said to him, 'what you say doesn't suit this *kaliyugam* with these youngsters any more! Our Anban doesn't even want to hear the word Pariah! You know that! You were alive in the days when we didn't know anything and we were innocent.'

'My time is over now, Velpakkatta. It's up to other people to run the world. I'm keeping quiet. You're the one who's come and stirred this up.'

I gave him two leaves of betel and three areca nuts and there we are, Sinnamma. Yesterday evening I thought I hadn't talked about my caste and I knew you'd ask me questions, you always want to know the why of things! I was sure you'd ask me why we're called Pariahs.

I'll tell you that I didn't know myself why we're called that. I found out by asking different people. I thought that it was because we aren't civilised, because we don't have beautiful teeth, because we chew betel, we carry our meals in earthenware dishes, because we neglect everything to do with cleanliness and dress. Today our youngsters have caught up in this way. Girls are in nylon saris, boys in terylene shirts, aluminium bowls have replaced earthenware pots. Subba doesn't make any wood trunks any more: he buys metal trunks from the market like everybody. We use soap to wash and *sikakai* for our hair. But we'll still be unclean, Sinnamma! Soap does not remove uncleanliness. That's what I point out to my featherbrained Anban who's always hanging about party meetings. Just because we're a little bit 'decent' now doesn't mean that we're going to be allowed into people's houses: and if we touch any utensils in a courtyard or at the well, women still rinse them with loads of water before they pick them up![2]

My son told me that in the past, in the time of the elders, there were no castes. People all lived together. One day the villagers went to Mailam, to the temple of Murugan. A crow hovering above them dropped a bone in the temple precinct. The man walking at the head stepped back and spat, saying, 'Tu, Sanyan, tu tu!' The one following him recognised that it was a beef bone. He picked it up and threw it aside. When the first one saw that, he said, 'Muruga! Muruga! You are a Pariah!!!' Murugan instantly decided to leave the temple which is in ruins today.

He took possession of the priest and said to him, 'I don't want to stay in the old temple which has been soiled by those Pariah beef eaters. I want a new temple to be built and Pariahs to be forbidden to enter it!' Since then we've been Pariahs. In the past, when we didn't know anything about anything, Murugan and the Brahmins agreed to divide the people up who used to be all together. That couldn't happen today!

Things happen differently in this *kaliyugam*, because Pariahs have started to go to Mailam again. I went there once on foot a long time ago. We had our meal on the way. When we got there our feet were as swollen as elephants' feet. I went back a second time after the marriage of Anban. There's the bus now, you only have to pay two rupees and you get out right at the foot of the temple. We saw all the paintings, it was really very beautiful!

Anban insisted that I go in. He said, 'De, calm down! We've spent our money to come here and instead of going into the temple, you want to go back home! What idiot claims we have no right to go into the temple?'

'No, my son! Don't do that! This god will take away your sight! People like us haven't the right to go into these places!'

'De, tchi!' Anban answered, 'be quiet! Why spend so much money if we don't see the sanctuary? Everything you're saying is tradition, stories from the old days!'

My son didn't want to listen and he always talks to me like that when I remind him we're Pariahs and that we should live humbly at a distance from the other castes. How many times have I told him, 'Pa, no, don't go to the *ur* in such a beautiful shirt, with powder on your face and ash on your forehead! Don't put on your rings. Leave all that at home. You'll be able to do what you want after work. We're poor. We are Pariahs. We live from day to day. We only eat if we're given work. Those people from the *ur* employ us. We have to be humble, more humble than them. If you go around dressed like that, they'll say, "What a nerve that Pariah's got to come and work for us in trousers and a shirt!" No, Appa, be humble and let's live like we used to!'

But he always says, 'De, tchi! Get away, you and your speeches! If I don't wear trousers and shirts at my age, if I don't put ash on my forehead, tell me, when will I do it? Perhaps you think only the rich have the right to dress up, to wear a watch or glasses? No one else? Not me?'

'My son! My son! Calm down! We Pariahs must live apart, discreetly!'

'But those traditions don't apply any more in today's world, little sister! Wake up a little!'

'Dei, boy! Yes, yes, I'm your little sister and I'm the one who should listen! I'll tell you again, I came to this village as a little girl. I've grown up. I've had twelve children. I've honoured my name. Now I'm on the way out. It's your turn to live here, to have children and to have a good reputation too. Listen to my advice. I'm your mother, I want the best for you!'

That's how he makes fun of me and how I try to argue with him!

God is the one who called us Pariahs, since there weren't any castes the day before that visit to the temple at Mailam. That crow's bone is what revealed everyone's true nature. Disgusted, the Brahmin stepped away from it and spat and the Pariah picked it up, as of course he would. (*Laughs.*) They also say that one of the people walking in that group broke his sandal and started sewing the leather loop back on. The Brahmin couldn't stand it any more and said to Isvaran, 'Sami! We can't live together any more! These people are too unclean! Separate us into castes, each one according to his occupation!' Isvaran heard his prayer and divided us up, saying to the Brahmin, 'You will be a Brahmin. You are vegetarian. Your task is to perform the *puja* and recite the mantra. You, since you've touched the beef bone and you eat this animal, you will be a Pariah. You will work the earth you've touched, you'll be a ploughman. And you who repaired that sandal, you'll be a cobbler.' He asked each one their trade and made a caste out of those who shared the same trade. When the men went home, they settled in different streets in the *ur* and the *ceri*, according to their caste. The beef eaters settled in the *ceri*, the others in the *ur*.

That's how come we Pariahs have moved into the *ceri* and lived our lives separately. But we need other castes in the *ceri* as well who can do other work. Otherwise who would wash our linen? Who would tan the hides? Who would work the leather? And we have to have a priest as well. We Pariahs can only work the land and that's why we've got our launderers, our barbers, our cobblers, our priests and our head of the *ceri*.

Besides, Sinnamma, there's people like you, the people who have land, the people who live in the *ur*. When one of them dies, what are

they going to do? Who's going to take the news to distant relatives?
Who's going to cut the bamboo, plait the rope, prepare the funeral
stretcher? Who's going to dig the hole or raise the pyre? Who's going to
play the drum? And for births? For marriages? And who's going to
guard the harvests? Who's going to go from door to door collecting
taxes? High caste people aren't going to do it. Nor are the Kudiyanar.
God destined us for that. He doesn't give us food just like that, for
nothing, when we're dying of hunger.

But we had to know which of us was going to do that unclean work,
who was going to dig the graves, or do this or that. So the elders
decided that those who live north of Guardian Street – that's to say the
people who worship Periyandavan and eat beef – would do that unclean
work because they're not afraid of being polluted. They're the Vettiyan.
Every year, in the month of Cittirai, we chose eight *totti* from the
Vettiyan: they're responsible for playing the drum at all religious ceremonies and taking care of funerals. The *urtotti* is responsible for carrying the news. The people from the *ur* talk to him, 'Listen Karuppan, go
and tell my family in Kuttirai that we will perform the ceremony of the
turmeric water on such a day!', or else, 'Karuppan! Sir is dead! Get
your men ready for the cremation!', or else, 'Karuppan! We've chosen
this date for the festival of Draupadi. Your men must come and play the
drum for eighteen days!' The *totti* get paid a few measures of grain and
some free meals for all this work. There's a rota and after a year each
totti is replaced by a man of his line: that way all the Vettiyan are *totti*
for a year. At the moment it's my brother-in-law's turn. Next year it'll
be my son, but that donkey doesn't want to. He claims that we shouldn't
do the Vettiyan's work generation after generation and he asks me, 'Why
us and not the Pannaiyar?'

I tell him, 'We eat beef and we bleed pigs for Periyandavan. They
don't do that: they've got Peramanar as a god and they give him an
offering of milk. How do you expect them to do all this work? They can
take a seat in a *panchayat* and stay there talking!'[3]

'Listen! You'll see that we can go on worshipping Periyandavan and
not be Vettiyan and not do this work any more! If they want us to do it,
they'll have to give us a real wage!'

'Ayo, little one! No, no! Not that! We've always been *totti*, let's stay
that way! We'll gain nothing by refusing – the opposite, we'll lose everything. The people of the *ur* have money and we depend on them to fill
our stomachs. We have to live. We have to marry our children. Where
are we going to find the money apart from our masters? Be patient, our

life will gradually get better. We can see changes everywhere. Look at things even here, in our colony. Sinnappan collects taxes, as his family has done for generations, but now he's left the *ceri*. Only his mother has stayed here. He and his wife have moved to Pondy. His daughter, who is very well-educated, is a member of the Assembly. They have electricity in their house. She gets paid by the government and they even give her money to send her children to school! Her brother works in a factory in Pondy as well.

Sinnappan has to run around everywhere telling people they haven't paid their taxes. The Reddiar are rich. They haven't got anything to worry about and they pay their taxes on time. But people with only a little land always ask for extensions. Sinnappan tries to arrange that and it's the accountant who does or doesn't accept the request and can say to him, 'Which house can't pay? Go on! Bring me back a cow or a goat from them and tie it up in front of the office!' Or if they haven't even got that as a guarantee, the accountant will say, 'Go on! Bring me their dishes!' Well, boy! Even though Sinnappan's our caste, he only knows how to collect taxes, because he's only ever done that. He goes to all the houses and calls out, 'Innanga! Don't forget the tax money!' He tells people well ahead of time and when he's collected everything, he helps the accountant tie up the big sack and they go and take it to Pondy under police protection. There are plenty of people in our village who pay those taxes: everybody who's got land. Even in the *ceri* there are some people who own half a hectare or a quarter or an eighth. They say that it's up to two hundred rupees a hectare! Well, boy, I'm telling you of all this to remind you that in the past Vengadesa used to walk all the streets of the *ur* to collect tax with his toothless mouth and a stick in his hand and he never got tired. But times have changed. His son Sinnappan has become a man of the city. But that hasn't meant he's given up his traditional job, because he's always collected taxes. And nor does he ever miss taking part in a *puja* in honour of Periyandavan!

EIGHTEEN

The blood sacrifice
to Periyandavan

We Vettiyan worship Periyandavan. He's the god of our line and when we make a vow, we offer him a pig. You have to spend plenty of money for that and two sacks of coconuts. I've already made an offering of a pig four times! The first time was after the death of my two eldest. My husband had decided to make a vow. He bought a piglet which ran away after five days: it was a bad sign, we were worried and we wondered what misfortune was coming to us. In fact, the piglet's running away was the sign of a miscarriage, which I had the next fortnight. The second time everything went well. We were offering Anban's hair and we wanted to bleed the pig and have a big ceremony to mark the occasion. My husband and I went to the Tomban to choose a piglet. He had one which was as handsome as a prince. Anyway we didn't really choose it, it came running up to us and let itself be stroked. It was a good sign. That piglet was a little more expensive than the others because it was speckled pink but, because it was for the great god, we didn't think twice about the price. My husband proudly took a ten-rupee note out of the fold of his *soman* and said to the Tomban, 'Done!' We went home with my husband carrying the piglet on his shoulders. It was a Wednesday in the month of Maci, an auspicious day. We decided to dedicate the pig the next day, also a favourable day. The custom is that the ceremony is paid for by my *pangali*, even if I'm the one who makes the vow. I buy the pig, I feed it, I carry out the *puja* up to the

172

day of the sacrifice. Then all the other expenses are the *pangali*'s. They should take part in the dedication of the piglet and give money for the sacrifice, because Periyandavan is not only my god, he's the god of my husband's whole line. We made up our minds, the piglet would be dedicated the next day.

There was barely enough time and we had to collect money fast. No one had enough money of their own. So everybody went to their master to borrow. We were about fifteen families. Everybody, depending on what they could afford, had to bring between twenty and twenty-five rupees, because everything was much cheaper then. Today you'd have to get sixty to sixty-five rupees a family! We had collected the money by midday because masters lend very easily when it comes to ceremonies like this: they're afraid our gods will make them suffer. Then all the women set off with baskets on their heads to do the shopping in Tirulagam. It was dark when we got back, weighed down like oxen. Our husbands were waiting for us on the main road at the wine stall, half drunk. They took our loads off us, along with the bottles of palm wine and curried tripes, and set off back home, staggering and talking very loud. We women walked behind. Once we got there, we set out all the baskets at my house, since that's where the dedication was going to be. We sat down on the *tinnai* and our husbands served us a little glass of palm wine with the curried tripe and a thick *ragi* gruel. We ate hungrily and discussed the arrangements for the next day's celebration. Everything was in order so people went home, the women having to meet again back at the well at four in the morning. There were two rules we had to observe: no relations with our husband that night and no attending the rites if it was our period. Otherwise the celebration would turn out badly, there'd be a misfortune in the family, or the piglet would run away. The second rule holds for all the five years the pig is growing. When I'm unclean, somebody else comes and feeds it and washes it until I can start doing it again. Women have to observe this duty without fail!

The next day we met up at the well as we'd planned. First of all we washed to purify ourselves, then we did our hair and each of us put on a *pottu*. Then I washed the piglet. I rubbed it very hard. I washed it again with lots of water. Once it was clean, I coated it with turmeric paste. I rinsed it and hung a thick garland of flowers round its neck. It was radiant! Now it had to be fed. In a brand-new earthenware pot we'd made it a rice and palm sugar gruel. That smelled good! The piglet seemed to like it and gave us a look after every gulp. The children who were there shouted, 'He likes it! He likes it! He's telling us it's good!' I was very happy hearing that. Everything was going well. It felt like a holiday. The smell of camphor and incense filled the *ceri* and we felt like we were in a heavenly world! In this joyful atmosphere, with all the shouting and noise, other families took advantage of the auspicious day to fulfil a vow: some offered their son's hair, others pierced their daughter's ears. It wasn't just 'my' celebration, it was everybody's and I still hear mothers saying today that they had their son shaved the day I dedicated the pig, and girls saying, 'My ears were pierced the day Velpakkatta dedicated the pig!' I'm very proud when I hear that, Sinnamma, and I tell myself that God has been good to me!

Once we'd revered the piglet, we made *pongal* for the whole *ceri*. Some cleaned the rice. Others grated the coconuts. A third group did this, a fourth did that. The good smells of cardamom and coconut milk mixed with the scents of camphor and incense. The *ceri* stopped looking anything like the picture of filth that the people from the *ur* make it out to be and people walking past on the road said, 'Hum! There's a celebration in the *ceri*. That smells good!' We were happy. No one went to work. We cooked. The men and kids were there, playing or watching us cook, and as we cooked the *pongal*, we women giggled and chattered away without stopping. The sun was high in the sky when it was all ready: *pongal*, chutney and vegetable curry, because everybody is vegetarian that day. Now we were able to make the offering of food to Periyandavan.

We led the piglet under the shade of the banyan tree and tied it up. All the *pangali* women then came in a procession from my house to the square with a new basket on their heads full of *pongal* and food. There was a crowd in front of them and although everybody was excited, they were still respectful. Soon the piglet was surrounded with the contents of the baskets: food, bunches of bananas, coconut, areca nut, betel leaves, camphor and incense. I took a big banana leaf, a very wide one, and put in it a good helping of *pongal*, some condiments, three bananas, seven coconuts and some camphor I'd lit. I offered the whole thing to Periyandavan. Everyone prostrated themselves in silence. Then I got up again, and I stretched the leaf out towards the piglet who didn't wait for a second: it swallowed it all in the blink of an eye, the leaf as well: that made the kids laugh! People went back to their houses straightaway. With the *pangali* women I started handing out the food from door to door. Banana leaves were spread out everywhere. We went down every street: we stopped at every house, missing nobody out, not even the gravedigger or the cobbler. Everyone had their share, and lots of it! When we'd finished handing it out, we went to eat at my house. Much of the afternoon had already gone and the ceremony of the dedication of the pig had come to an end. After the meal we talked about it for a long time.

The piglet, full up like us, was tied up opposite my door. He was there for five years, until he became a beautiful big fat pig and his tusks started showing. When we see the tusks coming through then we have to make the sacrifice without waiting a single day, otherwise the pig will bring misfortune to the family who's reared it. And if we don't have enough money to pay for the ceremony, we have to go into debt to make the offering straightaway, otherwise the pig could bring destruction on our household, right to its very roots. My husband and I consulted the priest who's in charge of auspicious ceremonies. He advised us to offer the pig on the first Monday of the month of Purattaci.

Preparations were going to take a very long time, because the sacrifice is not a simple thing. Lots of people outside the family take part in it and everything has to be organised perfectly, otherwise Periyandavan will be crossed. He is a good god, but extremely sensitive and quick-tempered and we are all afraid of him. When his wishes are not re-spected, he can throw himself into terrible rages. But the priest promised us that Periyandavan was in an excellent temper and ready to accept our sacrifice on that Monday of Purattaci, because he hadn't forgotten that in Karani our family owed him a pig. We were reassured and thanked the priest by giving him a coconut, a dozen bananas, some camphor and ten rupees on a tray. We asked him to come and celebrate the sacrifice on the arranged day.

We had a good week in front of us, but it seemed very short, because we could only get on with all the preparations after work and that made the days very long! The first thing to do was let the whole family know and collect the money we needed – which was was more than for the dedication. My husband ran to the Grand Reddiar's to borrow seventy-five rupees from him and he got them without too much trouble: I've already told you why! Since we were the ones who'd made the vow, our share was bigger. My eldest brother-in-law gave sixty rupees. The others between forty and fifty. It's because there are lots of costs: the musicians, the potter, the *urtotti* and all the rest have to be paid. It's not easy.

That evening, coming home from work, I stopped at the potter in the *ur* to order the earthenware things we needed: everything from jars to

hearths and containers of all sizes. Kandassami promised they would be
ready before the ceremony and that I could count on him. I gave him an
advance of ten rupees so he would start work the next day. Every day I
stopped to see how he was getting on. My husband and some cousins
went to Tirumangalam to hire the *pambai* and *udukkai* players. In the
ceri we've got all the musicians we need apart from those two. In the *ur*
Peramban the launderer plays the *udukkai* and Tirumala Gounder the
pambai, but they work for the high castes and they'd never come and
play for us. We understand that: a master and his serfs can never employ the same people. We have our own who don't all live in the *ceri*
anyway: we just have to pay them to get them to come.

So our men went to Tirumangalam to book the musicians. They took
them for a drink at the wine stall to discuss the price and they agreed
on thirty rupees. It was a good thing to have settled because you have
to have music and rhythm to make a sacrifice acceptable to a god: a
ceremony without musicians would be shameful, like food without salt!
Praises are sung to Periyandavan with the *udukkai*. Once he's drunk on
the music of the drum, he's easier to communicate with. That's why
there really have to be musicians. If the ones in Tirumangalam hadn't
been free, we would have had to run to Pombur, miles from here, and
that would only have added to the expense. But God is always there,
thinking of us: he only wants what's good for us!

The only thing we women talked about, at work or at the well, was
the ceremony. In the evening we stayed up late and the men joined us.
We wanted at all costs for everything to go off as it should: the ceremony had to please Periyandavan and the whole *ceri* as well. And I can
say that, up till now, my ceremonies have always been successful! Everyone remembers them and says about me, 'When Velpakkatta sacrifices a
pig, it's always magnificent!' Everyone in the *ceri* takes part in the ceremony, everyone helps with the preparations. My cousins, my friends
come and suggest things and give me a hand with the cooking.

The day before the ceremony we women set off with baskets on our
heads for Tirulagam market. We washed at the pump. We put on our
best saris. Our hair up in a bun, a *pottu* on our forehead, we made
ourselves as beautiful as for our wedding day. We walked across fields
under the sun, buzzing like worker bees. People waiting for the bus or
hanging about by the main road were dazzled: women in multicoloured
saris, under a blue sky, baskets on their heads – there must be something important happening in the village.

We had to buy lots of things that time and we couldn't find them all

in Tirulagam. It was time to go to town. There's no lack of buses to
Pondy. A private company's bus was about to leave. Without even thinking of the cost of the ticket, we settled down on the benches reserved
for women. The conductor threw us a look and then let us be. Eh, yes!
We were well dressed, like Tamils! No rags, no sweat. We weren't
blocking the aisle with big baskets of okra, aubergines or banana flowers,
or whey or yoghurt. And for once, the conductor didn't make us open
our purses to check that we really had the right money. Because it
wasn't an ordinary day. The conductor didn't ask any questions and nor
did we. I gave him thirteen rupees and asked for thirteen tickets: there
were thirteen of us, a lucky number! You must always be an odd number.

Half an hour later we were in Pondy. We walked to the Grand Bazaar
and started with the grocers. It was a quiet time and the shopkeeper
hadn't got too busy. He served us calmly and didn't get irritated by all
our questions, 'How much is the sugar? How much are ten grams of
cardamom?' The baskets filled up: sugar, cloves, cinnamon, cashew nuts,
cardamom, sugar candy, dried raisins, cumin, turmeric, red lentils, sticks
of rose, saffron and jasmine-scented incense, camphor, *kungumam*, and
scented ash. At the florists, we chose beautiful garlands of fresh flowers,
especially orange chrysanthemums. We also got a good dozen cubits of
flowers for our hair, keeping the rest for the women who'd stayed at
home. The baskets got heavier and heavier and the money went down
very quickly. But in such a heat, we couldn't resist treating ourselves to
a glass of very cold pink or yellow syrup. When we'd quenched our
thirst, we bought some *kelti* for dinner from the fish sellers, like we do
every time we go to Pondy.

We finished our shopping and walked back to catch the bus, which
we had to wait a good hour for this time. It was dark when we arrived
in Karani. Our men were waiting for us on the main road. They're well
aware that women who go to Pondy don't get back before the moon is
up. Because we can't read, the only problem is being given the wrong
information and getting the wrong bus or taking it in the wrong direction. Anyway, everything was all right and we went back home. We put
the shopping in my house. The whole *ceri* was there to inspect our
baskets. We gave flowers to friends and neighbours. The children, who
were waiting for us, demanded 'sweets from the city' but because there
wasn't enough for everybody, there was some shouting and crying!
Straight after that we started making the fish sauce: our husbands went
weak at the thought of eating *kelti*. It was a change for us from the
dried fish which Kumari sells us. We told the story of our day while we

were grinding the chillis. My husband told me that a messenger had come to announce that the Tirumangalam musicians would come and play for free. Our men had ordered three more demijohns of palm wine from the wine stall in a flash: the music will only be strong and the celebration cheerful if the musicians have had a good drink! The sauce was ready. I had got some rice cooked for the occasion and it all smelled good. The children had gone to sleep. My husband was sipping his palm wine sitting on the *tinnai*, his mouth watering. We couldn't hear the buses going past any more in the distance and it was late in the evening when at last we got to have a taste of the strong fish sauce. I didn't even need a drink of wine by then, I was so close to falling asleep! We kept a little sauce for the children and to season the morning's rice in water.

It was a short night because we had to start the rites to Periyandavan early in the morning. From the time the priest had fixed the date of the sacrifice, we'd stopped giving our leftovers to the pig and I'd had no more relations with my husband. That day the same thing would apply to all the *ceri*, and women with their periods couldn't be at the sacrifice otherwise the pig would turn nasty and try to run away. To tell you the truth, I didn't sleep much that night! I was excited and all I did was move around in my corner, turning this way and that. In my thoughts I was preparing the ceremony which would go like a play I'd directed. It was still night when the cock started singing. I went to the well to wash. Hearing the noise of the pulley, my sister-in-law Vanamayil woke up and she joined me. Gradually the *pangali* women and their friends turned up. The men went to take a bath at the pump in the Grand Reddiar's paddy field.

At daybreak everyone was ready. I went to find the pig to wash it. He let me do it without making a fuss and I took him back to the house. Then I put on a brand-new white sari, in the Brahmin way, and I tied my hair up on my neck. I hadn't chewed betel to keep my mouth clean. I drew a big, bright red *pottu* on my forehead and at last I signalled to everybody that we could begin. The ceremony was going to happen under the banyan tree on the square behind the *ceri*.

My husband and I walked at the head of the procession. He carried a pot of gruel which he made the pig sniff so he'd follow us. The priest walked beside us. Marimuttu, my eldest brother-in-law, followed us, reverently carrying the lance in both hands. The women came behind, with the earthenware dishes and the new baskets full of betel, areca nut, incense, camphor and spices. My young brother-in-law Ajakesan carried

the sack of rice which the Grand Reddiar had lent, two sacks of coconuts, some wood to build the fire and some large and small knives. The
crowd followed behind. The *ceri* was empty: everyone was following the
procession.

The sun was rising in a very blue sky. It was a beautiful Purattaci
day! We put the baskets on the ground when we got to the banyan and
that meant everybody could relax! We'd tried our best to calm the children down during the procession, but they couldn't stay still and it was
no good threatening them. We broke up into little groups. The priest
started preparing the place for the sacrifice. He took a pot of earth. He
mixed rice flour and water to get a firm paste and then he modelled a
lot of Pillaiyar of all sizes. He took particular care of Munnadiyan, who
was the largest with a very pretty round belly which made the children
laugh.[1] He put it in the middle and then planted the lance opposite it,
facing where the sun sets. He decorated the statue and the lance with
flowers and *kungumam* and lit the incense sticks in little clusters: the air
was filled with their smell. Meanwhile the men and women were busy
in little groups preparing the *pongal*, grinding the spices and cooking
the white rice.

I gave the pig its last bath and rubbed it with turmeric. My husband
drew ash markings all over its body. He was as handsome as a king and
grunted with joy. Lying under the tall banyan, he watched the crowd
working around him. He must have thought that we were going to hang
a garland of flowers round his neck, like a young husband. On large
banana leaves we put dozens of bananas, a good chunk of camphor,
some betel leaves, some areca nuts and coconuts, a basket of *pongal* and
white rice, some incense and some flowers. The musicians played the
udukkai and the *pambai*. The priest began to read the prayers.

The crowd was half following the reading when the priest signalled
with his head to my eldest brother-in-law. He was wearing a garland of
chrysanthemums around his neck and dressed in new clothes. He took
the lance in both hands and walked towards the pig, which had been
chained up. There was a great silence. It was the crucial moment. Everyone was wondering anxiously if the lance would go through the pig's
side as easily as cutting a banana. With a hard thrust, my brother-in-law
drove the lance in. The pig collapsed immediately, screaming. The men
crowded round to catch the blood which was spurting out and my
husband mixed it with the *pongal* straightaway. The musicians beat their
drums harder and harder, while my husband threw the *pongal* mixed
with blood in the eight directions for the messengers of Periyandavan,

who were waiting for it impatiently: if they didn't get it at the exact minute of the sacrifice, they'd slap us! By the grace of Periyandavan everything happened in the right way. We still had to finish the rites before Munnadiyan, the witness to the sacrifice. My brother-in-law dug a big hole in front of the statue. He put the rest of the *pongal* mixed with blood in and a share of what was on the banana leaves. He covered up the hole again. Munnadiyan had been thanked.

The rites for the gods had finished. Now we had to take care of everybody who'd taken part in our celebration. The men picked up the pig stretched on the ground. He was a beautiful colour, like a Tamil woman coming out of the bath daubed with turmeric. My brother-in-law called together the *pangali*, before cutting off the pig's breast: that part goes to the family. Then he continued jointing it for the whole *ceri*. As usual, we went to the door of every house to give out meat, rice, betel and coconut. We *pangali* still had a last rite to carry out. We had to keep the pig's breast, which we'd put aside, in water and revere it for seven days while keeping to the rules of purity: no sexual relations, only sleeping on the ground, changing the water every day and burning camphor. At the end of the week, we'd collect a little money and offer a last feast to Periyandavan.

But for then the feast was over. We heard the people from the *ur* coming home after the evening show at the Tirulagam cinemas. We were tired but happy. My husband and I – our hearts were at peace: Periyandavan was with us and he has never abandoned us since!

NINETEEN

This *kaliyugam*

Every day we hear on the radio in the *ceri*, 'Don't stay separate! Don't be divided! Down with castes!' Every day a car with a loudspeaker comes by as well and tells us, 'Come, people of the colony! Come and educate yourselves! Come to evening lessons, adults and children, for people who can't read and for people who can't write! You'll see that when you're educated, you won't be treated like you are now! You won't be a lower caste any more!' We're there in the evening, enjoying the cool air, and we hear them, 'Dear elders! Stay one with the young in the fight against the segregation of castes! Why do you send your children to work for half a rupee or a rupee and a half? And you women, why do you plant out for three rupees! Demand five! A measure of rice now costs two and a half rupees: the price must come down! If a landowner employs ten of you at three rupees a day, does that allow you to live? What are we making of our lives, from birth to death? What are we making of our families with so little money? Demand an increase in your wages! Five rupees for the women, ten rupees for the men!'[1]

That's what the party workers come and tell us every evening, Sinnamma! And we answer them, 'Ayo! With ploughs and sickles, our parents only showed us how to plough the land, how to manure it and irrigate it. They taught us to make our living from that. And now suddenly all of you start telling us we have to give up the hoe for the pen! So how are we going to live? Unlike yours, our parents did not

181

make us study. They were ruled by the laws of Him who divided us into castes, into Palli, Paraiyan, Komutti, Kosavan, and they raised us according to those laws. And look, here you are turning up now! You want our happiness. You want to wipe out these divisions to bring more justice. But we're too old for that! That will be in the next *yugam*, if there is one! You people who can write still need our work, you still need us manual labourers, and we're still dominated by you!'

Yes, the parties take all that to heart and fight for us. Look at M.G.R.: he'd give his life for us.[2] He's the one who sends his men to our doors. He tells us to hope, to struggle, to stay as one. But do you think, Sinnamma, we're the age to struggle, to fight? Life is behind us now. We're heading for the cremation grounds and I'll never see this coming together of the castes. That's why we women say to the political parties, 'You want to fight to bring us together and make caste disappear. But it's impossible. We haven't got a field or any land, nothing but the house we live in: so how do you expect us to live? If you really want to fight for us, the poor, give us some money to buy some land, or share out land for us to cultivate. Give us a cow, a goat, a pair of oxen and we'll be able to make our living, eat our fill and have plenty of children. They could study, have a job.'

In my day the school was here, but my parents didn't take the trouble to send me. They didn't understand anything. They didn't think of our future: they lived from day to day. If they had educated us, we would have earned more money, but they were ignorant! As for us we've only had one son. I wanted him to study with all my heart. I remember Karani school well! I built it with Anjalai, Pakkiam, Kannima, Managatti. We were young then. We laughed and sang a lot as we pounded lime and carried bricks. We worked on the building site until it was finished. I hoped that one day I'd put my son in that school – I hadn't had Anban yet. And after his birth, without saying a word to anybody, I put money aside to buy him new clothes and give him a silver chain instead of his red thread with an amulet. On his first day I dressed him in a new shirt and new shorts and I gave him a tray of sweets and another of sugar candy to give the teacher. The Grand Vattiar had just been appointed. Anban stayed with him for three years, but then a new teacher came. He beat the children. Lots of times Anban wanted to stop, but I always took him back to school. Once he won a running race and he got a cup: I sold it to our Reddiar who keeps it in a glass cupboard. When my eldest daughter got married, there was nobody left to look after the little ones for me. I had to take Anban out of school: she was the one who used to take them for walks when I was working. Anjalai had very young children. She understood that I was heartbroken and offered to look after my children as well so that Anban could go to class. I gave her some rice to thank her. But afterwards I had to stop working myself so that Anban could carry on. I really sacrificed a lot to educate him!

But I'll tell you the real reason he gave up. It was a time when my husband and I were arguing a lot. Sundari was still a baby and could hardly sit up, and my husband already wanted me to be his wife again! I'd had enough of being pregnant the whole time and I didn't want to let him. We ended up fighting and I went with the children to my brother's, who was in Madras then. I left Anban with my husband so he wouldn't miss school: he took good care of him for a few days but then he left him with neighbours to come and find me. First he went to Velpakkam where he was told I was in Madras and he came to my brother's. I didn't want to go back straightaway and he waited for me. Meanwhile the neighbours took as much care of Anban as they could. They gave him something to eat in the morning before going to work, and in the evening after coming back from the fields, and they told him to go to school on his own. Anban didn't have anybody to take him to school and he didn't have the midday meal: he started hanging round the village with other kids from the *ceri*. When I got back it was too late: he'd missed classes for too long and he'd practically forgotten everything. But he understands everything at the cinema and he remembers the words of the songs. He fumbles his way through the newspaper. He can do a bit of maths. He can only write his name. But lots of boys who were at school with him have finished their studies. Now they've got work in a factory or in an office in Pondy. He's stayed in the fields. Look at the brother of our Parasuraman: hasn't he gone off there? You know him well, Sinnamma! I'm not making anything up. He's definitely from our caste, but he's been recruited by the police, like a Naicker or a Gounder. His studies were what allowed him to make it.

When the Reddiar of Naliveli was elected, he gave desk-work to about twenty people from the commune. But Anban couldn't get it, because he couldn't write. Chandran and Kannan got jobs at the main hospital of Gorimedu, and Saktivelu became police inspector. All three of them now have land and irrigation pumps. Saktivelu bought his land in the village where his grandmother was born and he's moved in there, into the *ur*. He bought a plot of land and had a house built. But they say he's suffered losses for two years because it's so dry, even though he's had a pump installed. The land isn't as good there. If he'd bought here, he wouldn't have had those problems. But he would never have been able to move into the *ur* here: it makes no difference if he's an inspector, everyone knows perfectly well what caste he is! His brother, the Potbellied, has stayed in the *ceri* with us, and he's an agricultural worker. The Reddiar of Naliveli also found a teacher's job for our priest, who got his diploma in Tirulagam. Five or six others are at the factory, including Sinnatambi, who is an electrician. But to get there, you have to have studied, and that's not possible for everybody! Because we need everyone's wages in a family, the children's as well. The boys tend the cows, the little girls collect peanuts or come and plant out with us. And in the evening we tell our children stories instead of sending them to school: the story of the worker, the story of the crocodile, other stories about animals.

The world has changed in this *kaliyugam*. Today youngsters or adults who haven't been to class and want to learn to read and write can go to evening school. A teacher comes from Pondy to give lessons, there on the *tinnai*. That's how my daughter Sundari got to learn all by herself. We didn't have anything to do with it, and now she can write her name and read a little.

It also has to be said that nowadays more and more people send their children to school and leave them there longer. The government provides more facilities than it used to. Our virtuous father M.G.R. gives out uniforms free; shorts and shirts for the boys; skirts and blouses for the girls; and notebooks, books, slates, pencils, all they need, you know! He even gives the midday meal to schoolchildren. Parents don't have to worry any more about equipment, they don't have to make the midday meal and run not to be late. The government has tarmacked the *ceri* streets now and put in neon lighting. Children go and sit under them to do their homework quietly. Well, with so many facilities, why wouldn't we send our children to school? You've seen our children on their way to class, Sinnamma: perfectly neat, their hair well-done, the girls with two plaits. You'd mix them up with the children from the *ur*, wouldn't you? They say that our children are the biggest group in the school, which is in the *ur*. They're neatly dressed, so there's no harm in them going to the same school.

You know, lots of children used to stay away because they had to look after their little brothers and sisters at home: they couldn't keep up very well. Teachers didn't understand the situation at home and slapped them, smacked their fingers with the ruler or made them kneel on the sand in the full sun. Children stopped wanting to go to school because they were afraid of being punished. M.G.R. has thought of us again, and to help women with young children, he's had a creche built in every village for the little ones. Mothers leave their babies in the creche before going to work in the fields and that way the older ones don't miss school. Two Vanniyar women have been put in charge by the government. One comes from Gorimedu, the other from Pondy: she's Patti, Kannan's wife, who helps them with the cooking. They wash the very little ones, do their hair, put a *pottu* on their forehead, then give them the bottle. The bigger ones are neat and tidy when they get there: the boys with their hair combed, the girls with two plaits hanging down their back. They play on the seesaw and the slide. At midday they wash their hands and each one goes and takes a plate from the pile in the kitchen. They sit down in a row and are served a meal: rice every day, with lentils and vegetables. The smallest ones are helped to eat. After the meal, the big ones wash their hands and go back to playing, while the little ones are stretched out on a mat for their afternoon rest and no one is allowed to go into the house. Before it's time to go home, the big ones wash their face and arms. They eat a bit, a handful of fried chickpeas, and leave. The mothers come and find their babies. Then the two women have a wash and two young girls from the *ceri* give the creche a once-over with the broom. Finally the women take their bags and their umbrellas and go back home in the bus.

Now the creche is too small. Especially because the women from the *ur* want to be able to leave their children there, like the women of the *ceri*. They say the government gives all the facilities to the *ceri* and none to anyone else. To satisfy everybody, the government is going to build a new larger creche. It will be in the *ur* but the children of the *ur* and the children of the *ceri* will go there together. The women from the *ur* have agreed. Why should they refuse? Children are not unclean. When they plant out in the fields with us, their children play with ours all day while they wait for their mothers. And what idiot is going to refuse when they know they're washed and fed at the creche? There are poor Kudiyanar as well and the government usually helps them. But they're the ones who reject us because we're unclean: that's how it's always been. When everyone lived separately, there was no fuss. Now, when it comes to all these facilities we're being given to lift the poor out of their misery, everyone has to give way a bit. The Kudiyanar should accept us and we should make an effort. We used to be a joke in the past: slovenly, our hair never done, never washed. Now we're putting ourselves right.

The *ceri* has changed a lot. In the past we worked for a quarter of a rupee a day. We were happy with little. We filled our stomach with what we found on the verges of fields or just with water, and that was enough for us. It's not like that now. Everything comes from the city: bread, tea, petrol, sweets. Everything is bought with money. That's what civilisation is as well: money! You can do anything with money – eat, dress, live, be a higher caste, have all the rights. Our young have understood that and that's why they want to be educated and earn lots of money. That wasn't our goal. I remember before when times were difficult and there wasn't work in the fields, we didn't eat every day. All my grandmother would go and buy was a little oil for the lamp and she'd say to us, 'Little ones, we haven't got anything to cook today. We'll light the lamp instead of the fire, so you won't be afraid of the dark. Quickly go to sleep, you won't feel any pangs of hunger!' We'd lie down on our stomachs, all huddled together, and shut our eyes. Hunching our shoulders and clamping our teeth tight shut so as not to hear any noise, we'd fall asleep in a flash. Our parents would ease their tiredness and hunger by sharing a twist of betel. What child would do that today? Not even the poorest Pariahs! They'd roll around on the ground to make us buy them at least some bread or a cake: they're sold everywhere and they fill you up without having to light a fire. Rice used to cost only four *anna*, but we can't eat uncooked rice and now we can buy ourselves something ready-made for a few pennies. It has to be said that there are also more little shops in the village and Tirulagam market is larger. We don't have to wait for the weekly market any more. We manage to get some money: we borrow it, we pawn our crockery and pay it back when things are going better. Money gets around more easily, you know! It's true that in the past we only earned six *paice* for weeding. Then it went up to twelve. I remember buying one *paice* of salt, one of tamarind, one of chilli and one of salted fish! That didn't go very far, but we ate kodo millet and foxtail: that filled us up and gave us strength. Even the Komutti bought them because they were easy to sell. That's over now, they're not even grown any more. There's only I.R.30 and *ponni*.[3] My son doesn't even know what foxtail tastes like! As for kodo millet, the bran used to warm us up. Yes, Sinnamma, I can still see my grandmother, in the month of Kartik-kai, when it was cold and raining very hard, and next to her she had an earthenware pan full of hot kodo millet and foxtail.

But everything changes. The weather as well. In this *kaliyugam*, we wait for the rain. The sun heats up so it's almost frying the earth. Everything's changing in the *ceri* as well. We're putting ourselves right, we're becoming civilised. My husband tells me that Gandhi was the first to want all the castes to change in the right way. For that, the world had to be educated. And everyone has followed – them and us.

We understand things better now. I said to you that we used to be dirty, slovenly, disgusting. Only people who went to offices, for example, would use soap. I remember that the accountant, the taxman, Narayana Gounder and a few others would come to the well. They'd have soap. On our way to work we'd go past and we'd look at that foaming water with amazement. Now my Anban buys soap with different scents every month and I use it as well. You can find everything in Tirulagam or even in the markets: combs of all colours, powder, pencils for the eyes and the lips, *pottu* which don't rub off and we're gradually learning to use them. Take razor blades, for example. You can buy a blade for ten *paice*. In the past we used ash to remove the hair under our arms and down below. That hurt very much, so we didn't do it very often. So a juice drinker seeing us go by in the street would say, 'Eh! There's nothing as hairy as that garden! What a forest that must be!' It was humiliating having to hear that! Nowadays our girls shave themselves with a blade and they wear a blouse like all of you.

I'm the same as everybody. In the country I don't wear a blouse. A *paratchi* shouldn't wear one once she's had a child, it's not polite. But when I go into town, to your house, I'm not going to leave my shoulders bare! So I borrowed the blouse Kannima wears when she comes to Pondy. But I'd had enough of asking her for her blouse every time I came to see you. So I bought one, the red one with yellow flowers, at the fair in Vagur. And I liked it very much when you offered me a blouse with the sari you gave me at Dipavali – that way I've now got one spare. We don't give it much thought in the fields. We don't wear a blouse and the sari hides our chest. But we can't help uncovering ourselves when we're working and then we're like that in front of the Reddiar and the Gounder or the schoolmaster. How many times has the Reddiar's wife said to me, 'Eh, Velpakkatta! There you are, always showing off your nipples to the men! Hide yourself! Show a little modesty! If you put on a blouse, your breasts wouldn't look as big and you'd be better off!' But I don't listen to her because there's no shortage of pierced ears in the *ceri* and old troublemakers who criticise us bitterly, 'Will you take a look at them! They've had a bushel of children and there they are, putting on a blouse to strut about at the Reddiar's imitating their wives!' That's why, when I came to visit you, Sinnamma, I kept my breasts bare from the *ceri* to Tirulagam and then I put my blouse on before getting on the bus – because the conductors make fun of us or look at us with contempt if we travel without blouses! Coming back is the same. I take my blouse off and put it in my bag under a tamarind tree near Keva Reddi's house – a friend of our Reddiar who lives in Tirulagam in a two-storey house beside the grocer's. Once the Reddiar surprised me and said, 'Manikkam's wife, you look good with a blouse, why are you taking it off?' I was ashamed to hear that, but I left without my blouse, leaving him to think whatever he liked. That's what I do when I come and see you, Sinnamma.

It's the same with my hair: when I come back from Pondy, I undo my bun which I wear to go to town and with my fingers, without a comb, I gather up my hair and tie it up in a bun on the side. Eh, when you dress, you have to follow the customs of each country! Still, if you could see our girls and our boys in the *ceri* today! What clothes! What saris! What blouses! What hairdos! What haircuts! I'd even say that our girls beat you when it comes to clothes! You always wear cotton saris and no jewellery, while in the *ceri*, after work, our young are in nylon saris or shirts. The men from the *ur*, their mouths water when they see our girls and we hear them say, 'Look at that! Would you say that was a Pariah! She is so decent!' When everybody changes, why shouldn't we? In the past I'd always been clean and tidy when I could. Now I'm married, why not take a turmeric bath or put a *pottu* on my forehead like everybody else? But I'm afraid of backbiting. In the *ceri* no one thinks twice of slagging me off, starting with my own sister-in-law, especially when I come to your house in town. Just the other day I heard her say, 'But where can that whore be off to so neat and so dressed up? Just look at her: a nylon sari, a *pottu*, flowers in her hair'. Others asked me, 'Well, Velpakkatta! Where are you going by bus the whole time, dressed up like that?' And I tell them, so they don't ask me any more questions, 'I'm just going to my daughter in Katterikkuppam!' Danamma, Kitteri and Kuppamma know you. They know I go to your house and that my husband knows too. In an argument one day they shouted at me, 'We're not like you, leaving our husband planting out and our son working to go running into town every day!' Yes, Sinnamma, our women are very jealous and they love backbiting at the slightest opportunity.

Anban's now involved with the other young people in the association that's just been set up for them. The women's one has been around for a long time, but the young ones' is very new. They built a room so they could meet up and celebrate marriages. The young clubbed together to set up a lending fund. More than a dozen are old enough to get married and they give ten rupees a month. The day one of them marries, the association lends them the money, without interest of course, and on top of that sends a procession with bottles of soda, sweets, photos of actors and an envelope with five hundred rupees in it! Announcements are made by loudspeaker, 'Gift of the young people's association: five hundred rupees!' and everyone applauds. The political parties do that for the young. Sometimes in certain villages, K.S. himself presents the bride's *tali*: gold, of course, with the party symbol on top, the rising sun. It's so that we don't get into debt for the rest of our days, and even longer. When we married Anban, we borrowed from the Reddiar as usual. Anban didn't want to. He said we could make do with the money from the association. But I told him that if I borrowed, it would be from the Reddiar and nowhere else. Some months beforehand I asked for five hundred rupees and four sacks of rice. The Reddiar said he'd advance me three hundred rupees. But that's what the *tali* costs on its own, if it's two or four grams of gold, and, apart from that, you need the bride's sari, the drinks for the family, the meal, the *pandal*, the neon lights, the invitations. I pointed that out to the Reddiar: 'If you only lend me three hundred rupees, what sort of marriage will I be able to put on with that little?'

'Borrow from someone else, from the association!'

'But who knows me besides you? I am a serf in your household, nowhere else!'

'OK, OK! We'll see! But still, times are racing ahead now and everything's falling into place for you. Soon you'll be our equals, you'll become like our caste!'

And the Reddiar started laughing. My husband immediately said to him, 'Ayo, Sami! I'm not the one asking for that! It's people from outside who want me to become like that!'

In spite of everything, this Reddiar has a good heart. Deep down he thinks it's a good thing we're taken care of, and that we have to rise up and become decent. But people like Lakshmanan, Vira Reddi or Bangaru Reddi don't like it one bit. They're old rats, and jealous to boot! 'The government itself is on their side and fights for them! They give too many facilities to those Pariah dogs!' That's what they say when they see the *ceri* streets tarmacked and lit up. And it's true that there didn't used to be any order in the *ceri*. It didn't matter where houses were built. The streets were full of bumps. Even indoors, everything has changed today: there's aluminium tumblers, bowls and plates when they all used to be earthenware. Although I've got aluminium dishes, I still make sauces in earthenware bowls: I think they give a better taste. And I still go through the rice with an *alavu*, a type of broom made from coconut palms which I spread out on the jar. It's an old custom which we've kept up for years! Look at the water, that's changing as well, Sinnamma! There used to be only one well in the *ur* and one in the *ceri*. Now the government has installed taps: there are four or five for the *ceri*. No more need to go a long way, queue up and have arguments: we just turn the tap and the water flows! Well, not always! The government has put pipes everywhere – in the *ur* as well as the *ceri* – and if they're opened up too much down below in hot weather, by the basin, then the water doesn't reach further up, by the temple of Aiyanar, and the people from the *ur* are not happy. They say we use too much water and that it's our fault they don't have anything left to drink. We answer politely that the government put in taps for everybody and that we have to drink and our animals do as well. They're not the only ones, so why kick up a fuss? Now some of them come and get water from the *ceri* when they need it and, if our taps are broken, we go to the *ur*: I go to the Reddiar's, others go to the centre. There's no more pollution. The government sorted that out by putting in closed wells and water towers. The water is delivered by taps, so how could we pollute it? We don't lower our containers into the wells, since they're closed. We turn the tap and the water runs into our jar or into the people of the *ur*'s jars. That's why lots of the people from the *ur* now don't hesitate to come to the *ceri* to get water when they've run out. When we see them coming, we step aside out of politeness, and we let them help themselves first, 'Help yourselves, Amma, we'll go after you!' That's what we say to them. But there's always some who are too stubborn to come to the *ceri* and prefer to go and get water from the wells in the fields a long way away. Even so, lots of them allow themselves to be tempted because the *ceri* is nearer. When there's a fault in the *ur*, they even come from our Reddiar's household with a cart full of big containers: zinc basins, copper jars.

All this means that we talk to the people of the *ur* more, even though some of them don't like it. For example, I stop by the Little Gounder's veranda and catch up on news of his mother. Or coming back from work, just the other day, some Kudiyanar talked to me, 'So, Velpakkatta, were you away this week? We didn't see you at the Reddiar's, your daughter was collecting cow dung.' And I told them that I had taken time off work, I'd gone to Madras. You see, Sinnamma, in the past we wouldn't have done that. We'd go to work and then back to the *ceri* without hanging around in the *ur*. We didn't even know who lived there apart from our masters. The only reason we went to the *ur* was to work. The people down there couldn't do without us. Who'd look after their cows, if it wasn't for our children? Who'd cultivate their land, if it wasn't for us? Today there's more contact, because of the school and the water or just like that, for no reason. We still live in the *ceri*. We've got our customs, our ways, our own life, we're better off amongst ourselves, but we're not completely cut off from the *ur* outside of work. Apparently for the next election the *ceri* and the *ur* are going to be joined together, that's what they say in the men's meetings. I don't believe it. I don't think the people from the *ur* could accept it. But if it was true, I'd be afraid of what could happen! If I could choose, I'd go and live over by the stable at the Reddiar's, because we are his serfs. (*Laughs*.) All I wish for, Sinnamma (*Viramma's tone becomes serious again*) is that we get on well. If they decide to join us all together, there won't be the same respect any more. I'm afraid of that.[4]

Take an example: you were the one who came to me. I didn't go looking for you. What right would I have had to do that? I'm happy to know you, I love you like my own daughter. When it's just us, I talk to you with an open heart, I touch you when I talk to you. But could I behave like that with you outdoors? No! I owe you respect, you are a higher caste! Everything else is the same. They want to make us one, when God said, 'Each of you stay in your caste. Live apart. There'll be no arguments. There'll be harmony and the world will turn in the right direction!'

Nowadays people think the opposite. They want the world to be one, and everybody to be the same, all with the same rights. That is the *kaliyugam*! It's good people want us to be raised up, but it's better if we stay in our place. That's what I'm always saying to my son, but he doesn't want to hear any of it. He thinks I'm wrong and says, 'Who is this miserable God who made us Pariahs? We're all conceived in the same way! The husband screws the wife and we spend ten months in the womb! So why at birth do they become superior and us inferior? And we should have to accept that and work for a ten-rupee note? Who is the bastard of a God who's done that? If we ever meet him, we'll smash his face in! Why did he do that, that bloody God: them rich and us poor?'

My answer is, 'De, Anban! Don't talk like that! Be humble and polite. Don't throw away the people who employ us. Honour them instead, that will do us much more good. We earn money through respect. People must say that the boy born from Velpakkatta's womb is very polite, well brought up, respectful and not that he's arrogant and a rogue who picks fights.'

But he's always irritated by my advice. He says, 'De! You really belong in the old days! You ask me to go to work dressed like a pauper. Every time I put something on to wear you find something wrong with it. You make remarks about my haircut and the same when I powder my face!'

Angry, I say to him, 'Eh well, kid, get on with it, da! Powder yourself all you want and go off into the world without anyone's respect. You'll never have the name I had in this village. I got here when I was as big as that. I've had children and grandchildren. Your father was born here and now he's an old man. Look at the affection people feel for him. You, you're our absolute opposite!'

I lecture him kindly so he'll see sense, Sinnamma. 'If the master who employs you wants to hit you, bend down and let it happen. Seeing your attitude his heart will melt and he'll let his arm drop. But if you rebel saying, "So, how can you raise your arm against me just because we're a different caste? How can you hit me?" If you answer back, his anger will only grow and he'll tell you, "It's the party dogs who've made you so arrogant!"'

That's how it happens in the country, Sinnamma!

(*Anban is there with his hoe, listening and smiling. And he adds*) 'Mother is always strict with me, Sinnamma. She always argues in the old way. The truth is that the people from the *ur* don't want us to rise up and be educated like them. Why? Because if we manage to own a bit of land tomorrow as well, then they won't be respected any more, they won't find manual labour at a cheap price, they'll have no more serfs. That's what they're afraid of! That's why they insist on the old rules: I should always be half naked in front of them, I should speak to them with my arms crossed, I shouldn't wear my *soman* hanging down to the ground, I shouldn't walk in front of them or dress like them! And why should it be like that? They don't feed me, they don't dress me. I don't owe them a thing. I work and they pay for my work, that's all! The other day I met the Grand Reddiar. I was in a white *soman* with a nylon shirt, my hair was oiled and well combed. He said, 'Dei, Manikkam's son! Where are you going like that with your *soman* sweeping the ground? You're not in the slightest bit embarrassed to walk around like that! You've got a nerve!' I answered, 'Do you dress me? I work hard and I please myself. I pay for my clothes: why shouldn't I have the right to

wear them and walk in the street? Why condemn me for it, sir?' And he
said, 'Oh! You've got a real nerve now to be talking like that!'

(*Viramma interrupts*) 'Get out of here! Get out of here, idiot! Aren't
you ashamed to tell Sinnamma that?' (*Anban goes off, still laughing.*)

Don't go thinking he's got a pile of *soman*. The men have got two.
He's got four, two with a red and black border.[5] We women have three
or four saris. We don't change them every day for work, but we wash,
of course. On the other hand, when we're going on a journey, we always
dress better. If we don't have a beautiful sari, we can always borrow
one. If we have to go to a marriage or a funeral and be well dressed,
we'll ask a relative or a friend, 'Big sister, lend me the sari you bought
in Madras or Pondy. I'm going to a marriage at such a place: I'll give it
back to you when I get back'. The boys do that as well, but the men
hardly ever borrow.

Anban's got a watch, a pair of trousers and a nylon shirt. He dresses
like that for going to the cinema. He goes there a lot and even our
Sundari loves the cinema. Now there's three cinemas in Tirulagam.
They know all the actors: M.G.R. is unbeatable, Sivaji is a queer, Nagesh
is funny, Sujata is like that, Rajnikant is like this. They love all the
gossip. Ah! Anban's got a radio as well to listen to all the film songs, of
course. He takes it everywhere: working in the fields, spreading fertiliser,
at the well, everywhere, everywhere! I've ended up learning some songs
from hearing that radio. And I've even been to the cinema once or
twice, the girls insisted. But I didn't like it. The actors talk quickly and
their language is proper. I don't understand any of it, well, I mean not
all of it. And I don't like staying awake just to see embraces and dances.

TWENTY

'Talking like they did in the old days'

Quarrels break out in our caste like matches being struck and I don't need to tell you, Sinnamma, how particular our language is and how blunt: the Reddiar is very right when he tells us we speak a half-language. And that half-language betrays us every time we open our mouths, even when we're well dressed, even in the market when everybody's mixed together. In the buses people move away from us when the conductor says, 'That has to be the Pariahs!' We're recognised everywhere, at the temple, in the cinema. That's why my son listens closely to the politicians, to film dialogue and the plays on the radio. He pays very careful attention to what he says, so as to speak politely, clearly and with good taste. He always makes fun of me and when he comes to town with me, he always asks me to be quiet or he corrects me the whole time, saying, 'You talk like they did in the old days! Learn to speak properly!' I won't allow myself to be treated like that and I say, 'My little boy, you were born yesterday from this womb and now you're starting to correct me? Where have you seen that? For generations we've talked like this, how do you expect us to correct it overnight? It's like asking a sterile woman to give birth! People my age will never manage it!' When you say, 'But how could that jar have disappeared? You wouldn't happen to have seen the jar that I put down there?' we instinctively say, 'Eh, the whores! Which bitch stole that jar which was in the house! I'm going to fuck your husbands! I'm going to bite your nipples!'

And so on. (*Laughs.*) In our caste we never say people's names, like I do with you when I tell stories about them. We always give them nick-names: 'Coconut Palm', if he's tall; 'Shorty', if he's small; 'Crow' or 'Swarthy' if he's dark black; 'Duck' if he's got bandy legs. And if we want to say sweet things to a child, we'll say: 'my little fool', 'my little curse', 'my little juice drinker', while you'll say, 'my little pearl', 'my parrot', 'my sprig of jasmine'. We only use words like that in songs. When we're talking normally or even when we want to be affectionate, we have to have a 'whore' or a 'screwer of my husband' or a 'fucker of his sister'. It's a question of tone: those words can be kind, but they'll be insults if you say them in anger.

I won't tell you what our arguments are: you see them every day. If there aren't any – and that's rare – the people of the *ur* get worried and wonder what's happening, whether there hasn't been some misfortune in the *ceri*. Because there's no *ceri* without quarrels: Ayoyo! It's shameful! You don't have to go very far to see that. In my own family, I have a sister-in-law, you've seen her, she's the whore who looks for trouble for no reason. Yesterday she got my husband worked up again by telling him that no one knows exactly where I go in Pondy: is it really to your house or is it somewhere else, by the sea, for example. Do you get it, Sinnamma? Am I the age to go walking beside the sea? We quarrelled very fiercely. My husband had been drinking, and she took advantage of my absence to fill his head with nonsense. Otherwise, as you know very well, he's a gentle person. When he staggered back from the wine stall, he sang to me:

Ayo, I left, taking my hoe, very early in the morning,
Ayo, my charming bride will bring me my gruel very early in the morning,
I left, leading my oxen, at midday,
Ayo, my mate bringing my sustenance, fly away with me!

Hearing him, everybody bent double laughing. The palm wine doesn't make him nasty: the opposite, it makes him sing songs for me. And people say, 'That's not bad! The old man is still in love with you, Velpakkatta!' It makes me very proud, deep down, but I don't show it with those whores, you never know what trouble might follow!

I never say my husband's name – in the country, no one calls their husband by his name. I respect him and I don't talk to him in just any old way. With all my heart I say to him, 'O beloved, o kind one, tender one!' I say to him, 'O beloved! Come, we're going to go to Madras!' or 'Come, we're going to go to your daughter's!' Lots of people in our

caste call their husband 'Uncle': 'De, Uncle, come here!' I think that's
ugly. Others, without showing any respect, just say, 'De! De!' Not to lie
to you, I'll admit that I sometimes do that too, but only when I'm
impatient or worn out. If I shout from a distance, 'O beloved, de, come
here, the Reddiar is calling you!' and he doesn't hear or doesn't answer,
I use our half-language and say to him, 'De, de, come on, de, you're
still sitting around talking about women when the Reddiar called you a
good while ago!' That's all: I don't go further than that, even in big
arguments. I think there has to be dignity in everything, even in quarrels
and even in anger.

But you've seen how things happen in the *ceri*, there's no limits! The
other day when Kannappan was chasing his wife with a knife, she
grabbed his stones pretending to catch his *soman*! We all had a good
view! And he took us as witnesses, 'Look at this bitch who's crushing
my stones!' and he screamed in pain. What shame! A husband who gets
beaten by his wife will never be able to go out the next day with his
head high – you'll never hear that! But when a bastard is chasing you
with a knife, you're not going to put up with it. While waiting for
somebody to arrest him, women have found a clever way to get their
revenge. It's very effective you know! The men scream on the spot!
Kannima is fearsome at that. Last month a big argument broke out at
her house and she didn't control herself at all. She held him like that,
her husband, and shouted in his face, 'Dei! Mate, come to my house,
come to my mother's. We'll cut you in two! Think of my mother's
suffering when she sees what you're doing to me, you fag, you juice
drinker!' It's very wrong to say that to your husband, Sinnamma, but
it's serious as well hearing that bastard calling her a whore the whole
time! I say that you have to control yourself, but we're not restrained
and that makes us easily recognisable. We never look for quarrels with
other castes, but if two Pariah women are on a bus or at the market,
they'll abuse each other about something trivial, about a seat. If he can't
calm them down, the bus conductor stops the bus and makes them get
off. That's already happened, you know. And in Madras it's worse!

That's why I tell our young girls to be calm and patient. There are
two places, especially in villages, where quarrels explode like firecrackers:
at the well for women and at the wine stall for men. It's generally the
girls who start trouble at the well, and Sundari and Amsa are terrible
when it comes to that. Each of them turns up with two or three jars,
lines them up in the queue and starts chatting. That's how we learn
what's going on in the village. If you want to find out anything, you just

have to go to the well. The women talk, they get into huge discussions and forget their jars, so someone else fills theirs in front of them. And then it starts:

'Hey, you! I put my two jars ahead of yours!'

'I've got to go to work too! You think you're the only one in a hurry?'

All the insults start flying, they grab each other by the hair and slap each other. It's even worse in the *ur*. It's actually shameful for people like that: women throw jars in each other's faces. Going to work in the morning I've often seen the remains of broken jars: that's what's left of the day before's quarrels!

When I go to the well, I let the others go in front if they're in a hurry and I don't pick a quarrel if someone says to me, 'Sister, ayo! Let me past! I took the advance for planting out, I must be there on time! I can't queue for water for hours, you understand, please!' That happens to us all so you have to be understanding. It has to be said as well that the morning queue is mainly women fetching water, whereas the evening queue is mainly girls and they love wasting time. So when I'm there in the evening, I tell them, 'Girls! Instead of filling your jars, why are you always talking of going and shacking up in the beefwood grove or in the shade of the pumps, or here, there and everywhere, eh? If you're doing it, don't talk about it! That's what makes you say wild things about each other!' That makes them laugh.

I love the young, boys and girls, and I make them laugh by talking crudely to them, singing dirty songs and setting them rude riddles. They're always embarrassed by my jokes but at the same time they ask me to tell them. It reminds me of my youth. I loved hearing those sort of things told by a man who could have been my uncle. I remember this song best of all:

> Ayo! If you see Muttamma,
> Sami, just tell her to come here.
> She will give me betel,
> Sami, she will wipe away the sweat.
>
> O girl, where are you walking to like this?
> Ayo! Who are you making love with?
> O girl, I'll go anywhere with you,
> O girl, to the land of the river Ganges!
>
> Ayo! If you take shelter over there,
> Sami, I'll tell you a secret.
> Ayo! Every day there are quarrels,
> Sami, in this bloody Pariahs' *ceri*!

Ayo! What will it become,
Sami, my prince's body?
Ayo! How long must I irrigate for,
Sami, until the close of day?

Ayo! You on your way, all the same height,
Ayo! You on your way to the cow dung,
Ayo! Collecting the cow dung,
Sami, make up a good bed.

Ayo! The snake hiding in the dung,
Sami, won't it spring at them?
O girl, give me a kiss!
O girl, get yourself under cover!

Ayo! O girl walking over there,
Ayo! Give me a kiss!
O girl, hide me under your sari!
O girl, give me your nipples first!

That's an irrigation song. When the men on their shaft-wells saw us
going past with two or three jars on our heads, our backs straight and
breasts sticking out, they'd sing that song very loud. We'd pretend to get
angry. We'd shout at them, 'You minges! Shut up! You jam rags! The
only things you like are nipples! Hold on, we'll rub our wetness on your
faces! Come on then and graze our fannies!' What interests men is nipples,
whether they're poor or millionaires! What matters is to be able to have
a feel: work only comes later! On their shaft-well, they'd repeat the last
verse at the top of their voice and we'd laugh: that was a happy time!

When I see a group of young sitting down, I always chat with them.
They tell me their stories and they ask me to set them riddles. They know
mine are often rude. They get embarrassed by them and they start laughing. Just the other day Balu, Bojakkannan and Sankar were there. They
called me, 'O Anban's mother! Give us a riddle! Go on, Grandmother,
give us one and we'll get it first go! And make sure it's not smutty!' I
went on chewing betel and they insisted, 'Go on, Grandmother!'

So I said to them, 'I stretch it out for you and you put it on for me.
What is it?'

They started laughing.

'Dei, Bojakkannan! You think it's rude, but it's not at all. Think!'

And those fools, instead of trying to work it out, were laughing the
whole time and repeating the riddle.

'Idiots! It's a bracelet. At a bracelet seller's, you stretch out your arm
to try it on and he slips on the bracelet!'

They were surprised the answer was so easy. I asked them another
one.

'I open it and you put it on for me. What is it?'

They laughed again without getting the answer: it was a banana leaf. We give it out folded up and we open it out for the rice.

After that I asked them, 'What is the monument you climb before going inside?' They gave me lots of names: Mailam, Pajani, Sabarimalai. But I told them it was Sidimalai![1] They burst out laughing, 'Look at that old woman! She fooled us when it wasn't dirty but she still ended up talking about cunts.'

Another time it was morning and we were going to work. I was in a good mood. We women were walking in front. Soon the boys caught up with us with their ploughs and their oxen. We were all going to work Tambu Reddi's field on the other side of the river. I'd had enough of stepping over the channels and the dykes, so I started singing:

> Time to step over dykes and canals,
> Look, di! The cunt's opening its mouth!
> Look, di! The cunt's laughing and up to no good!

Hearing that the boys started laughing, slapping their foreheads and falling over each other.

Balu said at the top of his voice, 'That old woman is badly on heat! All she does is talk about fucking! If the old man would see to her every day, her frenzy would calm down! You're still rutting, are you, after so many children?'

I told him that he might be strong but he'd still find it hard to satisfy me and, ashamed, he hid his mouth.

You can see for yourself, Sinnamma, there's nothing bad about all that: I just love teasing the young and Bojakkannan most of all, because he's the shyest.

I also say to him, 'The more I put in, the more she stretches out. What is it?' Actually, it's scales; the more things you put on the tray, the more the needle stands up.

Or, 'The further you go in, the juicier it is. What is it?'

When he hears that, Bojakkannan hides his head in his *tundu* and says, 'She's more and more disgusting this woman! She really is on heat!'

And I answer him: 'Little fellow, there's nothing dirty about that, it's the cashew fruit!' You know, Sinnamma, that fruit has lots of juice. You put it right into your mouth so as not to lose any, and the more you suck it, the more it flows. Of course that makes you think of a man's thing and that's why it makes those young wall fuckers laugh!

TWENTY-ONE

Two stories

I told you that I don't like films very much, Sinnamma, and it's true that my husband and I prefer to listen to the stories sung by the beggars who go round the villages at harvest time. Han! Those people have lost everything – house, work, even family – and, with their mats on their heads and a few dishes, they go from village to village begging for grain: millet, *ragi* or other things. They often stop in the tamarind wood near the village. In the day each of them goes and begs in the *ur*. They're made to sit down in the courtyard, their songs are listened to and they're given either grain or money. In the evening, when we get back from work, they come to the *ceri*. On those days we eat very early. We give them a little bit to eat as well and after we've done the washing up, we gather around them and ask them to sing. Patchamma and I always like the story of Nallatangal the best: it's long, you know, and sometimes it can last two days.[1] When the beggars are there, we save money on betel so we can give it to them and hear the whole story of that widow:

> Apparently there's a marriage, marriage
> For the daughter of the king of Kasi
> Saying that there's a marriage
> I crossed the sea to give betel ...

When we break into this song at work we don't feel tired or the pains in our knees or our hands in the mud or anything! And what's more,

200

the work goes quickly! I learned a lot of songs from those beggars, Sinnamma. That's why when you came to the *ceri* to record songs, they called me to sing them to you and that's how I got to know you, my dear! But I'd like you to be able to hear these people with your own ears! Sometimes they come by and you're not here, or you're here and they're not. I asked Danamma, who's in Putrai at the moment, to tell us if they're coming to her village. Perhaps they've found work or gone much further away. It doesn't matter, there'll be others!

The launderers also tell stories, accompanying themselves on the *udukkai*. You know them, you even recorded some of their stories. The one about Brother Crocodile, the one about the lovers of Manjakkuppam. Sinnamma, put on your tape: we're going to listen to them for a bit!

BROTHER CROCODILE

One day, a young girl with seven jars on her head was taking the mid-day meal to her seven brothers, who were working in the fields on the other side of the river near the sea. When she got to the bank, the tide was high and the young girl didn't know how to get across. She saw a crocodile not far away, and she said to him, 'O brother crocodile! Get me across the river and on the way back I'll give you all the rice that my brothers leave!' The crocodile accepted her offer. He carried the jars one by one over to the other bank, then he put the young girl down there as well: she lifted the jars back into place and headed off to the field that her seven brothers were ploughing. When they saw her arrive, they dropped their ploughs and came and took their food. All of them left a little rice in water apart from the youngest one. All together, these leftovers filled a jar.

On the way back, the young girl was hungry, so she sat down at the foot of a tree and got through almost the whole jar. That's when she remembered her promise to the crocodile. She took a big handful of clay and rolled it in the few grains of rice left to make it look like a big ball of rice. The crocodile was beside the river, waiting for what he was owed. The young girl passed him the ball, which he swallowed in one. But what a disappointment when he realised it was only a ball of clay! In a fury and to get his revenge, he clawed the young girl so she bled. Then she washed her wounds in the river, put her sari back on, took up her jars and went back home. When her mother, to her complete surprise, saw her in that state, she asked her what had happened, and

where the blood came from. That young whore, who wanted to get her
revenge on the family's youngest son, told her mother that he'd beaten
her. Full of compassion for her daughter, the mother decided to punish
her young son severely.

When the boys got back from the field in the evening, they tied up
the animals and had a rest before supper. The mother had made them
fish curry. But she'd made something else for the youngest: snake curry!
She'd thrown the head in a jar of water, thrown the tail on the road,
and cut some good slices for her son. The youngest sat down, ate the
curry, as well as giving a little to the cat which had come up to him and
to the dog which wanted some as well. Both animals died straightaway
and he didn't last much longer either. To avenge her daughter's wounds,
the mother had killed her son.

Some time later, six or seven suitors came and asked for the daughter's hand in marriage, that whore! At last the marriage was arranged,
the auspicious day chosen and the date of the wedding fixed. But come
the day of the marriage, it was impossible to find any flowers. You could
travel the whole world and cross all fifty-six countries, no flowers! How
can you celebrate a marriage without flowers? Everyone in the village
was upset, when some little cowherds who were grazing their cows
came to speak to the panic-stricken family, 'Listen! There's a place in
the cremation grounds where thousands of flowers are growing, in whole
bunches, in the middle of the woods: roses, jasmine, *samandi*! Follow
us!' Relieved, the father and mother went to the cremation grounds, the
mother carrying a basket on her hip. They were overjoyed at the sight
of all the flowers. At last the marriage could go ahead. The mother put
down her basket and went to pick the first flowers. But as soon as she
touched a jasmine, it started singing,

> O Mother! O Mother! She said her brother beat her,
>   The bitch!
> Will my flowers stick out of her black bun?
> Will my flowers be cut to decorate the bun of that woman who's so 'pure'
> Can my flowers make the bun of that whore beautiful?

Hearing that, the mother started staggering and trembling all over. She
recognised the exact spot where they'd buried her youngest son, the son
she'd poisoned. And while the whole of the world had been deprived of
flowers, the earth had flowered there, on that tomb! That flower was
telling the truth when it sang the son's story, 'What? You poisoned me
when you heard false accusations against me and now these flowers are

going to that whore, for that whore's marriage?' Then the mother very humbly took her turn to sing,

> Little brother, little brother,
> Give a marriage garland for your little sister!
> A beautiful garland has to be seen
> On the marriage sari!
> Everyone must see the beauty of this sari with its flowers!

That flower which sang was the brother himself – you've understood that, haven't you? So, knowing full well that everything had to end like this, he stopped holding it against his family and when his mother had finished singing, he threw her a big bunch of flowers. Then the father took his turn to sing:

> Little brother, little brother,
> Give a marriage garland for your little sister!
> A beautiful garland has to be seen
> On the marriage sari,
> Everyone must see the beauty of this sari with its flowers!

And the plant replied:

> O Father! O Father! She said her brother beat her,
>   The bitch!
> Will my flowers stick out of her black bun?
> Will my flowers be cut to decorate the bun of that woman who's
>   so 'pure'
> Can my flowers make the bun of that whore beautiful?

But in the end he threw him a bunch of flowers. Then it was the sons' turn and their wives': each of them sang and each got a bunch of flowers. When there was enough they plaited all those flowers into great garlands. The preparations were going well. The groom's parents had done a good job: orchestra, songs, lights, the meal – it would all be ready on time.

But, the day before the marriage, the betrothed and all her family went to the neighbouring villages for the ceremony to ward off the evil eye. The path ran alongside the cremation grounds. The group were going past them, discussing things, when suddenly a skull appeared in front of the betrothed, laughing and baring all its teeth! She thought she recognised this skull which none of the others had seen! She stepped off the path, as if she was going to relieve herself and the skull followed. She looked at it closely, for a long time, and realised that it was her old lover who'd been taken by death. Full of emotion, finding him even more handsome dead than alive, she sang to him:

Ayo! My husband, my desire!
O my handsome Kamban
O my quick temper with the proud moustache!
O my mischief with the beautiful beard!
Here you are alone in the wood after you abandoned me!

She held the skull tight and kissed it with love. That was it! The skull
stayed stuck to her lips. How was she going to ward off the evil eye like
that? How was she going to get married like that, in front of such a
crowd of people? She covered her head with her sari and started walking
again, her head down. Getting to the village, she went to lie down with
her head covered in a dark corner of the house out of sight, so as not to
be overwhelmed with shame. How could she show herself like that?
What dishonour! What an insult for everybody! Outside the celebration
was going on. The evil eye was warded off but the betrothed couldn't
be found. Everybody was looking for her and her parents found her in
the end, tucked up in a ball in her corner. They thought she was overwhelmed by sadness at having to be parted from them, and they said to
her, 'Come, Ma! Come and put your money in for the ceremony. Stand
up! Come on!' She had to stay sitting down, and so she showed them
her face and the skull stuck to her lips and told them the whole story of
her old lover. Everyone was furious. What country would accept a
woman marrying when she's had a lover? Who wouldn't have made fun
of her, shouting, 'Her lover is stuck to her lips! Her lover is stuck to her
lips!' Wasn't it all scandalous? The ceremony was stopped. The betrothed was seized. Her head was shaved, and covered with red and
black dots. She was put on a donkey and made to ride round the village,
as they shouted, 'She's committed adultery! She's committed adultery!'
And she was burnt alive.

THE LOVERS OF MANJAKKUPPAM

A husband and his wife were walking along a road which bordered a
paddy field which a handsome lad was ploughing. The woman wanted
to go and relieve herself. She let her husband go on a bit and crouched
down out of the way, behind a dyke. The handsome lad, who'd followed
her with his eyes, saw that it looked as if she was writing something. He
said to himself that this woman, who'd got down into the paddy field,
must have hidden something without her husband knowing. He was
intrigued and, once she'd left, he went over to the place where she'd

crouched down. He saw a wet brick with turmeric marks on it on the damp ground. She'd collected her urine in her hand, sprinkled the brick with it and rubbed it with a piece of turmeric which she'd taken from her betel pouch. That's why he'd thought he'd seen her writing. Astonished, he stayed pondering this brick for a little while and then, with a decisive step, he went and unharnessed his oxen, put the plough on his shoulders and ran home. He tied up the oxen by the drinking trough and brought them two armfuls of straw, saying to himself the whole time, 'Oh! She wanted to tell me to go to Manjakkuppam!'[2] And without telling anybody, he set off. But once he got to Manjakkuppam, how was he to find her? What street did she live in? What house? With all these questions troubling him, he decided to sit down on the steps of the pond. Perhaps she would come here to draw water? He settled down on the bank under a banyan tree. And in fact he soon saw a group of about ten women coming and her with two jars on her head and another on her hip. He recognised her from a distance. Her brilliant complexion and her hips like banana trees leapt out at him. Like the other women, she drew water from the pond. She filled two jars which she put down on the bank. But taking the third one out of the water, she let the fold of her sari trail in the pond. She wrung it out and pretended to spread it out to dry. The young ploughman, who hadn't stopped watching her, understood the message, 'She's asking me to wait for her at the launderers', he said to himself.

He got up and went round the pond towards the houses of the launderers. He waited until evening. When night had fallen and it was so dark you couldn't see the fingers of your hand any more, the launderers went up to him and asked, 'What village are you from, Appa? Where are you off to like this?' He said to them, 'I'm from Karikam. I've been walking since this morning and I'm very tired. I've still got a long way to go to get to Saram. Could you offer me hospitality for the night, please? I'll be off again tomorrow morning.' A family welcomed him in good heart. The launderer told him to settle down on the *tinnai* for the night. The son of the house went to the village to get the evening meal. The young woman who served the meal put three jasmines in the rice. When the young son had come back, they put out an extra banana leaf and the young ploughman started eating. When he brought the rice to his mouth, he smelled the jasmines which troubled him. But once again, he understood the message, 'She's waiting for me in the jasmine garden.'

As soon as he'd finished the meal, he asked permission to go out and smoke a *bidi* and he went to the jasmine garden straightaway. It fronted

a beautiful, large house: well-off people had to be living there. He
jumped over the garden wall and hid behind a copse of banana trees.
Soon the woman came out of the house and joined him. She took him
by the hand and led him to another hiding place, under the arbour of
hyacinth beans. There they kissed, they embraced. They talked, they
laughed, they took each other's hand – in a word, they went through
their whole routine. Suddenly they heard knocking at the garden door
and a voice shouting, 'Amma! Get up, Amma! Where are you, Amma!
Amma!' It was the husband coming home. He had knocked on the front
door, then on the garden door. When he went back to the front door,
his wife quickly left the arbour and went up to the door, saying in a
sleepy voice, 'Yes, here I am! I'm coming!' She opened the door. Seeing
how she looked, her clothes, the flowers in her hair, he suspected something but didn't say anything. She poured out the water for him to wash
his hands and feet and served him dinner. Tired out by his day travelling, he went to bed as soon as he'd finished. His wife, using her baby's
tears as an excuse, said she was going into the garden to make it go to
sleep. She sat down, her legs stretched out like this, and rocked the
baby, singing:

> O the rustling hyacinth beans
> O the rustling hyacinth beans
> O the husband, o the prince,
> He has come, he is inside,
> Araro, araro, araro, araro
> He keeps watch on the palace

Once again the lover understood the message, 'Stay hidden in the arbour. My husband is back. I'll come later'. She went and put the baby
to bed and had a look at her husband who was snoring. Then she went
out again. The embraces and laughter went on under the arbour all
night, until the crow's first call, until the first glimmer. She tore herself
away from her lover's arms and went back to the mat next to her
husband for hardly any time: soon she had to get up to sweep in front
of the door, sprinkle the threshold with water and coat it with cow dung
before drawing a *kolam*, heat up the water for the coffee, and prepare
her husband's bath and breakfast. He ate and left for work. His wife
then started cooking a thousand things for her lover, of course! She
made *vadai* and *payasam*. She fried meat and eggs. She fried potatoes
and green bananas. Now the husband had left, she'd brought her lover
into the kitchen. The door was closed and the baby wouldn't talk! While
the preparations for the meal were making good progress, they loved

each other again, making a fuss of each other cheek to cheek and then getting serious. When they'd finished, she took her lover to wash in hot water, then gave him an oil bath and washed his hair with *sikakai*. While he was getting dressed, she chose a beautiful banana leaf and put all the dishes she'd cooked on it. Both of them started eating and laughing as they fed each other, when suddenly the husband burst in and caught them in the act. He'd been suspicious since the day before and, following his hunch, he'd wanted to surprise his wife. He took the two lovers to the village council straightaway.

There they were asked how they'd got to know each other. She described walking alongside the ploughman's field the day before. He told the whole story in detail: how the brick had fascinated him, how he'd deciphered the messages, how he'd come to Manjakkuppam, how, at the side of the pond, he'd understood what the wet fold of the sari meant, how, at the launderers', he'd guessed that he'd find the woman he was looking for in the jasmine garden. When they'd heard the whole story, the council asked the woman if she wanted to stay with her husband, promising not to carry on this affair, or if she preferred to pack her bags and leave with her lover. Her reputation now being stained, the woman said that she wished to leave with her lover. By asking her this question, of course the council made it easier for her to leave and took the lover's side more than the husband's. That's because the lover hadn't seduced her. All he'd done was follow the trail which she herself had left while he was honestly ploughing his field. He knew nothing about her, not even her name or her birth. It was planned that he would understand the messages. It was planned that the jasmine flowers put in the rice chosen by the launderer's son would lead him to her. It was fate. Nothing could change it. God had written that he would live with her. It was cut and dried.

In Karani as well, the *ur* council meets when there are problems, questions of dividing up a house, land or property, cases of adultery or even for arguments between women at the well. The *panchayat* always listens to Murugaiya Gounder, the *samiar*. He's the *nattam* of the village. Everyone respects him: his words are golden and no one contradicts him when he's spoken. He always says to people who quarrel, 'Don't talk to each other like that! Don't insult each other! You might be related tomorrow!' He also settles questions of adultery between different castes: a Kudiyanar woman with a Mudaliar, an Udaiyar woman with a Sanar. He questions the lovers to find out how the man seduced the woman, and where and when. Then, depending on how serious it is, he orders him to be beaten or to pay a fine.

'Viramma, what happens when an affair between a man of the *ur* and a woman of the *ceri* is discovered?'

'Ayo! Ayo! Ayo! Where could there be such a calamity, Sinnamma? In Karani, we've never, never seen a Reddiar or a Gounder marry or live openly with a Paratchi, with everybody knowing! Besides we wouldn't want that ourselves! Can you imagine? We'd be hit in public, our lives would be made impossible! The council would have a meeting that very second and say, 'Bring her here immediately! Show her to the whole world! You, a Paratchi, what a nerve you've got to come and take a husband here in the *ur*!' We'd be called every name there is! What a disgrace it would be!

Of course those affairs can happen. Nowadays our girls go to the cinema. They know how to dress, make themselves up, powder themselves like actresses. They don't look like Paratchi any more, they're like Tamil women! They're attractive and they turn people's heads. If a Pappan, a Gounder or a Reddiar wants to have an affair with a girl from the *ceri*, it will always happen in secret. There was a story here after I came to the village. The woman was called Kokilam. She had breasts like two measures of rice. She was the mistress of a Naicker from the *ur*. When night fell, she'd put a *soman* on her shoulders and, dressed in white, she'd go down into the sugar-cane field with him. From a distance people would think that it was two men taking the air and chatting. But one evening her husband found out. He beat her like a dog and sent her back to her mother's. In Velpakkam there was a case of a Reddi who set up house with a Paratchi from Perani. When he wanted to move to the *ur* with her, the other Reddiar were against it and sent him away from their ward. They had to live on their own far away from his old house. And then one day he found work in a trunk factory in Madras. They left for there. He covered her with jewels: it has to be said that she was as beautiful as a lemon! But the poor thing never had any children. They say the Reddiar's dead. He's buried in Madras and she still lives down there.

There are some affairs like that here and there. A beautiful girl catches the eye of a Reddiar or a Gounder. She allows herself to be seduced, and they secretly have relations in a sugar-cane field or paddy field or coconut plantation. But if some women agree, it doesn't mean we're all whores. It only happens if we want it to. Whether it's a Reddi or a Naicker or a Gounder or whoever, it can only go ahead if we agree. No one can force us, not even Isan who moulded us. You can shower her with all the gold in the world, but the woman has to give her consent, 'Come on, ya! I'll be at such a place. You'll be able to find me there.' That way, it can work. Otherwise, no! It's the same whoever the man is, whatever the caste: a Reddi, a Gounder, a Komutti or a Kosavan. Suppose I'm walking down the street. A man desires me and throws a little stone at me to catch my attention. I turn round. I look at him. I can very easily get angry and say, 'What do you want, you piece of crud? What have I done to you? Why did you throw a stone at me like that?' But if I take it differently and I want to go a bit further, I'll say to him, 'What's got into you? Why did you throw a stone at me like that while I'm walking quietly down the street? What have I done to you?' He'll reply, 'I'll tell you what, de! Love made me throw a stone at you. Why kick up a fuss in the street?' If I like him, I can let him talk to see what he's going to say, 'De, I'd love us to meet tomorrow, at such a place at such an hour. What do you say? Don't drop your uncle!' Then, if I don't want to have an affair with him, I can really slag him off, 'Hey, donkey! You want me to give you my blessing with a broom? You think you're Manmadan and you're calling me to be your wife? You piece of crud! You think you're better than my husband?' Eh yes! Nothing happens without the woman's say so, even if she is a Paratchi!

'And what happens when there's an affair between a man of the *ceri* and a woman of the *ur*?'

'Ayayo! Ayayo! Ayo! That's wrong, very seriously wrong! You mustn't say that! The world wouldn't accept such a thing! If a Pariah had relations with a Reddi woman or a Gounder woman, you could start counting his bones immediately! They'd be picked up from the ground and put in a basket! Anyway, I'll tell you, those women are always in their houses and they never go out on their own. They're not like us. We're always outdoors. We go to the fields, to the well, collecting cow dung. It's easy to meet us. They only see the men in their family. They have affairs amongst themselves: between sisters-in-law and brothers-in-law, between uncles and nieces. If there's a liaison, they sort it out between themselves, as well as they can, but that never gets to the village council!

It's different for the castes who can get divorced.[3] The *panchayat* meets and they have to tell everything, 'You are another's wife. Why did you get to know this man? Do you usually meet him? Who was your go-between?'

When everything's straight, the *nattam* asks the husband, 'You know your wife has been with another. Are you ready to make it up with her? Do you want to take her back or not?' He'll ask the wife, 'And you, do you want to stay with the man who bent down to tie the *tali* round your neck or with the man you have found for yourself and been together with?'

And she will answer, 'I want to leave with the man I found for myself. I don't want any more of my husband. I don't love him any more. That's why I looked for another man.'

So then the *nattam* sends the woman away with her lover, telling them, 'Live with the one you have chosen!' and he tells the husband, 'Go! Tell your family to find you a good girl and get married again!' Then the *panchayat* judges what sum should be paid. If the woman decides to leave her husband, she has to pay back the equivalent of the marriage costs. If it's the other way round, the husband has to pay the fine. And what should be done with the children? We marry early, we have children, but if the husband abandons the wife, how will she manage to bring up the little ones? That's also why the elders meet and discuss the fines to be paid. Sometimes the husband or the wife don't accept the money, saying that money doesn't make up for losing a person. They'll say, 'Take that money for the temple!' Then the money's shared out: half for the temple and half for the *nattam* and the council members who organised the meeting. On a large copper tray, the two parties hand out areca nuts and betel to all the members of the *panchayat*. Old people who've discussed the affair are not given money.

Sometimes discussing it in front of the *panchayat* leads to a reconciliation: Sandanam took his wife back and agreed to overlook the affair. But Rasatti didn't want to stay with her husband and she was allowed to leave. Because both parties have to agree, Sinnamma! You can't force anyone to stay or sleep with you. It's the same for all women, for you the same as me. Govinda created us all the same and no one can touch a woman unless she agrees. Between a man and a woman, both have to be willing, otherwise the man's hand will never be able to stroke anything!

It's obvious to me with Sundari, who I'm worried about. Well, really it's Anban who's fretting about her, because she's started looking for a husband on her own. Anban thinks people will make fun of him if they see his sister walking with a boy who her family hasn't chosen. Really he would have liked his sister to do the same as me. You know, Sinnamma, I was married very young to the Old Man. I only reached puberty afterwards. As for him, he married his niece, my granddaughter

Amsa, who hadn't come of age yet. But today girls are married later, years after their first period! In the end Sundari has found herself a good boy. He stayed at school up to class X, he owns a quarter of a *kani* and he's very serious.[4] Anban thinks the marriage should happen quickly, otherwise it would be an insult to the whole line. They'd promised to hold the marriage in Avani and then they put it back till Panguni. You have to understand them too. Two brothers to marry and two marriages in the same family – that's a lot of money to spend. In the past you could celebrate a marriage for fifty rupees. The suitor didn't have much to give. He'd give a sari and a silver *tali*, that's all. Today it's very different. The *tali*'s gold and it costs more than three hundred rupees. But it's true the bride's family pay the most because of the dowry. Nowadays the boy's parents ask for twenty-one things with the trousseau, including a watch, a bicycle, a radio, a fan, a bed, a cupboard, trousers and shirts. You'll soon see when you marry your son and daughter, Sinnamma! I must get to see that, ayo! Andava!

TWENTY-TWO

Spells and spirit possession

I told you that the beggars who sing came to the *ceri* not long ago, Sinnamma. Vairakkannu asked the *nattam* for permission and he took a collection for them. It was also the day of the milk *puja* to Periyandavan. The singers accompanied the procession that came back with the jar of *pongal*, and they sang to Kali:

> The raw carcass, you ate it, didn't you,
> All dripping with milk?
> All the bones lying around, you crunched them, didn't you
> Telling yourself they were sugar cane?
> The kneecap, you ate it, didn't you
> Telling yourself it was *murukku*?
> Gripping the club
> You strap on your breastplate and arrow!
> Gripping the lance
> You strap on your breastplate and arrow!

Hearing that, Amsa went into a trance and no one could control her. She was taken to Murugaiya Gounder's so he could give her an amulet.

Murugaiya Gounder is not just the *nattam* of the village, he undoes spells as well and he's a very good exorcist. You've seen the queue in front of his house. Now you have to take a number to wait your turn! Because he knows how to do everything, he can do everything! You want a child? Or you don't want one? He'll know how to set about it. He'll give you knotted threads, talismans, amulets. He exorcises with

212

margosa leaves. He can discover spells, but he never says the name of the person who cast them. He can also bewitch someone. For example, if someone wishes to seduce you, and you don't want to be, the man will go and see the Gounder, who'll make a spell and cast it over you. You'll forget everybody, your father, your mother, your husband, your family, and you'll follow the man who wants you. He'll take you to his village and you'll live day after day with him. Then your husband, full of sadness at the memory of all the lovely days you spent together, will go and find another exorcist to discover what spell you're under, because the person who casts the spell is never the one who removes it. There has to be someone else for that. Married couples can cast spells on each other as well. If a husband can't get his wife to obey him any more, he'll say to himself, 'She's become insolent, she doesn't talk to me respectfully any more. Perhaps she's found something better elsewhere?' And he'll go and see the Gounder to sort it out.

My niece got very ill because of that. She was a beautiful girl, very natural, always laughing. And then she started spending her days in bed, her head buried in her sari. She had headaches, shivers, her legs felt heavy. Medicine didn't do any good. Her parents were suspicious and took her to see a *pusari* in Erippattu. The *pusari* went into a trance. The god possessed him and he told everything: Virayi had been bewitched at the request of a man of such a colour, such a height and living in a house facing south. The *pusari* then asked for sesame oil, which he made Virayi drink. Then he gave her a medicine made of plants and she had to swallow a half-litre of *rasam*. Of course she had diarrhoea all day long and that's when a smooth little ball came out. The *pusari* said that the little ball with a spell on it had been dissolved in fish sauce. Virayi had swallowed it without knowing. The *pusari* told her to clean it and show it to everybody, to all her family, so they'd know what had happened. Virayi was laughing and cheerful again after that.

It all depends on your star. If Virayi's had been ill-fated, she could have died or just had miscarriages or her babies would have died very young. But there are spells and spells. When a spell is hidden in food, it's quite easy to remove it. But sometimes it's very dangerous if it's hidden in a tree: a male coconut palm or a banana tree. And if it's dissolved in the Ganges, then it's fatal. It'll only leave when it takes your head with it.

My grandfather Samikkannu said that an apprentice sorcerer always begins on a dog. A good sorcerer must be able to kill a dog in one stroke, otherwise he'll never be any good and if the dog stays alive it won't stop barking night or day. If the sorcerer fails, his mantra isn't strong enough. The imp doesn't obey him. Because the imp is the sorcerer's agent. He's the one who'll put the spell where it has to go: where someone's sleeping or where they're washing or collecting cow dung or working in the woods. Our Iyer who lives near the temple of Pillaiyar is also an exorcist. He gives out amulets and knows his mantras well. But we go and see Murugaiyar for serious cases, even though he's much more expensive.

Before Murugaiyar Gounder became an exorcist, we'd take our be-witched to Kuttavaram. If there was a case of demon possession as well, we'd go to Malayanur. That's where we went for the sister of my mother-in-law. I was a young bride then and I didn't have any children. We took crockery and food and set up on the bank of the Palar. At midday we put rice on to cook with an aubergine sauce and some saltfish. In the afternoon, about four o'clock, we set off on foot along the river towards the cremation grounds. Hundreds of people were walking along like us, each family with someone possessed. I remember there was a beautiful woman in front of us possessed by a demon. She was singing at the top of her voice:

> Near the tall banyan tree
> Isn't that true?
> It was near the tall banyan tree,
> That I met you,
> It was near the great banyan tree
> Nanna, na, nanna ...
> O demon, leave me be!

She had a thick rope tied round her chest and hips and five or six people were pulling her, but she wouldn't give in and she pulled the other way. The demon in her was fighting like that! Poor woman! Ap-parently she was from Maruttur. Like all the possessed, she went in every direction except the right one, towards the temple of Malayanur.

There's a pyre beside the temple which is alight. When they get near the temple, the possessed tear themselves away from their families and rush towards the fire. They shout there, they jump, they dance, they roll around on the ground. You really need courage to watch that! I don't know how I did it. And then there's a banyan tree covered in locks of hair. If you saw that trunk covered in hair, you'd understand how many people go to Malayanur! After beating it with margosa branches, the *pusari* gives each of the possessed a piece of a corpse dripping with fat. You can imagine that a normal person wouldn't eat that: it's those bloody demons who are treating themselves when the possessed chew that! On the road to the temple there's already some demons who won't go any further and they say, 'Let me go, I'm going back to my land!' Others leave near the pyre, 'I don't want any more, I'm going to leave her. I'm off. I'm going home.' But the stubbornest keep on fighting and they say, 'No! I won't let her go! Give me what I'm owed, otherwise I won't go!' Then the *pusari* offers a cock or a goat. He mixes their blood with rice balls and throws them in the faces of the possessed. The demon only gives itself up after that. It takes the *pusari*'s hand and swears, 'I won't possess her any more. It's over. I'm going to leave her. Take me back to where I must go!' Then the *pusari* takes hold of the possessed by a lock in the middle of their heads, which he twists round a thin spike. He leads the possessed to the tall banyan tree, and nails them by their hair to the tree trunk. Then he cuts the lock. He takes them back to the temple and puts hot ash taken from the pyre into their mouths. Then the demon leaves for good. We say that he's leaving for the mountain. It was only after she'd been to Malayanur that my sister-in-law could have children.

Murugaiyar Gounder was the one who healed us. My husband was sick and Anban as well, but my husband had it worst. If the Gounder hadn't been there, my neck would be bare today.[1] It all started like prickly heat, then a little bump started growing until it was the size of a children's toy jar. I made him poultices of betel and thorn apples. We thought it was going to get better. The growth burst. But a few days later, it started again and opened and then sealed over. The poor man was in a lot of pain. And with an abscess like that in your chest, how can you work, how can you go ploughing? We were losing money. That wasn't all. One day we found some jasmine in the sauce and then another day, we found a man's kneecap in the fire. Or a lemon in the cow dung I'd just collected. Another time Anban ran in, panic-stricken: there was blood in the jar of water we keep for drinking.

I'd had enough of all this trouble. I got an exorcist to come from Ottumedu and tell me the truth. But not all exorcists are honest. There are some who get paid a lot for nothing very much. He had me sit down in the middle of the house which I'd thoroughly cleaned, sprinkled with cow's urine and coated with dung. He drew some circles and squares on the ground. He put trays of offerings all around, sang some mantras, but he didn't find anything. He went away with five rupees. Then

Selvaraj recommended a guy from Pombur. That one asked for a full
meal as an offering, with white rice, yellow rice, meat and palm wine.
Then he sprinkled us with turmeric water. He threw lemon segments in
all directions as he recited mantras. But nothing changed.

I was very ill myself as well, so ill that I had to stop working at the
Reddiar's. So I decided to go and see the Gounder. Since people came
from every country to see him, why couldn't he cure me as well? But I
was afraid it would be very expensive. That's what everybody said. He
didn't ask anything for himself, but a large donation had to go into the
collection box. I couldn't afford it and I hesitated. But one day I plucked
up my courage and went to take a number and my husband and I saw
the Gounder. I said to him, 'Sami! We've been ill for months and we
don't know what to do. We put ourselves in your hands. Cure us!'

He shut his eyes. He muttered something under his breath and said,
'It's your own sister-in-law, your husband's youngest sister, who be-
witched you a year and ninety days ago with three eggs which she put
in three different places. Do you want to be cured of the spell without
taking your revenge, or do you want to turn it back on her?'

He doesn't decide those things on his own: he does what you ask him
to. I said, 'Sami, that woman is just a she-ass! She's got no brains, that's
why she's behaved like that with us. I don't want to copy her and sink
so low! I don't want to turn the spell back on her. Just cure us, that'll
be enough!'

He asked me to bring him the copper leaves which I'd bought from
the goldsmith in Tirulagam. He exorcised us with margosa branches.
Then he drew some circles and squares on the leaves and wrote something. He rolled them up and slipped them in silver tubes which he
gave back to us.

When we got home, I told the family everything that sister-in-law
had done. We spat on her. My husband was ashamed to have a sister
like that. Why did she hold such a grudge against us? We'd shared out
the parents' possessions fairly. The two sisters had been married in the
proper way. So why behave like that to us? It was pure jealousy! Because
we're serfs at the Reddiar's and, thanks to him, we've been able to buy
a few animals and marry off our children decently. And for a while I've
been going to the Reddiar's less and working more at home. All that
made her jealous. Besides she didn't come to Anban's marriage and we
didn't go to her son's marriage either. The *nattam* wanted to reconcile
us. 'You are the eldest, it's your duty to take the parents' place. Put any
grudges behind you and pay tribute to the ancestors.' But neither my

husband nor Anban agreed. I said that we'd send what we owed to the married couple – a *soman*, a *tundu* and a sari – but that we wouldn't do them the honour of attending.

When I tell you all that we suffered, I can't believe that she could have wished us so much ill. Anban doesn't want to hear anything else about the whole business and he says he doesn't believe in sorcery, 'De! Stop banging on, de! That one-eyed whore is meant to have put a magic lemon in your house and that made you ill? And you're saying it as if it was all true?'

I tell him, 'Ayo! Anban! Don't insult her like that. Just because she's got faults doesn't mean you should talk like that! She's a woman like me, after all!'

And it's true. I don't get on with her, but that's no reason to speak ill of her. Don't go thinking she's a whore, Sinnamma! No, no, no! But she's someone who can't control herself. She screams, she insults people for nothing. She doesn't respect anybody. She calls the Old Man, 'You piece of crud! You fag! All you love is your wife's juices! Your tail only works for her! We wonder why he puts her on a pedestal, that fag!' No! She's got no restraint. Let's forget that woman, Sinnamma!

Anyway the talismans Murugaiya Gounder made for us kept the spirits and demons away and they've protected us all up to now! I wear mine round my neck, with my *tali*. My husband and Anban wear theirs round their waist. If you've got problems or if someone in your house is sick, don't hesitate to go and see the Gounder, Sinnamma, even for your children or for sir. I'll go and take a number for you. He is a *samiar*, he has great powers! People come from very far to see him: from Mysore, Bangalore, Hyderabad, and he really is successful with everybody!

He is the one with *bhakti* in the village. He is the one who's pure. He has the power to go up to Murugan. Of course he obeys all the rules for that, but that's not enough. He can do it because he's got the *bhakti* of Murugan. He had the temple of Murugan built in Karani and he organises the celebration of Tai pusam every year. The first year the village celebrated Tai pusam, he had vowed to break a hundred coconuts on his head for Murugan. But the elders stopped him after ten. Every year for Tai pusam seven purifications are made to the Gounder: five of powder from freshly ground red chillis, one of milk and one of yoghurt, to refresh him. At the same time the pilgrims have needles put in where they are in pain: in the cheeks, the temples, the tongue.[2] This year people from the *ceri* came to see the Gounder to ask him what you must do to be a penitent and take the needles either as a sign of gratitude or to be healed, like Virayi whose chest has been hurting for months and months. He told them that you have to be pure, not have relations, sleep on a new mat, and only cook vegetables in new pots. He also said the days that you have to fast. The penitents fully respected what he said, even the little ones carrying *kavadi*. The Gounder himself sells pretty *kavadi* covered in coloured paper which he has made by the carpenter. Everyone can carry *kavadi*, even old women.

You saw hooks being put in the accountant's back to hang him up and spin him round with two other men, Sinnamma. Lots of people rush forward to put sick newborns in their arms. Ayo! Ayo! Some people come from a long way away to do penance. There are some who pull tractor trailers with hooks in their back. We were all afraid for the son of Kannan and the brother of Nettappakkatta: one pulled a little cart, the other a millstone. We never know! We are unclean and we can do something wrong without even realising. Maduraipakkitan had ten co-conuts hanging from two hooks in his back. We followed them shouting, 'Govinda! Govinda!' At the same time their relatives, all along the route, sprinkled them with turmeric water, shouting, 'Vel Muruga! Vela! Vel Muruga!' Thanks to God they went round three times without any trouble. When the boys reached the temple at last, the *pusari* took off their hooks. He put ash on their wounds. He lay them down on a mat, away from all uncleanliness, and sprinkled them with cow urine and turmeric water. Then he beat them with margosa branches. He made the sign of penitence over them many times and in the end sent them back home. They slept and gradually their memories came back. Their *bhakti* saved them. If they had offended, their flesh would have been torn, their wounds infected, and they could even have died of suffoca-tion. Someone unclean only has to look at them at that moment and Murugan will be crossed and he will reject them. That's why the *kavadi* carriers never come into the *ceri* and, apart from the penitents, very few people from the *ceri* take part in this festival. We just cook the *pongal* near the pond and watch from a distance. Only the children go up close to get a share of the offerings which people give to the Gounder when he goes by, pierced by a lance and walking on wooden sandals with nails in them as big as my finger! He's at the head of the penitents, all of them with a lance through their cheeks. Ayo! What a feeling! What tension! We shout, 'O Muruga! Muruga! O Muruga! Muruga! Muruga! O Muruga!' People come out of their houses with a cup of *kungumam* which they pour on the penitents going by. They sprinkle the Gounder with spice-bush and turmeric water. They put gruel with milk, rice and yoghurt, rice flour cakes and fried chickpeas at his feet.

I have never seen this festival so close as this year. Usually I watch it from a distance for a minute and then I get on, because there's always things to do: the cows, the goats, the *kanji* to carry. When I see the police with their batons I'm scared of being caught up in a beating. Above all, you have to have a lot of *bhakti* to see it. And we people in hell, although we try, we don't have that. I am afraid Murugan will be angry. I'm afraid he'll whip me or paralyse one of my legs or even tear me into strips! I've had so many children, I've had grandchildren, but I've never been over by the temple of Murugan. I've been too afraid. We never know, unclean as we are! But this year, Sinnamma, I tied up the cow in the morning, I gave her enough food for the day and, taking advantage of you being here, I came with the others, all very neatly dressed, to see the traditions of the devotees of Murugan.

TWENTY-THREE

The Pongal of the Oxen and the festival of Draupadi

I'm afraid of Murugan, Sinnamma, but I love Aiyanar. He is a god for everyone, he's great and good and we worship him a lot. He's in the *ur*, to the east.[1] We're never allowed to go into his temple, not even these days. I often go and make an offering of camphor which I give to the priest: he goes and performs the *puja* in the temple and then gives me the ashes. On our way to work or on our way back – because a lot of fields are over that way – we prostrate ourselves and put our hands together, saying, 'Father Aiyanar, keep us in good health here and protect us in the place we will have to go to later'.

When my brother-in-law was very ill and spitting blood every day, he made a vow to Aiyanar. He promised to offer him a sheep. On the day of the sacrifice he prepared the sheep well, with a *pottu* on its forehead and a necklace of flowers round its neck. Well, there was no need to show that sheep the way: it went and lay down right in front of Aiyanar's temple! The priest gave back half the offerings on the *puja* tray and kept the rest for himself. He gave the meat – between eight and ten kilos, roughly – to the family only on the day after the sheep had been sacrificed. My brother-in-law shared it out with all the *pangali*, along with some *pongal*. I went to make an offering to Aiyanar for my black cow, which was constantly having yellowish discharges. I made a vow. And when my cow had been cured, I took a measure of paddy, a coconut, some flowers and some bananas to Aiyanar and cooked *pongal* for him.

The priest offered it all to him and gave me back the *pongal*, which I shared out with my whole family when I got home.

We actually worship Aiyanar on Pongal Day.[2] It happens in the main square in front of his temple. Aiyanar is there with all his horses, ready to go hunting in the forest. Two young boys guard his temple. One, sitting down and playing the drum, is poor like us. The other, standing up with his stick and bag of money, is a rich man's son: he's the guardian of the west. All the statues of horses and guardians have been donated by the faithful. The whole world prays to Aiyanar. And since he protects the whole world, men and cattle, we take all the animals to his temple on Pongal Day.

We don't celebrate the Great Pongal. That's the Pongal for people like you and the Reddiar. The Reddiar have a full measure of new rice cooked in a large new pot, decorated with ginger and turmeric roots and with garlands of ears of rice tied round its neck. As soon as the rice begins to boil and the water overflows, they cry, '*Pongalo! Pongalo! Pongal!*' and they collect the water straightaway in a jar. In a large jar they mix this *pongal* water with water drawn from the Aiyanar's temple wells and blessed by the priest. Each of them should carry the water to his land – or his lands – very fast. Whether they own a bit of land or a lot, they must sprinkle their fields with this *pongal* water, to all the four corners, shouting, '*Pongalo, pongalo, pongal! Pongalo, pongal!*' Then everyone goes home and has a bath.

What's important for us is the Pongal of the Oxen, the Day of Meat and then the Pongal of the Calves. A week before the start of the month of Tai, my husband and the Reddiar get out all the ornaments for the cows and oxen: the bells and the *koppi*. He cleans them and keeps them ready. Next he goes to buy pots of paint from Tirulagam. The Reddiar chooses the colours: red, green, blue, yellow. Some people choose the Congress colours, others DMK's. My husband paints the horns of all the Reddiar's cattle – there are about thirty, at least – and with any paint that's left, he does the horns of our cattle as well. Then he gets ears of rice and millet, sesame stalks, bunches of treebine berries, young green mangoes, malacca and roseapple fruit, black bean pods and all sorts of plants – not forgetting coconut fibre: he brings back loads of that to make ropes. The Reddiar gives him two rupees and some *sikakai* and oil for a bath. Next morning he brings out the cows and oxen and takes them to the pond. He washes all the animals one by one and gives them a turmeric bath before putting a *pottu* on their forehead. Then he puts on the ornaments and takes the animals to the stable to feed them. He washes, has his oil bath and goes to the Reddiar's house where they give him a full meal on a banana leaf. After his meal, he hangs the garlands round the animals' necks and now they're ready for the parade. He changes, puts on the *soman* and *tundu* which the Reddiar has given him while he's eating and goes back to the *ceri*. He finishes getting our animals ready, which Anban has washed, and both of them hang the garlands round their necks. All the Pariahs who are serfs do the same. They prepare their master's animals and their own.

So, all the village's cattle are ready by about four o'clock. It's time for the great parade. Everyone joins the crowds with their herd. My husband leads the Reddiar's animals and Anban leads our own. You can hear the pariah orchestra's drums beating at the head of the procession: para para para para! (*Laughs.*) The *naiyandi* orchestra comes next, followed by the herds. Behind them come the carts full of children and we women round off the procession, neatly dressed with flowers in our hair, a *pottu* on our forehead and a basket of offerings for the *puja* on our hips. All of us walk like this down the main street which is jammed with animals. The oxen for ploughing walk proudly in time to their clappers: djalog djalog djalog! Can you imagine, Sinnamma: all the animals of the *ceri* and all those from the *ur* and not one left behind: that makes a huge crowd! The cows are overjoyed and they do little jumps with their bells: dim dam dim dam dim! As for the children, they're happy too and they shout for joy. Everyone heads for the main square of Aiyanar's temple, where we herd all the animals into the middle and make a circle round them. There's so many people that they can't escape! Then we wait for the gods Isvaran and Perumal to arrive, drawn by tractors and accompanied by the barbers' orchestra. The gods stop in front of Aiyanar's temple. Camphor is burnt for them, the orchestra begins playing very hard and our *totti* shout, '*Pongalo, pongal! Pongalo, pongal!*' Then the *puja* for Aiyanar is performed and the cows are chased. The children run after them through the streets shouting '*Pongalo, pongal!*' and trying to snatch stalks of sugar cane, young mangoes and ears of millet off the cows' necks.

While this is going on, everyone goes up to the temple with their basket of offerings: I give ours and my husband gives the Reddiar's: coconuts, bananas, camphor, flowers and sweet rice flour. We women then dance the *kondam*, singing *kavadi* songs, working songs and comic songs. Afterwards everyone collects their animals and goes home. My husband takes the basket of offerings to the Reddiar who gives him a little bit of everything: half a coconut, some bananas and some rice flour. And the Reddiar fills his serfs' stomachs by serving our whole family a real meal on banana leaves. There's all sorts of vegetables: fried aubergines, okra, beetroot, carrots and *sambar*. Everything is prepared in his kitchen. After the meal the Reddiar gives his serfs the year's clothes: his other workers get money. This year I got a red blouse and a sari with flowers on it. My daughter got a sari and a blouse as well. My husband, I told you, got a *soman* and a *tundu*. But because he's young, the Reddiar gave Anban a pair of trousers and a shirt.

We cook *pongal* in the *ceri* on the day of the Pongal of the Oxen as well. Everyone digs a hole in front of their house, makes a fire and cooks rice in a big new pot. All the houses are whitewashed and decorated for the event. It's Kapok who decorates the walls. I like that boy a lot. He often comes to my door to chat and I give him betel. His wife left him saying that he was impotent. Kapok is very thorough. You see him before Pongal trying out all sorts of plants on the ground to get his colours ready. He chooses the ones that last a long time: the greens are the most difficult. He grinds up brick too, like we do for rice flour. He helps me a lot each year with the *kolam* and he draws on my walls. He also helps get everything ready for the *puja* to our god. The tools have to be put in place: the hoe, the sickle, the billhook, and the plough and rice measures as well – and all of them have to be well-decorated with coconuts, bananas, flowers and camphor. When we've performed the *puja*, I give him a good helping of *pongal*. I put a bit of everything on another banana leaf and give it to my cows to eat.

The day after the Pongal of the Oxen is the Day of Meat. It's a great day for us! It's the one we look forward to the most! They sell beef in the *ceri* on that day. People even eat meat in the *ur* but there it's mutton, of course! I always buy two or three pieces of beef which I cook in a sauce to eat with the *pongal*: I make enough for two meals. We're very cheerful that day and we drink! As the proverb says, '*Karinal, verinal!*', 'Day of meat, day of madness!' That's just how it is in the *ceri*! Next day is the Pongal of the Calves. We cook a fresh *pongal* on a little fire in a little pot. We gather together all the little calves, then we chase them shouting, '*Pongalo pongal! Pongalo pongal!*' We also perform the *puja* for cow dung at the Reddiar's that day. We coat the stable in cow dung and make a pile of it in the middle. When the stable is ready, the Reddiar's wife arrives with a tray heaped with coconut, palm sugar flour, *kungumam*, flowers and camphor. She tells me to make Pillaiyars out of cow dung. I decorate them as she hands them to me: first with

red, then with flowers. Then I have to get myself ready. I wash my face,
which I rub with turmeric paste, and put flowers in my hair. The
Reddiar's wife lights some camphor on a tray which she gives to me to
present to all the Pillaiyars. Then I put the tray on the ground and we
prostrate ourselves before the Pillaiyars and the mountain of cow dung.
Finally I get up and stick about ten cow pats on the walls. I take my jar
to be given some *kanji* and hold out a fold of my sari. The Reddiar's
wife puts in half a coconut, a banana and a little palm sugar flour and
I go home with that.

I gave my first *pongal* to the mother of my black cow. I had bought her
at Nagapalaiyam market. My husband always prefers to buy oxen: they
work better and when they grow old, you can always sell them to the
butcher. But once I really insisted that we buy a cow. We chose a very
beautiful one with a big white mark on its forehead, but one day my
fucking son hurt her leg while she was grazing. Instead of getting up,
he threw a stone at her to make her come to him and he split her foot.
I was very sad seeing her come back in that state! I put some turmeric
paste on the wound, I did what everybody told me, but nothing cured
her. The Sakkili told me that his maternal uncle at Ambavaram knew
about that. Both of us went off to find him and he came straightaway.
He massaged her hoof and bandaged it: it all cost me more than thirty
rupees but nothing worked and my cow kept on limping. So we decided
we couldn't keep her any more. I cut off some hair from her tail as a
souvenir before we sold her to a butcher in a village a long way off.
That cow always brought us good fortune. We were fortunate when she
was here! And even now I light some camphor for her every Tuesday
and Friday and I pray.

   After I'd bought that cow I tethered her in the Reddiar's stall and the
Reddiar family drank her milk – all her milk – until she became pregnant again. I didn't hold out my hand even for ten *paice* for that milk
because the Reddiar gave us everything for Anban's marriage: the marriage sari, the rice, the coconuts and the *tali*. I have to admit that we
didn't have to feed her at all when she was in his stable. I used to give
her an armful of the Reddiar's hay on my way back from work. His
stable was almost empty then. Anyway, I always take very good care of
cattle because they are gods. You've seen the ox at the entrance of the
temple with his horns decorated: he's all clean, all beautiful, don't you
think? Well that's how cattle should be kept. The cow is sacred, it's
Lakshmi. Every Friday I coat the house in cow dung because the cow is

Sridevi. I collect its urine and sprinkle the house with it for good luck. We wash our faces in cow urine to drive away Mudevi, who puts us to sleep in the middle of the day while we're working.[3] There's a lot of power in this urine, great good fortune. It frees us from uncleanliness and we must drink it, especially during our periods: the elders pour a little into our hands like holy water. This urine is a form of *bhakti*. Once the daughter of my neighbour opposite came to ask me for a light. I said to her, 'Come in, help yourself'. That same evening I quarrelled with her mother and I was in pain: constant headaches and arguments with everybody in the house that never ended. I suspected something and went to see somebody who was possessed at Mangalur. As soon as I came near, he said, 'A young girl didn't come and ask you for a light, did she?'

'Yes!'

'She was having her period. Her unclean blood – three drops of it – fell in front of your door. That's the *dosham* which is afflicting you and that's why there's trouble in your house. For three days you must light lamps of three oils – groundnut, sesame and castor – after coating the house with cow dung and sprinkling it with cow urine. Offer some *pongal* on the third day to widows and sterile women.' I did what he told me and I was freed from that *dosham*.

On Friday I wash my oxen and cows with loads of water. I give the cows a turmeric bath, just like a married woman, and put a *pottu* on their forehead. Cows should always be bathed by a married woman and, with us, that's me. I think of Lakshmi as I do it and I say to my cow, 'We live well thanks to you, Mother Lakshmi. Mother, protect us!' She's the one who protects us women when we are unjustly suspected of having deceived our husbands. You know the arguments that go on between husbands and wives in the *ceri*, Sinnamma! The husband will say, 'You went to such and such a place that night, you slut! You cheated on me that night!' And, picking up a cow's tail, the woman replies, 'Mother, listen to what he's saying to me! It's a lie. You're the one who ought to give him an answer!' Because everyone knows you don't tell lies when you swear on a cow's tail, otherwise you'd go blind or even die. That's another reason why you have to look after cows with reverence. In the evening, when the lamps are lit, I offer them a tray of camphor. Lakshmi is wealth. It's thanks to her that we have several animals at home. Think how much you make with a pair of oxen and, with our cows, how much milk we can sell.[4] What blessings these animals bring us! Of course when there's no grass, we have to buy food for the oxen and the cows too. We buy them special feed at Tirulagam market: bran, sesame and groundnut cattlecakes. When the Reddiar is having sesame oil made, he leaves us some of those cattlecakes, but we get the groundnut ones from the market. Before milking we give the cows a gruel made of the cattlecakes, which we leave to soak in the morning before going to work. The paste swells and doubles in size, it becomes creamy like yoghurt and then I mix it with rice bran. When the cows eat it they produce lots of milk.

Twice a day I take my cows to the cooperative where we are members. The Little Gounder is the head of the cooperative. He got some money from the government to run it. The milk from the cows of the *ur* and the *ceri* goes to the cooperative and a big lorry takes it to Pondy. The milk is pure, without a drop of water. It's checked on the spot by a machine which tells you immediately if there's a drop of water in your milk. Two women from the *ceri* and one from the *ur* had watered down their milk a bit: ah well, they were sent home with it! It's because they need to make the milk into butter with a churning machine. The butter is sold at Pondy too. They give us two and a half rupees a litre which they pay us every fortnight. That makes me sixty to eighty rupees a month for two cows. If the cooperative workers milk the cows themselves, they keep five rupees a cow. But I know how to milk and Anban does too. We both go there with our cows: I milk, he measures and pours. If we miss milking time at the cooperative, then I make yoghurt which I sell at the market. But right now my black cow is pregnant and she's giving very little milk: we keep it for home, since my husband and children drink tea. If there's any left, we make yoghurt.

I asked the cow hospital to come and cover my cows because, if they do it, the stranger's bulls they bring are magnificent and enormous. We country people like them very much. Besides, all the cattle you see now at Karani are crossbreeds of those bulls and they make very good dairy cows. Mine give me three or four litres a day. That's why I prefer the people from the cow hospital to come. They ask four or five rupees a cow but I like paying them that much because it's never easy when you let them be covered in the fields. I can see that clearly when I'm with the little cowherds who work for the Naicker, Nadan Reddiar and Lakshmanan Reddiar. All those kids are friends, they herd the cattle together and I go and graze mine in the same place. When I see those heavy bulls mounting those tiny little cows so brutally, practically suffocating them, I get furious and chase them away, saying, 'Those cow lickers, they don't want to walk, all they want to do is fuck! Dirty fuckers!' The little cowherds burst out laughing when they hear this and say this to each other, 'Have a look at that old woman! Listen to what she's saying about those bulls! That's all that old woman of Velpakkam thinks about!' When we're all sitting in the shade by the pond, talking about this and that, I'll suddenly say to them, 'Eh, boys! Have a look at that tail that's hanging down!' That never fails: they all laugh, putting their hands in front of their mouths, and it amuses me to see them cracking up like that.

Last time I had to spend ten rupees to have my cows served but it can cost up to seventy rupees. The man took them one by one. He tied them to the tree in a quiet place behind the houses and he got the bull to mount them. Those people are doctors for cows. They know what precautions to take and what not to do. Thanks to God, it worked for the white cow, but, with the black one, the sperm spilled on the ground and nothing happened. It had been the same the time before when she hadn't stopped having yellowish discharges. The doctor examined her by pushing his whole hand in while I squeezed her head between two bars. She mooed with pain and then slowly she stopped: she seemed to get used to it. Then he injected the sperm. That's when I saw what a load of sperm they've got! I was given some medicines and told to come back a month later. The following month the doctor put his hand in again and told me there wasn't anything. He injected sperm a second time. When I went back, the doctor told me this time, 'She's two months' pregnant. You must give her gruel made of unsteamed rice and not take her to graze.' They give us food and special feed free for each pregnancy.

It was after that injection that my black cow gave birth to that calf without horns which you've seen. She's very fragile, very delicate, my black cow. She gave birth one day when I was taking her to graze. I could see she wasn't walking normally. After a few steps she'd lie down, then walk on, then lie down again. Her teats were as stiff as rods, her udders swollen, her flanks hollow and her stomach was touching the ground. She was dilating and having some sticky discharges. When I saw that, I understood that she was going to calve soon. My husband and Anban weren't in Karani that day, so I took care of it myself: I'm used to women and cows too. Anyway cows don't need anybody. Mine pushed all on her own. She lay down, stretched out her four hooves and pushed very hard. Some cows do it standing up but not mine. The calf came out head first and the rest followed. It's very important not to say the calf's sex out loud the minute it touches the ground: you must leave it to struggle, that's the way we always do it. Then I gently took the cow and her calf to the *ceri* for the placenta to come out. There can be some problems with that and, if so, we go and find a man from Kodik-kuppam. But this time it went well. I gave my cow some millet flour mixed with palm sugar flour. That picked her up and she pushed out the placenta which I didn't leave lying there for a second: I rolled it in straw and hung it high up in the banyan tree behind the *ceri*. We always fix them very high up so cats or dogs won't get them, otherwise the cow's milk will be cut off. It's even better if we can hang the placenta on a jackfruit tree. That tree has milk in its branches and it means the cow will have as much as a breast that squirts milk.

After calving, I bathe the cow for seven days in hot water that has been used to soak a measure of rice, and I sprinkle her udders and hooves with it. I get a yellowish milk at first, which I use to make sweets, and a yellow, shining cream, good and sweet smelling, which I put in the middle of the house to offer to our god. Then I take some of the cream to Mariamman's temple to offer it to her and I share it out with everybody afterwards and announce the calf's sex. The Reddiars do the same and often I get some cream that way from them. The Friday after calving I give the cow a turmeric bath and, just like a woman, mark a large *pottu* on its forehead. Finally, like on the day of the Pongal of the Oxen, I ward off the evil eye from the cow and her calf with some dry chilli and salt in a coconut.

I haven't said anything about buffaloes, Sinnamma, because the buffalo is the mount of Yama, the one who leads us away. We don't celebrate those animals the same as cows or oxen, we don't revere them. We don't decorate them except for on one day, during the festival when there's firewalking, when rice mixed with blood is thrown on Pakkasuran, and the cart is pulled by buffaloes washed with turmeric and with garlands round their necks.

On that day a Gounder dresses up as Pakkasuran to take a collection of rice in the *ur*.[5] He paints his face red, wears wings like Garuda and six thick ropes are tied round him, held by three people on either side, because he's drawn by demons. He shouts, 'I am Viran, da! Viran!' Each household gives rice, especially the Reddiar's and those people who've made a vow. All the jars of rice are carried in the cart of Pakkasuran, in front of his head, and put down behind the temple of Murugan near the pond, after the last houses of the *ur* facing south. Hundreds of people go and wait there to see the rice mixed with blood being thrown. We get that rice for free, but some devotees, especially ones without children, pay two or three rupees for it. It happens on the last day of the festival of Draupadi and only after that do people walk on fire.

You've seen the festival of Draupadi yourself, Sinnamma, it's the biggest festival in the village. It lasts eighteen days, when the *Bharatam* is read and everyone listens – those who understand its meaning and power and us, the illiterates, to atone for our wrongs. An Iyer is invited, whose trade is to read the *Bharatam* in the temples of Draupadi.[6] He sits down in the morning with his book and he doesn't get up until the evening when a lamp is lit and the crowd breaks up. You don't need to be nearby. A platform is built for him and he has a microphone. There's a loudspeaker on top of the temple and another near the pond in the *ur*, so that all of it can be heard from the *ceri*.

The third day after the new moon in Panguni, everybody who's going to lead the festival has a yellow string tied to their wrist: the musicians, the priests, the Iyer, the Gounder and the dancers who'll be brought from Mailam to play for the eighteen days. Then the date is set for raising the flag.[7] Murugaiya Gounder sends for the *totti* and says to them, 'Dei, we're going to raise the flag on such a day. You must be there with your instruments!' and he sends the *urtotti* to carry the news from village to village with his drum. Our *totti* are in attendance night and day at this festival. They accompany the processions from morning to evening, because both the Pariah's orchestra and the temple's orchestra with the *karna* have to be there for this goddess. Our musicians are always at the front: they're the ones who clear the way. Their drums ring out very loud, para para para, and when they hear them, people in the neighbouring villages start running, saying, 'The goddess has come out in Karani. There's bound to be some theatre. Let's go and see!' Thanks to the drums of the Pariahs, people come from everywhere, Sinnampet, Kodukkur, Tirulagam. There's always music and lights during the festival and our *totti* don't rest even for quarter of a day, because it's our duty to play the drum when a goddess comes out in a village. The barbers can't play, but we Vettiyan have to. We get what we're owed, like everyone else. We have our share of the harvest from the temple land – we Vettiyan, the barbers, the *karna* player and the launderer. Muragaiya Gounder gives each of us our share of rice. Each *totti* is entitled to four measures of rice and a little money, and it is not much for all that effort. That's why there's been an argument. I told you about it, our young wanted to be paid like real musicians.

Very early in the morning, even before we go to work, our *totti* set off with their drums under their arms. They go and sit down near the

temple to wait for the divinity to come out on a cart, and they warm up
their drums, beating them so they sound good: tang tang tang tang!
Everyone must be able to hear the Pariah orchestra from a long way
away, otherwise how will they know the god has come out and not miss
the festival? You can't rely on the barbers' orchestra for that. They're
right next to the cart, they play for the god. We announce his arrival,
we play for everybody else. We tell them, 'The cart is coming! Get your
trays ready!' The barbers only have to do their duty on one day, the day
of firewalking. The other days they play for people who can afford to
pay them. It's not the same for our *totti*, they have to be there morning
and evening.

I can't remember now which god comes out in the morning. Wait ...
It's Perumal. Perumal comes with Garuda. He goes round the *ur* very
early in the morning and looks for offerings in every corner, even by the
temple of Aiyanar. The priests are on the cart, bells in their hands, and
they present each of the trays that people bring to Perumal. The cart is
actually a wagon with tyres drawn by oxen, except for the day the
Reddiar pays. Then he mounts the god on a taxi. Because each of the
eighteen days is the responsibility of a family, and all the *pangali* take
part.

The accountant's family begins on the first day. It's a modest celebration, but the actors play. As soon as the date for the raising of the
flag is fixed, the accountant goes and offers betel to a troupe of actors.
The troupe changes each year: it can come from Mailam, but also from
Nettappakkam, Nellikkuppam, Kolappakkam ... The actors come and
move into the *ur* for eighteen days. Everyone gives them what they need
to eat: rice, vegetables. They cook their meals and sleep in the temple
courtyard. They don't put on a performance every day because not
everybody can afford to pay for a whole episode! But we can't organise
a festival without theatre either, that would be degrading! So the troupe
is hired for some dances and some individual songs.

On the second day a family of Udaiyar take over. Not much happens.
The divinity comes out, there are a few firecrackers and that's all. The
third day is Murugaiya Gounder's. That is magnificent. Everything is
lit up, there's firecrackers and fireworks. And the Gounder feeds everybody, the people who pull the cart, the dancers, the *totti*. The fourth
day is the turn of the Nadar. Very little goes on and there's no theatre.
The next day is the house of Ambadi, a small family as well and nothing
happens. But the Naicker organise the sixth, seventh and eighth days
and then there's everything! The god who steals butter comes out. We

see him on his cart eating butter. He's the one who plays the flute later. I've forgotten his name. He has his hair tied up in a knot to one side. Ah! It's Kishtan, yes, he's Kishtan![8] The statue captures his movements very well, as if he was real! The Naicker offer him a full jar of butter. There's theatre on those days: the troupe tells the story of Kishtan, who steals the butter, pays court to the girls and climbs the coconut palm. The ninth day is the thieves' – we call them 'the new houses'. They do it on a big scale, with lights and loudspeakers. The tenth day is a family of Gounder, who are well-off: there's theatre in the evening. I don't know who the eleventh and twelfth days are – Gounder, I'm sure, but there's no theatre. Tambu Reddiar takes over on the thirteenth day. Again it's magnificent. There's everything: firecrackers, fireworks, lights, theatre in the evening. What's after that? The fourteenth day? I don't know who does that or the day after. The sixteenth day, ah! the *kambattam* organises the marriage of Draupadi like a real marriage! There's no one in the *ceri* that day. Everyone's in the *ur* to see the celebration that must cost at least two thousand rupees! The matrimonial home of Mother Draupadi is in Kodukkur. It's her mother's home here in Karani. So women go to Kodokkur for trays. The goddess wears a red wedding sari on this day with garlands round her neck and a thick, gold *tali*. Coconut, betel, areca nut, rice and money are all tied on to her sari. And a meal is served to the *totti*, the actors and everybody: because it's a marriage! The next day Gopala Gounder's family is in charge of the festival and the pearl cart comes out. Everyone is fed, there's a firework display and of course, theatre.

Finally, the last day is the day of the carpenters and the descent into the fire. In the morning the battlefield is acted out next to the place where there's going to be firewalking. People are struck with margosa branches and the bodies are covered with a white shroud.[9] Ayo! The *Bharatam* priest carries on reading his book, while the carpenters prepare the fire. Two big rectangles fifteen feet long are dug near the temple of Murugan. The first is for fire, the second for water, the River Palar, because the people who walk on the fire get into the water afterwards.[10] From the morning onwards pilgrims bring wooden objects for the fire: pestles, mortars. Even the people from the *ceri* give theirs. Margosa trunks are sawn up and the logs lined up. Young wood can catch as well. You should see how it all burns, going kola kola kola kola. It's like a field of red hibiscus. The *bhakti* of that Mother is what makes this possible! In the afternoon the embers are spread out over the first rectangle. A lot of

our people from the *ceri*, devotees who've made a vow, pierce themselves with needles on this day, near the eyes, in the neck, in the temples, in the back, everywhere. We go to the *ur* very neatly dressed in
new yellow cloth, with a pot of turmeric water mixed with cow urine in
our hand. We buy tiny little needles in front of the temple which the
priests put in us. We prostrate ourselves and go round the *ur* shouting,
'Govinda! Govinda!' But some have long spikes, hundreds of spikes
going through their stomach. Others pull carts with hooks in their backs.
Their *bhakti*'s what protects them! The hooks are fixed into their flesh,
but they don't feel anything, they walk very slowly, taking little steps,
without making sudden movements. Someone guides the devotee and
takes him three times round the temple, then he leads him to the big
cart beside the embers near the pond. Then the hooks are taken out and
ash put in the wounds. You have to see the face of this Mother who's
there on her cart – it's like puffed sesame!

In the afternoon Murugaiya Gounder carries the *karagam*. He's done
penance and followed the rules of purity for many days. The devotees
have to obey those rules as well. He wears a knotted thread on his wrist,
as a sign of his vow, which will protect him when he goes down into the
fire. With his *karagam*, and his mouth gagged, because the goddess
could knock him over or slap him, Murugaiya Gounder comes out of
the temple with about ten devotees as faithful as him. Three times he
goes round the temple. He goes down into the fire first. Afterwards the
crowd of devotees follow him: big, little, old, young, even a baby a few
hours old which someone will have put in a devotee's arms. They walk
on the fire, a garland round their neck and flowers on their wrists,
shouting, 'Govinda! O Govinda!' And watching them, we shout
'Govinda! Govinda! O Govinda!' as well. Then they all get into the
Palar, and when they come out of the water, a priest gives each of them
a lash of the whip, even the *kambattam*. Even your grandfather had to
take it! You hear the whip snap, pada, pada, pada! Their skin changes
colour and blushes. Without this lash of the whip, they'd die! They get
another lash of the whip in the temple of Draupadi and then they
regain consciousness, their life returns to them – that doesn't come
from men, it's the mercy of God! Then ash is given to the devotees and
they go back to their homes.

We Pariahs can only watch, we can't walk on the fire. At the start of
the morning we leave the *ceri* in a long line which stretches to the pond:
all of us well dressed, with a clean sari, flowers in our hair and a *pottu*
on our forehead. We carry a basket on our heads, and in it, jars of

different sizes, ladles, a tray of offerings, rice, firewood, flowers, water –
everything needed to cook the *pongal*. Each of us sets up on the edge of
the basin, lights their fire and cooks their *pongal*. At the end of the
morning, we line up all the jars at the door of the temple and make an
offering of them. We finally go back to the *ceri* when we've seen the
firewalking and gone to the fair which comes to the village for the
festival. It's hard getting around, there's so many people. Sometimes
people die from suffocation because all the travelling salesmen are there
and the stallholders from Tirulagam bazaar have been set up near the
pond for two days. There are merry-go-rounds and you can find little
booths selling tea, bananas, sweets and dishes made of copper, aluminium
and stainless steel. The stallholders do well that day. Pilgrims come
from everywhere, from Andhra, Madras, Pondy and, of course, in ox-
carts, from Tirulagam and the next-door villages, to offer *pongal* to our
Mother Draupadi on the eighteenth day.

TWENTY-FOUR

Sharing the harvest

Our Reddiar has sent for the Brahmin today to consult the almanac. He doesn't do anything without asking his advice and he goes to Pondy as well to consult other Brahmins about his crops: they say that they're more knowledgeable. We consult our priests as well. For marriages we go and see the Valluvar, who lives next to the temple of Perumal. He'll say if the stars of the intended are compatible and if the couple is well-matched. For agriculture we go to the Pandaram. He has all the almanacs he needs, the old as well as the new, and he finds what we need to know about cyclones, floods or droughts in them. He tells us about the rains and which date will be favourable for this or that crop.

Because we don't just sow any day we want. The Reddiar only touches the seeds after the Brahmin has told him which are the auspicious days. Once the date is set, he comes and tells us, 'Dei, today is the eighth day after the new moon – or the ninth day after the full moon – you can prepare the seedlings!' Not just anybody can touch the seeds first. It has to be someone with an auspicious name, who brings luck or has green fingers. At the Reddiar's that's me. I pour seven measures of *samba* rice seed in a big earthenware pot for every quarter of *kani* and I cover them with water. Generally it's too much and there's some left for us. If I've got a field, I sow on the same day as the Reddiar and only consult our Iyer to see if my harvest will be a good one. After three days, the seeds will have sprouted and we'll see shoots. It's a pretty sight, shoots as thin as needles. The third day we'll sow. From the fifth day onwards the shoots will come out of the earth, and on the sixth, eighth and tenth days we'll see them more and more clearly. On the tenth day the stalk and its leaves will be visible: it's like a green light which leaps out at your eyes.

Amongst all the different seeds, there are some we sow directly without soaking them first. We call them *vilvirai*. We carry them at first cock crow as they are, on our heads, wrapped up in a jute sack. We have to get to the field before anyone else and not meet anyone on the way.

My husband and Anban always go and sow for the Reddiar. Men rather than women have to do that and there must be two of them. When they get to the field, my husband and Anban go straight to Sani's corner.[1] Anban puts down the basket for the *puja* which I've prepared at home. I've put some bricks in and a little stool, some flowers, couch grass, camphor, turmeric paste, red powder and cow dung. My husband prepares the *puja*. He puts the bricks on the low stool and, in front of them, he makes Pillaiyar out of cow dung. He coats them with turmeric paste and draws a red *pottu* on their forehead. Then he arranges the flowers and couch grass in the same way we women put flowers in our hair. With both hands, he takes the seeds and puts a pile in front of each Pillaiyar. Then he lights the camphor and, with Anban, prostrates himself. Then they go and prepare the seedbed. They make a square in the place they've chosen. They turn over the earth with a hoe before sowing and make it all level, so there's no holes or bumps. Each of them stands at one end with a winnowing fan full of seeds and they sow by lifting up the fan and turning it once back towards themselves; the seeds fall like rain, without leaving any spot uncovered. They carry on sowing like that until there are no seeds left. They mark the square by planting a margosa branch at each corner and then the sowing ritual is over. They go back to Sani's corner and keep the seeds offered to Pillaiyar, because they belong to them now. They go and wash at the pump and return home. Then I'm given the seeds. I put them on a tray in the middle of the house and all of us prostrate ourselves. In the afternoon I take those seeds, hull them and then pound them to make flakes. I mix them with palm sugar and if I've got some, I add sesame seeds – or you can add green leaves: that's very good too. First we offer this mixture to the god, praying to him that everything will go as it should, and that we'll live well and not go without food. Then we share it out with the neighbours and the women who've seen me pounding and have said, 'Sister-in-law, you're pounding seed from the sowing. Give me a little, de!' We eat the rest with the children.

At the Reddiar's, they don't make flakes on that day out of the seeds they've kept to offer to their god. They have their seed blown. I am the one who does it and it takes so long, I'm always crippled with pain and my hands are blistered from bursting the unhulled rice. When they split, the grains are like beautiful flowers and they have to be poured still burning into the mortar. The Reddiar's wife is in charge of that. There are two of us pounding and it has to be done in the right way, fast and to the same rhythm, without stopping for a single instant, because if we're too slow, we won't get flakes, just grilled rice. When it's all done, the Reddiar's wife mixes the flakes with sugar. She puts a share of it on a banana leaf to offer to the god, and she shares it out with her relatives. We get our share as well which we give out in the *ceri*.

Once we've sowed, we wait a few days for the shoots to come out of the earth. If the shoots come a finger's length out of the ground, with one or two leaves showing, then it's a sign that the harvest will be good: otherwise, if the seeds aren't good quality, the shoots come out here and there and rot or are completely burnt up. But when they suddenly come out like that, like a ray of light, on the eleventh or thirteenth day, we feel reassured and we say to ourselves with satisfaction, 'It's all right! The square I made has worked. The shoots are coming up well, soon I'll be able to plant them out!' When the shoots appear, we treat them so they won't be eaten by insects. We throw on something like the ash from cow dung which we use to brush our teeth. We only put on chemical fertiliser after that. They tell us everything about crops on the radio and now everyone has a set, all you need is to turn a button to hear it on your *tinnai*! They recommend I.R.8 or I.R.50, *kannagi*, horse-tail *samba* or *ponni*.[2] The grains are so small that once they're cooked they look like jasmine petals or pulao rice from Madras. And two hours after you've eaten, you're hungry again!

I have to borrow six measures of *samba* the day after tomorrow and of course I'll have to pay them back with interest: as you can guess, no one lends for nothing. Here it's the same as the fifty-six countries of the world. People do the same thing everywhere, the same as you, the same as the Gounder. The rule for cereals is double. If you borrow a *marakka* of *ragi*, after the harvest you've got to give two back. And we do the same when we borrow paddy by hundredths of a measure for a marriage.

I was able to lend a sack of paddy, by the grace of God, to my neighbour opposite when she married her son. She said to me, 'Sister-in-law, give me a sack of paddy, I'll give the sack back and the interest when your Anban gets married.' Another time Pakkiam came and asked, 'Viramma, Viramma! Give me a little bit of paddy! My granddaughter has come of age and I must prepare some turmeric water. I'll give it back to you when my rice has sprouted!' For a sack of paddy, you take ten *marakka* interest and you need three sacks of paddy to get two sacks of rice. That's because we need a lot of rice for a marriage. Everybody is paid in kind. The Iyer gets his measure of uncooked rice but we have to feed the musicians and launderer. Where can we find that money? We can borrow up to a certain amount from the Reddiar: he pays himself back out of our salary, interest first, then capital. But when we have to make up the amount, we manage to earn money some other way – by being day workers for other owners or by becoming tenant farmers on a little bit of either temple or public land.

We Vettiyan are entitled to two *kani* of temple land, like the musicians of the *ur* and the barbers. That land is for us and we share whatever we reap from it. But often we slave away for almost nothing because it's bad, dry land. That's why our young don't want to play as musicians any more because we get nothing from those two *kani* and the pay that they get apart from that is really very low: two and a half rupees for a gravedigger and now seven rupees for a musician. But let's forget about that, I've already told you about it. The public land is difficult to work as well because the water is a long way away. On the other hand, the temple owns more than thirty *kani* of good land which they rent out every year.

Up to now I've always got a quarter of a *kani* of temple land for eight sacks of paddy. By spending two hundred rupees on fertiliser and insecticides and by working ourselves – my husband, Anban, Sundari, Amsa and me – we can bring in three harvests, each of eight sacks. I give eight sacks for the rent and I share the rest half and half with the Reddiar, who irrigates for us. That's what allows us to eat or pay back what we owe or hold a marriage or give a relative a good burial. Some people even get richer by managing what they earn very carefully. You see some building brick houses for themselves or paying back everything they've borrowed from the Reddiar and releasing themselves from serfdom, saying, 'Ayya! I'm retiring, I haven't got the strength any more to keep on working for you, I'm leaving, Ayya!'

But this year we couldn't get any temple land because they've raised the rent to ten sacks. We can't risk that much because we're not at all sure that we can grow enough and if we have to pay ten sacks, what will

we have left? When you rent a field, everything has to be settled at the
end of three years because bids are made every three years. We've just
finished a lease. Six of us Pariahs got together to take one and a half
kani but this time we weren't able to match the new bids. What's more,
they wanted a bond, a mortgage this year. Only people who own land
could give one but no one wanted to do it for ten sacks. If the risk
hadn't been so great, some of the Gounder would have agreed to sub-
let us the land: the Gounder from Karimangalam, for example, because
he knows we will pay even if we make a loss, so as not to lose the
owner's confidence.

It's harder and harder for us to become tenants on privately owned
land because they're afraid that, after a while, we will take their land.
You know very well that we're not like that, that people can trust us in
this. But the government is for it and they encourage people who work
the land to take possession of it after a few years. They say that there
have been some court cases like this and that a Chettiar from Pondy lost
all his land that way. That's why it's very, very difficult to get some of
a landowner's land and when he rents it out, he splits it up and gives a
quarter of a *kani* to one and an eighth to another. You understand why
we poor are the Reddiar's serfs – it's to win their confidence. We haven't
got any land of our own, so each one of us tries to rent a little bit of
their land without middlemen and without a mortgage. They have to
trust us, otherwise how are we going to pull through without a scrap of
land of our own?

Some years when nothing grows, the administration comes to certify
that and then we pay nothing. The owner comes and sees that the ears
have wilted through lack of water. He goes off without claiming anything
and we stay there with our losses. What can you do? It's Mahadevan
who hasn't sent us any rain and my stomach is empty![3] Afterwards we
start all over again by borrowing a hundred rupees at ten per cent
interest a month. If we can't borrow anything, we pawn some copper
pots or dishes or a jewel with the Marwari of Tirulagam: he lends ten
rupees for something worth a hundred. People who have land can
mortgage it while they're still cultivating it and then get it back after
they've paid off the mortgage.

Since there are people from Pondy who work in the village at the
school, the dispensary and the creche, we can also borrow from them and
they lend money against sacks of paddy. I organised a loan this year for
Arayi who wanted to grow a little paddy but didn't have the money to
buy seeds. The nurse at the dispensary was looking for someone growing

paddy because she had five hundred rupees to lend. I acted as security because the nurse trusts me – she knows me from the births where I've been midwife. After her harvest, Arayi gave her back the five hundred rupees and two sacks of paddy. Sometimes it's not possible to pay it all back in one go so you give back the interest and then, little by little, the capital. It's the only way you can work it out. When a harvest makes a loss, you have to try and pay it back the next time. That's how farming is! But when it works, you make the most of it to buy a cow or put money aside to marry a child or repair the house. If the family-in-law has fixed the date of the marriage, we sell everything – the cows, the oxen, the sacks of paddy – and we'll start again with nothing, trying to buy back one cow and then the other. That's what we did for Sundari's marriage.

I asked the Little Gounder to rent me a quarter of a *kani* because it's important to get a little bit of land. It's the right season for sesame and that doesn't need much rain. You can plough the earth and weed it and then it'll grow by itself: all you have to do is harvest it. It would give me three or four sacks of sesame and a sack now costs between eight hundred and nine hundred rupees, half for him, half for me: because you don't count the person who provides water for sesame, or else you only pay for irrigation by the hour. I hope the Little Gounder will agree. His father's old and isn't involved any more, and he himself has a little less to do with farming since he got a government loan to open a bicycle-hire shop. Besides, he's got enough money and he could live well just on the interest on what he lends out! He rented out half his land last season – all the fields that are a long way from the irrigation pumps – and he said, 'If anyone gets tired of cultivating it, I'll be happy with a third of the harvest.' Yes, that's the way it is with dry land: if there's a loss, the tenant suffers it and if there's a profit, the owner keeps a third. We own nothing and we accept that. We work ourselves, without employing anybody, using our own oxen. I hope the Little Gounder will decide during the rainy season: he told me not to sell the fertiliser I've got left. Otherwise, to get a square mile of good land near the pumps which will yield three harvests, you now have to give two and a half thousand rupees as bond and fifteen hundred rupees for land that will only yield two harvests. The bond is returned at the end of the tenancy but you have to be able to pay out all that money and then cover it for months: that's not possible for us poor.

Some people in the *ceri* own some land. Some have a quarter of a *kani*, some half as much. There's very few of them in all, eight perhaps. They

say that my family owned land here at the time of my father-in-law and
his ancestors. But those widowers lost it all. Pariahs were ignorant in
the past. They pawned their land to the Gounder and the Reddiar and
they have never got it back. The *ceri* elders have often told me that the
family used to have a big house with a porch. A juice drinker set fire to
it because a daughter of the house had dropped him for someone else.
There was a terrible fire and the jars of sesame and groundnut oil
burned for a whole day and night. My husband had four brothers and
a sister. His mother had a lot of children but they were the only ones to
live. So my husband was the son of someone respectable and we could
see that when his brother came from Penang. Somebody cheated that
brother when he was a little boy. One day when he was tending the
cows, a guy kidnapped him and sold him to someone else who took him
over the water. But this boy remembered the name of his village and his
family and he found us again much later. He sent us his photo: I showed
it to you, it's on the wall at home. He also sent a money order which
Gounder's father signed for us so that we could have the money. So
first this brother got married over there to a woman from Tiruppakam,
but she didn't have any children. Then he got married again to a woman
from Porattur who gave him four children. He came here one day and
I saw him. He was very large and he had a gold chain round his neck
that was thicker than your one, Sinnamma, and rings on his fingers.
Everyone in the *ur* talked to him politely! He died this year and we held
the ceremony of the sixteenth day with his photo. My husband led the
mourning because he's the eldest.

They say that it wasn't difficult to have land in the past. Anyway,
even now you can clearly see that not all of it is cultivated. Ask anybody
for land and it's there. But what there isn't these days is water. Everything's dry, the channels, the ponds, the rivers, the wells, everything! It
rains very rarely and when it rains, the man with two pumps helps
himself first and the rest have none left, their crops are ruined. The
government does what it can. It puts taps near the houses and pumps in
the fields but their motors have nothing to pump. It was different before. It rained at every festival. They say that everything was green all
year round. The rivers and the channels were full of water, the paddy
fields were always irrigated and people could set money aside to buy a
cow or a quarter of *kani*, but our fools gave everything away to the
Gounder and the Reddiar. And now, when my husband works in the
Grand Reddiar's fields which are next to the Gounder's, if the Grand
Reddiar's father is there, sitting on his rope bed in the shade of a

coconut tree, he always calls out in his gruff voice with his Telugu accent, 'Dei, Manikkam! Dei, son of Patchayappan! Your forefathers heaped up land but they didn't know how to pass it on to their children and here you are now, slaving away on the land which your family owned in the past.'

Yes, it wasn't the *kaliyugam* in those days and the weather wasn't the same as today, as Toothless always tells me. Poverty wasn't so hard then. There were less people and they all knew each other, those virtuous ones. Toothless also tells the story of it all changing because a chaste shepherdess cursed the earth and that's why we suffer now from a lack of water. One day this shepherdess was carrying seven jars of *kanji* for her brothers who were grazing the cows. The top jar hit the sky and tipped over. The shepherdess was chaste and virtuous and she was in a fury: she cursed the sky, shouting, 'Get away from the earth and don't let us reach you, not even by unrolling ten cartloads of string!' The sky, which was very low, moved away from the earth and stopped watering it constantly like before. Coming back home, the shepherdess used to pick ears of rice to eat on the way, because everything grew within arm's reach. But she got jaw-ache from chewing the unhulled rice that grew then. In pain, she said, 'I feel the *kaliyugam* beginning. I am a chaste woman. My mother was as well. Let the rice be covered with a little hull!' And that's why we harvest paddy in this *kaliyugam* and not rice.

I remember a year of drought, Sinnamma! Nothing sprouted. We couldn't find anything to eat. A measure of rice went up from one and a half rupees to five and a half rupees. In a house of five people, what could you do to feed everybody? We ate like cattle, groundnut cattlecakes and green leaves. Even a measure of foxtail cost a rupee in the *ceri*. We didn't throw anything away when we harvested onions. We ate the shoots and the skin with foxtail. The world had become dry. Everything was scarce: rice, oil, salt. I'd sown marrows and pumpkins as usual and we ate those the whole time.

Another year – I was very young – the whole world roasted, no rain, no water. Wages were four cents then. They didn't sell rice during that famine by the measure but by the eggshell! When you bought rice in an eggshell, you didn't cook it directly. You started by wrapping it in a cloth which you plunged in boiling water for a few minutes and then you drank the water it had cooked in. You dried the half-cooked rice and the next day you put it back in the cloth to drink the water for the second time. It was only on the third day that you actually ate the rice.

In those days we cultivated different strains of rice than we do now. *Sirumani* was like real jasmine flowers. We called it the *samba* of Garuda because its grain has a curved tip like an eagle's beak. Other *samba* have longer grain like bananas. *Vaikundam, mukkutti, kammal* used to sprout in twenty-one days and we'd harvest them after seven months. All those strains kept you full for a few hours and when you kept rice for the next day it stayed good and hard. With the strains we've got now, we're hungry again almost immediately and we end up in Gorimedu hospital! These strains grow in no time and we can harvest them three times a year with the fertiliser they give us. We didn't use any of that in the past. We ploughed the fields and irrigated them well. There are pumps for the Reddiar's land. You just have to start them – one of his brothers is in charge – and the fields are irrigated. But they always need plenty of workers. My son's the one who finds ploughmen now. He asks everybody in the *ceri*, 'Big brother, do you want to plough at the Reddiar's? And you, uncle, are you coming?' They go over it several times. The first time with a ploughshare. The second with the big plough. The third time they smooth out the mud to get it good and level with one of our doors, an ox on either side and the ploughman in the middle. The earth has to soften for the next twenty-one days. Before, we used to strip the leaves off tulip tree branches, add some cattlecakes and pumpkin leaves and mix all that into the earth: that's what fertiliser used to be and it made all those strains of rice grow that kept us in good health, even if sometimes they failed us like the two times I've just told you about. It's true that nowadays we don't suffer famine any more like that. They look after us better and there are the ration shops.[4] They protect us, like the skull protects the brain: the world has changed.

Since then we've had to put out a *kodumbavi* doll almost every year to bring the rain. Our *totti* take clay from the paddy fields to the potter and then go and collect rice in the *ur* with their drums. A man carrying a torch goes with them. The potter in the *ur* makes a clay woman, the *kodumbavi*, and then the *totti* drag it through all the streets while a choir of women sing laments. The goddess has to be made to feel for us and shown how weakened and shrivelled we are by the drought. Then the doll is thrown in the pond by Aiyanar's temple and they watch to see what side it drifts towards. That's where the rain will come, either immediately or four or five days later.

Once we went without drinking water as well because of a cyclone. We had to go to the pond and dig in the sand for a long time. We used half coconut shells to draw water to fill our jars and when we got home, we had to use dirty water to cook the rice. I've seen a big cyclone twice in my life. The first time I was married but still living at Velpakkam. We found a large jar floating in the water, it took a few of us to get it out, and it was full of peanuts which we shared. Animals were floating as well, oxen, cows, lambs – some alive, others dead – rabbits, partridges, crows and all sorts of things: branches, tree trunks, trunks. I even found a five-rupee note! There was less damage in the *ceri* than in the *ur*. The water didn't reach us thanks to the canal which runs alongside the *ceri* land. We didn't lose anything in our house, but in the *ur* brick houses were hit and a whole family died when their house collapsed on top of them: nothing could be done for them. Since then I've had twelve children, I've had grandchildren, but no one has touched that ruined house and the land has stayed empty.

I was here and I'd already had children when the second great cyclone came. The houses near the pond were blown away. The roofs in the *ceri* were torn off or turned upside down. The Kudiyanar went to get the animals near the pond that were still alive but they left us the dead ones. My husband went to get the carcasses of cows and ewes with the other Pariahs. He also found a plough and a roller. Vayu Bhagavan sends all that, he brings down the trees and the houses and floods the land.[5] We also say it's because of two gods, a brother who wanted to possess his sister. To escape, she hid in a pumpkin which rolled, rolled, rolled down to the sea. They're still there today: the tall waves that break are the sister getting crushed first; the brother is behind, chasing her. If the male wave manages to catch the female wave one day, then that'll be the end. The whole world will be flooded. The fifty-six countries will be wiped out. No one will be left.

When the fields are ready it's us women who go and plant out the rice. The men plough the fields, sow, irrigate and uproot, but we plant out. The Great Reddiar says to me the day before, 'Velpakkatta! You must bring me thirty-two Paratchi tomorrow! Give them an advance from this evening.' They always pay a little money to keep the women otherwise they'll go to someone who pays more because, at planting out time, people always make higher bids, especially the Reddiar. Sometimes, even when they've got an advance, some women will go and work elsewhere but they keep their word when I've booked them.

We all go together on planting out day when we've finished our morning's work. First we clean the house. We sprinkle the floor with water and coat it with cow dung, then clean the stable and collect up the cow dung. Afterwards I have to run to the Reddiar's to sweep in front of the house, clean the stable and wash out the jars. They can also ask me to pound rice or winnow lentils, then they give me something to eat and I go home. I make the *kuj* there, add salt and water to thin it and send it to my husband in the fields. It's only then that we all leave: the serfs and the day workers, the mothers-in-law and daughters-in-law. We start singing on the way. If some old women come with us, we sing a lament for them:

> Ayo! Aunt! If you are carried off by a fatal illness that
>   shouldn't have struck you,
> If you are laid out on the *tinnai*,
> For you, aunt, I'll light sticks of incense,
> I'll buy a coconut palm.
>
> Ayo! Aunt! If you're carried off by a fatal illness
> If you are laid out in the yard
> For you, aunt, I'll light sticks of incense
> I'll go and find you the launderer's son.

And we start laughing when she says to us, 'Dei, why do you want to fetch the launderer's son for me? I've got my own children! Sons who can light my pyre!'

Once we get to the field, we don't sing because the Reddiar is there. We work in silence out of respect for him as long as he is under his umbrella. When he goes and stretches out by the pump, under the shade of the coconut palms, it's the turn of a female serf to oversee the work. At the Reddiar's that means me. 'You in the red sari, work hard! Plant them out good and close together otherwise the Reddiar will bite your head off!' When the Reddiar gets on his motorbike and goes off to eat, well then the field is ours! It belongs to whoever sings the strongest: lamentations, planting out songs, *sunnambu* songs. We've got to endure the pain in our legs and arms when we've had to plant out one or two *kani* and, in the hot sun, our stomachs are hollowed out by hunger: we endure it by singing. It's one o'clock when the Reddiar comes back. He checks everything and says, 'Velpakkatta, come here! Here's the money for the Paratchi.' I take the money and hand it out to everybody and then we go home because us women don't have the midday meal.

The men only have it when they're ploughing. When they work for our *kambattam*, you can count up to twenty ploughs. In an hour they're finished. They wash the oxen and the ploughs and then themselves and they wait for their gruel which comes from the Reddiar's. The old men still swallow it by the handful or it's poured straight into their mouths, but Anban takes a cup or makes one out of a palm frond. They rest a little in the shade of the pump and when the sun has changed sides, they start work again. They repair the dykes, spread fertiliser or insecticide and level the paddy field. The Reddiar comes back on his motorbike and asks from the edge of the field, 'Dei! That field down there, have you dyked it up properly? Raise up the dykes a bit! And have you put any fertiliser here? Everything's done, is it?' My husband's the one who replies. He gets the money and gives it out to each worker.

So we finish well before the men. On the way home we pick green leaves, amaranth and joy weed which we put in our saris. I sow vegetables as well round the edge of the Reddiar's fields and near his pump. In the past we'd irrigate with a shaft-well too, one guy at the bottom, the other on the pole and a big waterskin that poured out when the pole swang back up. The men always sang when they worked the shaft-well to coordinate their movements:

> Let Pillaiyar come!
> Let Perumal come!
> Let Siva come!
> Let Siva and Perumal come together!
> O Omavalli, I haven't seen you for a very long time!
> Muttamma and I, we've left for Patnam
> Give me a kiss, o woman, a kiss,
> And most of all, give me your nipples!
> (*Laughs.*)

We'd plant aubergines, okra and hyacinth beans near those shaft-wells. We'd make little *pandal* so courgettes and balsam pears would grow up them. The palmyra fruit I gave you this morning came from a tree I planted two years ago near the pump. Now it's very tall and it bears so much fruit we don't know what to do with them any more. We could grow all that near our houses, we'd have the seeds no problem. But it's a question of water: we don't have any and we have to go and find it to water them. We prefer to plant a little on the edge of the fields. A small family like ours can sow half a *kuji* near the fences of the chilli fields and grow okra or hyacinth beans. We can also sow brown hemp seeds. They grow without too much looking after and when they're a good size, we pick the leaves to eat. We steep them in the pulp of stems and branches and when they rot, we beat them hard against a stone and the hairs come off. We plait them with hemp ropes for the cows' nostrils and foreheads. If there's any left, I give them to people who need them.

When I'm renting a field, I manage to grow some aubergines after the rice. You have to allow at least three months and take lots of trouble. We wait until the shoots are as big as that to weed them for the first time. We water them well, they carry on growing and then we weed for a second time and put on fertiliser. When we see the fruit come out at last, we weed for a third time and put on groundnut cattlecakes. Then they give a good crop, and after three months we harvest fifty to sixty kilos of aubergines, sometimes even a hundred kilos. The traders come and buy them in the field.

If my aubergines and chillis don't take, I pray to Mariamman, 'Mother Mariamman, if my aubergines and my chillis grow well this year, I'll make you an offering of the first harvest'. The day of fire-walking, we throw out two or three kilos of chillis, or aubergines, mangoes, or drumstick beans. Everyone rushes to get them. Last time I was able to get three or four drumstick beans. I throw my offering by the temple of Mariamman on the first day of Cittirai. Others do it at the temple of Vinayagar. We throw them very high so everyone's got a chance of getting something; adults and children beg us, 'De, de, de! For me, for me, de, de!'

After the rice, the Reddiar tends to grow green lentils or peanuts. You should see the size of the pods! We can get this many lentils from each one. I only take children to the lentil harvest, all roughly the same age, small rather than big, because they're paid according to their size: one rupee for the small ones, two for the in-between and three for the big. The Reddiar oversees the harvest right to the end in case the kids pinch anything. He doesn't check on me, but I don't steal either. At the end I'm given a large measure of green lentils and a few plants. I winnow the lentils as well and sort them before putting them in the bag. At that point I get a big measure of cracked ones and two little measures of lovely lentils.

I hire the workers for the peanut harvest too. First I go to the *ur*, to the Kudiyanar: 'Tomorrow we're harvesting peanuts at the Reddiar's. Do you want to come and pick them?' Then I go to the *ceri*: 'De, youngsters! Come and pick the peanuts, we'll give you plenty. Tomorrow we're harvesting at the Reddiar's!' I also bring the children. Everyone picks and makes a pile in their row. I oversee. I go between the rows with my billhook to loosen the earth near the plants and I say, 'Careful, pick them all up! Lift up the plant properly! Pick everything underneath, don't drop anything on the ground!' I also check nothing's hidden in the folds of the saris. It's true that the pickers are poor like me. They

can pinch the nuts, but they mustn't go too far. What would happen to
the owner if each of them stole a measure? Think what that would come
to for twenty or thirty people! What would be left for the man who'd
made it all grow? He's the one who'd end up shaved! And that's why I,
his own serf, have to check the harvest and say, even to Kudiyanar, 'Put
back what you've hidden in your sari. Take a handful to eat and leave
the rest. So, you don't want to listen to me? You won't do it if I ask
you? It's got to be the Reddiar jabbing you with his umbrella and saying,
"What have you got in your sari?"' That's how I talk to them, otherwise
I'm the one the Reddiar will come and tell off or even shake, grumbling,
'What are you there for, eh, you Paratchi? You think your pot will boil
if they take everything? If it's on my land, your husband can eat, your
son can eat, you can eat. And even if I beat you, you know you can help
yourself on my land!' And that's why I say to the women harvesting,
'Be honest. You are Kudiyanar, I'm a Paratchi. The Reddiar will be
angry with me because of you. Take some peanuts and leave the rest!'

When the day's work is finished, everyone brings what they've picked
to a big square in the middle of the field. The Reddiar stands with his
notebook and my husband measures the harvest with a basket. Everyone
goes up to the square, one after the other, my husband measures the
amounts and pours the peanuts into the square. The Reddiar notes it all
down and pays everyone what they're owed, adding a handful of peanuts
for every basket collected. Fast workers can fill four or five baskets, old
women one and a half, children three quarters or a half, or a quarter if
they're very small. After that I have to sweep the field for all the peanuts that are left lying about. That's the hardest work. When I've done
it, it's my turn to go up to the square, all covered in sweat and trembling with tiredness, and the Reddiar says to my husband, 'Give some
peanuts to Velpakkatta!' And even if he is my husband, he'll still give
me three or four measures, no more and no less, exactly the same as
everybody else. But I tell you, Sinnamma, that I won't be satisfied with
what the Reddiar gives me for all that work. When I get to the field, I
fill a little jar with big, fat peanuts which are white as milk when they're
cooked. I hide the jar under a peanut plant. At the end of the day, I
quietly pick up what I've hidden, put the leaves I've picked for the oxen
on top of the jar and get going.

'And what if the Reddiar catches you out?'

Even if he sees me, he acts as if he hasn't noticed and he doesn't say
anything. But aren't we there to take care of the fields, to be bitten by
snakes and lizards, to oversee the harvests, because we're his own serfs?

Would Paratchi paid by the day care about all that like us? Would they do as much for him?

'And what about the others, when they see you doing it?'

The others don't say anything either. Why should they call me a thief? They're day workers. They come exactly on time and they leave exactly on time. I have to sweep three or four plots of land in the full sun. When I've done my work, if I'm paid, I take it, but I can also leave without being paid because I'm their own serf. I wear myself out for the Reddiar family, my husband wears himself out, my son does as well and our oxen wear themselves out for them too. We've worked for them for generations, men and women. Of course we can hide a few peanuts without being embarrassed. The others have no reason to call us thieves. But they can't do the same thing. So we pinch a bit here and there during the harvest. At the end, on the last day, when it's all been collected and bagged up, the Reddiar will give us eight measures: four for his serf, four for his Paratchi who collects the cow dung.

At the millet harvest I also get what's owed to me for collecting the cow dung. Then I get a sari-skirt-full: I look like a pregnant woman having trouble walking. When I hull that millet, it gives me half a sack of grain, not counting what I can keep in my basket and the two rupees I'm paid. I would never be told to give back what I've taken: it's my due, because I'm their own Paratchi. The others would not be allowed to do that, and they'd have to give back what they've slipped into their basket. I'll be told, 'Velpakkatta! Take the ears back from all those women. Search them one by one before letting them go!' After the search, when they've given everything back, each of them is given three ears and five rupees, and the field is checked as well to see they haven't hidden anything there: the landowners are on there on their dykes under an umbrella. They trust the children least of all and they chase them off, giving each of them an ear, 'Dei! Take that and go home!' That way mothers cannot hand the ears they've stolen to their children.

My husband and my son also get their due at the millet and sorghum harvest. A full basket for each of them, that's the serfs' share. The basket is well filled and someone gets on it to pack down the grain. The Reddiar watches, then says, 'Good! Right, have you filled it up well? Dei, lift it up to see how much it weighs?' Then someone will tell him, 'Well, it's about twenty litres ...' And the Reddiar will say, 'Good, take it away. That donkey's only got to take that and he'll have set up his whole family!'

Even though we're serfs, Sinnamma, we can want to live a little comfortably, maybe even buy a bit of land. But you have to behave

honestly. I can't go too far in stealing from my master. He trusts us, his
own Paratchi, his own Paraiyan. He leaves us alone with the day workers on the millet and *ragi* harvests while he goes and eats. I mustn't
betray that trust and steal four big measures of grain from him. It
wouldn't make me happy and anyway it would be useless. But if I take
within limits, then I'll live in peace. For their part, those who give us
work should say to themselves, 'Leave them be! Those poor work to fill
their stomachs. I'm not going to buy land, build another storey or sink
a well with that little!' In the *ur* there are some owners who are hard-
hearted skinflints, their eyes always peeled. Others like our Reddiar are
the opposite: they say to themselves, 'These souls live under our orders
and look out for us. Let them be.'[6]

There's no shortage of work at our Reddiar's, Sinnamma! During the
paddy harvest, which lasts ten days, fifty to ninety workers work for
him. They get five sacks of paddy per *kani* for fifty workers. During
that time, I light a big fire at the Reddiar's in the morning to cook the
workers' gruel. Everyone harvesting or baling straw gets a midday meal.
I light the fire and keep it going, there's no uncleanness in that. But
Kudiyanar do the cooking, because some of the workers are Vanniyar.
At our Reddiar's the meal is always the same: a well-cooked *kanji* of
rice, with preserved bitter oranges prepared a year before. Others will
give something else with the *kanji*, mango skins, for example. After
cooking, we go and join the workers in the fields. The women pass cut
ears to the men, who beat them for the first time to separate the grain.
The women beat them a second time, to make the grains fall out properly, and make heaps of straw. In the past a cart would take the bales of
straw to the stable, but now a tractor does it. The Reddiar hires a
thresher and there's half as many of us working as there used to be. In
that sun, we're soon dripping with sweat and our tongues are hanging
out. At midday on the dot, we're brought something to eat. Some
Kudiyanar hand it out. We pour *kanji* in jars to let it cool down, but
some, as I've said, drink it straight from their hand. Women with
children come with a container to share it with them. Sometimes the
Reddiar sees me with my grandchildren. Then he says to whoever's
serving it up, 'Dei, there are two children with Velpakkatta. Give them
a ladleful!' He's always there for the meal, to make sure the *kanji* is
shared out fairly. Sometimes he calls a server, 'Tell Velpakkatta to go
and have her meal at our house, she's our Paratchi!' and I'm given a
meal of rice and vegetables. Before going back home I ask if there's

anything to do. Sometimes I'll be told to fetch somebody and I carry
out the errand when I get back to the *ceri*.

The men who do the harvest finish their day by piling up the bales
on the rick. They take their wages and go. They're paid day by day and,
when the harvest is over, each of them gets six measures of paddy. It's
impossible to hide anything then! If you take a measure of paddy, that
will make you two days of rice: how can you be allowed to get away
with that? We are closely watched and the Reddiar doesn't let anything
go. He'll leave me the two last sacks of bits of paddy and stones. But
even if the quality isn't that great, the weight is. He'll give Anban a bale
of straw and a measure of paddy, because the minute my son's asked, he
makes the dykes, washes the cows, waters them and feeds them. He
does everything he's asked to, he even drives the cart and that's why the
Reddiar gives him that share and says, 'Dei, Ettiyan! Take it, it's for
you!' He gives my husband ten measures of paddy because he guards
the harvest at night. The last evening when everything's finished, the
Reddiar seals the harvest before going home. We sweep out the whole
area, heap the paddy up into a mountain, and make both sides level
with our hands. Then we burn a little straw: rice straw catches fire
quickly and leaves lots of ash. We mix the ash with two measures of
paddy and mark the harvest with that, making letters like in your notebook. After that no one can steal it. My husband quickly goes home. He
washes, has something to eat and sets off again with a lantern and a
stick to guard the harvest. He guards the Reddiar's, while others watch
the harvests of other landowners. All the watchmen meet up and spend
the night chatting and singing. From time to time, they strike the ground
with their sticks to show there's someone there and keep prowlers and
animals away. The next day the harvest is sold on the spot. Each year it
makes a full tractor trailer for our Reddiar, not counting the sacks he
takes with him.

They grow *samba* and another rice called *karai* which is used to make
pancakes. Those sacks of paddy are taken to the Reddiar's. It takes a
whole day to steam the rice. That day my husband and I work in the *ur*
without going home at midday. My husband brings the steamed rice
into the concrete courtyard and I scatter it with my feet, because you
couldn't do it by hand for that long. When I reckon the rice has finished
drying, I hold up a grain of it, saying, 'Look, not one grain is broken.
Can I sieve it and put it in a sack?' After they've had a look and hulled
a grain, they'll tell me that if the grain breaks when you're hulling it, it
has to dry more. In the past we did the hulling by hand, with an iron

pestle or even a pestle with a pole. Nowadays we put the grain through the machine. We count the sacks in front of the Reddiar. My husband puts them in the Reddiar's cart and yokes the oxen. He takes the reins and I sit on the sacks. The Reddiar goes in front on his motorbike and we meet up at the *kambattam* of Anaikollai's who's got a hulling machine. On our way back, when everything's done, my husband goes to the paddy storerooms and takes seven or eight measures in his basket. That's his real wages and the Reddiar won't say anything. That paddy is just for my husband. He'll go and sell it and keep the money for himself, to buy drinks, visit his daughter, buy something for the children or eat something he loves, a dish of meat or tripe or some *dosai*.

We don't often have the chance to eat that sort of thing. When we shell black lentils at the Reddiar's, we keep everything broken or eaten by animals. That can give me two little measures, as well as the one I get as wages. I mix them, leave them to dry in the sun, then cover them in oil, and keep them for occasions like Kartikkai or Ammavasai, days when I love making *dosai* and *idli* for the whole family. Otherwise, we used to eat mostly vegetables. In the past, aubergines and pumpkins grew everywhere, you just had to pick them. Coming back from work, we'd make a good sauce, well-spiced with lots of chillis, sometimes fried fish and peanuts as well. We wouldn't eat much rice, mainly millet grass and koda millet. The Reddiar has always grown aubergines and we'd get some from him as well. Chillis too: he always grows them and I get two big handfuls which I leave to dry in the sun with some rough salt for a week. After that the chillis keep well and smell good. My husband likes them in the gruel I send him in the morning. At midday, we drink *kuj* from the Reddiar's and each of us is entitled to a jar of *kanji*. My son and daughter come and eat some after grazing the cows. In the past, we used to do things differently. We'd pick things growing around us and gather up what we could. For example we'd go to the pressing shed to pick up any groundnut oilcakes that had fallen in the mud. We'd soak them in water to get them clean, strip the leaves off drumstick branches, brown the leaves on their own and eat oilcakes and leaves with foxtail. Nowadays we don't eat those oilcakes any more or use them as fertiliser – we give them to the oxen.

The Reddiar also grows some sesame on a quarter- or a half-*kani* and I do too sometimes. We harvest it for him. We tear up the plants and shake them to make the seeds drop off. We women winnow them to get rid of the earth and the stones and we put them in a sack. The sacks are put to soak in a big concrete basin, and pitch-black water comes out:

the colour and the dirt runs out. Then we scatter the seeds in the
courtyard and, with four pestles, we pound them, pushing them with
our feet. The shell comes off and the sesame becomes all white. We
winnow them another two or three times to get the skins off completely
and only keep the white seeds. Then we go to the oil presser in Tirulagam. The men take the cans and the women carry a big basket on
their heads along with four or five kilos of palmyra sugar as well. The
presser gives us back the oil in the cans and the scraps in a basket.
Sesame oilcakes are delicacies and after giving some to his relatives, the
Vanniyar and everyone who doesn't make oil, he leaves the rest to his
Pariahs. He keeps his oil for a whole year. It's like rose water! Other
landowners don't give out their oilcakes. They sell them to grocers in
Tirulagam who make them into little pieces and sell them for a good
price, because they're seasonal. I buy sesame oilcakes at Tirulagam as
well, Sinnamma! Because the world has changed: I don't buy groundnut
oilcakes any more, because I think they're too heavy and not very good.

Now we eat rice in the evening, a measure and a half for four. *Kanji*
in the morning, I've told you that, with an onion or a chilli if there are
no greens. When I've finished working at the Reddiar's in the afternoon, his wife sometimes gives me a pancake, some *murukku* or some
sweets which she's made. Depending on how I feel, I either keep them
for the children and my husband or eat them on the way home. Afterwards I take my basket and go to Tirulagam market with my grandchildren. I buy them sweets of every colour and pink ice creams or I
find a good fresh fish for the evening. In the past we wouldn't have gone
there on what we earned, and anyway there weren't all those stalls.

Yes, it was better for you in the past. You could employ us for a rupee
or a rupee and a half a day and we'd eat what grew at the edge of the
fields. Nowadays in this *kaliyugam*, ploughmen demand ten or fifteen
rupees. The government steps in and sets wages. Would we have seen
or experienced a government in the past that would take care of us like
that? We could only buy from day to day when we used to go to the
market. Now I can afford to stock up, to buy spices for two or three
days. I buy rice, salted fish and betel, and there's still a little money left
which I put into a loan fund or the women's association. If my son and
I get a full sack of rice, we keep half for the house and sell the rest at
a good price. Gradually we pay back our debts at the Reddiar's with
that. I'm paying them little by little by working as well and if I die, my
son is here to take over. He pays what he owes by working as well. And

if he doesn't want to be a serf any more one day, he'll sell the calves, the cows and the goats. He'll pay off his debt. He'll be free and he'll become a day worker.

Because there's work at the village! There are large fortunes in the *ur*, families with fifty, sixty or eighty *kani*. They need a lot of people to work that! And that's exactly why we're here. We're here to work for the people who have land. Their trade is to own, to be rich. Why do you want them to get down into the fields? Their place is in the shade of their house, or under the umbrella on their dykes. They're not made to work the land they own. We Pariahs, some Palli, some Padaiyatchi, the poor Kudiyanar – we're here to be agricultural workers. The owners need us, Sinnamma. How could the *ur* survive without us? It's not enough to own ten cows, it's not your son who'll take them to pasture, it's mine. Your child's here to study and to work sitting in the shade. So when a landowner says to a Pariah, 'I'll give you eight rupees to raise the dykes in my field. Are you coming?' the Pariah will answer, 'No, that won't work! I've got children, they have to eat and be decently dressed. What can I do with eight rupees?' In the past we'd work to eat and get married. The Reddiar was the only one who was always neat, with a pure white *soman*, a shirt, well-cut hair, rings on his fingers, and a watch on his wrist. Our men in the *ceri* only had a little *soman* rolled up round their waist and another knotted in a turban on their head: these were clothes that showed respect to the masters. Nowadays we wear the same clothes as you, but it costs a lot of money. We're not afraid of hard work, so we're ready to do all the work we're given. Look at Anban, I send him far away to work for a relative of the Grand Reddiar in Andhra Pradesh. He's given lodging there, he's fed and he earns twenty rupees a day! Even without having studied, we can still earn a reasonably good living nowadays.

Anyway, it's not always easier for those who've studied. People who've left Karani to start work at a factory in Pondy have come back to the village once the factory's shut. A Sanar set up as an ice-cream seller in Tirulagam, others now sell fresh or salted fish. And what do you do when you can't find work in the city? Because there's lots of people down there who've studied and are looking for work. They don't wait for our boys to get on with things in the office or the factory, while they're saying to themselves, 'Why work in the fields when we've studied?' Yes, but when you don't find anything, you're forced to go back to the land and at that point, people who've stayed teach the others how to plough, make dykes and transplant. Everyone must have a trade to feed themselves! Normally people who've studied and don't find work tend to try and open a little business in Tirulagam.

I go there every evening with my basket to do my shopping. I love hanging about the market, there are so many things to see and do! The other day, coming back from my daughter Miniyamma's at about four o'clock in the afternoon, I got out of the bus at Tirulagam and stopped there. I bought some fish, chilli powder, ginger and curried leaves for the evening meal. Suddenly, in all that noise, I heard someone shouting, 'Sister-in-law! Sister-in-law! Aren't you getting any green bananas or okra for this evening?' It was Selvaraj, our eunuch from Mangappakkam, who's a travelling grocer at Tirulagam. I went up to him and he said, 'Come, sister-in-law! Where have you come from? Have a little sit down. Here, chew some betel. It seems you go to Pondy a lot now, that's what people in the *ceri* tell me about you. You go and sing for Sinnamma.'

I was happy to see him again. He'd been selling vegetables some-where else for a while. So I sat on the ground next to him and said to him, in the same singing voice as his, 'Ayo! Come along with me to Sinnamma's one day. I'll take you to Pondy one time. We'll soon see if you can match me for a story or a song!'

He started a lamentation song straightaway and blew his nose on my sari at the end of the first verse. (*Laughs.*) All the travelling sellers sitting near the Muslim's stall – the ones who sell cassava, sweet potatoes and guavas – started laughing. Anyway as soon as we see him in the market, we go up to him, because he always tells stories or sings songs. He was the one who taught me the 'Lament of the telegram announcing bad news', and he told me, 'De! Go and sing that to Sinnamma, she'll be happy!'

That eunuch lives at Mangappakkam but he's from Periyambakkam. He's as beautiful as a bayadere and a great dancer as well; you must see him at the festival of Draupadi! During the harvests, the eunuchs come and sing work songs, comic songs or other ones. I like their songs a lot. I make them sit down and I give fifty or seventy-five *paice* to hear them sing and to learn their songs. That's how one day I put my hand in his s*oman* and said to Selvaraj, 'So, you've got no balls?'

'No, I'm a woman like you!'

'Give me a quick look so I can see!'

He didn't have any balls or anything! Ambigai and I didn't believe our eyes. We took him into a house and undressed him, touched him, everything: he really didn't have anything. Just a big scar there and flat like us. It had all been taken out! And when we started laughing at the sight, he said, 'Aye, di! Fuckers! Whores!' Ayo, Sinnamma! Their way of talking is very funny, very pretty. I love teasing him until he insults me just to hear him talk.

One day I'll take you to Nellipet to see Ponnuttambi. You know him, I've already pointed him out. At the festival of Draupadi, he sells green banana fritters, sweet lentils and semolina cakes. In his gestures, his words, his voice, he's a real woman, more real than a woman even! He is very nice, very kind. I bumped into him the other evening when he was going to Tirulagam market with some cans to buy oil. He had a string on his wrist for protection. When I asked him how he was, he told me, 'Ayo! Those pieces of filth, those faggots, those cocksuckers! They kidnapped me and abused me to their heart's content, Anban's mother!'

Hearing that, Sinnamma, tears came to my eyes and I even cried. He had been kidnapped by his relatives, juice drinkers who'd made him suck them off and then buggered him. They tore him open, the poor thing. Queers treat each other like animals! He was in such good health, with his beautiful hair tied up, big earrings and a handsome chest! He's a Chettiar – well, he's from the oil pressers caste. Normally he sells *idli*, *dosai*, fritters and when he goes to the *ceri*, he comes and sits on the veranda of the brick house in the launderers' quarter.

There are two others in his village I'd like to show to you. They got there not long ago. Both of them are beautiful, one black, one as light as a woman from the North. How they carry on! Our stomachs ache from laughing just watching them. They came to my house the other day with slides in their hair. They sat on the *tinnai* and said to us, 'So, ring doughnuts, how's it going?' They're always a laugh! They were made up like film actresses, the eyes done up very carefully. If, thanks to God, both of us go to Nellipet one of these days and you bring your recorder, we could get all their talk and have a good time listening to them again. The light one can't sing well. But the other one, yes, he's smart! And the care he takes dressing! He changes saris the whole time, always cotton. And jewels everywhere, on his feet, his fingers, and a *tali*: God made him a man by mistake. Their god is Kuttandavar and they wear the *tali* for him.[7] For the annual festival of Kuttandavar which happens in Pillaiyarkkuppam, they get ready months ahead. They sing at fairs, in markets, during the harvests, they go from village to village to get rice, grain and money. They buy billy-goats with that, because they have to offer rice mixed with blood. Thousands of eunuchs go for the festival, all dressed elegantly, with false breasts. They make offerings of their *tali* and throw bracelets to their god. Three jars of milk and seven jars of water are poured on them. That's their *bhakti*. There are lots of possessed that day. That's why a eunuch goes round the villages before the festival with a round drum with two hides, to announce that the festival is going to happen and that women more than three months' pregnant should not attend. They even say that the whole world is told by the *Dinatandi*.[8] Apparently the dry riverbed at Pillaiyarkkuppam is filled up by pump on that day.

I dream of going to see it one day. Will you come with me Sinnamma? But you are young: you must be careful. Ambigai has gone there. My daughter's sister-in-law got married at Vandipalaiyam, not far from there, into quite a well-off family who own a cart, two *kani* and a pump. For Anban's marriage, her mother brought a good tray. That woman invited us to go and see the festival of Kuttandavar, but we couldn't go because Amsa was possessed by a spirit. I must see that festival before I die.

TWENTY-FIVE

The way of the world

The Reddiar goes to Pondy on business very often and also, I think, for political business: he's won the elections twice. Don't ask me which party! I think it was the one with the spinning wheel. I don't understand very much about that.[1]

'Grandpa Gandhi, grandpa Gandhi, don't eat *bundi* ... ' That's what I remember from school songs, slogans and men talking about Kamaraj the traitor, uncle Nehru, Indira the chaste Mother, Annadurai our master, Karunanidhi the poet.

Apparently this country was ruled by a white king in the past, the ruler of the Kingdom of Pondy who had heaped up lots of money and hid it under his bum. Everyone here says that: the Vattiar's father, the Gounder, my father-in-law as well. Gandhi appeared after my birth. They say he was a trembling old man who looked like an earthworm. But he had a great heart and he spoke well. Out of all those people his daughter Indira Gandhi did the most.[2] That chaste woman fought for us poor. When she arrived, things went better for us. She brought water to the *ceri*: she had wells sunk, she told people with forty or fifty *kani* to give one or one and a half of them to the poor, so they could have enough to eat. She let it be known on the radio and by sending out cars that the government would distribute land near the pond and near the channels and that she was with us and was fighting for us. But the enemy party attacked her government. They say she went to prison.

257

The men were jealous of a woman in charge of the country. And in the end, she was killed by some juice drinkers, as I've told you. Poor Indira Gandhi! I loved her very much, even if I never saw her. The day she came to Pondy, I couldn't go even with the lorries that took us there. I had too much work that day, I had to collect groundnuts in the Little Reddiar's fields. But lots of people went to see her. They said she was as light as a White woman and her head was always covered. She was as beautiful as the moon. The chaste woman!

The blessed father Annadurai was one of the men who've governed the Tamil country. Apparently he fought for us a lot. But people who work for the poor don't live long. A widower from the enemy party cast a spell on him and that incarnation of the great gods died because of it. We can't stay longer on this earth than we're given. It ruined my heart hearing he'd gone. I quickly ran to Anjalai's, Kannima's and Araiyakka's and we sang a very long mourning song to pay homage to that man with a golden heart, the father of thousands of poor people. I began like this:

> O Blessed!
> You were the light that shone for the poor of this earth!
> O man of *dharma*!
> O generous one, is it true you're leaving us?
> Here we are, orphans today.

Our laments were so sad that the men started crying and they kept the songs going for a very long time. Later my husband took me to Madras by train. When I'd gone there with my father, he would never have dared step a hair's breadth out of the Pariah quarter. In those days we didn't visit anything. But everything's open to us today, even if we know where we have to stop! So I made the most of it by visiting everything: the college of the living, the college of the dead, the markets, and we went to see the *samadi* of Annadurai.[3] I laid a bunch of jasmine there. His tomb was covered with flowers and incense sticks. This earth is not just full of ingratitude!

That said, I never got anything personally from Indira Gandhi and Annadurai: not a scrap of land or one rupee. It's enough for me to know that some good souls are thinking of us, the poor. Now all the talk in the *ur* and the *ceri* is of parties, meetings and assemblies and our young are the first to get involved. The only thing I know is that it creates divisions, enemies, fights, revenge and murders. And it makes us women anxious because when our men and boys have been drinking, they stop

joking and humming a tune. They start swearing at each other and
fighting about their party stuff. Our young especially are becoming more
and more violent: luckily the older generation are there to calm them
down a bit. Anban is a master in all these party goings on, but if I was
to ask him to explain them to me, I wouldn't understand a word of it
and I wouldn't be able to tell you anything. When he comes back from
work, you should talk to him or my husband and ask them anything you
want. They'll be able to tell you lots of things on that subject. I'll listen
along with you.

(*The next day Manikkam is with his wife and he comes to sit down.*)
'Well then Sinnamma! After Viramma's life, do you want me to tell
mine?'

(*Viramma*) 'Yes, yes! You are older than me! You've seen and done
plenty of things: tell it all to Sinnamma! (*Viramma laughs.*) I've already
told you what we want you to talk about; parties, politicians. And don't
mess around with that equipment! (*Viramma points to the tape recorder.*)

(*Manikkam laughing*) 'Soon she'll have seen more things than me!
She'll be more civilised than me!'

(*Viramma*) 'We're not asking you that! Say what you know about the
parties. Go on, give it all you've got!'

(*And Manikkam begins.*) In the beginning there was only Congress for
us in India. I mean at the time of the war between India and the English.[4]
There was a second party as well, which had come from Russia: the
Communist Party. Political men who'd gone there had found that the
same things could be done here for the workers. The elections began
under the Whites: voting goes on for a whole day and the people choose
such and such a party which they like. The two parties both fight for the
poor, but they've got nothing to do with each other. In the Communist
Party it's the poor fighting for the poor, while in Congress, there's both:
rich and poor, sincere and dishonest. Congress's ideas were good and
they had some great souls: Indira, Kamaraj, Nehru, Gandhi. I think
Gandhi was the first. He travelled a lot. He met people in each region,
each town, each quarter, each street, and held meetings to teach them to
imagine the future. He said to them, 'It's by getting rid of ignorance that
a country can evolve.' Gandhi also fought against the English. He liber-
ated India. Yes, the Whites, the English set themselves up here saying
that the country belonged to them. Gandhi said to them, 'You have
cheated everybody. You came as guests and you took over our India. Go
back down the road that led you here!' And after fighting a lot, and
planting the Congress flag over the whole country, he got Independence.

Once I heard him. He spoke in simple words; 'Don't be afraid of anybody: neither the Reddiar nor the Gounder who put you to work. You
must conquer your ignorance first of all. This *kaliyugam* will favour you,
the Harijans. You should make the greatest efforts to conquer your ignorance. Ask the Reddiar and the Gounder if progress belongs just to
them, if they're the only ones who have the right to grow rich?' That's
what Gandhi said and he was the one who made us change caste, so we
became Harijans and stopped being Untouchables. But even with his
great heart and all this generosity, he was shot down. They say it was a
Muslim, a nabob, who killed him.[5]

At the same time, or a little later, there was the war between the
French and the Union. My father often told me that things were better
in the time of the Whites. In those days, everything was a reasonable
price. An *anna* or a fanon and a half was his pay. With that all the
family ate properly. A penny's worth of aubergine, a penny's worth of
spices: that was enough. Everything grew abundantly. There was water
everywhere: we'd find it by digging two feet down. We could easily
irrigate aubergines, pumpkins, *ragi*, groundnuts and sesame and the
poor made the most of it. Now you have to dig for more than a hundred
feet to set up a pump and we can't afford it. The Whites also used to
hire people to work for them in Pondy and the Gounder could hope to
see their sons get an office job. And the Whites drank alcohol, like us:
they ate beef, like us. We didn't want to get rid of them. But that wasn't
what the Reddi thought.

The Reddi from different communes met up and brought together
thousands of men. They armed them and sent them everywhere to
cause fear. Their coup was well organised. Goubert Papa and the Reddi
of Nilugarai, Cinnapalayam and Naliveli ran the whole thing.[6] They had
everything they wanted: jeeps, lorries, men and the Madras police. Bahur
fell first, then Nettappakkam and gradually they took the eighteen communes. Only ours was left. Apparently it wasn't easy to take. Karmegam
and Dakshnamurti Gounder did everything they could to resist, but of
course Gundurayan Reddiar was on the side of the other Reddi. He
paid some guys to come with *mattai* and iron bars and he also appealed
to the Madras police with their guns. Men were patrolling day and
night in Karani, in the *ur* as well as the *ceri*, but the Gounder didn't get
the help they were expecting from Pondy. One night when our men
were asleep, some armed men came in a lorry. They went into the
village firing into the air to frighten people and then, seeing that nothing
was happening, they started firing all over the place. Everyone tried to

run away, but where to? Tirulagam was already in Congress's hands. Only Sellipattu and Nellipet were left, but they heard gunshots coming from there as well. My parents-in-law put the children on their backs and went and hid with Muttuvel's family in the pandanus thickets, and they saw everything from there: blood, wounded, fires. The Reddi stepped in to stop the houses being burnt, because burning a house which hasn't been abandoned brings misfortune. But at the same time he gave the order that those who'd been captured should be thrown into a lorry and taken to Nettappakkam. At the same time other guys were wrecking the harvests. They mixed up all the grain they could find – paddy, *ragi*, foxtail, millet – poured petrol on and set them on fire. In the *ur* they stole money and burnt all the mortgage papers. When everything was over, the Reddi sent for rice from Mangappakkam and their men had a feast and planted the Congress flag.

The unrest lasted a good week and then, day after day, all the people who had got away started coming back. People who'd gone far away, to their relatives in town, came back two or three months later. And then the ones who'd gone to prison in Nettappakkam came back as well and they told us about the beatings with gun butts, the urine they'd had to drink. Everyone here talks about it as if it happened yesterday, and the old tell it to the new generation, laughing wholeheartedly. That's what we got from supporting the Whites.

Now we've got all the parties in the village: the Communist Party, Congress, DMK, Anna DMK, the Vanniyar Party, Janata.[7] All of them fight for the poor, for the Harijans. They're all for us, but we can only put one of them in power. So we choose by who's leading the campaign. DMK, for example. That's a new party. They added an M to the old party of Periyar, the DK, the party of the Adi-Dravidar. Anna formed the DMK.[8] It fought for the poor and against the division into castes. In the *ur*, the great DK campaigner is Ananda Gounder and, in the *ceri*, it's Kaliyappa. DK used to be a strong party and that's why DMK caught on well here in Karani. Now there's nobody left in DK, it's become an old party. After the death of Anna, Karunanidhi and MGR argued and that led to two separate parties. Out of us Anban is DMK. Those two parties think the same, they want democracy and to do something for the poor, but once they're in power, they stop taking care of us. They're all dishonest like that. In the beginning, in Anna's time, the party had a conscience. Those people used to tell themselves they should work for the poor who'd elected them. They had programmes. But once they were in power and they'd discovered money, those representatives

changed their mind and said to themselves, 'Why give so many facilities
to people who are under our orders? No! First we must fill our pockets
and make the most of it to get rich!' And we've stayed the same as
before, not being able to read or write. True enough, there's a Harijans'
office in Pondy, but we don't know how to set about making a demand
or signing. If you go in that office and know how to read and write,
you're well received and you get what you want. But when we go and
ask for something, they say, 'Come back in twenty days!' or, 'Wait three
months!' What we understand is, 'Build that dyke higher!', 'Hoe the
field!', 'Irrigate there, put fertiliser here!' And we're given fifteen or
twenty rupees a day for that.

Since we've been accepted into society and asked to vote, I've always
voted for Gopala Gounder. He was a worker as well. He understands
how difficult it is for us and, most of all, we can talk to him about our
problems and ask him to get us a few plots of village or temple land. He
understands things and at least he gives an answer. The Reddi live in
the shade eating fruit and drinking milk. They don't receive us when
we go and see them. We have to wait for hours before talking to them
or we have to keep coming back, 'Sir is asleep', or 'Sir is taking his
bath', 'Sir's not free'. Anyway they don't understand our worries. We
work for them, but we sympathise with the Communist Party. The
Communist Party is a party of the poor. Its goal is to fight for people
who have got nothing to give them a better life. What the other parties
want is to cream off money and land and make things better for the
rich. When Anna was alive, his party was honest, but now everything is
rotten.

One day there was a big drama with these parties. The Grand Reddi
didn't know I was voting for the Communist Party. He thought we were
all voting the way he told us to. One year, Gopala Gounder assembled
all his people for a demonstration on the day before the election. But
Kuppussami had gone to his daughter's and wasn't there to lead the
march with the red flag that time, so Gopala Gounder asked me to take
over. I was very unsure, because I knew the Grand Reddiar wouldn't
take it well! But I ended up by saying yes and the march went through
the *ceri* shouting, 'Long live Mr Subbaiah! Long live our party! Vote for
the Communist Party, the true party of the people!'

Unfortunately the party with two leaves had also decided to march
the same day. And they yelled, '*Podungayya ottu irattaiyilaiyai pattu!*',
'Vote with a clear cross next to the two leaves!'[9]

Both groups tried to shout louder than the other. When we got up to the temple of Draupadi the Anna DMK flag carrier tripped me up. I told him, 'Innappa! Don't do that, or else there'll be a fight! You carry on with your demonstration and we'll carry on with ours!' But his group tore the flag out of my hands to hit me with the pole. We fought back and broke them up in the end. But the police had been told. One of the policemen marched forward pointing his gun at me. I clung to him and turned out of the way. The Gounder who were there defended me and everything calmed down. Even so the police arrested me and a few others and I was taken to Pondy. In court the Gounder spoke up for me again and, in the end, after a night in the station where we were beaten up a bit, we went back to the *ceri*.

After that, when K.S. was elected, I left the CP. That very evening I went to see Gopala Gounder and I said to him, 'Ayya! I have fought for the party for a long time and yesterday was the same. The party has good ideas, but I've got children to feed. I need work, my son does as well. All my family are serfs at the Reddiar's and we eat the *kuj* he gives us. I depend on him completely. I have to run to his house to borrow when we've got nothing to eat, or when we have to celebrate an important event. I don't want to provoke his anger and we must vote for him. Please understand and forgive me!' Gopala Gounder told me he understood my reasons, and he added, 'All I ask is that your family give me one vote, yours for example. All the rest can go to the Reddiar.' That's how we voted and the whole *ceri* did the same.

Everyone thinks that Congress was very good in the past, with Gandhi, Nehru and Kamaraj. But we don't understand any more what's going on in the North. In the elections for Parliament, people vote for Congress out of loyalty for Gandhi, who fought very hard for the poor. He defended us loyally and he was the one who raised us to the rank of Harijans. And then what would happen with a Tamil party like DMK in Parliament in Delhi? DMK is a party for people who speak Tamil, for problems in the Tamil country. People used to vote for the *dharmaraja*, but since his death, the Anna DMK hasn't managed to pick itself up and Karunanidhi is usually in power.[10] He has been in the party from the beginning too and he fights for us. Our Reddiar has voted for Anna DMK the last few years and the people followed him. A *kambattam* should know who to support and who not to. Since the death of M.G.R., he votes DMK and the people do as well. We say to ourselves, 'I'll do what he does. I am a worker, he is a *kambattam*. I am his serf. If he prospers, I get four or five measures of paddy thanks to

him. Of course I'm the one who works hard and my family wears themselves out for him, but the pay is there'. So we vote like him. And then
we're looked after in our constituency: running water has been put in
for the poor, the whole *ceri* has got electricity, we can collect tamarind
fruits for three years, we have a rationing card, widows and disabled are
given rice and clothes and children are fed at school. Even a girl like
Shanti can study to go into the police.

But it's not enough to make everything all right! Communal land for
instance. It was rented out to us, but when Congress got back into
power, they took it back. Maybe the Congress Party fights for the poor,
but the people in it have money. They're the sort of people who are
offered tea or coffee when they go into shops. The sort of people who
sit out in their armchairs on verandas in the cool of the evening and
plan their move, make their decisions, which village head should be
given two hundred or three hundred rupees under the counter, which
accountant should be slipped some money to get the land register.
They're the people who get the land we should be given. And if we
fight to get that land, they'll come and tell the accountant, 'Innappa!
The Reddiar or the Gounder needs those fields. Cross out that name
and this one. Make sure that disappears from the register: there'll be
this much money in it for you.' And the village head, the accountant
and the *talaiyari* share it. The next day, there's an official there with a
chain who's come to measure the communal land and he tells us,
'Innappa! All this belongs to the Reddiar now. You mustn't come here
any more, otherwise you'll end up in prison in handcuffs!' And if we
refuse and stand up to them, they'll say, 'You sons of whores, you've got
a nerve to rebel against us!' and they'll have us beaten. But all of us
have already come out in protest. All the heads of families who voted
for the CP were there and we shouted,

> Long live the Communist Party! Long live India!
> Long live Subbaiah! Long live Gopala Gounder!
> Communal land for the poor!
> Let us farm the communal land!
> Down with the Government!

And we planted the red flag in the ground.

The policemen came to arrest us. They took us to the station with
our flags and said to us, 'Innappa! Why do you protest like this? You
must hand a petition to the Governor, the Chief Minister, the people in
government. You're protesting with the CP flags, saying, "Subbaiah!
Subbaiah!" Do you think he's the one who's going to give you the

commune's land?' 'Yes,' we told them, 'He fights for us! He's the most honest and we trust him. The rest only help the rich!'

After that activists from the other parties came running to the station, particularly DMK party workers, 'Let's go! We're going to get you all together to discuss this and make a quick decision. Let's see: how many households are there in the *ceri:* sixty, seventy-five? We'll give each family twenty *kuji*. No need to demonstrate! No need to protest! We look after you. Go on, go back to your homes. We will get in touch with you!'

That's what we hear each time we demonstrate, but we never see anything happen and the communal land is still given to the people from the *ur* and not to us. Sometimes one or two people from the *ceri* get a little land to rent before the elections. It's the same with the ponds. In the past we ate mussels, snails, crabs from the paddy fields and fresh water fish. No one else used to eat them. Now even the Vanniyar have started to and they're the ones who get fishing permits. They fish with big nets and they sell us their fish! And if I tell my son to ask for a fishing permit for part of the pond, he tells me that he's ashamed! But we are the ones who are the poorest. We only eat if we've got work, otherwise our stomach stays empty. So why not rent us a few plots of land or a pond – us, the landless? This is the reign of the rich and they don't worry about the poor.

That was plain enough when I went to see the Reddiar about Anban's marriage. I said to him, 'I have to marry my son. I'm going to look for a girl for him, Sami!'

'Hmm! You have to marry your son and find a girl for him? Han! How much will you need for that?'

'I need five hundred rupees and five sacks of paddy, Sami.'

Still sitting comfortably in his armchair, kicking his feet, he said: 'Hmm! You need five hundred rupees and five sacks of paddy. That makes a thousand rupees! When are you going to pay me back?'

'Innanga! I wear myself out for you, my son too and my wife and my daughter. All four of us wear ourselves out for you and you think you won't be paid back?'

'Good, so you think you can pay me back! Anyway, I can't give you that much. Take two hundred rupees and a sack of paddy. I'll buy the marriage sari and the *tali*. That'll make an impressive marriage! You'll pay me back those two hundred rupees and the sack of paddy later by working for me.'

'Sami, we've already done so much work for you! Won't you give us anything for that?'

'Dei! Your father died, I gave a hundred rupees. Your mother died, I gave another hundred rupees. When your brother died, I gave fifty. Every time there's a death or birth, you ask me for something!'

'It's true you give every time, Sami, but I always pay you back without fail. If you give me what I ask for now, it will come to fifteen hundred rupees with my savings. I'll be able to give my son an honourable marriage with that!'

'Ah no! I can't give you that: only two hundred rupees and a sack of paddy. Go and ask somewhere else!'

'How can I go and ask somewhere else, Sami? I'm a serf in your household. My oxen and my family work for you, and you're not going to do anything for that?'

'But I pay you a wage!'

'Yes, but a large measure of rice costs three rupees twenty. How can I live on that? If you'd give me a quarter of a *kani* to farm, I could cope. I'd get three or four sacks, I could save what I didn't eat and I'd pay you back.'

But it doesn't happen that way, for the simple reason that the Reddiar don't want us to cope. They say to themselves that if I managed to put two sacks aside from a quarter of *kani*, I wouldn't respect them any more: 'The next thing that one will do is cut his hair like us, put on a *soman* and a shirt, light a cigarette. But if we don't let him have that quarter of a *kani*, we'll keep him as a serf, with his loincloth and his turban'.

Because they don't want their workers to be respectable and civilised here in the country, Sinnamma. What they want is for us to stay backward and them to be advanced. We Pariahs are more supportive, we want what's best for the other, we help each other. If one of us is dying of hunger, a brother, a *pangali* will give him something to eat. If a woman comes to Viramma and says, 'Sister-in-law, I've got nothing to eat this evening. Can you lend me a measure of rice? I'll give it back to you tomorrow when my son brings his pay', we'll lend straightaway. If someone visits us unexpectedly, we'll run to the neighbour's to borrow some money which we give back the next day. We support each other in the *ceri*: we can't let people die of hunger!

But in your castes they want to bring Pariahs down. When you sweat, it's water. When we sweat, it's blood! Standing up under an umbrella making us work isn't tiring and you go and eat your meal, drink your coffee at the usual time. It's only about eight o'clock when I'm brought my first meal. At midday the Reddiar eats rice and lots of different vegetables on a beautiful banana leaf and I'm told, 'Dei! Go and wash

your hands!' and gruel is poured into them. In the evening I take off
my loincloth, I wash it, I tie on a *soman*, I politely cross my arms and
come and get my pay. I can only really rest after that. I buy myself a
few lentils, aubergine or salted fish.

'And you don't forget two rupees' worth of palm wine! (*Viramma
laughs.*)

'That's my one pleasure of the whole day.'

'OK, OK, carry on.'

If the Reddiar let me go earlier, I could eat and go to sleep early as
well, but, instead of that, I go to sleep late and get up early. And if I get
to work a bit late, the Reddiar hears of it and tells me off, 'Dei! Didn't
your wife let you go? She squeezed you tight in her breasts, did she?
You were well stuck in, were you?'

Why should they be the only ones who can sleep with their wife and
talk to them? Have they got the right to make children and not us?
We're men and women as well. We've got desires as well, and they take
us to midnight. Whereas they wash their hands at six in the evening,
their wife brings them food and then they go to bed to relax or play
with their wife: they don't feel tiredness. After we've hoed all day, we
eat in a rush and it's only then that we can speak, play, caress each
other, and be man and woman. That's our happiness.

We work like that all our life for a Reddiar and then, when we need
money for a very important matter, to light a lamp in a new household,
he goes and gives us two hundred rupees and a sack of rice. How are
you meant to manage with that? And the day after the marriage, if we
don't go to work straightaway as normal, he'll say, 'I gave money to that
Pariah for that marriage and look, he hasn't come to work. He's got a
nerve!'

So there you are: you're Reddiar, you've got the right to rest. You
high caste, you can say, 'That Pariah widower hasn't turned up yet!' But
then who's that widower who called us that: Pariahs, Pariahs? And all
the other widowers who call us Pariahs as well! We're not just poor, but
on top of that, we've suffered the great wrong of being born Pariahs.

'Dei! Get a move on with bringing in the cows or else you'll get the
stick!' That's how the Reddiar threatened me when I was little. Now he
wouldn't dare lift a hand against me, I'm the same age as him. And if
ever he couldn't control himself, if he hit me, there'd always be someone
around, a Gounder, a Naicker or even a Pariah to tell him, 'Innayya!
Even if he is a serf in your household, it's not good to hit a man your
age. You're hitting him without so much as thinking: even his parents

who brought him into this world, lulled him to sleep and fussed over him, cared for him and protected him, they wouldn't even dare do it.' Now the Reddiar respects me, because I'm a reasonable man, I'm fair, and I'm not extreme. I can stay in my place. But if someone picks a quarrel, I can defend myself, I can talk!

Six months ago my son Anban was hit. I got angry! It reminded me of the first time I was beaten very badly, when I was little. I was twelve maybe and I remember it very well. I had to graze a herd of about twenty and there were two oxen that were all stirred up and two cows that were always running off into the paddy fields. Impossible to graze them quietly. They'd hardly got out of the stable before those thieving cows were off grazing the Gounder's paddy field. He came up furious, saying, 'Innada! Maybe you think that because you work for a Reddiar, a *kambattam*, anything goes? Does your Reddiar think that he can graze his cows in my paddy field? Wait while I go and ask him that question!'

'Innanga! I am his cowherd, but I can't get all these animals to graze quietly with these cows that run off the whole time!'

'Well then! One of their hooves has to be tied to their neck!'

I pointed out that I had tied up one of the cow's hooves, but even so they ran fast and they'd got away. But he didn't want to know any of it and he started giving me an earful.

'Innada! Son of a whore! You motherfucker! If you were a good caste, you wouldn't behave like this! You really are a Pariah, you widower!' And he hit me on the thigh with his stick. That hurt very much and I immediately insulted him myself, 'You dirty Palli who's made it to Gounder! Son of a whore! You dare come here and hit me when my parents wouldn't dare touch me!'

Straightaway he ran to the Reddi's and said to him, 'Innayya! Your Pariah boy insults me without even taking my caste into account, as if there wasn't any difference any more between high castes and low castes! I am a Gounder and he's a Pariah and he tells me that I'm a son of a whore, that I fuck my sister! Is that any way to talk?'

I didn't go home at midday. I sent some other cowherds to the Reddiar's for my *kanji* while I kept an eye on their animals. When they got there, the Reddiar asked them, 'Dei! Where is my Pariah?'

'Innanga! He's looking after all the cows. He can keep an eye on all of them at one time and stop them running away. He wanted to stay there and asked us to bring his food.'

'OK, OK! There'll be a beating waiting for him tonight! Get on with it!'

When the boys told me that, I said to myself, 'Why does he want to hit me when the other one's already done it?' That evening I took the animals back to the stable and tied them up. I fed the cows, the plough oxen and the calves, then I went up to the Reddiar's wife and asked for a half-measure of rice. While I was getting the rice in my *tundu*, the Reddiar came up behind me, without me seeing, and hit me hard with a rattan. I yelled, 'Ayoyo! Ayoyo! Why are you hitting me?'

'Dei! What did you say to the Palli, the Padaiyatchi, eh?'

'Ayo, Sami! He's the one who called me a son of a whore and a motherfucker! That's why I swore at him!'

My father was working there and he came to defend me, 'Sami! If that cow trampled the Palli's harvest, all he had to do was confiscate the cow or complain to you and ask for compensation. But with these unruly animals, how do you expect my son to cope? And how much do you pay him? Six little measures of rice a month, because we're your serfs and do all the work for you and bring you our children.'

That was the first time the Reddiar hit me. He started again one other time. It was just before my marriage. Standing at the edge of the field he was overseeing the groundnut harvest: about fifty people were working on it. I was grazing a cow not far away. The Reddiar called me, 'Manikkam! Manikkam!' But I didn't hear anything because of the wind blowing from the south and all the noise the people were making and I stayed sitting down next to the cow without answering him. He picked up a tamarind branch and coming up behind me, hit me hard on the head. I fainted, unconscious. Everyone came together and started saying, 'What is this, a *kambattam* who hits a boy! A boy as strong as that, he could never have knocked him out: he got him from behind!' Everyone stopped work, leaving their tools and baskets where they were – women took advantage of it to fill the folds of their sari with groundnuts. They left, taking me with them to hospital. The Reddiar had gone home and said what had happened: 'I hit Manikkam with a tamarind branch. The workers gathered round and took him to hospital. Apparently he's in a bad way ... '

Then his mother bawled him out in Telugu, 'How could you hit that boy who we've brought up as a son? If he recovers, he'll be sure to get his revenge. He'll pay you back for what you've done to him. Maybe you think he'll be afraid of your money?'

They asked me at the hospital what had happened to me. I didn't tell them the truth because I didn't want it to get to the police and be told to lodge a complaint against the Reddiar: I have to work for him to live! And you have to be in court every time they ask you. I'm not rich enough to get involved in that. I'd rather die than have all that trouble. So I told the doctor that a trunk had fallen on my head. But he knew perfectly well that that wasn't true. He said to me, 'Don't hide anything from me. Don't be afraid. You can tell me the truth. Did somebody hit you?' I told him again that a trunk had got me on the head.

The Reddiar's father came to see me in hospital, and he backed up what I'd said to the doctor. But people went up to him outside and complained about his son's behaviour. He answered them, 'Yeppa! It wasn't me who told him to act like that! The harm has been done now. Tell Manikkam not to be angry.' He handed out twenty-five rupees so I could be given good meals in the hospital and bought a little brandy or beer. But my father said to him, 'I think of you as a father and you wouldn't have behaved like that. But how can money make up for what has been done?'

Meanwhile I was saying to myself, 'I'm not going to let this go, even if I have to stay there. He'll feel my fist! I'll get my revenge.' Once I was better, I didn't want to work for that Reddiar any more, but my father forced me to.

One day the following season, when I was picking up groundnuts with my mother, the Grand Reddi called her, 'Adi, Muniyamma! Adi, Muniyamma! Come here, di!'

I said, 'Mother, Mother, he's calling you! Instead of saying "Muni-yamma, come here!", he says, "Adi! Adi! Come here, di, vadi-podi!"'[11]

Hearing that, he shouted at me, 'Aye! Son of a Pariah whore! Let me fuck your wife, you sister fucker!'

His son came and hit me with his umbrella. I seized the opportunity and hit him on the back and the thigh with my hoe. Immediately he went off to call the police, telling them that a Pariah boy working for his household had hit him, and the day workers in the field took fright and ran away. I went home as well. Everyone was afraid I'd be taken to the police station for a beating. I just had time to wash when an inspector and a policeman arrived on a motorbike. The inspector called me, 'Dei! Come here!'

People gathered round immediately. I answered, 'How do you expect me to come over there without any clothes? I'm in the middle of washing!'

'Dei, right then! You've got a nerve! Come here immediately or I'll count your bones!'

'Go and look somewhere else! I've already seen police like you. You're not going to intimidate me!'

'Dei! You hit the Reddi and still you come out with arguments? We're going to bang you up and give you a good beating, boy!'

'Ayo! Earn some respect and respect the law! Don't overstep the role of policeman and don't push it too far with me! You think I'm a colony man, a Pariah you can insult and who'll be afraid? I won't go to the police station with you! You say I hit the Reddi? Well then, take me to the main police station in Pondy. When the magistrate summons me, I'll be there.'

'Aah, you're not coming! You want me to send people to Pondy! We're not going to get through with you till we've counted your bones!'

'Get going, ya! I've seen a bunch of people like you and they all wanted to count my bones too! Just try and touch me and you'll see. Go on, get out of here, instead of asking me for five or six rupees because I'm poor and the others for fifty or sixty. You're wasting your breath here!'

'And why's that? You are a Pariah boy and you hit a Reddiar instead of working!'

'They tell us, "Come here" and we come; "Go over there" and we go there; "Sit down here" and we sit down. They can hit us but if we give them the same back, they send for the police, we're taken to the station and beaten up.'

'What do you expect, ya! That's the way the world works! All you Pariah guys wear yourself out working and if you answer back, you've got to take the blows as well!'

'Yes, you take a backhander from the rich and then you beat us Pariahs!'

Sinnamma, if we talk to them straight, telling them what's what and slipping them a few notes, then they'll go and see the Reddiar and talk to him differently.

'Innayya! You make them work how you please, without having to follow any regulations or anything and then you beat them as well. Even if you've got all the police on your side, that's no reason to beat them. This boy wants to lodge a complaint. He wants to go over our heads. And if we beat him too hard, we'll be suspended as well. If you want, you can lodge a complaint as well!'

In the end they took me to the station and there I managed to give each of them ten rupees: you give what you can. They let me out after that and went to tell the Reddiar, 'Innanga! He wasn't at home. He's gone and hidden somewhere. Wait a bit for us to find him: we'll put him in the hole and then count the pieces!'

Two days later the Reddiar went back to see them, 'Well then, have you found him? Have you given him a beating, that delinquent?'

'Innanga! He's gone and lodged a complaint against you. You're going to be summoned the day after tomorrow for a confrontation!'

'Ah! That Pariah's got a nerve to take it as far as this! He can't have had the idea all on his own. Someone must have turned his head. I'm going to see how far this gentleman is going to go! Sir thinks he's rich! All he can pawn is his grass hut: where's he going to find the money from?'

And he went and complained to everybody, 'That Pariah has lodged a complaint against me and he's ready to pay for it!'

The others – a neighbour, a friend, even an Untouchable like me – said to him, 'Innanga! A Pariah has dared argue with you. You hit him as a punishment and he's paid you back. Where are we heading if everyone fights like this? The matter's closed now, so where is the Reddiar, where's the Pariah in all this?'

But the people who support the Pariahs said, 'What difference does it make if he's a Pariah? Does blood only flow in Reddiar's veins and not in Pariah's? It makes them laugh when we talk about Pariahs. But don't Pariahs have wives and children like everybody else? The Reddiar aren't the only ones with children. When it's a question of their children, they take great care. But the son of a Pariah is satisfied with very little: a little oil, a little *sikakai* to wash. The son of a Reddiar has that soap which smells good, what's it called? And he has meals with loads of dishes. The Pariah can't give his sons that. That's why he sends them to the Reddiar's to tend the cows, to be serfs and to get beaten up!'

And then there are other ones as well who go and say to the Reddiar, 'No, no! He mustn't be allowed to get away with it! He must be given a good beating to bring him into line!'

After that business, I stopped working for the Reddiar and all my family did as well. The stable wasn't cleaned out, the cow dung wasn't collected, the cows didn't go out. The Reddiar hired other people but the work wasn't done well. I knew the customs of the house. The others couldn't do the work in the same way as me and the Reddiar didn't have the patience to teach them to do what he wanted. I could be trusted to take a thousand rupees to a *kambattam* in a neighbouring village, apart from doing agricultural work. A newcomer couldn't be asked to do that.

For six months I stood up to him and I didn't want any of my family to work at that Reddiar's. I became a day worker and my mother did too. I pruned trees, I ploughed, I worked the well. And at the end of six months, the Reddiar said to himself: it's not working at all without those Pariahs. I've tried other people but they don't work the way they should. So he told the Reddiar that Ambigai works for to send for me. He said to Pajani Gounder, 'The Pariah from the Grand Reddi's has done this and he's done that. He hit him and hasn't come to work since. Tell him to come back!' And Murugaiya Gounder called me as well, 'Innappa! Apparently you've stopped going to the Reddiar's over there. What's happening?'

'Yes, Sami, I don't want to work for him any more. He doesn't pay me well. He doesn't let me have a plot of land to farm and he hits me. Why should I go and work for him under those conditions?'

'OK, OK. All of that is not good. He should look after you like a mother looks after her child, and you should end your days in this Reddiar's household. You shouldn't go anywhere else.'

'No, Ayya! Let him come and find me himself if he wants me. Otherwise he'll say to himself, "Oh, he's had a really hard time! That's why he's coming back now!" Let the Reddiar come and call me, "Come, da! Come, Manikkam!" Then I'll go. But I won't go back of my own accord!'

And the Reddiar came to call me. The people were around us. I said to them, 'I got very little for my son's marriage. I was beaten and injured. The police arrested me. Is that an honourable way for a *kambattam* to behave? Does he look good coming to call me today? What's he doing with his reputation?'

An elder of the *ceri* added, 'Yes! He always thinks Pariahs are afraid of the Reddiar and that they just have to be called to come running. He mustn't think that.'

Sadayan said, 'Dei! Let him go and look elsewhere. He's dropped you for six months! He beat you, he handed you over to the police, he lodged a complaint against you, and now he comes and says, "Come, da, Manikkam!" like a prince.'

Hearing that, the Reddiar understood that he really was in the wrong, that all the Pariahs had realised that and that they were saying it at the tops of their voices. So he said, 'OK, OK! Come on! I won't do anything to you from now on! You will work honestly and with dignity and you will eat with dignity what I give you. You'll have a little land to farm. But I want my property to be well looked after!'

Then somebody else answered, 'Would you hit your son like that? He's the child of a rich man: he's entitled to be treated differently. We have no means of support. We're beaten. We're sent to court. You've got money and you can read! We're Untouchables, we're poor and we can only live by your side!'

'OK, OK!' the Reddiar answered, 'you can ask for what you want, but Manikkam has to come and do his work!'

When all the elders of the *ceri* had finished talking, Murugaiya Gounder started, 'OK! You've said what you had to say. But when a *kambattam* comes in person to find his worker, he has to go. You know the customs of the family, their stories, their way of living. They have to have you. Go there!'

And I went off to be a serf again ...

(*Viramma picks up the thread of her account.*) This year we got the ballot papers for the elections very early. My son and my nephew got them as well. There were lots of people at the Reddiar's and the *kambattam* of Ariyanallur and his wife came and stayed with him. There were visitors night and day. There was a big party, a meal for all the voters and loudspeakers playing music. It was like a wedding! The Reddiar called us, the Paratchi, to winnow the rice: there were four sacks to feed that many people! We didn't cook at home at all because we were given what was left over. There was a big *pandal* in the street and rows of narrow mats with banana leaves in front of them: they were for the Kudiyanar, the serving castes and the Pariahs. No one missed the meal, even though there was no meat. It's not often we get to eat as well as that! The important people, like the Gounder, the Naicker and the Udaiyar, came without their families. Their meal was served on the first floor of the house. Apparently there was brandy and chicken from a big restaurant in Pondy. Pakkiri, the cobbler's wife, told me: she picked up the dirty leaves at the end of the meal. There were masses of them! The Reddiar's wife was very generous, she gave her a very pretty sari, an underskirt and a blouse. But Pakkiri doesn't wear a blouse so she gave it to her sister-in-law. We only got five rupees each for winnowing the rice, but I'd rather earn less than do a degrading job.

Everyone handed out the ballot papers for their party for this election: the Reddiar for their side, the Gounder for theirs. We vote the way we want: I vote for the Reddiar who I work for, another woman will vote for her master, or we can also vote for who we like. Afterwards we can make things up and tell the others that we voted for them. But we take everybody's money! Because they've all got money. We had five parties at one time. The ploughmen's party gave twenty rupees and a bottle of brandy; the two leaves party twenty-five rupees and a very brightly coloured factory sari; the cow and the calf party twenty-five rupees and some groundnut oil; the spinning wheel party fifteen rupees, and another one gave fifteen as well.[12] We tell them all we'll vote for them and we take their money. But anyway, everybody's only got one vote and you have to vote for just one person. Everyone gives, but we can't vote for everybody who's given! You can't vote twice because you've got two hands!

Ayo, Sinnamma! There's lots of people at the place where we go and vote: a little bit like queuing for the cinema. There are two police trucks, policemen, inspectors, nurses. The policemen are standing there with their sticks and saying, 'Go on! One by one! Through this door and go into that room!' We take what we're given and at last get to the man with the list, who calls out in the order of the list, 'Manikkam', then 'Wife of Manikkam: Viramma', then 'Anban'. When I got there I was asked, 'What's your husband's name? Show me your card!' Someone old enters everything and checks it: 'Look and see if her name's there. Her husband's name. Where's the ballot paper?' We form two queues: one for men, one for women. The ballot papers we get at home are not valid. We have to take one from there. When we get to the booth, we take the stamp and make a mark in front of the sign we want, and then all the ballot papers are put in a box.

Once I made a mistake: I should have stamped the rising sun and I put it on the hand. When I came out, my husband told me off, 'Can't you tell the difference between a rising sun and a hand?' Of course I can, but when it's all drawn on paper, it's smudged and I can't make anything out. He was in a rage, the others too. I said to them, 'Leave me alone! I'm trembling all over in front of all these men. How do you expect me to make something out? We'll see at the next elections!'

Nowadays, just before each election, they do new works in the *ceri*. Look: the streets are well marked out and tarmacked in the new *ceri*. There's a tap on every corner and there's street lighting. It's really nice and we're not afraid any more going home at night, whereas before, in the dark, guys used to hide in the sugar-cane fields to come and pester us. Everything that was cramped in the old *ceri* is roomy now, on a bigger plot of land: it all depends on the size of the family. We got nothing because we already own our house and we've only got one child living with us. They told my husband, 'You can stay where you are. Your family home is big enough for you. But your brother will be entitled to a plot in the new colony.' That's how they do it. If brothers live together, then one out of two or two out of four get a new plot. And everyone builds their house as best they can on the plot of land the government gives them.

Everyone in the *ceri* owns their house now. I have to redo my roof. I'm waiting for the sugar cane to be cut to hire a cart and go and collect the leaves. You have to allow for two full days of work. We take advantage of the harvest in Cittirai to redo the roof. In the past we'd also use *karudai samba* thatch and that would last for more than two years. But with the new types of rice we've got now, the thatch doesn't last like that. Yesterday I saw they were redoing the thatch on the house of Sinnappan, the *talaiyari*, who's living in Pondy now. He comes and spends a month here with his family each year for the festival of Draupadi. All the people who've left the village keep a house like that to come back from time to time. The government has recognised his work. There's only me who works as the midwife for nothing or almost nothing. Sinnappan's wife is the president of the women's association here. She looks like you, Sinnamma. You'd think she was a woman from the *ur*, not at all like a Paratchi. The association has got a hall in the new colony now and Sinnappan's wife comes to talk there with other women from Pondy. I asked her about me being paid a wage for my work as the midwife and I asked Kaliyan, the *nattam*, as well. But neither of those sons of a widower did anything about it. No one wants to put in a request for me.

I talked about it as well to Murali, a boy from the *ceri*, who's well educated. He passed all his exams and now he's working in a government office in Pondy. He is in the rising sun party. He could say a word to the people in his party, but he always answers me, 'Wait, aunt. Don't be in a rush: you'll be given notice to attend!'

'Yes, yes!' I tell him. 'I'll get it when I'm in the cremation grounds!' (*Laughs.*) That boy is very helpful all the same. He puts in our requests to the Office of Harijans. It's through him that I got a loan to buy a pair of oxen. I gave him twenty-five rupees and the *nattam* as well. Both of them go to the offices for all these requests and they slip two or three people some money to get the signature they need. If we don't pay, we never get anything!

Murali keeps our young ones up to date with what's happening in the parties. He gets them worked up and it ends in fights. 'The Reddi doesn't pay you enough: you have to rebel!' 'This one's a traitor, that one's a real thief!' That's what our young ones talk about! That's all that interests them. Our masters can't scold them any more because they react straightaway. That's exactly what the political parties preach. The cinema turns their heads as well and gives them ideas. One day I saw the son of Kannima go to Kuppussami's teashop and ask to be served. Kuppussami politely asked him to bring his glass, but that boy demanded to drink out of one of the shop's glasses and he started abusing Kuppussami. That really is some nerve! Just because at the cinema you see those misters drinking out of everybody's glasses doesn't mean that you have to do the same! What will happen to Kuppussami's business if Pariahs start drinking out of his glasses? No one from the *ur* will go there any more![13]

It comes from listening to all those politicians. Of course they don't have to worry now. By the grace of God, we, their parents, can still work. But there'll come a time when we can't any more. Then they'll have to go and ask our masters for help. You can't keep the stomach waiting. It's not their party or the men in government who are going to feed them. Thieves cannot live on what they've stolen for ever. One day they have to go back to living a normal life. Well then, our young can't always live on politics either! They're brainless birds. They whistle noisily and end up drowning in the drinking trough. We've got to find a way to feed ourselves somehow. Can we pawn something to borrow money from the Marwari of Tirulagam? The only things we've got are our hands. The day we go without our *kuj*, we can run to the Reddiar's and he always ends up by lending us a few measures of rice or a few rupees. That's why I always teach respect and obedience towards our masters. And that's also why I vote for the Reddiar myself ... My conscience always tells me to vote for him. I work for his household. He protects me and I should give him my protection as well. Everybody thinks the same as me: we're not dishonest towards the one who feeds us! The Gounder gives out lots more money than the Reddiar to get our votes. He tells all of us, 'Don't vote for your Reddiar! Vote for us!' But the Reddiar has married off all our children! Even if I vote for the Gounder, they won't do anything for us. They think of us before the elections, but afterwards they don't even know where we live!

Three elections before this one, Sinnamma, there was a fight here. Our young ones had decided to stop voting for Perumal Gounder's party and vote instead for the new party of M.G.R. There were quarrels for days between the men of the two parties. One evening, Perumal

Gounder's men came with sticks. One of the leaders was a Gounder called Vadivelu, who always comes and shows off round the *ceri*. That time he said, 'Dei! You sister fuckers! Who gave you so many facilities here? It's got to be the man who governs Pondy, hasn't it?'

Every evening they came in a group like that, after going drinking, and that Vadivelu would shout at us, 'Dei! You slits, they say you're all high and mighty and that you're not going to vote for us? Eh! No one's forcing you, you know? Vote for us if you want to, or else hang on to your votes!'

We listened to them in silence, but there were always some young ones who shouted back, 'It's all over now, you playing the wise guy! Nowadays you can't swing your dick like before or put a cap on our heads! You used to be able to trick us, but it doesn't work any more!'[14]

Luckily the elders calmed them down. Next day we went to see the Reddiar and the elders of the *ur*. 'Sami, our elders! We haven't done anything and yesterday evening Vadivelu the Gounder came to our *ceri*. He threatened to beat us. He insulted us crudely. We had difficulty restraining our boys!'

The Reddiar had the Gounder called straightaway and he gave him a severe telling off, 'Innada! You went drinking yesterday and wanted to beat these people: terrified, poor people, hiding like animals in the forest!'

And the Gounder replied, 'Innanga! It was because they took the money and then didn't want to vote for me. That's why I went to their homes!'

We left satisfied that the Reddiar had stepped in. That Vadivelu is really the only one who comes and swings his dick in the *ceri*!

Another time, long ago, it was much more serious. I still had my fifth daughter in my arms in those days and there was no water. Our stores of paddy were used up and we had to buy some in the market. I'd go every day to Naliveli, Mangappakkam or Nellipet to collect groundnuts. I couldn't work by day because I had the baby to feed and the owners wouldn't have put up with me stopping like that several times a day. I took the baby with me and simply went and picked up what the day workers had left: little shells or ones that were hard to pick. That would make me between one and three measures at the end of the day which I'd go and sell for three or four rupees. It hadn't rained for months, everything was baked and we were dying of hunger. My father was working in Madras and we decided to go to him to try and find work.

My husband left us there and he started working for a group who were smuggling for a nabob of Cuddalore.[15] They made bootleg alcohol in the villages out of palm sugar, bark, spices and mandarin peel and my husband transported it. He also dealt in cigarettes and gold for the nabob. He was paid twenty-five rupees a day, plus drinks and food. How else could we cope? We had to find something: a measure of rice was so expensive! But once he was caught and he went to prison, after we'd come back to Karani.

It was before an election and every day a car with a loudspeaker came to Karani telling us to vote for the Reddi of Naliveli who was standing against our Reddiar. No one in the *ceri* or the *ur* stopped to listen. The Reddi of Naliveli realised that he couldn't count on our votes and one day the car came to threaten us, demanding that we vote for him, but no one took it seriously, no one believed it. We said to ourselves, 'What on earth can he do to our village, and who on earth would really vote for that monkey face?' The elections went off peacefully and we didn't see anybody for two days. And then, one disastrous morning, on the third day when everyone was still at home, we saw a lorry arrive full of good-sized *mattai.* The lorry stopped between the *ceri* and the *ur.* There were only two guys inside. A little later two other lorries drove up full of men. We'd just got up and we hadn't really taken in what was happening. And suddenly all the guys jumped out of their lorries, took the *mattai* and spread out in all directions.

They went into all the houses (*Viramma laughs*), and started beating everybody they came across, smashing the dishes and looting. We tried to flee. The Grand Reddiar and his family left by car on the lane that goes behind the village. Some, like the Vattiyar's parents, managed to get on the bus and left for Pondy. Others hid in the pond and the trees. It was like an anthill that had been crushed. Everyone ran away. There were plenty of jewels stolen from the *ur*! Two lorries full of men to beat us or kill us! They took us out of the houses, 'Dei! You didn't want to vote for us, this is for you!' Luckily my husband wasn't there, or else he would have been beaten as well. I had my daughter in my arms. I was sitting in the sun with the old cobbler, when three guys came up, as large as Bhima, and told him, 'Dei, old man! Get up!'

But he said, 'How do you expect me to get up, Sami? I'm trembling, I've got old legs!'

They kicked him over, then left for Pakkiam's and said to her, 'Aye! Get out of there with your kid, you whore! So you didn't want to vote for us, eh?'

I don't know how I managed. Their punches had completely stunned me. I found myself on the road to Velpakkam without really being aware of it, I was so scared. They'd destroyed and wrecked everything and set fire to the registry office next to the Reddiar's. There wasn't anybody left in the village: not a soul, not a speck of dust. They could loot in peace. Only Rayappan had been seriously wounded. He was taken to Pondy hospital on a stretcher and he stayed there for days. When he came back he was like a Muslim corpse with bandages everywhere! (*Viramma laughs.*)

We came back little by little the next day. The registry office was still burning. Some animals had run away, others were dead. Loads of things were destroyed or stolen. In the *ceri*, all the dishes were broken, the food trampled on, the stores of grain either had holes in them or had been looted. Life was hard because we had to start again with almost nothing.

But, Sinnamma, that Reddi of Naliveli made a quick getaway!

'Where to?'

To *vaikundam*! (*Laughs.*) For two nights and three days, all you could hear was the poor cursing that dog: 'I wish that cuntlicker would die! That demon fucker can die with his mouth open! May his line disappear! I hope someone takes off his wife's *tali*!'

And we said to ourselves, 'Innanga! Is it just whores in this *ceri* and *ur*? Isn't there a single chaste woman so that at least her curse will be heard?'

Some time later we were working in the Little Reddiar's field and that's when we learned that that Naliveli dog had died of a heart attack! We dropped everything and set off with our children, the women in front. The men came afterwards. When that guy who screws Yama was dead, we wanted him still to hear us and our curses falling on him. They tried to push us back, but there were too many of us wanting to settle the score with him: 'Rotten cunt! You sent your men to beat us, but God took care of you sooner than you expected! Make your journey, no one will miss you on this earth!'

Hum! What a noble man! When he paid his workers, he didn't keep the money in a bag or in the fold of his *soman*: he put it on a spade and threw it on the ground so he could see the day workers knock each other over to pick it up! When he saw Paratchi walking past in the street, he'd shout at them, 'Aye! You sister fucker! What are you hanging around here for?' Always words like that. He could afford to leave on a funeral stretcher covered in flowers, but those flowers wilted under our curses! Seeing our anger and all the unrest, the family and politicians decided not to keep the body very long. They brought forward the time of cremation. Everything was rushed and the rites were slapdash. He'll have to wait a long time in that cremation ground before being reborn seven times and ending up impaled: that's what Isvaran can give to creatures like that!

Something like that couldn't happen in this *kaliyugam*, Sinnamma. They come and find us and pay us to vote, and our young ones have put ignorance behind them. The government itself works for us. In the past, the owners made the poor work and gave them their food. They made the law. No one came and asked us what we wanted. And then they wanted us to vote and today, we Pariahs are becoming civilised. There's more people as well than there used to be, more poor, and they are making demands now. For my part, I work for a house which carries a lot of weight and everyone is well off. Thanks to their *dharma*, I live well too. My children are married. I've got grandchildren. I don't go without anything. I live without starving, Sinnamma.

Notes

1. A CHILDHOOD IN VELPAKKAM

1. 'Serf' has been used to translate the term *adimai*: the agricultural worker whose family has been attached to and dependent on a landowner's family for several generations. *Adimai* are one of the types of 'bonded labour', which is now illegal in India. They are not their master's property and they have a certain amount of autonomy, allowing them to work as tenant farmers or as day workers for other landowners. But they are primarily bound to their masters by an inherited state of dependency. This means, on the one hand, being always available to work for low pay and, on the other, that they have guaranteed employment and the relative security of loans at important moments in family life – ritual ceremonies, marriages, deaths. But the ensuing debts, which are handed down from parents to children, have led to generations of debtors working for generations of creditors. In principle this form of dependency has ceased – landowners preferring to reduce *adimai* to a minimum and pay workers by the day – but its traditional relationships are still very strongly internalised by Viramma's generation, particularly the respect due to powerful landowners such as the Reddi.

2. Aunt in this case does not refer to one of Viramma's blood relatives. Adi, the sister of Viramma's father, Nadesan, is the only aunt by blood that Viramma refers to in the book, but throughout she follows the common practice of using titles of relations – grandfather, grandmother, big brother, big sister, sister-in-law and brother-in-law – to address her fellow villagers. Viramma will call her mother-in-law, for instance, 'aunt'.

3. The inhabitants of the *ceri*, who are mainly Paraiyars in Karani, tend to call the inhabitants of the *ur* Tamils: a mark of respect but also a purely ideological practice since, ethnically, they are just as much Tamils themselves. Their custom reflects the social exclusions that have been a defining feature of the ideology of Untouchability.

282

4. The Indian custom is for a child to be born at its maternal grandparents' home, the expectant mother returning there to give birth, as Viramma herself will do.

5. Viramma, like Virayi, is a woman's name derived from the god Viran.

6. Sinnamma is the name given by Viramma to Josiane Racine throughout their conversations. It could be translated as 'little mother' or 'young lady'.

7. The Indian squirrel has three stripes on its back and orthodox sivaite Hindus (particularly Brahmins) mark the three stripes that symbolise Siva on their foreheads after completing a *puja*.

8. 'The castes above us' is a literal translation of *meljatiar*. For a Tamil Dalit, the expression can mean the middle castes as well as the higher castes. But Viramma never uses the superlative and, for her, 'the castes above us' means the high castes, *uyarnadajatiar*, far more than all the castes which, indiscriminately, are above Dalits.

2. THE MARRIAGE IS ARRANGED

1. Dipavali, or Diwali, is one of the great Hindu festivals, celebrated throughout India. It is held on the day before the new moon in Aippaci (mid-October to mid-November) to celebrate Krishna's victory over the demon Narakasura – the firecrackers people throw recall their fight – and all the participants wear new clothes.

2. The trident (*sulam*) is an attribute of Siva.

3. The pledge of marriage (*nitchayam*) concerns only the two families, whereas the engagement (*pariyam*) is public and friends and neighbours are invited to the ceremony as well as relatives. The third ceremony is the warding-off of the evil eye (*nalungu*) and the fourth, the next day, is the marriage itself.

4. Days contain lucky and unlucky or inauspicious hours, specified by almanacs and daily calendars. Most people take this distinction very seriously, refusing to start an enterprise or journey at an unlucky hour, but there are formal ways of circumventing it, for instance by a symbolic, false departure before the unlucky hour and then a real departure at a time whose inauspiciousness has been neutralised by the symbolic early start.

3. 'BECOMING A WOMAN'

1. The maternal uncle (the mother's younger brother) is a key figure in the family. Traditionally, his agreement is essential for a niece to get married, since he has a pre-emptive right to her hand, and marriages between maternal uncles and nieces are still common. Along with the elder brother, he has a duty to look after his niece if necessary.

4. THE WEDDING NIGHT

1. Velpakkatta means the woman from Velpakkam. It's common practice to call a woman by the name of the village where she was born.

2. Mahadisvaran means 'The Great Isvaran', i.e. 'The Great Siva', and so someone of exceptional strength.

3. Colony is the more neutral or euphemistic modern name for the *ceri*.

4. Tiruvannamalai is a famous place of pilgrimage about sixty kilometres from Karani. At the festival of Kartikkai Dipam, the priests of the temple of Arunachala set light to an enormous fire with a wick soaked in a cauldron of oil.

5. '*Mattai uri*'. *Mattai* is a coconut still covered in its fibres, which people tear off sitting down, holding the coconut between their feet. The position, therefore, is when one partner sits on top of the other and squeezes her, or him, between his, or her, legs.

5. 'HE STILL DESIRES ME!'

1. The *annakkayiru*, the thread tied around a child's waist either at birth or at its first illness. It either has knots in it or carries an amulet as protection against illness and evil spirits and an adult keeps the amulet knotted round the waist all his or her life.

2. Symptomatic prejudice. Relations between Hindus and Muslims in the South of India are peaceful, but Hindus do hold a number of received ideas about Muslims, particularly that they are worryingly versed in sorcery.

3. A colloquial Tamil expression meaning that the sickness is incurable.

4. 'The great sickness' is leprosy, popularly believed to be the culmination of certain venereal diseases.

5. Viramma uses the word *sukkumattadi*, which refers either to the staff of the *sanyasi* mendicant, which is endowed with divine energy, or to the club held by the gods' guardian statues in village temples. The word implies superhuman force, and can also refer to a magic wand.

6. A *sanyasi* is a man, or sometimes a woman, who has renounced the world, and lives as either a hermit or a wandering mendicant in search of spiritual wisdom and liberation from the cycle of reincarnation.

6. A MOTHER TO TWELVE CHILDREN

1. The usual way of asking if a woman has had her period.

2. Generally in India a pregnancy is considered to last ten months, counting from the end of the last period. In Tamil Nadu it is marked by various ceremonies of *varisai*, when women from the mother's house bring trays of food in a line (*varisai*). The *arrasor*, the rice of mid-pregnancy, is handed out in the fifth month; the *mudugunir*, the ceremony of sprinkling water or milk on the back, is held in the sixth or eighth month; and *simantam*, the ceremony of wearing jewels, is held in the seventh month.

3. 'Go to the garden' means to defecate.

4. Cooling foods and warming foods are categories of *tridosha* theory, which is the basis of traditional Indian medicine. It is assumed that health results from a good balance between three corporal elements: air, heat, coolness. Heat and coolness do not refer to the feeling one may have when eating or drinking, but to the heating and cooling effects various types of food have on the body.

5. 'Sister' has passed into the Tamil language to mean nurse in general, without Christian connotations.

6. The sixteen gates are the different ways the soul of a dead person can

leave the body. They are divided into three groups and influence the soul's fate after death. Viramma uses the concept generally to mean that Yama, the god of death, will open the way of liberation and spare her reincarnation.

7. THE DESTINIES OF CHILDREN

1. Katteri, a menacing goddess who wanders through the forest after being cursed by Siva, is worshipped as a provider and protector of children. But the Katteri are also evil spirits who prey on pregnant women, as Viramma explains in chapter 8.

2. Children are only named definitively at the ceremony when their heads are shaved for the first time and they are dedicated to the god of their line. Amongst Dalits, this ceremony can be very late – four or five years old – mainly for financial reasons. It happens much earlier in more prosperous castes, and the first name is given at about six months when the baby starts sleeping in a cradle, away from its mother.

3. Sundari is one of the names of Draupadi, the heroine of the *Mahabharata*, the epic which Viramma calls the *Bharatam*. Viramma's allusion to fire partly recalls the *Mahabharata*, where Draupadi is born out of the flames of a sacrificial fire lit by her father Drupada and becomes the wife of the five Pandava brothers who eventually defeat the hundred Kaurava, their cousins, at the battle of Kurukshetra. But, more specifically, it refers to later myths and the sacrificial fire lit by one of the Pandava's descendants, King Sunidan, six generations after the *Mahabharata*. Draupadi emerges from this fire to cut off the thousand heads of the demon Asurapputtiran and then decrees that she will protect mankind if they build temples to her and celebrate her festival over eighteen days, the duration of the battle of Kurukshetra. Described in chapter 23, her festival culminates in walking on fire.

4. Ayodhya is one of Hinduism's holy cities and the glorious capital of Rama's father, King Dasaratha, in the *Ramayana*.

5. In each verse, the barren woman makes offerings in a different temple but, 'even so', she remains childless like the Pandava, all of whose children were killed in the battle with the Kaurava. Kaliyamma is Kali the Mother (the woman models her in clay), Puttupputtan one of the forms of Aiyanar, Selliyamma the eldest of the seven virgins born of Siva's hair, Patchaiyamma one of the forms of Sakti; Chidambaram in the Tillai forest is where Siva appeared as Nataraja, the divine dancer, and Mayavaram, on the banks of the holy river Kaveri, is the city of Vishnu as Maya, the god of illusion. '*Yelama yelam*', '*nana*' and, in the next section, '*Arigari*' are all purely onomatopoeic, without meaning.

8. IRSI KATTERI, THE FOETUS-EATER

1. The conch shell is the symbol of Vishnu, the trident the symbol of Siva.

2. The expression 'to die in good shape' means remaining active until one's death, without becoming weakened or bedridden.

3. Kerala, the neighbouring state to Tamil Nadu, where Malayalam is spoken. Malayalam is a Dravidian language which split off from Tamil over the course of several hundred years, between the 4th and 13th centuries AD.

4. The *magudi* is the snake charmers' wind instrument with a gourd and a long neck. 'Taking the photo' is the common expression for the cobra standing up and opening its hood.

5. Member of the Legislative Assembly of Pondicherry, Karani being in his constituency. It's common practice to call politicians by their initials.

9. THE GOD OF TIRUPATI

1. Tirupati, in the south of Andhra Pradesh, is the most important place of pilgrimage in the South of India. The main sanctuary is dedicated to Perumal (Vishnu), who is called Venkatesvara or Venkatapati, the 'Lord of the Mountain', there, as well as Tirumal. Viramma's declaimer, 'we're unclean but we believe deeply', reflects the fact that Dalits are drawn to worshipping secondary divinities, or secondary forms of major divinities, because of their status and the fact that they're forbidden from entering the temples of major divinities in the *ur*. The great pilgrimage temples are more accessible because of their anonymity but, significantly, Viramma says nothing about Venkatesvara in her account of the pilgrimage to Tirupati. She recalls mostly the temple of Mangavarttama (and its statues of Kali) which she stopped at on her way to Tirupati, and, at Tirupati itself, the barbers at work.

2. The sign of Vishnu consists of a vertical red line (*namam*) with two white oblique lines shaped as a V either side. Basil is the symbolic plant of Vishnu.

10. MARIAMMAN AND KALI

1. Mariamman, etymologically 'The Mother of smallpox', is one of the most important goddesses in Tamil-speaking areas, particularly amongst Dalits – in Karani, she has a temple in the *ur* and the *ceri* – and she was integrated into the Hindu pantheon by the myth which Viramma tells in part. Siva had taken the form of a wise man and Parvati that of his wife, named Renukka. As she was drawing water one morning, Renukka admired the reflection of a divine messenger and so broke the spell that allowed her to collect the water and flowers needed for her husband's *puja*. Siva, therefore, had one of his sons cut her head off as she was hiding in the arms of an Untouchable, the wife of a cobbler. Siva's son got permission to bring her back to life but, in the confusion, he put her head on the Untouchable's body and the Untouchable's head on hers. It was then that Siva condemned this ambiguous being – half-Brahmin, half-Untouchable – to sow smallpox in the world and receive both vegetarian and non-vegetarian offerings.

11. THE FESTIVAL OF MARIAMMAN

1. In other words, twenty rupees for a man, fifteen for a woman and ten for a child.

2. The consecration of a temple of second rank – which temples in the *ceri* are, since the priests are Dalits of the Valluvar caste – is the one occasion when a Brahmin may agree to enter a *ceri*. Viramma specifies that he is an *artchagar*, a professional priest who is a Brahmin of the second rank, and Mariamman, in this case, is considered as a form of Sakti, the principal feminine divinity.

3. Narikara is a contraction of Nari Korava, the 'Korava of the foxes', the most important Korava tribe who sell, amongst other things, cheap necklaces.

4. Viramma indicates the repertoire of the *kuttu*, the popular theatre played by semi-professional or, sometimes, amateur troupes at religious festivals. The *terrukuttu* troupes specialise in the epics: Lakshmanan is one of the heroes of the *Ramayana*, Bhima and Arjuna, their wife Draupadi and their enemy Karna are characters in the *Mahabharata*. The *nadakan* troupes draw on the Hindu myths of the Puranas and traditional Tamil myths such as the stories of Kattavarayan and Madurai Viran.

5. The 'guy from Pondy' is an activist of the DMK party, a Dravidian regionalist party.

12. THE SEVEN VIRGINS

1. The pig rearers are members of the very low, but not 'untouchable', Tomban caste. They have never lived in the *ceri*, but their social status has generally confined them to living on the outskirts of the *ur* rather than in its heart. The changes Viramma describes here represent government initiatives, particularly by the DMK, to erode the segregation that is one of the main manifestations of untouchability. As she points out, educated Dalits from outside are accepted in the *ur*, but low caste members of the *ur* will not agree to live in the heart of the *ceri*.

2. The hunters are probably members of the Irular tribe which used to live in the forests round Gingee and Tiruvannamalai. In the *Gazetteer* of the South Arcot District, published in 1906, W. Francis records that the Irular had long since left their forests and settled on the outskirts of villages, making their living from hunting, harvesting and as watchmen. Viramma's account indicates a further stage in their assimilation into the dominant society and economy.

13. A FAMILY FUNERAL

1. The Reddiar of Tamil Nadu originally came from Andhra Pradesh and they have kept their native language, Telugu.

2. Manmadan is the god of love, who rides on the parrot, and Rati his wife. Numerous songs celebrate them as the ideal of beauty and love between a couple.

3. Harichandran is the mythical king of Ayodhya who, having given his word to do anything the sage Vishvamitra demanded to save his kingdom, underwent every sort of abasement, culminating in working as an Untouchable in the cremation grounds.

4. In many villages the cremation grounds function as cemeteries. There are separate grounds for Dalits and for people from the *ur*.

5. The lance is the attribute of Murugan, Siva's son. Viramma's declarations that Pariahs don't pray or have gods in their houses should not be taken at face value, since Dalits have an intense religious life and all their houses contain religious icons, the signs of Siva or Vishnu and so on. They are rather an example of the alienation which leads to Dalits' devaluing their own spiritual life because it does not take the same form or follow the same rules as high caste religious practices.

14. DEMONS AND *DHARMA*

1. According to some popular beliefs, the soul is not reincarnated immediately after being judged by Yama but, depending on his decision, it first goes either to heaven or one of the many Hindu hells. But it's agreed that if the manner of death is abnormal or the funeral rites are not properly carried out, the dead will become a spirit and return to torment the living while it awaits reincarnation.

2. The Budam is a supernatural being, like a giant, who terrifies those he appears to. The Katteri and Mohini are evil female spirits and the Minisuprayan, sometimes known simply as Mini, can be either male or female and can slit their victims' throats.

3. Five months after Indian troops stormed the Golden Temple at Amritsar, where Sikh separatists had established their headquarters, Indira Gandhi was shot by two of her Sikh bodyguards on 31 October 1984. The announcement of her death was delayed and Rajiv Gandhi, her son, was appointed Prime Minister the same evening.

4. Viramma alludes to the serious outbreaks of violence in North India at the start of November 1984, when thousands of Sikhs were killed or wounded.

15. THE CASTE OF THIEVES

1. The State of Emergency declared by Indira Gandhi's government between June 1975 and March 1977 was marked by a number of operations against corruption and large-scale, or organised, crime – previously under certain forms of political protection – which were intended to compensate for the suspension of the democratic process.

2. Ayittalamma are two wives of a Chettiar of Karani, Ayi and Talamma, who were deified after being burnt on his pyre, long ago.

16. HIGH AND LOW CASTES IN KARANI

1. Viramma's list is not exhaustive and needs a certain amount of explanation. Of the castes in the *ur*, the Udaiyar are farmers and landowners like the Reddiar and Gounder – the Reddiar being the most powerful caste of landowners and the Gounder the largest. There are no Mudaliar in Karani in the main sense of a high caste of landowners, but the Kepmari – the caste of thieves – give themselves this title. Tulukkan is a general name for Muslims and Viramma is probably thinking either of the civil servants sometimes appointed to the village or the tradesmen from Tirulagam. Viramma leaves out the main caste in the *ceri* – the Paraiyar, with their two sub-castes, the Vettiyan and the Pannaiyar – and she describes them in the next chapter. The Vannan here are the launderers of the *ceri* and the Sakkiliar the very low caste of cobblers. There are no Koravar – members of the Nari Korava tribe – in the *ceri* as such, but some pass through and the Sakkiliar are often treated as being like them. *Talaiyari* is more a profession than a caste – the position of assistant to the village accountant described at the end of chapter 17 – and the Tomban are misleadingly described as being completely outside the caste system. Their low rank confines them to

the outskirts of the *ur*, as was made clear at the start of chapter 12, and Viramma's exaggeration could be due to her argument with a particular Tomban which she goes on to describe.

2. Kartikkai, the eighth month of the Tamil calendar (mid-November to mid-December), when the festival of Kartikkai dipam is celebrated. Lamps are lit in every house to evoke the ceremony to Siva at Tiruvannamalai on the same night, as noted in chapter 4, note 4.

3. The rules governing the exchange of food are an essential aspect of the caste system. The orthodox view is that cooked food can only be accepted from someone of an equal or higher caste. So, although the Kudiyanar are economically dependent on the Tomban, they assert their caste superiority by refusing cooked food. Raw food and basic foodstuffs, like grain, are exchanged more freely – as Viramma goes on to say, the potter accepts grain from her.

17. THE PARAIYAR

1. The Paraiyar are the largest caste of Dalits in Tamil Nadu and, through contact first with the Portuguese in the sixteenth century and then the French and English in the eighteenth century, their caste name has become a general term in its Europeanised form of 'pariah'. Muniyan gives one of its mythical derivations: 'the people of the drum' – *parai* being the specific leather drum played by the Paraiyar providing the drummers for the *paraimelam* orchestra. Michael Moffat, in his book *An Untouchable Community in South India. Structure and Consensus*, suggests that *Paraiya maraiyade* refers to a piece of beef, rather than a drum, which the four sons of Siva and Adi were meant to share.

2. Viramma uses the English word 'decent' as a synonym for the social practices and standards of hygiene and dress – set by high castes – which she describes as 'civilised'.

3. The Vettiyan and Pannaiyar are sub-castes of the Paraiyar, the latter being of slightly higher rank since they offer their god a sacrifice of milk, rather than a blood sacrifice, and they, rather than the Vettiyan, occupy the seat reserved now by law on the *panchayat*, the village council.

18. THE SACRIFICE TO PERIYANDAVAN

1. Munnadiyan, 'the one who comes first', is a secondary divinity who guards a principal god. The Munnadiyan of Periyandavan roughly resembles Pillaiyar, one of the Tamil names for Ganesh.

19. THIS *KALIYUGAM*

1. This conversation dates from 1983. Wages at Karani in 1990 were roughly twenty to twenty-five rupees a day for a ploughman using his own oxen: eight to ten rupees a day for a woman weeding a paddy field and ten rupees a day for a woman planting out rice. Wages, therefore, have increased but, as Manikkam points out in chapter 25, so has the price of rice.

2. M.G. Ramachandran, a famous film actor and the treasurer of the DMK until he left in 1972 to set up the Anna DMK. He led the government of Tamil

Nadu from 1977 until his death in 1987. Karani is in fact in the State of Pondicherry which has been governed, for the most part, alternately by the Congress Party and the DMK, but Viramma is justified in giving M.G. Ramachandran credit for changes in the village – free school meals and a creche – in so far as the ideology of the Dravidian parties, the DMK and the Anna DMK, has influenced the State of Pondicherry.

3. Varieties of high-yield rice.

4. The implication of the *ur* and *ceri* being joined together is that Dalits would officially be allowed to settle in the *ur*. There isn't a law legalising segregation, but nor is there a law putting an end to the traditional practice of dividing up villages on caste lines.

5. Supporters of the DMK wear *soman* with a red and black border. The Anna DMK's *soman* have a red, white and black border.

20. 'TALKING LIKE THEY DID'

1. The wordplay is on *malai*, 'the mount'. Many places of pilgrimage – Mailam, Pajani, Sabarimalai – are temples built on hills and *sidi* is a vulgar name for the vagina. *Sidimalai* is therefore a less poetic version of the Mount of Venus.

21. TWO STORIES

1. According to this popular story, Nallatangal took her seven children, against her husband's advice, to stay with her brother Nallatambi during a famine. But her sister-in-law refused them water and food and, full of remorse and anger, Nallatangal threw her seven children down a well before herself committing suicide. When Nallatambi found out, he had his wife shaved, paraded around the town on a donkey and then put to death.

2. The etymology is helpful in understanding the details given here: in Tamil turmeric is *manjal*, and *kuppam* is a place close to water, hence the damp ground.

3. Divorce, although sometimes practised, is not considered respectable amongst high castes and widows are forbidden to remarry. Other castes – particularly Dalits – tend to divorce more readily, by mutual consent in front of a village council, and separation without actual divorce is common. Effective polygamy, therefore, is not rare, without necessarily implying the sort of cohabitation that Viramma describes in the case of her grandfather's wives in chapter 1.

4. Indian schooling begins with Class I. Class X is for children of about fifteen – most Dalit children having left by then.

22. SPELLS AND SPIRIT POSSESSION

1. Her neck would be bare because widows take off their *tali*.

2. The festival of Tai pusam is named after the star, *pusam* – the eighth lunar constellation – and takes place during the full moon of the month of Tai. It is characterised by spectacular acts of penance – cheeks pierced by lances, hooks in people's backs with which they pull heavy objects or hang themselves off the ground – and its overall purpose is to cure illness: the needles Viramma mentions being stuck into affected parts of the body. As the son of Siva, Murugan is

a high-ranking god and thus particularly terrifying to Viramma. The rise of his festival in recent years in Karani is due to the influence of Murugaiyar Gounder, the local *samiar*. The festival of Draupadi, which involves similar acts of penance, has traditionally been the main village festival. Brahmins lead its rituals and all the castes play the symbolic roles that reflect their place in the ritual hierarchy of the village – Pariahs, for instance, lead the procession with their orchestra but are considered too unclean to walk on fire.The Tai pusam, however, affirms a different model of spirituality. Murugaiyar Gounder is of one of the middle-ranking castes and Dalits do not participate as a social group but, as individuals, they can perform the necessary acts of purification and thus do penance to Murugan.

23. THE PONGAL OF THE OXEN AND THE FESTIVAL OF DRAUPADI

1. In Tamil Nadu, Aiyanar is considered to be the son of Siva and Vishnu – the latter in his female form of Mohini – and he is the protector of villages. His temples, therefore, are either on the outskirts of the village, as at Karani, or at a distance and they are remarkable for their clay statues – monumental statues of the god, his guardians and horses and numerous small statues of horses given as offerings by worshippers.

2. Celebrated in mid-January at the time of the rice harvest, Pongal is the main agricultural festival, at which both cattle and the earth are honoured. The last day of the month of Markaji is a preliminary day, Bogui, when houses and agricultural implements are cleaned and decorated. Viramma describes the four days of the festival itself: the Great Pongal, at which newly harvested rice is cooked, the Pongal of the Oxen, the Pongal of Meat and the Pongal of the Calves.

3. Lakshmi is the wife of Vishnu, the goddess of prosperity and beauty, who is invoked for temporal and spiritual blessings. Sridevi is another of her names and Mudevi is one of her sisters, an inauspicious goddess who brings bad luck and difficulties.

4. Agricultural workers who own a pair of oxen for ploughing are paid almost double what they would be if they ploughed with the landowner's oxen.

5. Pakkasuran is an *asura*, a demon, in the *Mahabharata* who terrorises a village by demanding a cartload of rice every day and eating both the carter and the rice. He is killed by Bhima, one of the five Pandava.

6. Contrary to what Viramma believes, the reader of the *Bharatam* is not an Iyer (a sivaite Brahmin), but a Reddiar whose appearance explains the confusion.

7. The raising of the flag, *kodi ettram*, is the first day of the festival of Draupadi and the firewalking is the last, the eighteenth. The complex rites involved in raising the flag – mantras are recited in the eight directions on the outskirts of the village and specific gods are invoked at each of the eight cardinal points – are designed to protect the village and prevent any god or demon disrupting the festival.

8. Kishtan is the popular pronunciation of Krishna in Tamil-speaking countries. Viramma lists the well-known episodes of his youth – stealing butter, playing with the cowgirls – the *gopi* – and hiding in a tree to watch women bathing.

9. The eighteen days of the festival of Draupadi evoke, in general, the eighteen days of the battle of Kurukshetra between the Pandava and the Kaurava in the *Mahabharata*, and the last day does so specifically. Performers lie under a shroud which recalls the shrouds covering those killed in the battle.

10. The rectangle of water symbolises the Palar, one of the holiest rivers of Tamil Nadu.

24. SHARING THE HARVEST

1. Sani or Saniar corresponds to Saturn, one of the nine planets, and a god who guards the north-east, one of the eight cardinal points. Before starting ploughing or preparing the seedbed, a propitiatory *puja* is performed in the north-east corner of a field.

2. These are modern, hybrid strains which give high yields and grow faster than their older counterparts. The main rice growing season, *samba*, lasted from June/July to December/January and traditional *samba* strains of rice took six or seven months to grow. Well-irrigated land can now yield three harvests a year. Strains like *ponni* take four and a half months and are sown in August. *Kannagi* and the I.R. strains 8, 20 and 50 take less than four months and are grown either in the *sornavari* season, starting in April/May, or the *navarai* season, starting in December/January. Viramma lists some of the older strains a little further on: *sirumani*, 'little glass pearl'; *mukutti*, 'jewel for the nose'; *kammal*, 'earring'.

3. Mahadevan: 'the great god', one of the names of Siva, or, occasionally, Vishnu.

4. After the food shortages of the mid-sixties, a network of 'ration shops', or 'fair price shops', selling essentials for less than market prices was set up all over India.

5. Vayu is the Vedic god of wind.

6. Viramma lists the responsibilities of a master to his *adimai*. The Reddiar should tolerate small-scale pilfering, give Manikkam and Anban paddy, millet or sorghum at harvest time and, generally, be prepared to loan them money when necessary. In return they should not abuse his trust by stealing too much. Viramma constantly emphasises the personal nature of their relationship. They are 'his own serfs' and 'his own Paratchi or Paraiyan' and, as such, to be distinguished from another type of 'bonded labour' that, through a network of middlemen, are uprooted from their homes and sent to live and work in quarries or building sites often in another State.

7. According to the myth of Kuttandavar, Aravan, the son of Arjuna, was beheaded in the battle of Kurukshetra and his sacrifice should have ensured the victory of the Pandava. But Aravan was unmarried, which made the outcome uncertain, and so Krishna became Vishnu again in his feminine form of Mohini and married Aravan who then became known as Kuttandavar. After Aravan's death, Mohini threw away her *tali*, an act which eunuchs repeat at the festival of Kuttandavar. Arjuna himself displays the same sexual duality as Vishnu. According to popular stories, he lived for a year as a homosexual after being exiled in the forest. The *Mahabharata*, however, only says that he spent a year at the court of King Virata disguised as a eunuch and the master of the dance.

8. *Dinatandi* is one of the main Tamil daily newspapers.

25. THE WAY OF THE WORLD

1. When Viramma or Manikkam say that the Reddiar or the Gounder won an election, they mean the candidate of the party they supported won, rather than that they did so personally. 'Vote for the Reddiar' means voting the way he wants. Ballot papers in India contain the symbols of the different parties, the spinning wheel being for a long time the symbol of the Congress Party.

2. Gandhi and Grandpa Gandhi refer to Mahatma Gandhi who entered national politics in 1919 – well before Viramma was born – and was assassinated in 1948. Jawaharlal Nehru was the first Prime Minister after Independence, from 1947 until his death in 1964. His daughter Indira Gandhi – no relation of Mahatma Gandhi – was Prime Minister from 1966 to 1977 and from 1980 to 1984, when she was assassinated. Kamaraj was the Congress leader of the State of Madras – subsequently the State of Tamil Nadu – from 1957 to 1963, and then the national President of the Congress Party. No doubt he is called 'traitor' because of the split in the party in 1969 when Indira Gandhi broke away from him and his supporters. Annadurai – also known as Anna – founded the DMK, the regionalist Tamil party, in 1949, and in 1967 he became Chief Minister of the State of Madras until his death from cancer in 1969. M. Karunanidhi succeeded him until 1977 when the Anna DMK, founded by M.G. Ramachandran in 1972, won the elections for Legislative Assembly. M.G. Ramachandran's death in 1987 brought M. Karunanidhi back to power from 1989 to 1991, when Jayalalitha and the Anna DMK again won a sweeping victory. M. Karunanidhi and the DMK won again in 1996.

3. A *samadi* is the tomb or cenotaph of a famous person. The 'college of the living' is the zoo, 'the college of the dead' the museum.

4. Manikkam refers to the period before Independence dominated by the nationalist movement, which was led to a great extent by the Congress Party.

5. Gandhi in fact was assassinated by a Hindu extremist who accused him of having made too many concessions to Muslims and thus opened the way to Partition.

6. Goubert Papa is Édouard Goubert, the representative of French India at the National Assembly in Paris who, in 1953, supported the Congress Party in their demands that the French territories be returned. Chandernagor rejoined India in 1949 and the other trading posts – Pondicherry, Karikal, Mahe and Yanaon – were handed back, de facto, by the Mendès-France government in 1954. The transfer was confirmed *de jure* in 1962 and, despite violence of the sort Manikkam describes, the suggestion that there was a war between India and both France and Great Britain should be understood metaphorically.

7. Members of the Vanniyar caste, essentially farmers and peasants, go under numerous different names – Kudiyanar, Palli, Padaiyatchi, Gounder and even Naicker – and constitute the largest caste in the north of Tamil Nadu. They have formed various political parties: The Farmers and Toilers Party and Commonweal Party in the 1950s and 1960s and, at the 1989 elections, the Pattali Makkal Katchi. Janata was created in North India in 1977 out of the opposition to Indira Gandhi's Congress Party. Janata Dal defeated Rajiv Gandhi in the 1989 elections, and organised the large coalition which was called to power after the elections in 1996.

8. E.V. Ramassami Naicker, known as Periyar (the Great), formed the anti-Brahmin Self-Respect Movement in 1925, and the Dravidar Kajagam, the

Association of Dravidians, in 1944: a social reform movement aimed at emancipating the south of India from the hegemony of the north and the higher castes. Members of the DK, led by Annadurai, formed the DMK, a political party with the same principles, in 1949. Etymologically, the Adi-Dravidar are the First Dravidians, perceived as the indigenous population of India, as distinct from the Aryans who settled North India in the third millennium BC, and Dravidians are taken to be the peoples of South India – the States of Tamil Nadu, Andhra Pradesh, Karnataka and Kerala – who speak one of the Dravidian family of languages. Adi-Dravidar can also be used to mean the Dalits of Tamil Nadu.

9. Mr Subbaiah led the Communist Party in the Territory of Pondicherry before and after the unification with India. The two leaves are the symbol of the Anna DMK.

10. A Union of States, India has two types of assembly: the Legislative Assembly at federal state level and the Parliament, Lok Sabha and Rajya Sabha, at national level. As Manikkam points out, Congress candidates are generally elected as Members of Parliament whilst the DMK and Anna DMK, reflecting their regionalist programme, dominate the Legislative Assembly of Tamil Nadu. The *dharmaraja*, the king of *dharma*, is M.G. Ramachandran, the founder of the Anna DMK.

11. The formulation 'Adi! … vadi-podi' conveys a sense of contempt.

12. The ploughmen's party is the Janata Party, whose symbol was once a plough. Two leaves are the symbol of the Anna DMK. The spinning wheel is the original symbol of the Congress Party which was kept by Old Congress or Congress Organisation after the split engineered by Indira Gandhi in 1969. The breakaway party, New Congress or Congress-I, adopted the symbol of the hand. So, when Viramma goes on to describe stamping the hand instead of the rising sun, it means she voted for Congress-I instead of their main rival, the DMK.

13. Village teashops having two sets of glasses – one for the Dalits, another one for higher castes – is a typical example of persistent Untouchability practices. Less discreet is the ban on Dalits entering the temples in the *ur*.

14. 'Put a cap on our heads' means to trick, from the popular story in which a travelling salesman falls asleep under a tree with his supply of caps beside him. A troupe of monkeys steal the caps and take them up into the trees. The salesman gets his merchandise back by making a great show of putting on the one cap they've left him. The monkeys then climb down to imitate him and put all the caps on his head.

15. The word 'nabob' here means simply that the instigator of the smuggling business was a Muslim based in the town of Cuddalore, which is about twenty kilometres south of Pondicherry.

Glossary

Adi fourth month of Tamil calendar, mid-July to mid-August

alam turmeric water mixed with lime; 'performing the *alam*' means presenting this water, along with betel and lit camphor, on a copper tray and turning it near the face of whoever is being honoured

Ammavasai day of the new moon, particularly celebrated in the months of Adi, Purattaci and Tai in honour of ancestors

anna In the old Tamil currency, an *anna* was a sixteenth of a rupee, or 12 *paice*; decimalisation was introduced after Independence and a rupee became 100 *paice*, but 4 *anna* is still used to mean a quarter of a rupee or 25 *paice*

Anna Dravida Munnetra Kajagam (ADMK) political party created by M.G. Ramachandran after splitting from the DMK in 1972; Anna here is a diminutive of Annadurai, the founder of the DMK

asuras heavenly beings, a kind of very powerful Titans, generally translated as 'demons', implacable enemies of the *devas*

Avani fifth month of Tamil calendar, mid-August to mid-September

ayo! exclamation conveying surprise, grief, pity

ayoyo! emphatic form of ayo!

ayya a respectful form for Sir

bhakti intense love for a god, combining devotion, surrender and confidence, which is also reciprocal: the god giving himself to his devotee

295

bidi   cheap cigarettes

bonda   fritter made out of black lentil paste, with cumin seeds, ginger, green chilli, onion, coconut and peppercorns

bundi   sweet or salted fried chickpea-flour balls

ceri   also known as the 'colony', the *ceri* is the part of the village, the ward, where Dalits live; it is separate to the main body of the village, the *ur*, where all the other castes live

Cittirai   first month in the Tamil calendar, mid-April to mid-May

Congress   political party associated with the nationalist movement; after Independence in 1947 and Nehru's death in 1964, it underwent numerous splits but still dominated Indian politics – other than in Tamil Nadu, where it was ousted from power by the Dravidian parties in 1967 – until the 1990s

de!   interjection showing affection towards girls or women

dei!   interjection usually showing contempt, but sometimes affection, towards boys or men

devas   divine heavenly beings, translated as 'gods' in opposition to their enemies the *asuras*, the 'demons'

devi   generic term for goddess, queen or wife

dharma   the civic and religious duty of every individual, as dictated by their social status and what is necessary to preserve the order of the universe

dosai   type of pancake made of a paste of fermented rice and lentils

dosham   type of spirit possession, which, in children, takes the form of diarrhoea and dehydration

Dravidar Kajagam (DK)   'Association of Dravidians'; a social reform movement, created in Tamil Nadu in 1944 by E.V. Ramassami Naicker – known as Periyar – to promote the Dravidian states (South India) against the hegemony of North India and the higher castes

Dravidar Munnetra Kajagam (DMK)   'Association for the Emancipation of Dravidians'; a regionalist political party created in 1949 by C.N. Annadurai on a similar ideological basis, at the start, to that of Dravidar Kajagam

fanon   an eighth of a rupee in pre-Independence French India currency

idli   steamed cake of rice and lentils

Innada, Innappa, Innayya, Innanga   ways of addressing a man according to his status, Innanga here being the most respectful, Innada the least

Iyer   the title of the sivaite Brahmins in Tamil Nadu; significantly, the sivaite priests of the *ceri*, who are Dalits of the Valluvar caste, give themselves this prestigious title

Janata political party created in North India in 1977 out of the opposition to Indira Gandhi's Congress Party; Janata Dal defeated Rajiv Gandhi in the 1989 elections and came to power again in 1996

Jaya mangalam auspicious hymn, song of victory

jilebi pastry twists in syrup, eaten at marriages

kali thick gruel made of millet or *ragi* – *kuj* is a thin gruel with the same ingredients

kaliyugam in Hindu thought, the Iron Age or Dark Age – the age of Kali and disorder in the world – which Kalki, the tenth avatar of Vishnu, will set to rights; Viramma uses it to mean the present and the changes in the social order since her childhood

kambattam a landowner, but more specifically, the largest landowner in a village and the head of the oldest and richest landowning family

kani surface area of 5350m^2, divided into 100 *kuji*; Viramma often mentions a quarter of a *kani*, roughly 1338m^2

kanji mainly the day before's rice, kept in water and eaten the morning after; it can also mean a gruel made out of crushed rice

karagam a jar filled with water, covered in margosa leaves – like the *kumbam* – and used in processions, where it represents Sakti

karma the past and present actions of an individual and the effect they have on the individual's destiny – beneficial, if the actions conform to *dharma*, detrimental if they contravene it

karna a long metal horn which, because of its weight, is played upright

Kartikkai eighth month of the Tamil calendar, mid-November to mid-December

kavadi decorated wooden hoop, carried by worshippers of Murugan on their shoulders at the festival of Tai pusam, which recalls the yoke on which the defeated demon Itumpan brought Murugan offerings; the 'songs of *kavadi*' are songs in worship of Murugan

kodumbavi clay figure of a sterile woman used in rites to ward off drought

kolam auspicious, geometric patterns drawn on the ground with rice flour; a popular art form practised, with variations, by women of all castes

kondam a roundelay sung by women

koppi small brass cones, hung with little bells, which are put on oxen's horns

kuj millet and *ragi* gruel; a staple dish, usually taken to the workers in the fields at midday

kujidosham possession near cremation grounds resulting in serious diarrhoea for children

kulam pond or pool of water, generally near a temple

kumbam a jar filled with water, covered in margosa leaves – like the *karagam* – but kept in the house, where it represents Mariamman

kungumam paste made out of water, lemon juice, lime and powdered saffron for the red *pottu* on the foreheads of married women

kuttu puree of lentils and either vegetables or leaves

laddu sweet balls made out of chickpea flour, with cashew nuts, raisins and cardamom

Maci eleventh month of Tamil calendar, mid-February to mid-March

marakka a measure of grain in Pondicherry, corresponding to 3.2 kilos

Markaji ninth month of Tamil calendar, from mid-December to mid-January

mattai baton or truncheon made from coconut palm

murukku fried savoury, spiral-shaped, made from lentils and rice flour

mysore pak dry, crumbly pastry made out of chickpea flour

nadesvaram large type of oboe, used on auspicious occasions

naiyandi orchestra made up of young Pariah volunteers, specialising in love songs and comic or caustic songs

nalungu the ceremony of warding off the evil eye held on the day before the marriage

namam the vishnuite mark: a red stripe from the bridge of the nose, surrounded by two white stripes in a V shape

nattam traditionally, the hereditary position of head of the village who presided over the village council, the *panchayat*; no longer an official authority, but often still a village notable who is frequently consulted

ottu wind instrument with a deep tone

paddy unhulled rice; the rice produced by threshing after the harvest

paisa a hundredth of a rupee; *paice* in the plural

pambai double drum, fixed to the waist, played by *naiyandi* orchestras

panchayat elected village council

pandal an awning of palm fronds built on a bamboo frame in front of the house for ceremonies when there are numerous guests

pangali a complex term of kinship which etymologically means 'those who have a share'; essentially the men of the husband's line and, by extension, their wives

Panguni twelfth month of Tamil calendar, mid-March to mid-April

Pappar, Pappan generic name for a Brahmin in Tamil

paraimelam the Pariahs' ritual orchestra which plays at funerals for all castes, except Brahmins, and at the *ur*'s festivals, where they lead the procession

payasam dessert made of milk, green lentils, vermicelli and tapioca, flavoured with cardamom, cashew nuts and raisins

pey evil spirits of suicides or victims of violent death

picacu spirits created by Kali to fight the *asuras*

pongal 1. dish prepared at festivals, made out of rice boiled in milk, animal fat, lentils and spices; 2. Pongal: harvest festival, where, on the second day, oxen and cows are given *pongal*

pottu auspicious mark worn on the forehead by women, except for widows – traditionally black for young girls and red for married women; symbolically it represents the 'eye of Sakti', the eye of destruction, which Sakti, the divine female principal, will give to Siva

Purattaci sixth month of Tamil calendar, mid-September to mid-October

pusari priest who is not a Brahmin

puttu steamed rice flour with sugar and coconut, served at the ceremony marking a girl's puberty

puja the act of prayer and making offerings to a divinity, marked by a more or less elaborate ritual

ragi *eleusine coracana*, a cereal common in South India

rasam digestive tonic, made from peppery water and tamarind

samba 1. main rice-growing season from June/July to December/January; 2. traditional strains of rice historically grown during this season

sambar lentil and vegetable sauce

Sami generic term for God, or any male god, and by extension a master

samiar a holy man with spiritual powers

selavu powder made of ginger and crushed cumin, mustard and ammi seeds

senai a smaller version of the *nadesvaram*, an auspicious wind instrument related to the *shenai* of North Indian classical music

sikakai   soap-pod wattle (*acacia sinuata*); the pods are used to make shampoo

Sinnamma   etymologically meaning either 'little mother' or 'young lady', this is the form of address Viramma uses to reflect both Josiane Racine's younger age and her higher caste; usually used for the youngest aunt or for young married women by the castes who work for their family and know them well

sitalam   the group of illnesses marked by fever and chills

soman   white cotton loincloth, unsown, worn by men; wearing it down to the ankles is more respectable than tucked up to the knees

sunnambu   lime; '*sunnambu* songs' are those sung by women working on lime kilns

Tai   tenth month of Tamil calendar, mid-January to mid-February

tali   gold jewel worn on a necklace by married women all their lives, until their husbands die

Telugu   a Dravidian language spoken mostly in the State of Andhra Pradesh

tinnai   the open space outside a house, lined with columns and on a slight platform, which separates the front door from the street; visitors or inferiors who are not welcome inside the house can be received here

totti   seven members of the Vettiyan sub-caste of Pariahs who make up the *paraimelam* orchestra each year

tundu   cotton shawl worn by men on their shoulders and sometimes, among the lower castes of agricultural workers, as a turban

udukkai   hourglass-shaped drum played by *naiyandi* orchestras

ujakku   the smallest measure of grain and so, figuratively, a small person

uppuma   ground wheat or meal snack fried in spices and onions

ur   the village itself, as opposed to the *ceri*, the separate hamlet where Dalits live; every other caste, from Brahmins and landowning castes to the service castes like the barbers, lives in the *ur* and it contains the village's main temples, dedicated to Isvaran (Siva), Perumal (Vishnu) and Pillaiyar (Ganesh), which Dalits are forbidden to enter

urtotti   the *totti* responsible for announcing the village's news and liaising between the *totti* and the *ur*

vadai   fried dumpling or doughnut made from a base of lentils, chickpeas and black soya; some are whole, some ring-shaped, the latter being a vulgar name for girls or women

vaikundam the resting place, or heaven, of Vishnu, either on Mount Meru or in the Septentrional Ocean; 'to go to *vaikundam*' means to die

Velpakkatta literally 'woman from Velpakkam'; a name given to Viramma

Yugam in Hindu thought, one of the four ages of the world which continually succeed each other: Kritayugam (the Golden Age), Tretayugam (the Silver Age), Dvaparayugam (the Bronze Age) and Kaliyugam (the Iron Age). The four together are called a Mahayugam (a Great Age), which consists of 4,320,000 years. Viramma uses it more simply to mean an era or a generation in her lifetime

Gods

Aiyanar old Dravidian divinity, integrated early into the Brahminic pantheon as the son of Siva and Vishnu in his female form of Mohini; the guardian of the fields and the armed protector of the village's territory, his temple being always on the fringes of the village

Andava one of the names of Siva

Anjaneyar one of the names of Hanuman, the Monkey God and ally of Rama in his fight against Ravana, the King of Sri Lanka, in the *Ramayana*

Draupadi wife of the five Pandava brothers in the *Mahabharata* who has become a popular goddess

Ejumalaiyan 'He of the Seven Mountains', one of the names of Vishnu

Ettiyan guardian of the cremation grounds and assistant to Yama, the god of death; the sub-caste of the Pariahs, the Vettiyan, to which Viramma belongs, consider themselves descendants of Ettiyan – hence their ritual tasks connected to death, such as grave-digging

Govinda 'The Finder of Cows', one of the names of Krishna, i.e. Vishnu in his eighth incarnation

Guardian Kavalkaran, a minor divinity whose sanctuary is five roughly triangular stones

Isvaran or Isan 'The Master', one of the names of Siva, the most common in Tamil areas

Kali one of the terrifying forms Siva's wife assumed; Kali or Kali Ma (the black mother), with her necklace of skulls, is the destroyer of men, who demands blood sacrifices

Kamatchi   a form of Parvati condemned to twelve years' exile on earth by Siva, which she spent meditating in front of a clay lingam (Mannarsami) in a garden beside the Kampa river; cursed a second time, she took the name of Patchaiyamma and created seven guardians, the Muni; her likeness is shown on little copper or brass oil lamps which are kept next to household altars

Lakshmi   the consort of Vishnu, goddess of prosperity and beauty, invoked for temporal and spiritual blessings

Mannarsami   the clay lingam, the phallic symbol of Siva, in front of which Kamatchi meditated for the twelve years of her exile on earth

Mariamman   goddess of smallpox, one of the forms of Sakti whose head was joined to the body of a young Dalit woman from the cobblers' caste

Muni   the seven guardians created by Patchaiyamma, as Kamatchi was called after Siva cursed her a second time

Murugan   second son of Siva, god of masculine beauty, youth, war and the mountains; he rides on a peacock

Parvati   Siva's wife

Patchaissami   an incarnation of Vishnu, the greatest of the seven Muni who guarded Patchaiyamma

Patrakali   terrifying form of the goddess Kali in a fury

Periyandavan   'The Great God', Siva's double, created by his father-in-law, Daksha; the god of Viramma's line

Perumal   the most common Tamil name for Vishnu; his mount is the giant eagle Garuda

Pillaiyar   the elephant-headed god also known as Ganesan (Ganesh), Ganapati and Vinayagar; he bestows riches and ensures the success of every undertaking

Poraiyatta   goddess of the limits and guardian of the territory of the village

Sakti   goddess personifying divine energy or power, who assumes multiple female forms, such as Parvati, Siva's wife, Durga the warrior, Kali the destroyer; secondary goddesses like Mariamman are also considered forms of Sakti

Viran   secondary divinity, fearsome, a carnivorous, alcohol-drinking god; according to some myths, he is the son created by Siva to kill his father-in-law, the king Daksha, who hadn't invited Siva to a great sacrifice to which all the gods had been invited

Yama   the god of death

Castes

Note: The ending *ar* is used for defining the caste as a whole. It is also honorific, and not commonly used for the so-called low castes when referring to a particular individual.

Ambattar, Ambattan   caste of barbers, who provide an orchestra for auspicious ceremonies

Brahmins   traditionally the priesthood caste, the highest caste of all; known as Pappan in Tamil, Brahmin priests only officiate in temples dedicated to the major Hindu deities

Chettiar, Chetti   high caste of Tamil tradesmen; many castes involved in commerce use Chettiar as a title

Gounder   most common name for members of the Vanniyar caste, a caste of farmers

Kepmari   caste of thieves, some of whom are now farmers and call themselves Mudaliar

Komutti   caste of tradesmen who speak Telugu

Koravar, Koravan   semi-nomadic tribe of hunters; Koratti is the common name for women of the tribe

Kosavar, Kosavan   caste of potters

Kudiyanar   the poorest members of the Vanniyar caste who have been agricultural workers for several generations

Marwari trading community from Marwar, in Rajasthan, whose members are found all over India; many of them are pawnbrokers and money-lenders

Naicker farmers, the highest rank of the Vanniyar caste

Padaiyatchi members of the Vanniyar caste

Palli members of the Vanniyar caste

Pandaram Dalit priests, sivaite

Pannaiyar sub-caste of Paraiyar

Paraiyar the largest caste of Dalits in Tamil-speaking areas; in Portuguese, French and English their name is rendered as Pariah

Paratchi colloquial Tamil name for a woman of the Paraiyar caste

Reddiar, Reddi high caste of landowners of Telugu origin

Sakkiliyar, Sakkili caste of cobblers, considered one of the lowest castes of Dalits

Sanar caste of collectors of coconuts and palm wine

Udaiyar caste of peasants

Valluvar Dalit priests, vishnuite

Vaniyar, Vaniyan caste of oil pressers

Vannar, Vannan caste of launderers

Vanniyar caste of farmers, the largest caste in the north of the Tamil-speaking region; depending on their status, members of the caste call themselves (or are called by others) Naicker, Gounder, Padaiyatchi, Palli or Kudiyanar

Vettiyar, Vettiyan sub-caste of Paraiyar with ritual tasks connected particularly with funerals

Routes to emancipation

A DALIT LIFE STORY IN CONTEXT

On 17 July 1997, the eve of the fiftieth anniversary of the country's independence, K.R. Narayan was elected President of India. Supported by an alliance of India's principal political forces, ranging from communist parties to Hindu nationalists, he won 95 per cent of the votes, the best result ever obtained by a presidential candidate. It was the first time a member of the castes known in the past as Untouchables, and now as Dalits, had been elevated in such brilliant fashion to the highest position in the Indian Republic.

A few days earlier, on 30 June, nine Dalits travelling in a bus in the district of Madurai in Tamil Nadu were attacked by a gang with sickles. Six were killed outright; one of them, K. Murugesan, was beheaded and his head thrown in a nearby well. Several weeks before, K. Murugesan had become President of the village council of Melavalavu after a troubled election. For the first time, the practice of creating 'reserved' constituencies – usual in elections for national parliament and state assemblies – had been extended to local elections: only members of the 'scheduled castes' – the administrative euphemism for Untouchables – can stand as candidates in these constituencies, so that their community can be guaranteed representation in the elected bodies. A group of higher-ranking – which does not mean high-caste – Hindus at Melavalavu did not agree with this form of positive discrimination and were prepared to do anything to prevent an Untouchable presiding over their village.

The most remarkable Dalit of this century, B.R. Ambedkar, chaired the Drafting Committee which was responsible, immediately after Independence, for preparing the Indian Constitution. Since 1950, the principle of reserving places in colleges, universities and the public sector has given thousands of Dalits access to positions of high administrative responsibility, and there are now elected Dalits and Dalit ministers in all the Indian states where Dalits live, as well as in the national parliament and central government. But over the same period, the mass of Dalits have remained prisoners of age-old poverty, illiteracy and the prejudices and relations of power which debase them. Worse, the atrocities committed against Dalits have never stopped. Hundreds of murders, thousands of rapes and acts of police violence are perpetrated each year, whilst millions remain humiliated, crushed and oppressed, often indebted from generation to generation to a landowning family to whom they are, to differing degrees, bonded.

Crushed, oppressed: this is precisely the meaning of the word Dalit, the self-definition chosen by the so-called Untouchable militants and writers in Maharashtra who formed the Dalit Panthers in 1972, echoing the Black Panthers who were active at the time in the United States. For the militants who have popularised it as a substitute for Untouchable or ex-Untouchable – the meaning we give it in this short essay – the word Dalit is in itself a mark of autonomy. Contrary to Untouchable, which was common under the British colonial regime, it denies the presumption of uncleanness and underlines that debasement is not a fact of nature or divine retribution but the result of historical oppression, economic as much as ideological. And, contrary to the neologism Harijan – which was chosen by Mahatma Gandhi in his campaign against Untouchability in the 1930s – Dalit is intended to challenge a form of Hindu paternalism.

Untouchability is a scourge which has marked Indian society for centuries, but whose origins historians have never been able to ascribe clearly. The Laws of Manu, the code written around the third century AD, give one of its first justifications by drawing up a normative picture of the 'ideal' social order, structured in four *varna* or orders: Brahmins, the men of knowledge and ritual; *kshatriya,* the men of power and war; *vaishiya*, the men of exchanges and commerce; and the *shudra*, made up of the service castes – artisans, barbers, launderers – and the peasant castes, including, in South India, the powerful and respected castes of landowners. The Untouchables come outside the *varna*, but not outside the caste system, since they themselves are organised into castes.

At the heart of the belief in Untouchability is the idea of pollution: according to traditional thought, Untouchables are literally 'untouchable' because they are considered unclean. Contact with them, direct or indirect, is deemed polluting for all those of 'higher' status. The orthodox considers himself sullied if he touches or is touched by an Untouchable, or if he drinks water from a well where Untouchables live. Objects touched by an Untouchable themselves become polluting: the bucket with which he draws water, the glasses at the tea stall where he drinks tea, even if they're washed and clean: cleanness is not purity. Untouchability (not the caste system, as is sometimes supposed) has been abolished by law – the Constitution makes it a criminal offence – but it hasn't yet disappeared as a practice, even though things are changing. Today, Dalits may be able to go into the great pilgrimage and city temples, but they're still not able to enter those in their village where the local 'touchable' castes go. And in a society where caste is based on endogamy – people marry their own caste – Untouchability is hereditary.

In contemporary India, the traditional identification of caste and work has become looser in certain respects, just as the basic inegalitarianism of the caste system has been challenged by different groups. But these changes in status have taken place largely within the traditional ideology and not in opposition to it. And it is an ideology which both justifies the low status of the majority of Dalits – they have bad *karma*, the fruit of previous existences which has caused them to be born among the despised – and commands them to fulfil their caste duties in the name of *dharma* – the obligations everyone has, relative to the status they have been born into, to guarantee both the social and the cosmic order. And so, for example, the Vettiyan will be agricultural labourers, whose *dharma* is to be humble towards 'the high-born', obedient and respectful to the master who employs them, and ready to fulfil their distinctive ritual duties (as drummers, and those in charge of funerals). In other words, Dalits are traditionally excluded, debased and subject to segregation and, at the same time, essential components of the social organisation which needs them both for the village economy and for the ritual functioning of the community.

This old ideology has been criticised, refuted and contested for a long time, but progress has been slow because there have been such divergent approaches to reform. In a sense, everything depends on one question: is Untouchability an aberrant deviation of Hinduism or its logical consequence, even one of the foundations of its hierarchical principles? Mahatma Gandhi believed the former, much like some reformers now, who think that the fight against Untouchability and the emancipation of the Dalits will regenerate Hinduism. Others, like Ambedkar (and indeed the more radical groups today), have called for the 'annihilation of caste'. More broadly, regional political parties, like the DMK, have attempted to unite all the castes of South India – apart from the Brahmins – in the name of a shared Dravidian identity which is categorically opposed to the caste ideology and Brahminic hegemony of so-called 'Aryan' North India.

Reform movements may have had varying results in the past, but what is happening today is different. Improvements conceded by 'the high-born' are no longer enough. More and more militant Dalit groups are demonstrating and making themselves heard. Dalit intellectuals – Hindu, neo-Buddhist, Christian, Marxist, feminist or otherwise – are seeking effective, if more or less radical, ways to protest against the dominant culture and society which maintains the hegemony of 'the high-born', whether in the form nourished by Hindu tradition and caste ideology, or in that of liberal democratic secularism. We will not repeat here the debates among Dalit intellectuals and militants: unity is not going to come tomorrow. But meanwhile the fervour grows among men and women wanting justice, empowerment and an affirmation of their dignity and their place in the nation.

How is one to situate Viramma's account in this historical or ideological context? Over ten years, throughout the 1980s, we listened to Viramma. She was an agricultural worker, employed by a powerful family, and known for her repertoire as a singer and her talents as a lamenter. She was also midwife to the women of the *ceri*. Meeting after meeting, year after year, confidence and then complicity grew between two women, both Tamil. Listening to Viramma was to hear those who normally do not speak, who humiliation renders circumspect or even silent in the presence of others.

Viramma was born in Tamil Nadu, which has a population of about sixty million. Like many illiterate people of her generation, she does not know her exact age, but she is undoubtedly now in her sixties. Married as a child, she has lived since puberty in her husband's place of birth (Karani, as we have called it) in the Union Territory of Pondicherry. The largest caste traditionally labelled as Untouchable in this part of

Tamil Nadu is the Paraiyar. Literally this term means 'the people of the *parai*', the *parai* being the drum used by the *paraimelam*, the ritual orchestra which the men of the Vettiyan sub-caste – Viramma's and her husband's sub-caste – form each year. From this Tamil word, Paraiyar, the Portuguese, the French and the British have derived the universal term Pariah.

Depending on how it is used, this word can sound either like a deliberate insult, a condescending mark of contempt or an inescapable fate. Unlike her husband and her son, Viramma has always used it, and so we have kept it, even if it is no longer used publicly and even though many people, including the government of Tamil Nadu, call for all caste names to be abandoned. But we have kept it, above all, because Viramma has always seen herself as such, accepted herself as such and stayed faithful to the language of her everyday life: *paratchi*, a Pariah woman; *paraimelam*, the Pariah orchestra; *paraceri*, the *ceri* of the Paraiyar, the separate quarter, or, in progressive and administrative language, colony, which is situated away from the main body of the village, the *ur*, where all those who aren't Untouchables live. Bearing witness to her words and her vision of the world, we have not wanted to put the term Dalit artificially in her mouth. She was unaware of the word throughout the ten years of our conversations and she still didn't know its meaning in 1996. Neither have we toned down her forthright language, considered by more puritan or more hypocritical local mores to set her caste apart, nor added an echo of the atrocities committed against Dalits in Tamil Nadu or elsewhere to make her account more dramatic or enrich its impact.

The testimony we give after listening to Viramma is not a Dalit text – in the sense that Dalit literature can be said to have specific aims – but it is the text of a Dalit. It is not, in a primary sense, a text attacking oppression, but it is a text which tells how an oppressed woman lives and thinks. Viramma is not taken in by the inequalities of the system: she knows she wears herself out and burns in the sun in the service of the landowners because she has to 'fill her stomach'. She has not, however, rebelled or adopted a militant attitude. Viramma lives out her oppression like the majority: the harshness of existence does not preclude release through family, hope, the intact faculties of laughter, song and the imagination. And at the same time meaning is found in a place, a community, a framework of life and thought, and an order of things, even if that framework and order also claim to justify oppression or limit emancipation. Hers is essentially an example of the internalisation of oppression, which must be understood as an ideological system representative of the old order of the world. In telling her life, in expressing her philosophy, Viramma does not formulate a damning critique of that system: she simply tells, in her own words, how it functions in the village space, in the heads of 'the high-born' and 'the low-born'. And her portrait of the 'the low-born' makes us understand both how the system has held for so long and why it is cracking apart today.

Observers of Indian village society have proposed different ways of interpreting the reality of Untouchability. Some, like Michael Moffat, have stressed the significance of consensus. Others, like Joan P. Mencher, considered that Paraiyars neither adhere to nor are taken in by the caste system. Viramma's husband, Manikkam, a communist sympathiser, and her son Anban, who is connected to the DMK, bear this out. As Anban says, the powerful do everything to deny his community access to even a scrap of land, and consequently access to autonomy and a greater sense of dignity. He and Manikkam have both rebelled in their own way, Anban refusing for a time to perform the ritual duties demanded by his caste status and affirming his right to walk through the village the way he wants, rather than always keeping himself humble and half-naked in the presence of the masters.

This is already too much for Viramma, who finds her dignity elsewhere. The ideological shift which has brought limited material progress to the *ceri* worries her: Viramma is afraid of the spread of new ideas and the politicisation of youth, and nervous about losing the protection of her master, who is more significant to her than the promises of politicians. She fears the capacity of the powerful for reprisals and repression, and their displeasure at seeing her community make progress, however small. So she advises her son to remain humble, denounces the young who no longer want to perform in the *paraimelam* and disapproves of the hotheads who argue for only one set of glasses at the tea stall. Viramma certainly aspires to a better life and does not fail to note everything that has changed for the better since her childhood, but she hopes only for improvements granted by 'the high-born'.

In Marxist terms, Viramma can appear a stereotype of alienation. In her alienation itself, in her certainties as well as her anxieties, she presents the universal figure of those women and men who cannot or dare not conceive of a new world, of those who have borne for so long the logic of oppression that they believe in the order that debases them more than in those who wish to overthrow it. But at the same time she offers a richness, a courage and a strength which, despite the hardship of her condition, fill her daily life with an intense humanity. What alienates her makes her life itself, of course. But to liberate all the Virammas of India, all the Virammas of the world, it is necessary fundamentally to understand and to respect them.

Such an approach in no way denies the atrocities of which Dalits are the victims, nor does it underestimate – quite the opposite – the efforts aimed at eradicating Untouchability. Emancipation is not won without struggle, on all levels. But whatever the future holds, Untouchability will only disappear when the dignity of the crushed and the despised is recognised, and first of all recognised by themselves.

We would say to those Dalit militants who will find Viramma too submissive: please, hear this voice. Doesn't it remind you of your mother, your eldest aunt, your grandmother? Does it not provide an authentic account of subjugation? Preserving this voice and this memory of the past is, we believe, to contribute, however modestly, to the building of a future which will give each woman and man their share of dignity, their share of the truth. Viramma doesn't understand that emancipation is underway and in this she is naive. But she is not ashamed to call herself Paraiyar and here she is right. In the end, perhaps what Viramma provides is a vision of village society and a generation *before* revolt. May this account therefore contribute to that emancipation which seems impossible to her and which will mean that those humiliated for generations will finally gain their place in a society where everyone will honour the simple title that Unjai Ranjan gave the Dalit journal he edits: *Manusanga*, Humans.

Josiane and Jean-Luc Racine
September 1997